PRAISE FOR *THE DEA*

**WINNER OF THE ROYAL S
OF LITERATURE ONDAATJ**

**WINNER OF THE DOL
TRAVEL BOOK OF THE YEAR**

"You may not want to visit Jamaica after reading *The Dead Yard*. Thomson interviewed Jamaicans across the social spectrum: their voices speak for the violent discordant society, and are underpinned by his thoughtful discussion of his history of this multicultural, postcolonial world. . . . Vivid and evocative, a fine expression of the spirit of place and the best kind of travel writing."   —PENELOPE LIVELY

"A marvelous, revelatory trawl along the back roads and into the homes, kitchens and hearts of Jamaican all-sorts, leaving you steeped in the island's culture and conundrums."
                    —*The Scotsman* "Books of the Year"

"Thorough and elegant."
                    —ANTHONY HOLDEN, *Daily Telegraph*

"Thomson is strikingly brave. . . . Much of the book is both subtle and telling. . . . Thomson is a fine and tough-minded guide to what he calls this 'corrupted Eden.'"
                    —ANDREW HOLGATE, *Sunday Times*

"*The Dead Yard* is required reading for the rare traveller to Jamaica who wishes to learn what's going on beyond the grounds of an all-inclusive resort hotel."
                    —DAVID SHAFTEL, *Financial Times*

"Thomson braves dangers to bring home some fine set pieces. . . . Good on the sweep of history. . . . This book offers a thought-provoking insight into modern Jamaica and should enjoy a long shelf-life."
                    —ANDREW LYCETT, *Sunday Telegraph*

"Thomson brings back traveler's tales we need to hear from a Third World basket case."

"In his exhilarating new book, Ian Thomson catapults himself into the troubled heart and soul of raw Jamaica, taking the reader on an unforgettable journey. . . . Jamaica is exposed, scars and all. Thomson reveals a magnificent, snarling, wounded animal chewing on its own paw. Without fear he walks up to it and strokes it; he peers right down inside its open mouth. These modern tales are deeply considered, thoroughly examined. There is nothing throwaway here: a fascinating account of a beautiful, treacherous country."

"Ian Thomson's compelling book combines history and travelogue to paint an insightful picture of modern-day Jamaica . . . this is a powerful and enlightening book that deserves to be read."

"If you are planning to go to Jamaica, don't buy a guidebook, buy THE DEAD YARD, it takes you to the heart of Jamaica before you even get on the plane. . . . A well-observed look at a small but complex nation. Ironically it also tells us much about England and other parts of the Jamaican diaspora. There are streets, buildings and people I know in this book. The brother got it right. Ian Thomson has captured the tension, the politics, the heat, the chaos, the beauty and the music of Jamaica. . . . He got down with the people, he took risks, but Jamaicans do that every day."

The Dead Yard

The Dead Yard

A Story of Modern Jamaica

IAN THOMSON

NATION
BOOKS
New York

For Pat Kavanagh and Jim Ballard

Contents

The stranger who comes to Jamaica with his head full of romantic ideas of charming walks and lovely groves, shaded and adorned by aromatic trees and shrubs, perfumed with a thousand flowers, refreshed by limpid streams, and harmonised to the melody of the bird of Paradise, will find himself grievously disappointed.

J. Stewart, *An Account of Jamaica and Its Inhabitants* (1808)

Murder was the case that they gave me
Dear God, I wonder can you save me.

'Lil' Ghetto Boy', Dr Dre

Acknowledgements

This book could not have been written without the generosity of all those in Jamaica who shared their stories, suggestions and personal recollections with me. I owe a special debt in this regard to a number of people in Kingston. P. J. Stewart (PJ) not only fed and gave me shelter, but introduced me to Jamaicans I could not otherwise have met. Valerie Salmon, PJ's housekeeper, likewise offered me counsel and support, while Butch, Peedles and Sexy enlivened the PJ household in their own way.

The help and advice of Annie Paul (*Small Axe* journal) and Anthony Miller was decisive in helping to open doors to Kingston's music community, and the staff at the Institute of Jamaica, Kingston, were gracious and accommodating of my requests for material. Sheree Rhoden of the *Gleaner* library archive went out of her way to obtain microfilm newspaper records for me. Among others who helped me in Kingston I must also acknowledge Professor Roy Augier, Professor Barry Chevannes, Dr Carolyn Gomes, Leeta Hearne, Professor Mervyn Morris, Andrea Hopwood, Lady Golding, Mark Golding, Cookie Kinkead, Mary Langford, John Maxwell, Sonia Mills, Veerle Poupeye, Justine Henzell, Jackie Ranston, Rachel Manley, Bas Ogden, Paul Stockhausen, Ainsley Henriques, Valerie Facey and Bella Endeshaw (Tekle-Hawariat).

Herman van Asbroeck deserves a special mention for putting me up at his home in Kingston. I am extremely grateful to him, as well as to his partner Eunice, who went to considerable efforts to ease my way in the city. Elsewhere in Jamaica, many others were kind enough to share their thoughts and point up further contacts, among them Leonard 'Sparrow' Dillon, Joyce Francis, Geoffrey de Sola Pinto, Freddie Hamaty, Richard Jones, and June Gay and Frank

Pringle, who let me stay with them. In Morant Bay, Evelyn Matalon was especially supportive of this book and generously gave of her contacts as well as her hospitality and wisdom. Sally Henzell and the late Perry Henzell provided constant support; I owe Sally a heartfelt 'thank you'.

In Canada, Richard Greene and Father Brian Massie SJ were of immense help in helping me fathom Jamaica's legal system and Catholic death row chaplaincy. In Britain, the base for much of my research, I was given helpful advice by Donald Hinds (author of *Journey to an Illusion*), who guided me through his old Brixton haunts and was tolerant of my intrusiveness. *The Dead Yard* began in conversations I had some time ago with Jamaicans in London. I would like to thank James Berry, Jean Besson (Senior Lecturer in Anthropology at Goldsmiths College), the Reverend Les Isaac, Arthur 'Jimmy' Lee (treasurer of the West Indian Ex-Servicemen's Association in Clapham), Connie Marks (chairman of the Friends of Mary Seacole), Gladwin 'Gladdy Wax' Wright, Patsy Robertson, Charles Riggon, George Walters and Cecil Wilson. I am also indebted to the Co-operative Friends of Jamaica for their invaluable leads in locating returnees.

Evan Jones was always encouraging to me, and gave me advice regarding an early draft of a chapter. Mary Turner of the Commonwealth Institute, London, provided me with key contacts in Kingston. Caroline Butler introduced me to her Jamaican neighbours in Brixton (Thelma Genus, Pearl Willis) and was vital to the chapter on returnees. J. G. Ballard suggested that I go 'somewhere depressing, like Chechnya – what about Jamaica?'

Anne Walmsley, Frances Wilson, Sue Gaisford, Nick Gillard, the late Amanda Saunders, Bill Schwarz, Bryan Claxton and Sarah White (of New Beacon Books) offered more useful assistance, while Tony Pawlyn (chief librarian at the National Maritime Museum, Cornwall, Falmouth) went to considerable efforts to obtain material for me on aspects of the maritime slave trade. Vanessa Salter, Keeper of Social History, Hull Museums, Monument Buildings, offered advice on how to navigate the complicated Wilberforce House archives. Tony 'Ras' Goldbourne, Chairman of Hull's Afro-Caribbean Association, showed me round the city's Jamaican community and introduced me to Denzil Johnston, whose reflections on Jamaica's role in the Second World War were invaluable. Claire Taylor of the Methodist church in Hull shared many generosities with me.

Several people did me the honour of reading pages in progress and demonstrating their enthusiasm (or lack of it) for the way I was going about this book. Among them were my friends James Ferguson, Herman van Asbroeck, Miranda France, Mark Thompson and Maurice Glasman. Their thoughtful comments were adopted in nearly every case. Jessamy Calkin of the *Telegraph Magazine* sent me to Jamaica in the first place; my thanks to her.

Neil Belton, whose gentle but persistent encouragement urged me to efforts I may not otherwise have made, commissioned this book. And his assistant, Kate Murray-Browne, was a model of tactful criticism. Paula Turner at 'Palindrome', the copy-editor, has my profound gratitude for her attentive and punctilious reading, while Peter McAdie proofread the text and Alison Worthington prepared the index. The late Pat Kavanagh, my agent, I shall miss very much. She guided, encouraged and launched so many authors over many years.

Laura, my wife, gave me encouragement and advice for this book; I offer her a special toast to all the years together. Maud, Sidney and Henry had the good sense to choose Laura as their mother; I thank you for tolerating the time I spent on 'Majaica'.

My apologies to those who should have been mentioned but are not, and to those who would have preferred not to be mentioned but are (even if their names have been changed). *The Dead Yard* is not 'the' truth, it's only as I saw it.

Finally, I am happy to acknowledge the Society of Authors for the provision of an Author's Foundation Grant.

Preface to the U.S. Edition

In May 2010 a state of emergency was declared in the Jamaican capital of Kingston. Schools and businesses were closed down as armed vigilantes were roaming the streets. In Tivoli Gardens, a west Kingston housing project, gang members began to stockpile weapons to prevent the arrest of their leader 'Dudus' (Michael Christopher) Coke, revered locally as a Robin Hood figure, reviled in the United States as a master of drug cartels.

Tensions had been simmering for nine months at least. The previous summer, in August 2009, the United States had served an extradition notice on Coke, who was wanted in America on charges of murder and drug trafficking in the New York area. At first the Jamaican government refused to extradite Coke. What crimes, exactly, had he committed? Weeks passed, and still the authorities hesitated to hand Coke over. Jamaica's Prime Minister, Bruce Golding, seemed intent on shielding Coke from U.S. law. (The extradition treaty, he objected, was based on illegal wiretap evidence and therefore inadmissible.) As Golding continued to demur, relations between Jamaica and the United States were increasingly strained.

The reluctance to extradite Dudus Coke was, it seems, politically expedient. Tivoli Gardens is a neighbourhood controlled by Coke; it also happens also to be Golding's constituency. In Jamaica, the link between politics and crime is pronounced; politicians have long enjoyed the electoral support of 'garrison' constituencies like Tivoli Gardens in downtown Kingston. In exchange for his continued political allegiance, Coke was allegedly lavished with public contracts and other government favours.

In recent years, however, Jamaican politicians have sought if anything to distance themselves from 'ghetto' strongmen like Coke. In a role reversal, a new type of don—the narcotics don—has begun to dictate the terms to the politicians. While downtown Kingston has produced songwriters, musicians, and sportsmen of world renown, the neighbourhood has its corrupt side, too. Back in the 1970s, community enforcers such as Claudius Massop, Aston 'Bucky' Marshall and Lester Lloyd 'Jim Brown' Coke (Dudus Coke's father) ruled their Kingston turfs through intimidation and a gangster-man largesse; they paved the way for latter-day dons like Dudus Coke.

The power wielded by Coke in Tivoli Gardens had evolved in the absence of proper government. Without state provision, Coke alone was prevailed upon to settle local disputes, ensure adequate schooling, and create employment. In short, he provided public services that the Jamaican government did not, and still does not. One of the world's 'most dangerous narcotics kingpins' (in the words of the U.S. Justice Department) was, for the inhabitants of Tivoli Gardens, a benefactor and a godfather of sorts.

Born in Kingston in 1969, from an early age Coke had been acquainted with violence. His father, Lester Coke, mysteriously burned to death in a maximum-security prison cell in Kingston in 1992. During the 1980s Lester had led Jamaica's feared Shower Posse gang. On his father's death, Dudus assumed control of the Shower Posse and set up a number of outwardly licit companies in Tivoli Gardens, among them Incomparable Enterprises and Presidential Click (which continues to organise the neighbourhood's weekly *passa-passa* street party).

A man this powerful would be hard to bring to justice. On 17 May, however, after months of pressure from the Obama administration, Prime Minister Golding finally agreed to sign the extradition order and issued a warrant for Coke's arrest. A bounty of $60,000 was put on his head, and, in a televised address, Golding apologised for the delay in processing the extradition. (His government had become improperly involved in Coke's case, he said.) As the manhunt got underway, Coke loyalists surged onto the streets in the thousands to show solidarity. 'Jesus died for us,' they chanted, 'so we will die for Dudus.' Quite how many had already died for Coke, nobody yet knew for sure. Coke's fear was that security forces would kill him in order to hush up the extent of his ties to politicians.

In the clamour to find Coke, reports came through of extra-judicial police killings. Like the ghetto hero of the Jamaican film *The Harder They Come*, he managed to evade police dragnets and frustrate police intelligence. Perhaps he had fled to Venezuela? Or perhaps he was still in Kingston—in Denham Town, or adjoining Jones Town? The Jamaican government's inability to find Coke was now an embarrassment to Golding; on 24 May, thirty-six weeks after the extradition, he launched a last-ditch offensive aimed at cornering Dudus. As gunmen redoubled their resistance in Tivoli Gardens, the casualty toll climbed, and Kingston Public Hospital filled with bodies. At funeral homes in Kingston, meanwhile, people turned up with photographs of missing loved ones, hoping that staff might have seen them, dead or alive.

*

As the violence raged, a friend in Jamaica asked me, 'Will they distribute *The Dead Yard* over here now?' It was a question that I found difficult, as most bookshops in Jamaica had declined to stock *The Dead Yard,* owing to its alleged 'sensitive content.' While I had not anticipated any legal problems (in fact, there were none), Jamaica has a long-entrenched culture of litigation. The island's Libel and Slander Act of 1851 (amended by the Defamation Act of 1961) is considered by some to be an obstacle to press freedom. Not surprisingly, Jamaican newspapers favourable to Prime Minister Golding had been careful not to dilate on his alleged links to Coke.

But why, my friend persisted, this aversion to *The Dead Yard* in Jamaica? (It seemed absurd, 'and for that matter *unfair*,' that people outside Jamaica could read the book, while Jamaicans could not, he said.) Perhaps the answer lies in this: for good or ill, *The Dead Yard* exposes a dark side of island life at odds with the 'paradise' island of travel brochures. What I found at times was a vexatious, fear-ridden nation that had slipped painfully and not entirely from British rule onto a path dictated by the crime and business interests of the United States and its Caribbean neighbours. The Coke affair shed a glaring light on the longstanding complicity in Jamaica, as well as in the Jamaican diaspora, between politicians and gang leaders.

*

As the manhunt entered its second month, Coke was at last taken into custody. The police had detained him on the morning of 22 June at a routine roadblock in Kingston; with him in the vehicle was a local evangelist, the Reverend Al Miller, whom Coke had asked to help turn him in at the American Embassy. (Coke had not trusted the Jamaican police to turn him in alive.) The preacher had been on his way to the embassy with Coke when their vehicle was flagged down. Bizarrely, Coke was found to be wearing a woman's wig and in possession of a second (pink) wig, along with a pair of women's sunglasses. By this disguise he had sought to evade police detection.

Later that night on television, Coke's well-fed, healthy face gave an impression of loneliness, sadness, and disappointment. Two days later, on 24 June 2010, U.S. Federal Agents were seen escorting him off the plane in New York. On the advice of his lawyers, Coke had chosen to waive his right to an extradition hearing in the Jamaican courts. His capture was a victory of a kind for the U.S. Justice Department, but a calamity for the thousands of Jamaicans who had relied on him for a livelihood. ('No Dudus, no Jamaica!' they say.) If convicted of the charges against him, Coke may spend the rest of his life in jail. Dreadfully, the five-week manhunt had resulted in the deaths of over seventy people, among them police and civilians, as well as armed gang members. Whatever happens in the New York law courts, in Tivoli Gardens there will always be a Mr Michael Christopher Coke, the drug lord known as Dudus, whose sins, some argued, paled beside his largesse.

Ian Thomson
London, November 2010

Introduction

A History of Paradise

'What are you doing in Jamaica?' the woman said to me. 'Have you come to stare and make fun?' We were at a meeting of the Jamaican Historical Society held in the capital, Kingston. The woman was an elderly white Jamaican. Once, like other white Jamaicans at the top of plantation society, she might have been able to distance herself from 'the troubles' (as she called them) of her birthplace. Now she was not so sure. She resented voyeurs of Jamaica. 'Do we really need another book on Jamaica?' she went on. 'You visitors are always getting it wrong. Either it's golden beaches, or it's guns, guns, guns. Is there nothing in between?'

As I journeyed deeper into Jamaica, I realised that my critic had a point. The many wonderful things about Jamaica – its extraordinary music-making, its physical beauty, its athletic prowess (six gold medals at the Beijing Olympics) – contrast harshly with the crime, the violence and the political corruption. Tourists rarely see anything of the twisted side of island life. Yet Jamaica, the 'paradise' of travel brochures, is just as often derided as a criminal backwater. *Is there nothing in between?*

*

To the British, Jamaica is the best known of West Indian islands. But what, after three centuries of enforced rule, is the relationship between Jamaica and its former colonial masters? Jamaica was the brightest jewel in the British slave colonies: a prize and inhumane possession. During the period 1700 to 1808, sugar – the end-product of British slavery – became so profitable a commodity that the prosperity of English slave ports such as Bristol and Liverpool was derived from commerce in what one historian (Sidney Mintz) has called the 'tropical drug food'.

So Jamaica provided a sweetener for our tea and coffee. By the late nineteenth century, cut-price jam (one-third fruit pulp to two-thirds sugar) had begun to appear in the larder of every working-class household in Britain. When Atlantic slavery was finally abolished (last of all in Brazil, in 1888), cheap sugar was sustained by indentured labour from India and China. The influx from the East coincided with a period of Crown rule, during which Jamaica was governed directly from London, instead of through a local parliament of English slave-owners and traders, as before. The end of the slave trade, however, brought economic decline: Jamaica, a waning asset even under Queen Victoria, was demoted to the imperial category of 'minor colonies'.

Nevertheless, during the long twilight of colonialism Jamaica acquired a cosmopolitan character all its own. Immigrant Asia – as represented by those contract labourers from India and China – began to marry into the African slave population, creating a multi-shaded community of nations which was both parochial and international. Jamaicans are not all black; many gradations – Chinese, Indian, Lebanese – can exist within a single Jamaican family. So Jamaica in the high imperial age after slavery became the oddly 'modern' society. *The Dead Yard* explores, among other things, the island's bewildering racial and ethnic diversity.

Even as Jamaica declined, sugar sustained the island. Prices rose significantly during the Great War – sweetening the rations – and slavery cast its shadow as field-hands were overworked by their employers. Cruelty had been implicit in Jamaican life for the 300 years of British rule ('Jamaican history,' wrote Karl Marx, 'is characteristic of the beastliness of the true Englishman.') Throughout the 1930s resentments simmered again on the plantations, along the Kingston wharves and in the great overcrowding of the ghetto. The common man, said the lawyer and future Jamaican prime minister Norman Washington Manley, would no longer endure inhuman conditions; he was prepared 'to raise hell' to have them changed. Amid this civil strife, Jamaican nationalism was born.

As the 1930s gave way to the 1940s, trade unions, co-operative societies, reform leagues and other bodies developed into political parties. By the end of the Second World War Jamaican nationalist leaders with mass support were agitating for self-rule. Norman Manley, appointed the colony's chief minister in 1955, made independence his priority. Both he and the British government considered it impractical for islands in the Anglophone Caribbean to 'go it alone', so the idea of a British West Indian federation was drafted. Jamaicans tolerated the idea for four years.

In a referendum called by Manley in 1961 Jamaicans voted categorically to leave the federation and within a year made ready to greet independence. As the clock struck midnight on 5 August 1962, the national colours were raised and the Union Jack lowered for the last time. The British farewell ceremony, held in Kingston's newly opened National Stadium, drew a crowd of 20,000 people. Tears were shed as 'God Save the Queen' was played, followed by the Jamaican national anthem. The new flag had a St Andrew's cross designed in black, gold and green – the gold and green symbolic of hoped-for rebirth and the black a recognition of continental Africa. Not all Jamaicans cared for it. 'Black gold' had been slave-trader parlance for captive Africans; moreover, the flag appeared to be loosely modelled on the Union Jack.

Once down, the union colours were neatly folded by the duty-soldier and passed on to the sergeant-major, who passed them to the officer-in-charge, who passed them to the governor, who passed them to the sovereign's representative, who passed them to an aide-de-camp. Britain's withdrawal was presented (by the British) as a triumph of statesmanship, by no means a sign of national weakness. Jamaica was not *getting* independence; rather, Great Britain was *granting* Jamaica independence.

A clamour of songs exhorted the Jamaican people to join in the 1962 festivities and jump for joy. Derrick Morgan's 'Forward March' opened with a military bugle clarion, its chorus: 'The time has come when you can have your fun'. Queen Elizabeth II had sent her sister, Princess Margaret, as a symbol of gracious British retreat. 'But we have further been graced,' enthused the Jamaican press, 'with the attendance of Vice President Lyndon Johnson of the United States, a token of the esteem our great northern neighbour holds for us.' Prescient words: fifty years on, Jamaica has become a quasi-American outpost in the Caribbean; many poor Jamaicans in Jamaica dream of American citizenship.

The following day, 6 August 1962, Princess Margaret handed the new constitutional documents to the Jamaican prime minister. And with this gesture Jamaica moved, at least in theory, from the protection of the British Crown to self-government. The princess wished the fledgling nation well, and welcomed it to the British Commonwealth.

So, officially, ended imperial rule in Jamaica. The process of 'decolonisation' was marked by the usual contradictions and conflict. Jamaica's two-party Westminster system (assiduously put together during the last years of British control) was bolstered; but, at the same time, African Jamaican historical figures who had been denigrated, abused or simply ignored by the colonial administration were rehabilitated and made semi-official 'national heroes'. Among these were Sam Sharpe and Paul Bogle, rebel Baptist preachers who had championed the Jamaican poor.

Undoubtedly, Jamaica stumbled in the years following independence. During the Cold War in the 1970s, the United States intruded blatantly on Jamaican affairs. A nominally socialist (and outwardly anti-American) government was seeking to nationalise foreign-owned industries, redistribute land and empower the black majority. Jamaica's proximity to communist Cuba was of the gravest concern to Washington. The United States was determined to 'rescue' Jamaica from the threat posed by Fidel Castro. In subsequent years, Jamaica fell deeper into the clutches of North American financial institutions, incurring debts it could ill afford.

However, the burden of Jamaica's post-colonial political failure lies not with the United States or with slavery or British imperialism, but with the Jamaican people themselves. A system of 'clientism' has evolved in the years since independence, in which patron-politicians provide their client-supporters with jobs, protection and a flow of money, as well as narcotics and firearms, in return for their loyalty. The failure of local politicians to use independence virtuously has become entangled with a culture of violence; this is aggravated in turn by the rate of broken homes and absent fathers in a society already burdened by the legacy of the plantation and the lash.

The reality, for most Jamaicans, was that independence in 1962 brought only disappointment. For all the promises of prosperity and social justice, thousands of country folk continued to drift hard-broke into Kingston in search of non-existent jobs. The island's class and racial divides remained stubbornly in place. The problem of the colour-line continues to haunt Jamaica. The lighter your complexion, the more privileged you are likely to be. An insidious 'shadism' has ensured that a minority of white (or near white: what Jamaicans call 'local white') inhabitants still control the plantations and other industries, while the black population remains separated from them by the powerlessness or poverty of their lives. The frequent appearance in *The Dead Yard* of white and upper-echelon Jamaicans might suggest a skewed image of island society. However, white Jamaicans still wield huge (if not uncontested) power; the Jamaica created by the merchant-capitalists of slavery has survived. So anxious are some Jamaicans to 'whiten up' that they use skin-bleaches – a sad after-effect of the aristocracy of skin nurtured by the British during slavery.

For good or ill, British culture remains a significant part of what it means to be Jamaican today. The independence constitution of 1962 – still in existence today – had recognised Queen Elizabeth II as the Queen of Jamaica and the Governor General as her chosen representative. In spite of the British legacy (or because of it), Jamaica currently has one of the highest illiteracy rates in the English-speaking West Indies. Though Jamaica has a vibrant literature of its own, reading seriously, at any age, is often associated with reading for examinations.

Instead, the history and mythology of the Jamaican people are fabulously revealed in music. Music is a very serious business in Jamaica, influencing every aspect of life from dress to speech. Reggae, specifically deejay-based dancehall, now dominates the music scene, but old-time gospel and mento (a type of calypso) can still be heard. Chapter titles in *The Dead Yard* are taken from reggae (or reggae-related) songs. Reggae was – and is – the musical voice of Jamaica, just as rai is the musical voice of Algeria or flamenco that of Spain; it is a trance-inducing music out of Africa that I have come to love.

It may be salutary to reflect that the only time Jamaica prospered economically was during the sugar boom of slavery. The view that Jamaica was 'better off' in the British system (even if that means slavery) is held by some Jamaicans; yet it is not one that I share. The passing of the British Empire was good for Jamaica (independence came about *because* the Empire was opposed to Jamaican national interests); and it was good also for Britain, which by 1962 lacked the strength to carry out its overseas responsibilities. The Empire – Rudyard Kipling's 'dominion over palm and pine' – had created in Jamaica a white man's country within an impoverished black majority.

All the same, a surprising number of Jamaicans remain nostalgic for imperial glories, or at any rate a notion of British law and order, and deference to authority. The conviction that things were once a lot better is often voiced by older Jamaicans or returned Jamaican migrants. After their long years of expatriation in Britain or North America, returnees may come home to find Jamaica changed beyond recognition. In all likelihood this nostalgia has more to do with emotions invested in the remembrance of the past – the legendary period of their youth, when lives were organised and given meaning by the Union flag. To the post-imperial reader it may seem surprising – even shocking – that some Jamaicans should hold romantic opinions of Empire or at least display a pious Anglo-patriotism. Yet, as one Jamaican (certainly not an imperialist) asked me, 'What has Jamaica *done* with its independence?'

Pro-British Jamaicans, young and old, are so much a presence in *The Dead Yard* that I have had to consider (if only to register my impressions) whether the new-born nation did not in fact lose something after 1962, when the United States – the 'Colossus of the North' – began to strengthen its influence, and the island which had been overrun by one kind of empire was overrun (in a different way) by another.

Anthony Trollope, during his 1859 tour of the Caribbean, predicted that England would one day be 'no more than a name' in the West Indies: Uncle Sam would soon take the upper hand. Currently, the United States absorbs the majority of the 15,000 Jamaicans estimated to migrate each year. Britain is no longer such an attractive destination, not least because Jamaican nationals must now have a visa to enter. The legislation, passed by Tony Blair's Labour government in March 2003, was intended to curb the number of Jamaicans entering the United Kingdom as drug couriers. Yet most ordinary Jamaicans come to Britain to visit family and friends; the visa requirement is deeply offensive to them. Britons do not need a visa to go to Jamaica (or any other Caribbean island); why, then, should Jamaicans need a visa to enter Britain?

While it is true that many of the Caribbean drug kingpins in Brooklyn – 'Little Jamaica' – were apprenticed in the slums of Kingston, America's influence on Jamaica is often wrongly seen as a malign one of consumerism, bling and guns. The US–Jamaican exchange has been – and remains – far more positive than that. The Harlem-based newspaper *Negro World*, which offered an important ideal of black emancipation to African Americans, was founded in 1918 by the Jamaican race leader Marcus Garvey. In the 1920s, Jamaicans were active in the black American arts movement known as the Harlem Renaissance that coincided with the Jazz Age. Today, around 350,000 people in the East Coast cities of New York, Baltimore, Philadelphia and Boston are thought to be of Jamaican origin. The majority of Jamaican-descended Americans – from the eastern shores of Virginia, across the industrial heartland of Ohio and on to the Rocky mountain states of Colorado and New Mexico and beyond – had voted for Barack Obama in the presidential elections of November 2008. The first black president of the United States (in so far as it is necessary to designate Obama's race at all) is seen my many Jamaican Americans as a Franklin Roosevelt for the twenty-first century.

*

My impression of Jamaica was often of a baneful place. Nearly every Jamaican knows someone who has been threatened with a gun or knife – or murdered. With an annual murder rate of around 1,500 in a population of less than three million, Jamaica is now one of the most violent countries in the world, on a level with South Africa and Colombia. A recent report by Amnesty International, 'Let Them Kill Each Other' (April 2008), depicted a nation in tragic disorder. Reports on child labour, domestic violence and murder clog the national press. Kingston remains locked in cycles of political and gangland violence; to live there today calls for special qualities of endurance.

No doubt Jamaica's reputation for violence has been exaggerated by foreign reporters and in any case is only part of the picture. Rural Jamaica especially has an alluring atmosphere which cannot be guessed at behind the walls of the all-inclusive beach resorts. *The Dead Yard*, the fruit of three visits made to Jamaica over a three-year period, explores the present reality of island life with all its hospitality, charm and intrigue.

A word, finally, on the title. In Jamaica, the 'dead yard' refers to the house of a recently deceased man or woman; relatives gather respectfully at the dead yard for a wake that can last up to nine days. The term is linked to 'The Yard', a colloquial name for Jamaica, the 'yard' also being the area round one's house.

1

(Black Man) in Hammersmith Palais

I began my journey in south London, where James Fairweather had lived since 1947 after serving in the RAF. His Peckham house stood in a Victorian terrace which had been occupied once by horse omnibus inspectors and bank clerks; now, increasingly, by refugees from Africa. On greeting me, Fairweather led the way down a dimly lit corridor to the kitchen. Above the fridge hung an oilskin map of pre-independence Jamaica and, next to it, an out-of-date Page Three girl calendar. In his pinstriped waistcoat, Fairweather was prepared for the interview.

Another man was seated at the table, drinking white rum ('the whites', he called it). He introduced himself as George Walters, a building contractor. Walters had left Jamaica in 1966. Like Fairweather, he was natty, dressed in a pork-pie hat and a tie with a Top Cat motif. 'So when are you off to Jamaica?' Walters asked me, interested. 'Next week,' I said. He winced slightly. 'Mind how you go out there,' he said.

Fairweather's Jamaican childhood, as he described it to me, seemed very remote, a golden age when Jamaica had been an outpost of Britain's sovereignty. He loved Britain, he said, and the British royal cult with its fripperies and rituals (increasingly meaningless to young Jamaicans). On display in the kitchen were a Union Jack sweet tin and a 1952 coronation mug, as well as souvenir shire horses. Fairweather's wartime service was prompted by the anti-Nazi film *In Which We Serve* starring Noel Coward. The film inspired him to join the RAF. 'We all thought Hitler would bring back slavery and repatriate us to Africa if he won the war.' In 1943, after training in the United States as a wireless operator, Fairweather was transferred to Scotland, where his white superiors showed him a soldierly respect. 'There was no place for prejudice back then,' he explained. 'A war was on, and it was to be fought by black and white alike.' Some 8,000 Jamaicans served in the RAF during the 1939–45 conflict.

While on leave in wartime London, Fairweather joined white servicemen at the Hammersmith Palais, and in the smoky nightclubs off Jermyn Street. He was filled with patriotic zeal and felt a pride in being a citizen of the Empire. In 1947 he returned to Jamaica for ten months. The island was recovering from the hurricane of 1944 and many Jamaicans were tempted to book a one-way passage to Britain in search of a better life. Fairweather, who was now an important source of knowledge about jobs and money in the so-called mother country, encouraged them to go. Britain, he told his Jamaican friends, 'was the best place for a black man to be'.

George Walters, who had been listening to the conversation, turned to me. 'But hear me now on this, my friend. England was a *bad* disappointment for me at first.' He could not believe that London could look so old and dead and poor – so plain *different* from the way it was depicted in the posters back home. In the grey, inner-city streets lined with scruffy, bay-fronted houses he desperately looked for somewhere to live. His biggest surprise was not the glum clothes or the shut-in, unsmiling faces of the landladies, but the cockney they spoke. 'After the high-class English they taught me in Jamaica, cockney sounded low class,' said Walters, 'it sounded bad and coarse.' Saying this, he sighed heavily.

Understandably, Walters had expected British people to be exactly like the white missionaries and colonials he had known in Jamaica. So the spectacle of white people doing menial work shocked him. 'Road-sweeps? I nearly died.' It was a quite astonishing reversal of roles: Caucasian hands doing a black man's work. Other shocks were in store for him. Englishwomen wore their hair in rollers in public; dogs came to sniff the packets of bread left by the milkman on the doorstep. What kind of life could spring from such squalor?

Inevitably as a West Indian 'room-seeker' Walters experienced a degree of racism. He was surprised to find himself categorised as 'coloured'. ('Room to Let: Regret No Kolored' ran the typical advert.) In Jamaica the term 'coloured' applied to people of mixed race; in England it was one of the basic words of boarding-house culture and of polite vocabulary in general. Usually, there was no violence: the aggressors, once stood up to, turned on their heels. Walters was prepared to fight back, though. 'First try rebuke by tongue,' he told me, 'then fists.'

Fairweather, like Walters, had family responsibilities in Jamaica, and routinely sent remittances. Would I take out a sum of money to his older brother Roy? Roy was a farmer who lived twelve miles outside Kingston in Spanish Town, the capital of Jamaica when Spain ruled the island. 'He talks a bit raw-chaw – rough, you know – but he's arright.' I agreed and later, with the money in my pocket, I caught the bus back home from Peckham.

*

Sunday morning: the sky a poisonous pink, and Kingston was going to church. Women in spidery hat-veils got on the bus to Spanish Town, clutching bibles. I sat in the back, limp with perspiration. A hurricane had left Kingston in a mess of blown-over billboards and telegraph poles trailing wires. Spanish Town, where Roy Fairweather lived, was said to be no less storm-battered, and the road out of Kingston was flooded in parts. As the bus picked up speed I felt a stab of apprehension. Some of Jamaica's toughest ghettoes flanked these Kingston outskirts, places of extreme violence controlled by politicians and their gangster-henchmen. The possibility that Jamaica was a failed nation – a country in despair – seemed to increase as the bus driver, tailgating recklessly, almost hit a pedestrian and, shaking his head at her accusingly, sped on.

Smoke hung over the shanties in gauzy, thinning clouds, with the morning sun breaking through. Gangs of dogs, cowed-looking, slunk through a roadside litter of plastic bottles, old mattresses, discarded KFC boxes. Shuddering and jerking on creaking springs, we ground to a stop at Spanish Town's bus terminus on Bourkes Road. Inside the terminus, hemmed in by razor-wire fencing, teenagers with street-tough eyes were hustling and making chat. *Bumbo claat! Raas claat!* In their flat-top hairstyles, string vests and trainers they looked NYC ghetto-sharp. I took in the bombardment of impressions down Bourkes Road. Dancehall music, a numbingly insistent rap, blared from the meagrely supplied shops. Early morning pool-hall gamblers seen dimly though a doorway stood gathered round a table, cues raised. Higglers or market women were working their stalls with the industry of ants. Over it all, an odour of charcoal fires, kerosene, rotting vegetables. And here and there, duckboards had been laid down across the post-hurricane mud.

Roy Fairweather was eighty-four, his wife Helen eighty-one. They lived in the Willow Dene neighbourhood of Spanish Town on a street named Piccadilly Drive. If there was a criminal character to Willow Dene I did not see it. Women in white robes and white head-ties milled outside a concrete building, flanked by almond trees with whitewashed trunks, that stood for a church. The houses, many of them, had scrubby gardens with scarlet-flowered ackee trees. It looked as if low-income, church-going Jamaicans lived here. Some of them may even have had regular clerkly jobs in Kingston.

A network of footpaths connected the homesteads and their occupants into a human community. At a cinder-block bungalow with a 'Beware The Dog' sign affixed to tall sheet-metal gates I called out hello. There was a barking as someone came to loosen bolts and chains. The gates jerked open to reveal a tall, thin man in bare feet. Roy Fairweather's face was quizzical as he looked at me. 'Brother Jimmy sent you?' I nodded and, restraining his Alsatian, he led me across a yard of packed dry earth sheltered by a corrugated plastic roof; the yard was bare except for two leafy mango trees, one with old rubber tyres suspended on ropes from its branches: swings for grandchildren, maybe.

'So how is brother Jimmy?' Roy Fairweather asked me as we passed into semi-darkness. I said he was good. The room smelled of disinfectant and the sweet, wet smell that I associated with West Indian rum shops. Roy gestured me to a sofa – 'Sit down and relax yourself' – as his gaze passed quickly from my shoulder bag to my shoes to a room somewhere in the back. 'Mammee!' he raised his voice. 'Come to greet the gentleman from England!' Mammee was his wife, I assumed, but she appeared reluctant to emerge. A giant blue teddy bear stared at me from one end of the room. 'Drink?' Roy asked, as he opened a wall cupboard well stocked with bottles. 'Yes, Jimmy live inna Peckham now for a long time,' he said, his

Jamaican drawl languid. 'They say him have a lounge with TV, hi-fi, video, everything nice.'

Round his neck Roy wore a gold chain, and another on each wrist – a man of consequence. He had been the first of the family to leave for England. 'See that?' he said, pointing to a huge cocktail cabinet. 'I bought that in Herne Hill.' On the top were several gold plastic models of Big Ben – shooting-gallery prizes. The cabinet spoke to Roy of a previous era, of London south of the river. After a pause I handed Roy the envelope containing the remittance; with a nod he slipped it into a trouser pocket, finished his rum in two hard swallows, set the glass down sharply and called out again, 'Mammee!'

Roy's wife was now standing in the doorway. 'What you doin' with such a big glass, Roy?' She clucked her tongue and shot me a searching glance. 'And what bring you to 'Panish Town?' she asked, not too friendly. I said I had come with greetings from Fairweather junior. 'London?' Helen scowled. 'Jamaicans are like flies in London now. But you can't trust nobody there.' News of the Al Qaeda bomb attack two days earlier had brought images of shocked and bloodied London commuters into Jamaican homes: fifty-two murdered on a bus and crowded Tube trains.

Helen was acquainted with violence herself. In 1985 her first husband, a public works employee, had been murdered in Spanish Town after he got into a dispute with a gang over land ownership; his killers were never brought to book. What used to be considered a crime in Jamaica, Helen said, is now judged a non-crime – even murder. 'There's no respect no more,' she said. 'Is Satan take over now.'

Roy, shaking his head, asked his wife permission to pour himself another glass of rum. She set the bottle down on the table at his side, dang-danging under her breath as she did so. He tipped out a shot, mixing it with a pink-coloured syrup to take the edge off the 'overproof', and downed it. My impression was that he and Helen had barricaded themselves in against Jamaica. 'We don't like it no more in 'Panish Town,' Helen said; Spanish Town was out of control, individuals were caught up in drugs, rubbing each other out. The place was 'a creation of the Devil', agreed Roy.

'Yes,' Helen went on. 'The bad men are getting badder, and to tell the truth, I really getting to frighten up and worried.' The violence knew no respect or boundary. 'Is sufferation time,' she said; her eyes seemed full of fight and fear.

In the summer of 1962, just one week after independence, Helen set sail from Jamaica for England with 1,100 other Jamaican migrants, none of them coming to the mother country merely to claim from social services (as the British tabloid press would often claim), but determined to work. By migrating to Britain, Helen believed she was exercising a birthright; she had 'UK – Right of Abode' stamped into her passport, and considered herself a Britisher to the bone. Britain was going to rescue her from poverty.

Menial jobs awaited her. By occupying the poorest, dirtiest and most low-paid jobs – nursing, milk delivery, sewage treatment – Jamaica, a poor country, was providing Britain, a rich country, with a form of development aid. 'Colonisation in Reverse', it has been called. To Helen's further dismay, most English people assumed she was African. African? She came from a Europeanised, Christian, English-speaking island in what used to be known as the British Caribbean. 'They think we all just drop from the trees in the jungle like black monkeys,' she said to me, describing a not uncommon experience. Living in 'Missus Queen's' country was not at all what Helen had expected. Britain, still rebuilding from the ruins of the Empire, did not care to make distinctions between West Indians and West Africans; all were black, all were non-British. 'A lot of English didn't even seem to care about the Commonwealth and that class of thing,' Helen continued. 'And it vex me – cos I always flew the Union Jack in my heart.'

In London, Helen was employed as a cashier in a Battersea police station canteen. Only the Irish constabulary treated her as an equal. ('I think I understand the Irish,' the Jamaican author Claude McKay wrote in 1921, 'my belonging to a subject race entitles me to some understanding of them.') The rest of her time in London Helen worked as a nurse in old people's homes. News of her homecoming in 1989 spread rapidly through Willow Dene; parties were held in her honour amid a popping of corks. 'It was a very happy day for me,' she remembered.

But now she and Roy were tired, tired of the everyday struggles in Jamaica, and seemed to be the loneliest of people. As I left, Helen gave me a bagful of mangoes blown out of the tree by the hurricane. 'Watch your step, my dear, and walk good.' Her husband, taking my hand, said he longed to see brother Jimmy in Peckham, but feared it was too late. 'You live until you die,' he said with finality. 'It nah matter how you go; dead's dead.'

Out on Piccadilly Drive the afternoon air, rinsed of dust by the rains, had brought up a heavy, asparagus smell from the earth. I made my way back to the bus terminus on Bourkes Road where I saw a man brandishing a broken bottle at passengers. 'Ah mark you face!' he shouted, mechanically wrathful. The rage in him died away quickly, and I climbed on board a bus. The market stalls along Bourkes Road were deserted now, surrounded by a drowsy half-silence of cicadas, and a barking of dogs in the distance. On the way back to Kingston we were overtaken by a hearse; it was big, black and expensive, and it sounded a horn as it surged through the hurricane waters.

*

In the build-up to the hurricane, religious evangelists had spoken on the radio and television of an avenging beast come to cleanse our souls. Far from being a tropical depression to be monitored by the meteorological office, the hurricane was a divine visitation. Hurricane Dennis ('Dennis the Menace', Roy Fairweather had called it) hit with such destructive force that I could almost believe that it was a judgement on the 'sinnery' of modern Jamaica. First, the air in Kingston turned very close, then a low mutter of thunder could be heard as reports came of a swell down by the harbour on Marcus Garvey Drive. By early afternoon all Jamaica had been put under 'hurricane watch' as the government closed down schools and businesses. By four o'clock the winds had risen dramatically, with the eye of the storm now said to be about 200 miles east-south-east of Kingston – and coming in fast.

Downtown, street hustlers did a brisk, last-minute trade selling the provisions necessary to 'ride out Dennis': tinned mackerel, condensed milk. Most of the shoppers reportedly were women: the men were busy bracing themselves with rum.

I was staying uptown in the house of an English-born painter, Penelope Jane Stewart, or PJ, as she is known to friends. PJ had lived in Jamaica for over thirty years. The country's social malaise seemed to be of genuine concern to her, as she did good works for Catholic charities downtown, and was admired by a wide circle of Jamaicans of all backgrounds. Her house radiated an air of tranquillity; and tranquillity is what distinguishes well-off Jamaican homes from those downtown, amid the ghetto. But there was another reason why the house was enjoyed by many different people: PJ's attitude to her staff. While some wealthy (especially 'hurry-come-up' or newly wealthy) Jamaicans treat their domestics with an ill-concealed contempt, PJ was at pains to give hers the all-important respect.

As the hurricane gained strength, PJ brought in items of garden furniture; some uptowners were rumoured to be submerging metal chairs and glass-topped tables in their swimming pools. By eight o'clock a heavy rain was beating down. A few neighbours, braving the hurricane-gusts, dropped by for drinks. The storm seemed to have unleashed a tipsy excitement in them. They began to speak in raised voices of the devastation caused in Jamaica by other hurricanes. Hurricane Gilbert, in 1988, had left forty-five Jamaicans dead and one-third of the population in shelters. In the period of 'national reconstruction' that followed, Jamaica's pro-Reagan government announced that the island would not this time turn to Britain for aid, but to the United States. This was a turning point in Anglo-Jamaican relations, as Jamaica moved further into the Washington camp and the US Agency for International Development (USAID) imposed hard-to-repay 'financial assistance'.

I went to bed and tried to sleep, but the night was sticky with heat. At four o'clock came a terrific explosion and wailing – a thunderclap had set off car alarms in the neighbourhood. I stood transfixed by the window as the palm trees, lit up by lightning, banged their heads on the lawn, then whipped back like dry-fly rods.

*

When I woke next morning I turned on the television. Vegetation for miles round Kingston had been turned to pulp; flash floods had driven 2,000 people into shelters. In the worst hit of Jamaica's fourteen parishes, St Thomas, graves had been uprooted, while in the Kingston suburb of Portmore a crocodile had been washed out of a gully. It took five men five hours to truss it with ropes and cart it off to the city zoo.

Yet Jamaica had got off lightly. At the last moment 'Dennis the Menace' had veered north towards Cuba, becoming a mere tea-cup typhoon. The morning rush-hour traffic heading downtown was nevertheless infernal, owing to the hurricane floods. Trucks, motorbikes, animal-drawn conveyances moved at an agonising pace along Constant Spring Road. For some reason, bright yellow butterflies had proliferated in the wake of the hurricane; the roadside *Lignum vitae* trees were covered in them.

Most of the bus passengers (including me) had been cajoled on board by the driver and his team of conductors. Competition to fill bus seats in Kingston is fierce as drivers vie aggressively to scoop up passengers from the kerb. The essence of Kingston – the place where the noisy, violent and frequently humorous quality of the city's life unfolds – must be the bus. A white man seen on a bus has either lost his mind or his place in society; like the 'walk-foot buckra' (white man) who had no horse in the days of slavery, I was looked upon as a misfit – a loser, even.

Parts of Kingston, as seen from the bus window, resembled a tropical Surrey: statues of Queen Victoria and squat-towered Anglican churches abounded. But America ruled now, and with American values had come Burger King outlets and air-conditioned shopping malls. With over 900,000 inhabitants – almost 30 per cent of Jamaica's population – Kingston is unquestionably the greatest urban concentration of the West Indies. But it is not a pretty city and I doubted it ever was. While the French and Spanish had built beautiful outposts where they settled in the Caribbean, the British had allowed Kingston to grow in ugly parallel streets down to the sea's edge.

Further downtown stood the old slave depot, where sallow-faced merchants had waited to buy 'cargo' newly arrived from West Africa. On disembarkation the slaves were fed, washed, shaved and rubbed with palm oil until they gleamed 'healthily' for the market place. Lying about the wharves were also hundreds of decrepit slave-ship sailors known as 'wharfingers', who no longer had commercial value, but crawled into empty sugar casks to die. All this human wretchedness was in the trivial cause of sweetness: sugar. Jamaica was pilloried, appropriately, as 'the Dunghill of the Universe' (in 1788, in the *Massachusetts Centinel*).

I got off at Kingston's high-rise financial district, with its lush botanical parks and colonial King's House. A hush seemed to lie on this part of the city after the hurricane, people's faces strange in the close, steamy light. I had been warned not to go downtown. 'People are very grudgeful down there,' uptowners would tell me. 'You have to know what you're doing.'

Orange Street, a dark, narrow strip of asphalt, had once been Kingston's business sector, but now it was full of barren yards, and lined with little wood shacks and shops. A reek of spoiling meat, or perhaps sewage, hung in the air. Most of the dilapidation was the work of sun and rain, but man had done the rest. One store owner, exasperated by the use passers-by made of his shopfront, had put up the polite notice: 'Please Don't URINATE (PIST) Here. Thank You man COOL'.

Hot and in need of a drink, I headed further downtown in the direction of Coronation Market ('Corrie' to Kingstonians). A slight wind was up when I got there and blue plastic tarpaulins flapped over the stalls. Built in 1936 on the accession of George VI, the market was a higgler's domain full of bargains and trash: mango-sellers had set down their country load and tripe-vendors were yelling prices amid spillings of rice and brown sugar. Wealthier Jamaicans rarely venture down to 'Corrie'. The few who do first leave their jewellery at home, then put on a hostile 'screw face' to ward off filching hands. With its hustling sales pitches, Corrie was a world away from the American-style supermarkets uptown; it was more like a residue of West Africa, overflowing with tin plates, plastic mirrors, scissors, razors, assortments of hair beads and hair braids.

The market felt more edgy the closer I got to Tivoli Gardens, a ramshackle housing project, where porters were pushing handcarts at speed. Tivoli Gardens, formerly the Back-o-Wall slum, had been built in 1966 by the Jamaica Labour Party government or JLP. The inhabitants had been loyal to the opposing political party, the People's National Party or PNP, and the government wanted rid of them. On the morning of 12 July 1966, armed police dispersed the residents with tear gas, batons and rifle-shot, then bulldozers rolled in behind the police, flattening the shanty. The newly installed JLP strong men were afterwards supplied with firearms ('vote-getters') in exchange for their continued political allegiance. With the construction of Tivoli Gardens, the lines were drawn for generations to come: JLP or PNP? For or against? Today when rival gunmen chase each other through the market stalls, as often happens, bystanders get hit, most of them women.

Women make up 46 per cent of the Jamaican labour force, the highest per capita ratio in the world, and Coronation Market was effectively a matriarchy. In their heavy leather shoes and wide straw hats the higglers stood, hands on hips, over pyramids of yams and salted cod fish. Sometimes they travel for miles into Kingston by *jitney* (mule cart), and they run the peasant economy on which the Jamaican capital depends for its daily food. One higgler, glancing at my Bible-black notebook, addressed me: 'You a preacher man?' When I said no, she tried to sell me a 'roots' drink said to aid sexual potency. 'It big you up nice, my dear, and make you evva ready for love.' Jamaicans call these concoctions 'front-end lifters'. I do not think they work.

In my imagination, downtown had been a volatile place where white people inevitably become a target. ('I went to the place where every white face is an invitation to robbery,' Joe Strummer of the Clash said in 1977 of Kingston.) Instead I had found only friendliness and, in the market anyway, a sociable atmosphere. At the exit, a dreadlocked man was calling out to passers-by from a pile of lavatory rolls he had for sale. 'Everyting mus' go!' To my (and possibly his) surprise I bought a roll. 'Arright, man, rispeck,' he nodded.

*

Today I was going to the funeral of a High Court judge, Ronald Small, who had died in Kingston aged ninety-seven. The Jamaica of Judge Small's childhood had been hidebound by colonial red tape, its justice system overwhelmingly white and stuffed with antiquated, precedence-ridden lawyers from the Inns of Court in London. I could imagine that Small had grown up with a complicated understanding of what he was and what he was not – at a time after the First World War, when Jamaica had not much hope of independence.

The funeral was held in St Luke's, an Anglican church at the Cross Roads section of midtown. In the pews sat august-looking members of the Jamaican judiciary in chalk-striped suits. It was a very British (or Anglican Jamaican) occasion. The Small family were conducted to their seats by an usher in a clerical dog collar. Among them were the poet Robin ('Bongo Jerry') Small and the human rights lawyer Richard Small.

We learned that Judge Small had been a 'very British' Jamaican, who liked to relax at weekends in Edwardian knickerbockers and gave his daughter five shillings every time she recited a stanza of Gray's *Elegy*. To be a Jamaican of this sort, it was implied, was to be a little eccentric; yet Judge Small's pre-war education, with its jingoist myopia and labyrinth of Empire-era prohibitions, had been no less strange. School essays were set on such subjects as how to build a snowman at Christmas, scarcely relevant to semi-tropical Jamaica.

The deceased was praised as a 'public servant' who had practised the 'major export' of the British Empire: British justice. The 'sober, upright seriousness' of the British judiciary together with the 'stoical uncomplaining character' (as Judge Small saw it) of the British were therefore honoured. 'Never put your wishbone where your backbone ought to be,' Judge Small had liked to tell his children.

Afterwards the organist struck up 'Waltzing Matilda' and the congregation filed out of St Luke's into a downpour of warm rain. In the doorways people were putting up umbrellas. 'I hope your father's death was an easy one,' I said to Richard Small, the lawyer. (My own father had just died; I felt real sympathy.) Small looked at me sadly: 'Oh yes, you know, at his time of life – he died of old age.' We agreed to meet later at his Kingston legal practice.

*

At the legal practice, the noise of the traffic on Seymour Avenue was muffled by whirring fans. Richard Small, seated behind a desk, now seemed more wary of me. The values and standards of colonial Britain had not been as attractive to him as to his father. As a law student in 1960s London Small had been involved in the Caribbean Artists Movement, a Pan-African group which aimed (like the Harlem Renaissance in pre-civil rights America) to rehabilitate African identity in West Indian art, literature and music. He had also helped to set up the London-based Campaign Against Racial Discrimination, or CARD, which sought to combat racial injustices in 1960s Britain.

Having returned to Jamaica, Small was part of a growing body of intellectuals who believed that Jamaica must separate constitutionally from Britain and become a republic. Republican sentiment had been more prevalent in Jamaica in the 1970s, when the ruling PNP had absorbed the orthodoxies of Black Power and sought to distance itself somewhat from Queen Elizabeth II (who had claimed that *The Black and White Minstrel Show* was among her favourite television programmes). But in those days Jamaica had more trading links with Britain, and the trappings of British colonialism had been more visible, more numerous and, for Richard Small and others, more deleterious.

I asked Small what Jamaica had achieved in the four decades since the Union Jack came down: the fruits of independence, it could be argued, had failed to ripen.

' "Failed" is the right word,' said Small, relaxing a little. 'We got a new flag in 1962, a national motto, a national anthem, a flower, a fruit, even a national bird. But what has Jamaica *done* with its independence? That is the question.'

He added, 'Corruption is a very serious problem in Jamaica but we haven't bothered to address it. Unfortunately,' he went on with a rueful expression, 'if you lament the corruption of drugs – the corruption of politics – Jamaicans may take you for a neo-colonialist who wants to return Jamaica to the days of British law and British order. Well,' he concluded, 'I'm not going to get trapped into that foolishness.'

After the hopes and frustrations of 1962 – the bunting, the maypoles, the float parades of the great independence party – why is the illusion of British power still so strenuously maintained in Jamaica? Jamaican senators, Jamaican cabinet ministers, Jamaican judges of the high courts must all swear allegiance to 'Elizabeth the Second, by the Grace of God, Queen of Jamaica'. Jamaica's prolonged union with the royal family, surely, is a last vestige of colonialism – a subject people's obeisance to Britannia and to that ghost of empire, the Commonwealth. What has Jamaica's reward been for its loyalty? Few British people today take much interest in Jamaica or Jamaican affairs. 'It's not just ignorant British people who don't know or care where Jamaica is,' Small commented, 'it's *by and large* that British people don't know or care where Jamaica is.' Really? Back in the 1960s, Small insisted, most Britons thought the West Indies had to do with India. And now Jamaica, once Britain's most profitable sugar-bowl and slave depot, was being repaid with British neglect and, Small reckoned, abandonment to the United States.

Unsurprisingly, republicanism is growing in Jamaica. In October 2007 Prime Minister Bruce Golding (of the ruling JLP) pledged to take steps to replace the Queen with a Jamaican president to be chosen by the Jamaican people. Elsewhere in the English-speaking Caribbean – St Lucia, Grenada, Antigua, St Vincent – the monarchy is also under scrutiny. Less affection will be shown to Prince Charles when and if he succeeds to the throne; he is too associated with 'shame and scandal in the family' (to quote the title of a Trinidadian calypso) to enjoy the uncomplicated reverence shown 'Missus Queen'. In the meantime it was hard to disagree with Richard Small that the Union Jack had yet to come down completely on Jamaica. Having shaped Jamaica's past for ill, Britain had not helped to shape its future for good. As Richard Small accompanied me to the exit, he said that in Jamaica, as elsewhere, conflict has been the legacy of empire.

2

Trench Town Mix Up

PJ's housekeeper, Valerie Salmon, was a wise, self-contained woman in her early fifties, who flip-flopped round the kitchen in the mornings frying plantain and boiling green banana. 'Jamaica always was kinda in a certain bankruptcy,' she told me one day, 'but after Hurricane Dennis it a whole lot worse.'

Valerie's was a typical story of rural migration to Kingston. Thirty years ago, in 1976, she had arrived in the big city with money sewn into her coat lining. The crime rate was no deterrent to her; Kingston was – still is – the island's industrial and economic dynamo. Each week the city is pushed a little further outside its boundaries as countryfolk like Valerie continue to migrate there in search of work, and the government is obliged (if reluctantly) to bring services out to the proliferating shack colonies. It was to a government housing estate – a tenement yard – that Valerie arrived, travel-stained and bewildered, in the summer of 1976.

Firearms were ubiquitous and the inhabitants took advantage of Valerie as a newcomer. The guns offended her countryside propriety but what could she do? Life in the ghetto, thrashed and twisted, was controlled by gangsters who did the bidding of the politicians. 'If you didn't have gun,' Valerie said to me, 'the drug men kill you – if you did have gun, them kill you even worse.' In her view, there will always somebody at the top in Jamaican society who dictated the terms to those below. All Jamaicans had 'prejudice': even the poor in the shack dumps uptown looked down on those in the squatter colonies downtown. 'I don't know if it's a master–slave thing or what,' Valerie said, 'but is so life go.' Jamaicans call this social ordering – the sense that a hierarchy lies beneath all social interaction – 'ranking'.

'Uptown Top Ranking', the pop-reggae hit of 1978 (sung by the teenage Jamaican duo Althea and Donna), while hardly a social commentary, emphasised the distinction between Kingston's wealthy uptown and its impoverished downtown. In recent years the distinction has blurred as crime has crept uptown, and now even middle-class areas with their tranquil, shaded gardens are affected by inner-city violence. Everyone in Kingston – uptown, midtown, downtown – seemed to be frightened of everyone else. The fear had spread like a contagion up into the hills to penetrate the burglar-barred communities there.

But down in the ghetto, you are still in the presence of the aftermath of slavery, said Valerie, 'the giant evil', and you are not allowed to forget it. See for yourself, how the men and women stand by the roadside for hours – sullen, numbed; how the children are un-childlike; the women, hardened. The ghetto folk have become the 'property' of politicians, turned into 'things', judged Valerie. She was a woman of formidable intelligence with a tough yard-woman wisdom and a very Jamaican lack of sentimentality.

Trench Town, the ghetto I was to visit that morning, had been developed in the 1940s to accommodate West Indian troops returning home after the war. It had decayed into a violent place, disaffected. Trench Town's tenement yards gave rise to the much misunderstood term 'Yardie', meaning a Jamaican who lives or operates overseas, often but not necessarily in the criminal sector. Kingston gang members are getting younger; they feel they must kill and carry ever 'better' weapons in order to rank themselves higher. Today Trench Town is known as 'Fatherless World', 'Congo Zone' or 'Hellhole' – names that had once applied to the Chicago housing projects where Barack Obama had cut his teeth. It might have been dangerous for me to visit on my own, so a Kingston pastor, Bobby Wilmot, was to accompany me. I was told to wait for Pastor Bobby outside the Kentucky Fried Chicken outlet in Halfway Tree, midtown.

Halfway Tree was heaving with early morning commuters, a hectic interchange of cars and buses. The congestion in Kingston eases slightly between eleven in the morning and two in the afternoon. Second-hand cars from Japan – 'deportees', Jamaicans call them – have worsened the traffic and made life in the city intolerable for many. Maids and other domestic staff were riding buses uptown to serve the comfortable classes there, much as Soweto's black inhabitants travel into Johannesburg. Not least because of the distance involved, the journey north is an ordeal for these people, involving hours of travel on cratered roads. The inhabitants of the ghetto seem to come home only to sleep.

I kept my eyes fixed on the hazy mass of traffic crawling my way: Japanese deportees everywhere. I was about to phone the pastor when from the petrol-fumed depths of the traffic a voice called out to me, 'Morning, Mr Ian. Glad to see you lookin' so well this Lord's honest day.' I climbed into Pastor Bobby's Japanese jeep. Three mobile phones were clipped to his waist like grenades and a sticker on the dashboard proclaimed, 'No Jesus No Life. Know Jesus Know Life'. Bobby Wilmot looked happy and, at forty-four, he looked good, too, a beaming, good-natured man of transparent kindness. He was one of several Trench Town evangelists who acted as brokers among the ghetto's warring gangs, working hard to regenerate the area.

My impression was that Pastor Bobby liked the glamour that went with forging turf truces. 'The job keeps me busy,' he said as we stalled in traffic on Slipe Road, exhaust fumes coming in through the window. We were heading for a primary school in the heart of Trench Town, the 'Joy Town Learning Centre', and were making slow progress. Rastafarians sped enviably past us on their bone-shakers; they at least had the right idea.

On the ghetto outskirts, Pastor Bobby seemed to be much liked. People called out to him from the roadside 'Highly bless!' or 'Pastor B!' and I felt a warmth of understanding between them. He spoke of his work like a tent-show revivalist, in passionate, declamatory outbursts. 'Yessir,' he said to me, teeth flashing with confidence, 'you mustn't be a lone ranger in Trench Town – you must *fellowship* on the street.'

The heat was blistering. 'Here, boss, step out of the sun,' the pastor manoeuvred me into a patch of shade as we got out of the car by the primary school. Zinc-fenced shanties stood to our left and right; there was a clump of palms, and through the branches a tin roof glinted. Mopping his brow, Bobby explained why the school, on its inauguration in 1994, had been named 'Joy Town'. 'We wanted to get rid of the *entrenched* – the Trenchish Town mentality of Us and Them. So, for a mental readjustment we hit on Joy Town.' In its previous incarnation the school had been a Women's Institute; Pastor Bobby showed me the cornerstone laid in 1947 by 'Mrs H. M. Foot', wife of Jamaica's then colonial secretary Sir Hugh Foot (brother of the British Labour Party politician Michael Foot). British colonialism had extended even to women's welfare. Pastor Bobby parted bead curtains at the doorway, and ushered me into a hangar-like room full of empty desks; the children had yet to arrive. A sour smell of chicken pervaded the air.

The school stood on the infamous JLP–PNP borderline of Seventh Street. Back in the mid-1970s when Kingston had been riven by political violence, Seventh Street was a fire-scarred danger zone that served to divide and even destroy families. Those on the Rema side of Seventh Street were centre-right JLP (or 'Jelly'); those on the Arnett Gardens side, socialist PNP (or 'Peanut'); and down the middle, well, they might have been informers. Even today, just walking on the wrong side of Seventh Street can be a potentially fatal act. 'There's no safe middle ground in Jamaican politics, never has been,' said Pastor Bobby. 'Either it's PNP or JLP. Black or white.' In this land of extremes, he reckoned, there wasn't even much of a middle class any more. What Jamaica needed, in Bobby's view, was an alternative to the old two-party Westminster system bequeathed by Britain.

Moving off, we drove across scrubland, the morning still hot and shadowless as we continued on past the razor wire and watch-towers of an abandoned remand centre, and through vacant lots of tall, spiny grass until we came to one of the neighbourhood's most volatile zones: Rema, a JLP-loyal garrison constituency.

On street corners, pariah dogs prowled round heaps of burning rubbish. 'I've seen quite a few shoot-outs here in my time,' the pastor was saying, 'and the cowboy shows are *still* running.' He had no sooner spoken than a crowd of tense-looking women emerged by a roadblock of tyres and corrugated metal sheets. Bobby slowed down as one of them shouted out to him, 'Pastor B!' She looked flushed with rage, affronted. I quickly put away my notebook (it gave me a provocatively official air) while Bobby addressed the woman through the car window. 'Wha gwaan?' We soon found out.

A youth from Federal Gardens, an adjacent gang turf, had been executed that morning by the police; now another young man, Courtney, had been killed. Right here, in Rema. By the police? No, by a rival gang. The roadblock was to prevent retaliatory drive-by shootings.

Bobby got out his handkerchief, wiped his brow. 'Lord of mercy,' he said, and with a distressed expression added: 'Me a tell you something, Ian. Misery cause people to act desperate and kill. And idleness, Ian, it breed vice. And you see what happen when a man idle? You see when a man hungry? A man go tief! A man go kill!'

We pulled up in front of Rema's community centre. Painted over the entrance was an effigy of Her Majesty Elizabeth II, Queen of Jamaica. Her face, beneath a gimcrack tiara, bore the pockmarks of bullets. The building, weed-encrusted and splashed with urine, seemed part of the nightmare. I followed Pastor Bobby to the entrance, where a short, sleek man with a scarred face was standing draped in Nike-brand clothes and gold neck chains. A Rema don, I guessed, ranked by his labels. I kept a distance while the pastor went up to him and began to speak. 'But it retard progress!' I heard him say in reference, I guessed, to the morning's killing of Courtney. The man lowered his head, then flicked me a hostile look; instinct warned me not to hold his gaze.

Upstairs we met Ziggy Soul, a fellow evangelist, who had a box-like recording studio where teenagers were encouraged to lay down their beats and rhythms. The walls were pasted with big adverts urging the love of God. 'If the kids can't record, all they talk about is dissing people up,' said Ziggy Soul, a self-styled 'Distributor of the Holy Writ'. Violence was now so deeply ingrained in the local culture of 'respect', Soul went on, that to be in charge, you had to 'batter' people. 'That's the way it goes' – Soul's voice was casual but I could see the concern in his eyes.

Presently a tall thin man called Sledge Hammer (not, need one say, his baptismal name) turned up. 'Yo, wuzzup?' he looked at Pastor Bobby, then at Ziggy Soul, but not at me. Sledge had embraced Christianity under the pastor's guidance, but if he knew something about Courtney's murder, he was not going to say. Informers are despised in Jamaica; they can take the brunt of the rage that is always unleashed in a community following a murder; the rage is directed against the police, the judiciary, the undertakers – anyone involved in the Jamaican death business. It is best to keep quiet about what you know.

Sledge was a big man about my age – forty-five – but he looked younger. He was supposed to be a law-abiding sort now that he had found Jesus Christ. Bobby asked him how the world was treating him; Sledge lit a cigarette, said, 'Okay, pastor.' His sister Deborah worked in a literacy school nearby, Operation Restoration. She might know something about Courtney's death. 'You cyaan ask her.' Saying which, Sledge exhaled smoke, standing his ground.

At Operation Restoration the principal was distraught. 'Pastor!' She made a sharp noise with her breathing. 'I'm tryin' to keep my thoughts orderly. What's goin' on?' She stamped her feet. 'The police kill a man – you know that? And now Courtney's got killed. A war's on, Bobby, and the children are getting' scared and aggressive.' Apparently they had begun to jab at each other with pencils.

Sledge's sister was nowhere to be found. For the moment, only the bullet holes above the entrance showed how lethal the area could be. Pastor Bobby said to the principal, 'I'm as much 'fraid as you are, Lorna, plenty 'fraid.'

Lorna Stanley, a Jamaican in her late fifties, kept a poky office, with the blood spots of squashed bugs on the wall under a sign, 'Relax. God is Control'. She made to cross her heart. 'It give me the chills,' she said; a rumour was circulating that Sledge had killed Courtney. 'If Sledge is out there again, we might as well forget about it.' Sobs broke up her sentences as she sat down and dialled a number. 'Sledge? . . . That you? Oh Sledge. If you've left us . . . I beg of you, Sledge, *please* . . .'

Pastor Bobby was about to say something when the phone rang again. Lorna grabbed it. 'Operation Restoration. No, them nevva kill Courtney for drugs.' Courtney, well liked locally, had dis-respected somebody. '*Now* what must I do?' Stanley bit her lip. 'Even if the gunshots are audible out there, at least the children are safe in here with us. So we've been blessed. And I'm holdin' straight. But today for the first time I feel like *giving up*.' Suddenly her head was on the desk and she was crying.

For thirty years Stanley had worked in Florida as a journalist on the *Palm Beach Post*. Thousands of Jamaicans had migrated to Florida in the 1930s and 1940s in search of work. They ended up, many of them, on cane fields and citrus groves, where they created distinctive communities. By the 1990s, however, their reputation had become tarnished by Yardie gunmen, who gave the majority of honest, law-abiding Jamaicans a bad name. (As long ago as the 1970s in Canada, a police 'ten most-wanted' list included a picture of a dreadlocked man described as 'a Rastafarian'.) Jamaica's increasingly negative image abroad distressed Stanley so much that she decided to go home and set up as a social worker in Trench Town. Her life's task, she said to me (with a touch of rhetoric), was to 'help the forsaken of the ghetto'.

The day she opened a kindergarten in 1994 in Trench Town a turf war broke out. 'There was like a *barrage* of shots – all day long. Rat-tat-tat-tat. Oh my golly G!' Parents, fearing a full-scale gang battle, kept their children at home, which meant taking time off from work and losing money. Some children became gun-carriers or sold drugs for 'top rankers' high up in the distribution chain.

Guns, said Stanley, provided the 'respect' the poor so badly needed. 'The moment you're walking with steel,' she said, 'is the moment you have the power to boss it over others. Yes, a youth with a gun is a youth to be feared and looked up to: murder is his badge of honour.' She paused, nodded staunchly. 'But a child who can read and write, well that's different, that child is less open to the bad man's bidding; less gullible. I mean, look at Pops,' Stanley suddenly announced, looking up at the boy who had entered her office carrying a tray with a plate of rice and peas. Pops, the school cook, put the food down in front of me to eat, while Stanley explained, 'Pops used to flip hamburgers for a living, but then he knifed someone nearly to death. Now Pops has dropped his fist-fight ways and he's learnin' to read and write. Ain't that right, Pops?' Pops replied mechanically, head bowed, 'Yes, Miss Stanley. I used to feel like a dog, but now I don't feel like a dog no more.'

'See?' Stanley said to me with an air of triumph. 'Pops used to be dark [meaning 'ignorant'] but now he feels good, he *knows* the book is better than the gun.' Pops gave Stanley a sidelong glance, then drifted away.

In Stanley's view, Jamaican politicians had kept the poor in ignorance because it paid them to do so. It is much easier to manipulate the unlettered and use them (in Stanley's expression) as 'election fodder'. Illiteracy rates in Jamaica currently stand at between 13 and 15 per cent of the population, reaching 70 per cent in the Kingston ghetto: this ranks among the highest in the English-speaking Caribbean. Stanley said she was no longer so sure which politicians controlled which gangs. 'All I know is, there are four gangs out there within a *whisper* of each other, and they're killing each other for nothing – for nothing at all.' In this degraded world, cash ruled. Twenty thousand Jamaican dollars will be a man's reward for killing someone (what Jamaicans call doing 'a little ting'). Stanley said, 'That's a lot of money. Well, what would *you* do?'

At that precise moment Sledge's sister Deborah happened to walk in; tall, slender, she had corn-rowed and beaded hair.

'This gentleman a friend of yours?' she asked Stanley.

'We never saw him before,' Stanley replied, 'but he know Pastor Bobby.'

Deborah said 'Oh,' and shrugged.

Stanley, getting down to business, asked Deborah, 'So who killed Courtney?'

'You asking me? Ask Pastor Bobby. I don't really know.'

'I'm asking you.'

'Keep asking,' said Deborah. She was staring Stanley down.

'I'll ask you another one: can you *swear* Sledge isn't involved?'

Courtney was killed by persons unknown, Deborah said eventually, and he was killed because he defected from one gang (the Ninjas) to another (the Action Pack).

'A traitor?' I said.

'Pathetic, yes,' Stanley said to me, 'there's no escaping it, but things like that happen here all the time.'

Time was when Deborah used to 'preach badness' herself: she hid guns from the police, she sold drugs. She was not a fallen woman exactly – she had nowhere to fall to. Then, like her brother Sledge, she saw the Christian light, divorced her gunman husband and joined Operation Restoration. Her almost Victorian story of self-help was one of many in Trench Town. Stanley put it this way: 'The can-do spirit in Jamaica is amazing. Who says Jamaicans aren't reformable? We're the best at everything. The best athletes. The best musicians. Well, yes, the best murderers, too.'

With Deborah's help, Stanley ran a pressure group, 'Strong Woman of Trench Town' (SWOTT), which campaigned to keep guns off the streets. What was incongruous to me – Jamaican women taking on Jamaican men – was less so to Deborah and Lorna. 'We as strong as men,' Stanley laughed. 'We break heads, we mash up people same as men do.' Caught up in a 'district code' warfare, where turfs are respected on pain of death and the trigger for death is sprung tight, Jamaican women had to be strong.

*

'The Yardies call the shots,' Pastor Bobby told me; he should know. In 2000 a church mission in south London, the Ascension Trust, had appointed him its 'Jamaica consultant'. The director of the Trust, the Reverend Les Isaac, had begun to despair of the number of black youths he was having to bury in London following 'Jamaican-style' gang murders – death by gun; death by knife: every fifty minutes in London, a knife crime. South London gangs such as the Cold Hearted Crew and Beg For Mercy were fighting over the control of postal districts. Though most members were – are – substantively British (the grandchildren of post-war West Indian migrants), they were copying the personalities and methods of Jamaica's homicidal narcotics trade; and, once armed, were dangerously empowered.

The Reverend Isaac felt he needed to go to Jamaica to see how broken homes – absent fathers – were giving rise to generations of angry teenagers disengaged from society. Roadblocks of blazing tyres greeted his arrival. 'I thought I was in a war zone,' he told me from his office in Brixton. 'All that was missing was Martin Bell of the BBC.' More than the barricades, however, Isaac was shocked by the virtual absence in Trench Town of the elderly. 'Once a kid's so much as *touched* a gun,' he explained, 'his life expectancy's down to zero.' Almost half of Kingston's population – an astonishing 42 per cent – is below the age of twenty. The usual way out of the ghetto (by now it was obvious) was prematurely in a coffin.

The levels of despair and hopelessness in Trench Town struck Isaac as incurable. The church, the police and other powerful establishments had moved operations uptown. Thus the Jamaican state was failing to provide human security for its poorest population. Charities, free-food programmes and other inner city agencies no longer wanted to go downtown: they were too frightened. Parts of downtown have become a state within a state, where the residents pay no rent or utility bills; and the dons give themselves titles like 'President', because they pretty much rule the place. The only hope for downtown – the Reverend Isaac reckoned – lay in churchmen like Pastor Bobby, who were taking the gospel out to the street. 'Everything is politics,' he added. 'Including the word of Jesus.'

In some respects twenty-first-century Jamaica, with its mass poverty, its social resentments, its skewed distribution of wealth, is like pre-Revolution France; only in Jamaica there is no sign of a revolutionary movement, no glimmer even of organised political protest. So the wealthy will have nothing to fear: the poor are too disorganised, too ill-educated, for social revolution. There is, however, something far worse: thousands of empty, wasted lives, and an endemic of violence, in which God is a US-import Glock.

3

Strictly Come Dancehall

I was sitting in a bar on Marcus Garvey Drive called Oysters and Conch, trying to refresh myself with a pineapple Ting and ice. It was Saturday morning, and a thick sticky heat was closing in off the Kingston waterfront. The bar was a hang-out for youths who liked to come here to listen to the latest chart hits and, true to stereotype, talk about sex, money, what kind of rims to put on their cars, but above all music.

In Jamaica, music is the vital expression. Night and day, amid the heat and narrow lanes of downtown Kingston, rap, ragga and reggae boom from giant loudspeaker cabinets: a heavy musical beat. Few know more about Jamaican music than Gladwin 'Gladdy Wax' Wright, who ran a record shop in Stoke Newington, north London, not far from the gang-blighted Somerford Grove Estate. The shop, stacked with collector's vinyl, had served as a meeting place for Jamaicans living in London and a place to exchange news of home. I was an occasional customer, and before I left for Jamaica I went to see Wright.

We were sitting at the counter drinking instant coffee with condensed milk – Jamaican-style – when Wright said to me: 'How can anyone *not* like Jamaican music? Man, it give you a big lift up of the spirit.' He rocked slightly on his chair as a bass-heavy sound pulsed from speakers on a high shelf. Wright had grown up outside Spanish Town in the early 1960s, but had lived in England now for over forty years.

His father had come over in 1955 on the SS *Auriga*, a converted Italian troopship. Norman Washington Manley had just become prime minister in Jamaica, and his party, the PNP, was encouraging Jamaicans to provide labour for the mother country. The British presence in Jamaica was apparently for the benefit of Jamaicans, and Britain's greatness – as measured by its possession of Jamaica – was a source of pride to many Jamaicans. Over a quarter of a million Jamaicans – one-tenth of the island's population – migrated in the 1950s.

Wright's father, working first as a carpenter in the north-west, bought himself a house in Birmingham for £1,800. Ten years later, in the winter of 1965, his five children came to England accompanied by their mother, who was Cuban. At Southampton the family were directed to a 'boat-train' destined for Victoria, where they were met by a relative, who drove them up to Birmingham in a borrowed car. That year saw one of the coldest winters on record in Europe. 'It was so cold,' Gladwin recalled, 'that me and my brothers had to wear pyjamas under our Terylene suits.'

In Birmingham, a city with an already large West Indian community, Gladwin and his family settled in his father's house on Hatfield Road. Jamaicans had first moved to the area in the 1950s because of the opportunities for work. Between 1953 and 1958 the West Indian population of Birmingham had swelled from 8,000 to 30,000. But in the grey, inhospitable Midlands of those days, Jamaicans found most social clubs were reserved for whites, with pubs excluding black drinkers from their lounge bars. So Jamaicans held 'bashments' or 'blues parties' at each other's houses: in festively crowded front rooms West Indian mento and American R & B would be played into the early hours. Wright spent most Saturday nights standing by stacked speaker boxes, tie loosened, foot tapping, with a can of Harp in hand (Red Stripe came later).

In 1967, he installed a sound system in his father's sitting room. 'It had a 10-watt valve amplifier,' he recalled, 'and it made a good impression.' Competition was fierce among rival sound-men on Hatfield Road, so the 'Gladdy Wax' sound-system grew ever more loud. Complaints from neighbours were ignored: the idea was to 'blow the street to full watts'.

With West Indian expatriate life teeming in 1960s Birmingham, skinheads began to listen to Jamaican ska, a speedy jazz-tinged shuffle-beat. Ska had begun in the early 1960s as a Jamaican twist on black American dance music – 'upside-down R & B', as the guitarist Ernest Ranglin put it. Scooter-riding Mods had originally adopted it as a supplement to their diet of imported American soul, and soon a taste of Trench Town swagger was brought to Britain, through such Jamaican groups as the Skatalites, and the Jamaican singers Derrick Morgan and the late, great Desmond Dekker.

Oddly, given their racial antagonisms, skinheads rarely beat up Jamaicans (by 'niggers' they usually meant Pakistanis). Ska's driving, dance-floor rhythms appealed to their passion for uptempo black music, sharp clothes, short hair. Sometimes, if suitably dressed in crombies and two-tone Trevira suits, Jamaicans were even allowed to join skinhead gangs. Jamaicans were seen as less satisfactory when they 'acted clannish' or 'kept to themselves': in other words, when they failed – like the 'Pakis' – to assimilate into British culture.

Ska was, triumphantly, a Commonwealth music, that took hold in Britain's inner cities where Caribbean migration was at its most dense. 'My Boy Lollipop', sung by Millie Small with a pert under-age suggestiveness, was one of the earliest pop-ska hits. It swept Britain in 1964, followed by other novelty ska numbers such as Prince Buster's 'Al Capone'. For a while this sort of music brought the poor whites and poor blacks of Britain together. By the early 1970s, however, with football hooliganism a fact of British life, skinheads were increasingly seen as National Front recruits. Enoch Powell had evoked images of a sanguinary race war in his 1968 'Rivers of Blood' speech, and life in Britain no longer seemed so tolerant of minorities.

Gladwin Wright meanwhile had witnessed ska evolve into its languid offshoot of rocksteady (a rhythm said to have been adapted from waves hitting the sides of a slave ship), and finally into reggae, which, with its slowed-down, marijuana-heavy beat, would absorb happily into the middle-class hippie culture which the skinheads professed to despise. The word reggae, originally spelled 'reggay', had first appeared in 1968 with a Leslie Kong-produced hit called 'Do the Reggay' by Toots and the Maytals, and is believed to be of African – possibly Yoruban – origin. 'Reggae really is an African music,' Wright said to me, beating out a rhythm on the shop counter. 'Its heart belong to Africa. Its beat to Africa. Yes, man, it's the rhythm of the heartbeat – of the African drum beat.'

35

When Wright first came to London, in 1981, he recalled that he was 'bedazzled' by what he found. 'Trafalgar Square! Where'd I been all this time?' The stone lions on the Embankment were symbolic, in his star-struck imagination, of the Rastafari Lion of Judah, otherwise known as King Emperor Haile Selassie of Ethiopia, the Rastafari Black Christ. In between jobs Wright worked at 'Ital Records', a Jamaican music shop at 112 Stoke Newington High Street, run by two dreadlocked aficionados, Judah and Burt. Wright began to take the 'Gladdy Wax' sound system to Notting Hill for the summer carnival, his huge speaker boxes blasting out roots reggae by Gladdy and the Groove Syndicate, and the Pathfinders, his own bands.

Wright's big break came in 1987, when a pirate radio station in Jamaica appointed him its London deejay. British audiences began to tune in to Radio Supreme just to hear Gladdy play his selections of ska, rocksteady and reggae. Four years later, in 1992, he opened his record shop on Northwold Road opposite the entrance to Abney Park cemetery on Stoke Newington High Street. 'And sometimes it really humble me,' he said, 'people come here and say they recorded *every one* of my radio shows. Yes, man, my music give them plenty pleasure.' In December 2005, after fourteen years of trading, the shop closed and Gladdy moved on to the internet for trading. It has been replaced by the inevitable 'Perfect Fried Chicken' outlet.

*

One Friday afternoon, humid after rainfall, I found myself on South Camp Road in south central Kingston. I was looking for the Alpha Boys' School, a Roman Catholic orphanage founded in 1880 for 'wayward youth'. The building was protected by high, compound-style fences. Sister Maria Goretti, the current superintendent, came to greet me at the entrance and led me across a courtyard surrounded by classrooms, where 165 orphans were learning to read and write. 'We try to keep the boys in check, ' she told me. A New Zealander, Sister Goretti had lived in Jamaica for over twenty years, she said.

The orphanage is famed throughout the West Indies for its musical education. Many of Jamaica's greatest musicians were tutored there, among them the alto saxophonist Joe Harriott, now regarded as a pioneer of free jazz. Harriott had been part of a wave of Caribbean jazzmen who settled in London in the 1950s and early 1960s (the saxophonist Harry Beckett, from Barbados, was a contemporary). In England Harriott began to forge his own version of avant-garde music by fusing a Charlie Parker-style bebop with elements of his own Jamaican musical sensibility. The result was something unique, a lyrical 'abstract' jazz of tremendous originality and attack, which emerged independent of John Coltrane and Ornette Coleman in the United States. *Free Form* and *Abstract*, Harriott's greatest albums, were commercial flops but are now revered as black British Jamaican modernist works in which Parkerish improvisations zigzag across mento, calypso and other Caribbean dance tempos. Harriott died at the age of 44 in 1972, the year reggae began to filter into Britain with the Jamaican film *The Harder They Come*. The epitaph on the altoist's tombstone in Southampton reads: 'Parker? There's them over here can play a few aces too.'

Jamaican popular music would not have flourished in the 1960s and 1970s – with magnificent hit after magnificent hit – without the orphanage school on South Camp Road. Its orchestra, originally a drum and fife corps, had furnished the ranks of Jamaican military brass bands; by the 1950s, however, with vinyl recordings of swing and jazz arriving from Black America in the suitcases of Jamaican returnees, it began to produce its own swing and ska-jazz combos.

Greatest among these were the Skatalites, Jamaica's premier ska ensemble (founded in June 1964), whose trombonist Don Drummond was nine when his mother sent him to the school. Drummond remained a troubled individual and in 1966 he murdered his common-law wife, the singer and rumba dancer Margarita. He died three years later in a Kingston hospital for the insane. Mental illness was not uncommon among the black urban poor in post-colonial Jamaica, and Drummond was most likely schizophrenic. In his hands, however, the trombone took on a melancholic, minor-key sound that mirrored, wonderfully, the Revivalist religiosity of Jamaica.

The school's bandmaster, Winston 'Sparrow' Martin, was rehearsing in a field by the back entrance when I met him. 'As you were, boys,' he said, dismissing his class. Martin had known the more famous Don Drummond but taken a different path. He had played with Jimmy James and the Vagabonds, a British ska (or Blue Note) group popular in 1960s London but long since forgotten, and later was a session percussionist on the first Bob Marley and the Wailers album, *Catch a Fire*. The sound of early Wailers hits, Martin insisted, was due to Alpha musicians. 'And I'm talking about *real* musicians,' he said gravely, 'not the American-type rap dancehall stuff. That's not music: it's computer rhythms. Here at Alpha we preserve the old-style sounds.'

We went upstairs into the music hall, a large, barn-like room containing a blackboard chalked with musical staves and photographs of alumni on the wall. Don Drummond's trombone, polished to a gleam, was displayed on a shelf above the blackboard. Seats had been arranged on a stage for the musicians. I was to be treated to a concert.

The fourteen-strong Alpha orchestra trooped into the hall. Once seated (a couple of them scowling quizzically at me), Martin exhorted them: 'I don't want the wrappings or the tinsel – just the gift! You hear? All right, let's go!' The orchestra kicked into 'Eastern Standard Time', a Drummond number with elements of a dirge. The trombonists played soulfully, then picked up rip-roaringly, until the full orchestra joined in, the tune gathered momentum and I felt I was beginning to levitate out of my seat. 'Yes sir!' the bandmaster exclaimed. 'That does my heart *very* good.'

Next came a mento-calypso called Mango Walk (Jamaica Rumba), composed in 1938 by the Australian musicologist Arthur Benjamin. Martin made quick feints to right and left with his shoulders, marking out the rhythm. Not a false note was played; this was exemplary musicianship: the trumpeter finished his solo and dropped into the background while the clarinets took over, all adding to the harmony until, with 'Down Comes the Rain' by the Royals – one of the most haunting of all reggae songs – the band was playing too well to stop. In Alpha hands, even Bert Kaempfert's saccharine 'Wonderland by Night' had an up-tempo beat that could only be Jamaican.

Outside, after the concert, I leaned against a wall and got out a cigarette just to have something to do with my fingers. The Alpha orphans practise every day and they make music that you would not believe. I had been amazed. In the field ahead of me, pupils were sitting in front of their music stands, revising for their Royal School of Music exams. Somewhere saxophone music was being played: it came from the orphanage faintly through the sticky afternoon, and moved me more than I can say. Why? It seemed to belong to calmer times, when independence was briefly enjoyed in Jamaica, and it was assumed that Jamaica would make headway at home and in the wider world. I could not see how this extraordinary institution at the Alpha Boys' School would last.

*

Next day I telephoned Carlton Smith of the Tamlins, a vintage reggae trio well known in Jamaica. Kingston's 'tougher than tough' edge was reflected in the Tamlins' Philly, soul-inflected sound, and I was keen for Smith to give me a tour of Studio One, midtown, where the trio had recorded in the 1970s. I had met Smith earlier on the flight from London. 'Fus time to Jamaica?' he enquired – the Tamlins had just toured England and the concerts had gone well. 'Hackney was a boom – we mash up the place!'

Now I was sitting opposite him in a room upstairs in Halfway Tree's KFC. 'How you doin' mi breddah?' he greeted me. He had on a furry Kangol cap and a variety of gold chains beneath his leather jacket. With his neat moustache and sharp features he looked dangerous. In fact he was feeling murderous, he said. The other day a man on a motorbike and two others in a car had tailed him from a cash machine in uptown Kingston, and robbed him at gunpoint. Smith had taken aim with his gun (he is always 'strapped') but fortunately failed to kill anyone.

'When they find out who I am – what they done – they'll die for it,' Smith said, his eyes hot with anger. 'Yessir, I'll put them on ice.' He lifted up his shirt to reveal the butt of a Glock semi-automatic tucked into his waistband. 'It's licensed,' he said, and added (none too reassuringly), 'it's loaded.'

We made our way to Smith's Mercedes parked in a lot behind the Aquarius recording studio, not far from Studio One. A group of musician friends of his was chatting and smoking there when we arrived. Among them were 'Bunny' Simpson and 'Judge' Ferguson

of the sleek, roots-reggae band the Mighty Diamonds, in white
trousers, skintight at the hips, and Hendrix-style fedoras. Simpson,
with his broad pockmarked face, greeted Smith affectionately, but
Smith was not in the mood. He told Simpson of the mugging and
his intention to kill the muggers. With a slow smile Simpson told
him, 'You a bad-john, Carlton, you always was.'

A short man in a torn T-shirt was now standing next to me. Smith
introduced him as Headley Bennett, the Studio One saxophonist,
ex-Alpha School. Bennett, friendly, offered to sell me a copy of his
latest CD, *Deadley Headley*. He had a plastic carrier bag full of
them; I bought one. As I stood talking to Bennett, another man
joined us. For a long moment he stared at me, then he opened his
bag and took out a knife.

'What you think?' he asked, tendering me the blade. I hesitated,
not saying anything. 'What's holdin' you?' the knife-carrier said.
Was he all right in the head? With a qualm of fear I flicked a finger
across the blade. 'Ah, yes, man, don't be frighten,' he smiled,
snaggle-toothed. 'I'se never without a knife, yunnerstand?' My
voice sounded tight as I replied, 'Never?' If the man had been trying
to make me uncomfortable, he had done a good job. Now he was
looking at Carlton Smith; his voice remained low and
conversational as he said to him, 'Your friend *like* my knife.' Smith
seemed to know the man; so did Bennett, Simpson and Ferguson –
they all ignored him.

Smith glanced at his wristwatch. 'Let's go,' he said; I followed
him to his expensive German car. He turned on the car radio.
Rocksteady by the Melodians – flawless vocal harmonies – drifted
on the Kingston night as we lurched over the unsurfaced roads past
billboard advertisements offering fantasies of semi-naked, pale-
skinned Jamaican women.

It was hard to reconcile Smith's sweet tremolo of a voice – a
tremendous voice in reggae – with his intention to put three
muggers on their backs. After meeting a blade-wielding joker in a
car park and a pistol-carrying reggae singer, I was ready to think of
Jamaican men in terms of guns and violence. Some Jamaican men
feel compelled to defend their corner for fear of appearing weak or
'pussy'. George Walters's admonition to me in Peckham – 'Mind

how you go out there' – came back to me as we set off downtown to Studio One on Brentford Road.

Studio One turned out to be a glorified shack; an unlikely birthplace, at any rate, with its decrepit filing cabinets and scuffed linoleum floors, for some of Jamaica's most sublime music. Clement 'Sir Coxsone' Dodd, the Jamaican jazz enthusiast who took his nickname from the Yorkshire cricketer Alec Coxon, had set up business here in 1963 and in many ways Studio One became the foundation label of reggae. From this shack 'Sir Coxsone' (sometimes spelled 'Coxon' or 'Coxson') launched the careers of, among others, the Skatalites, the Heptones, Alton Ellis, the Abyssinians and the organist Jackie Mittoo. On his death in 2004, at the age of 72, Kingston went into mourning. There was much to mourn. The advent of dancehall music – the digitalised reggae that Jamaicans sometimes call 'ragga' – had helped to kill off Studio One's ordinary human business of recording musicians.

'Hail up, Tamlin!' It was Clement Dodd's widow, Norma Dodd, sitting at the entrance, solemn and imperious. Smith flinched slightly at her address: perhaps it seemed disrespectful to him, coming from a woman. We continued down soundproofed corridors and towards studio doors marked 'SILENCE'. Then we went into the dusty yard, where the solitary mango tree had provided shade for the young hopefuls as they waited their turn at Dodd's Sunday morning auditions, Carlton Smith among them.

*

In Kingston, as elsewhere in the West Indies, one can pass from enclaves of immense wealth to utter desolation in a matter of seconds. So it was that one night I sped from the gleaming Pegasus Hotel, midtown, to the grimy Spanish Town Road, downtown. I was in search of a street party, or *passa-passa*, organised in Tivoli Gardens by a group of local dons. The time was two in the morning and the dirt road stretching to the housing estate was ghostly. As we sped along, I could smell downtown – the odours were by now familiar: petrol, burning rubber, KFC fat. Now and then we overtook a lorry carrying higglers into Coronation Market, sleepy faces peering at us over the tailgates. Once, long ago, Spanish Town Road had been a prime residential district; a few of the old music hall theatres with their art deco colonnades were still standing. But they were abandoned now, or else they were 'coke shops' – crack dens.

Within thirty years of independence, Spanish Town Road had become the territory of the 'grudgeful', of crack-heads, and of stick-up artists, and was ordinarily dangerous. But tonight was Thursday night – *passa-passa* night – and any driver seen on the road was under the protection of the Tivoli dons. 'No violence will be done to us,' Bas Ogden reassured me as he stepped on the accelerator. All the same, Bas had not stopped at the red lights but had looked both ways instead and accelerated. It was an unwritten rule that you never stop at night at the traffic lights on Spanish Town Road.

My guide, Bas, was an uptown Jamaican with a clear-sighted concern about the plight of his country. Each Thursday for the last three years he has gone downtown to take part in the *passa-passa*: he liked the music, the deejay's art, the make-up – and the make-believe. He offered no visions of downtown remade and rejuvenated: Tivoli Gardens was JLP turf, and parts of it gangster turf. It would remain that way for as long as Jamaica's immovable two-party system – PNP versus JLP – kept its iron grip on political life.

We arrived at the quarter-mile stretch of the road marked out for the *passa-passa*. The trees here were festooned with coloured electric light bulbs and their branches glowed invitingly by the roadside stacked with reggae speakerboxes. Ganja mist, resinous and sickly, wafted on the night air. Perhaps 200 people were crowding the street, smoking, drinking and laughing. On the far side, a deejay named Alonzo was scatting and talking over records – 'toasting', Jamaicans call it – while moving the crowds. In Jamaica a good deejay must be able to chant in tune with the beat, as well as throw up witty nursery rhymes and nonsense lyrics, pull off verbal thrusts and parries. Jamaicans, not unlike the Irish, have a great admiration for the elegant control of language. And tonight's deejay, Alonzo, was a master of the turntable or, as Bas put it, 'lyrically active'.

Bas was a useful man to know and his contact in Tivoli Gardens was George Miles, owner of the 'Miles Enterprises' general store which had been trading here since 1944. The store was open and we went in. A dim light came from a bulb hanging from the ceiling.

My eyes focused on the stock: luminous Christs, bottles of jinx-removing incense, postcards of the Catholic saints, store-brand corn chips, canned sodas, caramel corn, mini-pretzels, 'fun-sized' candy bars, powdered doughnuts, chili-cheese nachos and other American trash. Also on display were jars of skin-lightening cream: in dancehall culture, the more fair-skinned a woman is, the more 'trash' or fashionable – hence the blonde wigs also for sale. Marcus Garvey had banned adverts for skin-bleaching chemicals from his 'black pride' newspaper *Negro World*. Bleaching one's black skin white implies that black skin must be lightened before it can be considered beautiful.

George Miles, an elderly Jamaican Chinese, threw Bas a welcoming glance, and came over to shake my hand. He had on a string vest over a pair of loose-fitting khaki trousers. Like most Chinese in Jamaica he was a Catholic (the Catholic Church is seen in Jamaica as the church of the commercial class), and a man used to dealing with money – a kind of politician. A photograph of the JLP leader Edward Seaga (pronounced 'Sea-a-ga') hung on one wall. It might seem strange that politics should still mean so much to the poor of Tivoli Gardens. In Jamaica, though, politics are often purely about resources: if the JLP lost an election, Tivoli Gardens stood to lose the housing schemes and public contracts, the guns and other favours that Seaga's party had given them in return for their votes.

I asked Miles, 'Surely Seaga had his . . . tricky side?' (The dark arts of ballot-stuffing and bribery were not unknown to his supporters.) Miles sucked his teeth and gave a smile of kindly contradiction. 'Seaga was a good man, don't nobody tell you different.' The slightest trace of a challenge was detectable in what he said. Miles may have been a lawbreaker (or had a relaxed attitude to the law), but he was a lawmaker as well: a man who was *feared*.

His store also served as a bar, and it was filling up now for the *passa-passa*. A girl with a gold ankle chain sat at the counter, lifting a bottle of beer to her mouth; I watched her as she sucked on the bottle, blew smoke out of her mouth, sucked. The store seemed to be a refuge for the poor who came here to be 'uplifted' by the music. The drinker at the bar with his hunched spine, the woman scarred by burns on her face, the five scrawny youths who said they were part of a dance team called the Gervaise Squad: for a few hours at least they could allay the bitter knowledge that they were not worth much in the eyes of the wealthy.

As the ragga boomed loud from outside, Bas got out his packet of Black Cat cigarettes, shook one loose, stuck it in his mouth and distributed the rest round the bar. He was a man of largesse, evidently; I noticed that Alonzo mentioned his name every time he spun a new record. Yet Bas was careful not to talk to the locals in *patwa* (Jamaican patois or Creole), which might have insulted their dignity, and possibly led to violence.

Violence is now ingrained in dancehall music, as it is in gangsta rap, which borrowed much from Jamaican deejay styles of delivery, dubbing and 'toasting'. (Dr Dre's revered 1992 album, *The Chronic*, teems with Jamaican influences, even Jamaican voices.) In turn, an element of nightmarish west coast G-funk ghetto violence has influenced Jamaican dancehall with its homophobia, misogyny and celebration of bitches, guns and cash. ('Life ain't nothing but bitches and money,' harangued the Los Angeles combo N.W.A., in a neat reversal of Marcus Garvey's vision of 'black improvement'.) Jamaican dancehall in the twenty-first century seems to present black people to the world in terms the Ku Klux Klan would use: illiterate, gold-chain-wearing, sullen, combative buffoons. It seems to have lost its moral bearing and declined from street celebration to the degraded soundtrack of venality, with scarcely any ideology left in it.

Oddly, as the soundtrack to modern blackness, dancehall rarely promotes black as beautiful. Reggae, with its righteous pre-slave-ship spirituality, had offered hope of deliverance to 'downpressed' Jamaicans and encouraged a generation of British-born black West Indians to confront a part of their heritage – Africa – that their parents had largely shunned. Magnificent Afro-centric albums emerged in 1970s Jamaica, among them *The Right Time* by the Mighty Diamonds, Bunny Wailer's *Blackheart Man*, *Marcus Garvey* by Burning Spear, Augustus Pablo's *King Tubby Meets the Rockers Uptown* and – most righteous of all reggae albums – *Satta Massagana* by the Abyssinians (quoted by the Clash on their album

London Calling). These records have a hymnal, incantatory quality and infectiously heavy bass lines that few white groups could hope to emulate. They can also be almost Stalinist in their insistence on repatriation to Africa ('The whole world is Africa,' chant Black Uhuru) and the wickedness of the white man. Yet dancehall has given up the fight entirely and regressed to dull, computerised rhythms. The journey from Horace Andy's 'In the Light' to Sean Paul's 'Shake That Thing' cannot easily be called progress.

In recent years, the homophobia of some Jamaican dancehall celebrities has tarnished Jamaica's image abroad. Few commentators can agree on the source of the homophobia. Evangelical church groups have not helped; neither have Jamaican politicians, who cynically foster a dislike (or worse) of homosexuals. During the 2001 general elections the JLP adopted the song 'Chi Chi Man' by T.O.K., which urged the burning and killing of male homosexuals or '*batty bwoys*' (literally 'arse boys'). The opposition PNP, not to be beaten, used 'Log On to Progress' as its 2002 election campaign slogan – a reference to 'Log On' by the singer Elephant Man, which similarly advocated kicking or stomping on homosexuals. The British Home Office has refused entry to dancehall stars known for their anti-homosexual *liriks*, most infamously Buju Banton and Beenie Man ('I'm dreaming of a new Jamaica, come to execute all the gays').

Fear and loathing of homosexuals – in which British colonial rule is implicated – has a long history in Jamaica. The island's anti-sodomy laws, an inheritance of the imperial Victorian administration, state:

> Whoever shall be convicted of the abominable crime of buggery (committed either with mankind or an animal) shall be liable to be imprisoned and kept to hard labour for a term not exceeding 10 years.

The prohibitions, deriving from the English Act of 1861, show to what a dismal extent Jamaica has absorbed values from colonial Britain. The island's anti-homosexual laws, endorsed to a certain degree by the black nationalist middle class, have percolated down to the poor, who are easily manipulated by holy-roller Churches: Pentecostalists, Seventh Day Adventists. Similar laws exist elsewhere in the Anglophone Caribbean, as well as in Fidel's Cuba and in many countries in Africa and Asia. Yet Jamaica is outwardly the most homophobic of the West Indian islands. A white man seen on his own in Jamaica (as I discovered to my exasperation) is often assumed to be in search of boys. Homosexuals are occasionally stoned, 'cutlassed', shot and raped (sometimes even at police stations). According to a recent poll, 96 per cent of Jamaicans are opposed to any move to legalise homosexual relations.

Jamaica has a vibrant homosexual community, yet the consequences of being 'outed' are so dire that homosexuals may themselves resort to expressions of violent homophobia just to deflect attention. One might have expected Jamaicans, with their brutal past under imperial Britain, to have some empathy for minorities and difference. Instead they have fallen into a mean-spirited and self-enslaving ignorance. In August 1997 the Jamaican government announced that condoms were to be distributed in Jamaican jails as a preventative against the spread of AIDS. The mere implication that a portion of Jamaican prison life was homosexual was enough to turn 'straight' inmates against 'chi-chi' inmates, sixteen of whom were murdered in riots within the jails.

It has been pointed out how deeply 'feminised' Jamaican culture is. Baby boys are coddled as little princes; and Jamaican men, as in parts of West Africa today, may be pampered and indulged by their mothers. Edith Clarke, in her classic (if now rather dated) study of rural Jamaican life, *My Mother who Fathered Me* (1957), spoke of the 'grandmother household' where grandmothers – especially maternal grandmothers – are the childminders for their daughters who go out to work. Today the chief female in most families – what Jamaicans call the 'woman-a-yard' – continues to be the grandmother. Many reggae songs glorify mothers and grandmothers (such as 'Mother's Tender Care' by the Ethiopians or 'Mother' by Burning Spear) but no reggae song that I know of honours the father. Fathers are not obviously a part of Jamaican popular music; the father is the parent most likely to be absent.

So Jamaican mothers, with their spoiling ways, have helped to create an 'almost entirely feminine' environment for their male offspring, argued the Jamaican journalist Morris Cargill in a 1965 essay. Unfortunately, there is no father-image to leaven the imbalance; so while the boy may, and usually does, grow up into 'a fine example of the masculine physique', according to Cargill, his attitude to life is 'extraordinarily feminine'. Jamaican men may compensate for their 'femininity' by a precarious, over-exaggerated masculinity, which can express itself, like a long-pent-up balloon, in eruptions of violence and even sexual peculiarity.

In 1998, for example, the Jamaican dancehall singer Bounty Killer released a song, 'Can't Believe Mi Eyes', which expressed incredulity that men should dress in tight trousers: in his view, tight trousers were an effeminate display of gayness. Yet some dancehall stars, with their shaved eyebrows, diamond earrings, white suits and lovingly manicured nails, present an almost Gloria Swanson-like image of womanly adornment. In Jamaica a homosexual man is sometimes called a 'Maama man'.

In compensation for its ideological nullity, dancehall culture has developed a seamy jargon, *dancehallese*, as lively as any eighteenth-century thieves' cant. The sublanguage seems to celebrate Kingston as a place glutted with sensation: lurid, sexually dangerous. 'Batty riders' are tight pants disguised as shorts; 'bumper riders' likewise expose a woman's 'bumper' (bottom); 'cargo dung' is extra-showy jewellery. The word 'buffilous' was translated for me (by Bas) as 'sexy'; 'punnani', vagina. 'Go low' means to have oral sex (considered unmanly in thrusting dancehall culture); 'roach killas' are shoes; and 'twin cam' is a bisexual man. 'Bashment', or party, has been replaced by the pidgin Spanish *'passa-passa'*, in island patois, 'confusion' or 'mix up'.

Bas smiled brightly. 'And I have another one for you – "anaconda".'

'Penis?'

'Right.'

As with hip-hop, parental discretion may be advised with Jamaican dancehall music (sometimes known as 'Yardcore').

At about five o'clock the party mood changed as flotillas of expensive-looking cars began to arrive. The women passengers, dressed in Lycra batty riders, tumbled shrieking out of the four-by-fours and – that ultimate symbol of inner city success – the 'bimmer' (BMW). Soon the women were skanking and flexing in the middle of Spanish Town Road, their men break-dancing in vaguely lewd James Brown routines.

A first paleness of dawn, and the *passa-passa* was still fairly bouncing with metallic ragga and deejay patter from Alonzo. I watched transfixed by the raw display of flesh. A woman naked save for a brief V of black lace was gyrating with a man on top of a giant speaker, their embrace only a little short of copulation. ('Rub-a-dub', the erotic body language of the Jamaican deejay, is well named.) When the girl with the gold ankle chain asked me a question – 'Wan compn'y?' – it was time to leave. Back at PJ's house, in the oyster light of dawn, Kingston looked almost romantic, the old imperial slave depot tinged with silver-greys and greens.

4

Slaving

Jamaica's oldest sugar estate, Worthy Park, was founded in 1670 and is still in operation. It stands in fertile plains an hour's drive from Kingston, and one day I was invited to lunch. The sound of cocktail-making – a clinking of crushed ice against glass – greeted my arrival as bow-tied waiters served at a long table draped in linen. The elite of Jamaica's sugar industry was enjoying French wine and chilled soursop juice. They ate well – steak, lobster mayonnaise – and many of them turned out to be related to each other.

The estate is run jointly by Robert Clarke (whose family own Jamaica's *Gleaner* newspaper) and Peter McConnell. Tough white country folk, they lamented the decline of the island's sugar industry and the ruinous state in general of Jamaican agriculture. McConnell, a silver-haired man in a pink sports shirt, said to me, 'We've lost the know-how. We can't run sugar efficiently any more.' Sugar has been in crisis in the West Indies ever since the plantation system collapsed under Queen Victoria. Between 1848 and 1910 the number of plantations in Jamaica shrank from 513 to seventy-seven, many being sold for less than the price of their sugar boilers. In 1897 a Royal Commission was sent to the British Caribbean to investigate the dilapidated industry. It was recommended that the islands diversified their crops, as dependence on a single industry hindered development. Once sugar was dethroned, however, Worthy Park was plunged into debt; and Jamaica, no longer vital to the British economy, became one of the Empire's many dark slums.

Like the rest of Jamaica, Worthy Park was today waiting on a government promise of money, otherwise it might not survive. McConnell and Clarke, ahead of the game, had diversified into non-sugar crops such as citrus and pineapple; they produced the

Tru-Juice fruit drink known to all Jamaicans. Yet every year the estate lost thousands through praedial larceny (crop theft), a crime for which some Jamaican planters would like to bring back flogging. 'A few strokes with a tamarind switch never did anyone any harm,' I overheard a guest say. (Flogging was abolished in Jamaica only in 1998.) Worthy Park employs armed rangers to keep out the thieves; the shootings, sometimes fatal, are not always reported to the police.

The waiters, with their plantation-bred obsequiousness, hurried to whisk away flies from our plates. Though most of the guests were white, few of them seemed to be afflicted by Anglophone pomposity or snobbery. (Robert Clarke's wife, Billy, came from Kentucky.) Until independence, Jamaica had been largely and inevitably British, but the island is increasingly American now, which is a change not always for the worse. The United States Peace Corps, for instance, has been in Jamaica since 1962, working in HIV/AIDS education, birth control, water sanitation and environmental projects.

However, America displays no greater openness towards Jamaica's black community than the colonial British did. It would have been unusual for a Worthy Park planter to marry a black Jamaican. Blackness, in the white (and perhaps also the black) Jamaican view, connotes not merely colour, but also ill manners and a lack of culture. The prejudice has passed into modern Jamaica from the days of slavery, when a black skin signified captivity and a lowly, field-hand status.

The McConnells had come to Jamaica from Ireland in the nineteenth century, lured to this sad green island perhaps by the promise of wealth. Opposite me sat Joanie Desnoes, Peter McConnell's wife, a frail, blue-eyed blonde with ringlets. 'You're a writer,' she said to me, in lightly Americanised English. 'Do tell me what you think of Jamaica.' I made some polite remark, which seemed to satisfy her. She was an heiress to the Jamaican Red Stripe beer family and, to judge by her French surname, descended from French planters who had fled from revolutionary Haiti during the slave uprising there of 1793 to 1804. Like most of the guests, then, she had been born in Jamaica out of hybrid, transplanted identities.

According to the eighteenth-century historian of Jamaica, Edward Long, the 'Creolised whites' of the island had peculiar characteristics that distinguished them from Europeans. The men tended to have 'deeper' eye sockets, for example, as a guard against the sun's glare. I looked round the table: no deep eye sockets, only a striking whiteness of complexion.

Most of the Worthy Park guests, being wealthy, carried guns. Violence was never far away; in 1967, Peter McConnell's mother was murdered by her chauffeur, a killing that shocked even Jamaica. The killer, twenty-five-year-old Joseph Spencer, strangled Nora McConnell after he had been sacked by her.

By five o'clock the last of the guests had left Worthy Park. Robert Clarke, a stop-watch on a cord round his neck, offered to take me on a tour of the estate. In his jeep we drove past ruined sugar-grinding and boiling houses, which had produced the coarse brown *muscovado* granules that fed the British sweet tooth. When the estate was at its peak of production, in the mid-1700s, Britain was importing 100,000 hogsheads (63-gallon casks) of sugar a year from the West Indies. The value of British imports from Jamaica alone was five times that from Britain's thirteen mainland colonies in North America; Worthy Park's sugar, destined for the docks and refineries of Liverpool and Bristol, was king.

No longer. A decayed planter's house, redolent of days of gambling and dissolution, lay mouldering in guinea grass. Beneath it were shacks built to accommodate the estate's 700 workers today. Among their other duties, the workers must clear the land for irrigation canals, cut cane, cut bush and gather field trash for fuel. Robert Clarke, bouncing behind the wheel of his jeep, made some barbed remark about the 'sociologists' who complained of a white man's injustice. 'Don't talk to me about slavery,' he said. 'We run a clinic, we provide facilities for football and cricket teams. So our slaves' – he joked – 'are well looked after.'

Thirty years ago, in the 1970s, boxing matches were held at Worthy Park, when overseers laid bets on the cane-cutters as they fought in the ring. Jamaica is a land with a continuous memory of slavery and slavish abasement. Slavery runs through island life like the black line in a lobster. Even today the cane-cutters are not encouraged to leave the plantation or to sell their services elsewhere; they are considered the property of Worthy Park.

*

In London I met James Berry, the Jamaican poet and children's author, who lives in a retirement home in Turnham Green. Though Turnham Green is not an obviously Afro-Caribbean part of the British capital, nevertheless I had come to speak to Berry about slavery. When I arrived he was listening to Duke Ellington's *Black Brown & Beige*, a sympathetic beatnik figure in turned-up jeans.

'God! What a country – Jamaica!' Berry exclaimed.

Every time he returned to his birthplace there was trouble: political violence, corruption. Things had not been too bad once – in the days when people still had 'respect'. But how Berry disliked going home now. There was nothing left, he said – everything was rotting into the sugar-cane fields. In his more recent poetry Jamaica emerges as a byword for all that is most despairing about the British West Indian condition:

> Me not going back to dat hell Jamaica.
> Me have more pain there than I can tell.

But surely, I asked, things had been 'worse' under the colonial British. 'That's what you'd like to think', Berry replied. 'But, you know, there was discipline back in them days. Look at the roads now, they're like hellholes. We can't even build a decent road! And the estates – they've run to seed, they're full of emaciated cattle.' Berry added with anger: 'Jamaica's stagnancy *sickens* me – what progress have we made since independence?'

Slavery, in Berry's opinion, had not been entirely erased from Jamaica. Violence was central to the system of slavery and the spirit of this violence continues to haunt modern Jamaica. The island was still run by overseers; only today the overseers were a motley of party bosses, armed 'badmen' and corrupted police. 'Does that not remind you of slavery?' Berry knocked back a tot of rum, then tilted out a jigger more. 'The greed of the few over the manifold misery of the many? Oh my Lord,' he said. 'Oh my good Lord.'

When Berry left Jamaica for England in 1948, at the age of 25, the crush of humanity on board the immigrant ship made him think of the Middle Passage – the feared Atlantic crossing of slaves from Africa. By the journey's end the SS *Orbita*'s stairs smelled of vomit and urine. Sixty years on, however, Berry felt no sadness at leaving Jamaica as the island still had nothing to offer. But what really troubled him was unutterable: he could hardly put into words, though he said it anyway, 'Jamaica has not been better off since independence.'

Something had gone terribly wrong in Jamaica for Berry to say that. He too had had a vision of a modern Jamaica freed of imperial Britain, where there was equality among black, white and brown, and life was transformed for the better. That dream had yet to be realised. An old man in Turnham Green, Berry was happily fulfilled as a writer, or almost fulfilled, yet bitterly disillusioned with his birthplace.

*

For three centuries slavery had been the only reason for Jamaica's existence. Jamaican society was created from slavery. Jamaican customs and culture were fashioned by slavery. Typically, British planters cast Jamaica aside like a sucked orange once they had exploited their estates in order to fritter their fortunes at home in England. Outside Georgian London the greatest concentration of absentee and retired Jamaican planters was in the Bristol suburb of Clifton. There, in their cocked hats and fashionably buckled shoes, the new men of capital were envied for their conspicuous and easy wealth. George III, the story goes, was peeved to encounter a 'West Indian' (as white planters were then known) whose coach was more resplendent than his own. 'Sugar, eh?' the king loudly proclaimed.

In books, plays and poems, Jamaica was depicted as a dangerous place where the British were undone by greed and licentiousness. A popular drama of 1771, Richard Cumberland's *The West Indian*, satirised planters as boorish but essentially lovable types who gleefully overturned English standards of civility. Belcour, the 'West Indian' of the title, visits England accompanied by a retinue of Jamaican slaves, his trunks bulging with 'rum puncheons' and other island exotica. Always drunk, he disgraces himself with other men's wives, and is shunned as a parvenu of empire. Later, in a show of remorse, Belcour blames his wayward behaviour on his 'cursed tropical constitution'; if only he had never left Jamaica:

Would to heaven I had been dropped upon the snows of Lapland, and never felt the blessed influence of the sun, so had I never burnt with these inflammatory passions.

Eighty years later, the 'degeneracy' of West Indians was more memorably evoked by William Thackeray in his novel *Vanity Fair*. The novel provides a glittery panorama of sugar impresarios, plantation heiresses and remittance men who have died (or are about to die) of drink or yellow fever in the Caribbean. Miss Schwartz, the novel's egregious 'West Indian', has 'earrings like chandeliers' and is consumed, like Richard Cumberland's Belcour before her, by wild amorous lusts. When not drinking, she haunts London's 'Tapioca Coffee-House' (in reality the Jamaica Coffee House on St Michael's Alley) for news of her Caribbean properties.

Real-life Belcours and Schwartzes populate the diary kept by Lady Nugent, wife of the governor of Jamaica, during her four-year residence on the island between 1801 and 1805. Vast planter meals were endured by the prim and very proper Nugent, who commented of one breakfast:

> I observed some of the party, to-day, eat as if they had never eaten before – a dish of tea, another of coffee, a bumper of claret, another large one of hock-negus [wine punch]; then Madeira, sangaree [sangria], hot and cold meat, stews and fries, hot and cold fish pickled and plain, peppers, ginger sweetmeats, acid fruit, sweet jellies – in short, it was all as astonishing as it was disgusting.

Behind this strenuous dissolution lay the 'triangle merchants' who motivated the slave trade between England, Africa and Jamaica. A typical 'triangle voyage' carried trading goods (such as beads, rifles and gunpowder) from England to Africa, then slaves from Africa to the Caribbean, and finally sugar, coffee, cotton, rice and rum on the home stretch to England. It was one of the most nearly perfect commercial systems of modern times, a flawless loop of supply and demand, that linked a network of overlapping (not always 'triangular') trading routes and merchant-capitalist systems across Europe, Africa and the Americas. The Middle Passage foreshadowed the greater cruelties of the plantations in Jamaica, as

Africans were herded on to slave ships, branded with irons, flogged and ferried in stinking holds to the imperial sugar fields.

The African side of the Jamaican 'triangle' – sometimes called the 'black trade' because it was controlled by non-Europeans – was exemplified by the slave castles which the British operated along the Gold Coast of Africa until slavery's abolition in 1807. The castles served as holding centres for Africans captured by and sold into servitude by fellow Africans; it was from these 'castle doors of no return' that thousands of men, women and children born in Africa were transported to Jamaica. Conceivably, the forebears of British Jamaicans today passed through those warehouse-dungeons on the South Atlantic Ocean.

The realisation that European slavery depended upon African slavery disillusioned James Berry, who told me in a tone of disbelief, 'My *own* people – my African ancestors – had sold and abandoned us to the white man. Oh, that was a sorrowful shock for me, I felt a tremendous betrayal, even a hatred for Africa.' African complicity does not diminish the white man's responsibility. It was the British who supplied the vessels of profit and despair that made Jamaican slavery possible; it was the British who evolved a new, modern, economic system out of human beings. African rulers who profited from the British triangular trade were often shocked by the antics of their British counterparts, who appraised their 'cargo' like cattle, prodding and examining orifices for signs of disease.

Few in Britain acknowledged that each sweet teaspoonful dissolved in tea (that 'blood-sweetened beverage', the abolitionist poet Robert Southey called it) was an added measure of black mortality. The misery of untold numbers of Africans barely registered in pre-abolition Britain: slavery was, quite simply, an un-questioned, widely accepted, morally neutral trade which yielded immense profits for some and a sweet pleasure for millions.

Since Jamaica was riddled with disease, insects and reptiles, the British plantation owners became absentee landlords if they could. Or else they liquidated their tropical holdings outright. Still others never even set foot in Jamaica. The Gothic novelist William Beckford's sole attempt to sail to his properties in Jamaica, in 1787, took him no further than Lisbon: sea-sickness, combined with a fear of shipboard cockroaches, detained him. The few planters who did stay behind aimed to send their children 'home' to England for their education. Tobias Smollett, the eighteenth-century Scottish novelist, having married a 'home-comer' from Jamaica, appointed a London agent to oversee the sale and purchase of her slaves. Typically, funds were slow to arrive, as slaving agents were inefficient and, often as not, drunk. 'That cursed Ship from Jamaica,' Smollett complained in a letter of 1756, 'is at last arrived *without* Letter or Remittance.' Smollett and his wife could hope to earn £80 for each 'Negro man' sold in their behalf – a considerable sum in those days.

In the absence of their owners, Jamaican estates were run by attorneys or family relatives. Often these were ignorant, limited men (family black sheep, army deserters, youngest sons) who wanted only to fight duels, smoke cigars, 'humbug' absentees, make money and spend it. Their wives, according to an account of Jamaica published anonymously in 1808, were little better, as they suffered from a slothful, bed-bound inertia, or squandered their time in drinking 'corkers' (strong rum punch) and reading 'trash' novels sent out from England. Like their husbands, they had come to Jamaica to acquire a fortune and a social status that would have been denied them at home. By the end of the eighteenth century, when Jamaica enjoyed remarkable prosperity, only one in ten of the plantation great houses was occupied by a proprietor.

*

The first slaves to arrive in British Jamaica, however, were not Africans, but white 'bondsmen' and women shipped out from England in the 1600s as convicts, debtors, political dissidents and other 'undesirables'. Many of these transportees were Royalist casualties of the English Civil War, prisoners of Oliver Cromwell sold as 'redemptioners' to the West Indies. From the start, then, British dominion in Jamaica rested on coercion rather than voluntary settlement – the land was held and worked by violence.

Cromwell had seized Jamaica from Spain in 1655 as part of his great 'Western Design' intended to halt the spread of Catholicism in the Hispanic New World. It took him five years to clear the Spanish out of Jamaica, however, and his new territorial jewel was far from attractive in the short term. Disease soon wiped out the white slaves; Cromwell therefore agreed to import slaves from Africa. These arrived from the Gold Coast (today's Ghana), the Bight of Benin (today's Togo, Benin and south-west Nigeria), and the coast of Sierra Leone (on today's map, Guinea-Bissau, Guinea, Sierra Leone, Liberia and the Ivory Coast).

However, it was not until the Restoration that Jamaica became to England what India later became – a showcase mercantile colony where Britons sought easy wealth and a future. John Evelyn, the Restoration diarist, worked as a civil servant for the Council for Foreign Plantations, a seventeenth-century equivalent of the Department of Overseas Trade. His job was to oversee the maintenance of Jamaica as a colonial and commercial outpost, and to that end he devoted his energies to an investigation of Jamaican soil conditions and forestry. The Council met each month at the Earl of Bristol's house in Queen Street, Lincoln's Inn Fields, and had no scruple about the brutality of the 'Negro trade'. All that mattered was that Britain rivalled Spain as a slaving nation and inflicted piratical raids on Spanish territories along the Panama trade route to Europe.

For that reason, Kingston was turned into a slave depot, while Charles II worked with Parliament to establish the legal existence of slavery. Kingston was protected against Spanish attack by a ten-mile spit of land with the citadel of Port Royal at the seaward end, which served as a British navy base, as well as home to Jamaica's lieutenant governor, the former pirate Captain Henry Morgan. By the time Port Royal was hit by an earthquake and tidal wave in 1692 the city had earned its reputation as 'the wickedest' on earth. Merchants, pimps, prostitutes, mercenaries and criminals of every stripe came to gorge on Port Royal's free-flowing wealth, much of it generated by the government-sponsored pirates who had marauded the Caribbean with Lieutenant Morgan, disposing of the Spanish. Only one tenth of this rackety boom town survived its 'Biblical destruction' by wave and tremor (the rest still lurks a few metres beneath the surface of the sea). It says something for British Jamaica that it began life as both a pirate and a slave base – profit and criminality conjoined on the high seas.

*

I set out from Kingston to visit Arthur's Seat, a plantation house on Jamaica's north coast. Arthur's Seat had been the centre of a very prosperous banana and pimento business in the 1770s; the English owners of that time, the Hepworths, had given their name to the outlying district known as Epworth. (Jamaicans can have a cockney-like difficulty with their aitches.) After slavery's abolition, however, Arthur's Seat collapsed as a commercial enterprise; bush smothered the cane fields, the slave quarters were burned down and the remaining servants occupied the empty great house. (Great house was the name given to a plantation home in Jamaica during the slaving era.)

Almost forty years ago, in 1970, Marjorie and Jacqueline Parkins, a black Jamaican mother and daughter, moved into Arthur's Seat. They live by selling bric-a-brac and giving tours of the old plantation home. Some tourists (the majority of them American) would ask the Parkinses if they could meet 'the owners' of the house; others wanted to know if 'white people' had bequeathed money to the Parkinses, so they could live like well-heeled sugar ladies. By inhabiting Arthur's Seat, the Parkinses seemed to upset the notion of white freedom and black servitude. In reality, slaves had been owned by 'people of colour' (to use that unattractive phrase), and in a few exceptional cases Jamaican slaves were even owned by freed slaves.

St Ann parish, as I drove across it from Kingston, had the appearance of English parkland. Cattle grazed on green meadows, and green fields rolled towards the sea. On my left, just before I reached Arthur's Seat, a mammoth cotton tree stood perhaps sixty feet tall in a dip of the land. Cotton trees, with their bulging steel-grey trunks and banyan-like buttresses, are sacred in Africa, and sacred also in Jamaica. Their branches are believed to harbour spirits or 'duppies'. Cotton trees rooted in graveyards are particularly feared; a spirit known as Old Hinge hangs her skin on the branches, and travels about at night, making mischief.

Marjorie Parkins, the mother, had the worn and disappointed look of one who had spent her best years in public life. In 1962, immediately after independence, she was posted to New York to serve as Jamaican consul. Jamaica's conservative JLP government under Alexander Bustamante had sided with the United States on Cold War issues and shared America's disapproval of the Soviet influence in Cuba. So Marjorie Parkins was made to feel welcome. On her return to Jamaica eight years later, in 1970, she bought the ruin of Arthur's Seat and filled it with modern furniture freighted in from Brooklyn. 'But,' Marjorie said to me, 'the American furniture didn't really suit a British great house, so we got rid of the American stuff and filled it with antiques.'

Every room was crammed with a neo-colonial accumulation of rosewood and mahogany furniture, much of it for sale. Sunlight, dispelling the frowsy atmosphere, streamed in through open jalousies on to a collection of porcelain dolls, a metal 1960s Red Stripe advert, and an immense Victorian bird cage. An air of unreality pervaded the place. Some of the furniture was pseudo-antique, with much gilt trimming, brass studs and lacquer like an east European coffin. Jacqueline Parkins, Marjorie's daughter, told me about the people who had visited Arthur's Seat. Not so long ago a group of thirty British tourists were taken to see the property's slave dungeon, where the ventilation slits could still be seen. Jacqueline had described to them how the English-born Hepworths had whipped and branded their slaves, and hanged them by their necks from the cotton tree. As she dilated on their brutality, some of the visitors turned away and stared fixedly at their feet, while others seemed most distressed. 'Oh no, please!' They begged Jacqueline to show forgiveness – forgiveness for Britain's slave-trading past.

I asked Jacqueline: 'Do you like the British?' and her big, gentle face stirred with impatience.

'Not always,' she replied. 'You British expect to find a paradise of sea and sun and sand in Jamaica – you don't want to be reminded of historical realities.' Some of the visitors that day had become really quite hysterical. 'I thought we'd have to call an ambulance,' she said. Jacqueline's mother, looking at me, interjected grimly: 'Or a hearse.' She added, 'Those English people – they were white, of course – they just weren't expecting to be lectured on slavery by two black ladies living in a plantation great house . . .' Amid the antique gloom of Arthur's Seat, mother and daughter had further reversed the old planter 'rankings' by keeping a black staff of their own.

In 2007, during the bicentenary of the Abolition of the Slave Trade Act, British guilt for the 'Africa Trade' was expressed in various ways. Tony Blair offered a tokenistic 'deep sorrow' at Britain's involvement in the 'shameful' commerce, yet his government made no official apology (John Prescott, the deputy prime minister, made a woeful attempt at it: 'Everybody should feel the sorrow, pain and regret . . .') An apology by the Church of England in February of that year was ridiculed in some quarters; the word 'sorry', it was objected, hardly atoned for the crimes committed. Whatever could?

Thirty years after Cromwell had wrested Jamaica from Spain, in 1687 the scientist-collector Sir Hans Sloane arrived on the island to act as physician to the British governor. Sloane became a founder of the British Museum (his collection of Jamaican curiosities was purchased by Parliament in 1752 for £20,000 and donated to the museum), but he was no philanthropist. For the crime of 'rebellion' he recommended that slaves be pinioned to the ground and burned with a flaming brand 'by degrees from the Feet and Hands . . . gradually up to the Head, whereby their pains are extravagant'. For 'lesser' crimes he recommended 'chopping off half of the Foot with an Ax'.

Slave resistance – what Sir Hans chose to call 'rebellion' – took many forms: sabotage, withdrawal of labour ('laziness'), protest in words and song, escape, outright revolt. Punishment records in the Wilberforce House Archives, Hull, add 'stealing rum', 'insolence to overseers', 'refusing to pump water', and 'making use of improper language' as punishable offences. On Parnassus Estate in Jamaica, amputation appears to have been inflicted, as the overseer notes for the year 1779 that his slaves had 'lost both hands', are 'without fingers' or have 'only one foot'. They have been given Classical names such as Pompey, Caesar, Cupid and Juno, which seem to mock their servile condition. Most of them died of overwork or disease: the Hull records say they are 'pox'd' or 'laid up'; they have 'yaws' (a form of leprosy), or they are 'troubled with fitts'.

Britain's complicity in what John Newton, a former slave-trade captain, called the 'disgraceful branch of commerce' should be acknowledged and taught in British schools, as a matter of education. But apologised for? Tony Blair could not feel personal guilt for the slave trade, yet surely apologies are meaningless without any show of remorse. 'Deep sorrow' is probably the best the British can offer.

Meanwhile, the impression of something sinister in the heart of Arthur's Seat was enhanced (for me) by a local legend of recent vintage. During Hurricane Dennis in 2005, Epworth district was convulsed by such a loud commotion that it was assumed the old slave mansion had 'exploded'. One of the cotton tree's elephantine branches had cracked off in the storm. It was believed that from the tree's dismembered limb the spirits of hanged slaves had been released. 'Ever since that night, if one person dies in Epworth,' Jacqueline Parkins said, 'two more always follow. Well, the locals blame the hangman's tree for that. They blame the British.' Jacqueline had recounted this story with excited, wide eyes; and as she did so I wondered how she and her mother could live so isolated, without transport or a working telephone, in this haunted place.

5

Massa Day Done?

On a dreary day in Hull, under a damp North Sea drizzle, I visited Wilberforce House. A statue of the English abolitionist, with thin mouth and serious eyes, stands outside the red-brick Jacobean manor where he was born in 1759. Inside I saw a recreation of a British ship's slave-hold, complete with life-size models of enchained Africans and a recording of a slave captain's yelled abuse ('Get out of my way, filthy animals!'). A teacher was accompanying a group of primary-school-aged children. 'See,' he said to them, 'the slaves were treated like pieces of meat-cargo'; and with dour Humberside understatement he added: 'It wasn't luxury-class cruising, it was horrendously cruel, children.'

In the bicentenary year of the abolition of Britain's slave traffic, 2007, William Wilberforce was feted by Humberside City Council. From 1788 onwards he had been the British MP synonymous with the Parliamentary campaign to ban the slave trade in the British Empire. Under Wilberforce was a group of other high-minded Englishmen (many of them Quakers) who opposed a brutish, mercantile greed and its arsenal of chains, whips and leg irons.

Thomas Clarkson, a clergyman's son, was Wilberforce's chief lieutenant. In search of evidence against slave-ship brutality, he scoured the waterfront taverns of Bristol and Liverpool. His famous diagram of a seagoing 'Guineaman' – the top, side and end views of the Jamaica-bound vessel tight-packed with Africans – became an iconic image of the abolitionist movement. Clarkson submitted his findings to the House of Commons and, after years of lobbying, a Bill was passed on 25 March 1807 that outlawed the carrying of slaves by British ships. The Bill marked the beginning of the end of slavery. Jamaican planters, fearing that abolition would precipitate the collapse of the British Empire (and loss of profit for them), burned Wilberforce in effigy, while Jamaican slaves prayed to 'Saint' Wilberforce.

Abolition was hastened by the Haitian slave uprising. In the New Year of 1804, to the alarm of British Jamaica, slaves toiling on the neighbouring island of Saint Domingue finally overthrew their French masters after more than ten years of revolt and declared independence. The French name of Saint Domingue was replaced by the aboriginal Indian word Haiti ('mountainous land') and the white band ceremonially ripped from the French tricolour to create the modern Haitian flag. French planters were massacred but many escaped to Jamaica, where their descendants can be found to this day.

The prospect of a free black state founded on the annihilation of its white community horrified slave-owning Britain. Planters in Jamaica, outnumbered ten to one by their slaves, spread stories of black (but not white) cruelty in Haiti: infants impaled on pikes, pregnant (always pregnant) women raped. Quite suddenly it seemed the whites were on the defensive. And in 1793, fearing that the 'contagion of revolution' in Haiti would spread to Jamaica, King George III sent 27,000 troops from Kingston to Saint Domingue. The occupation turned out to be one of the greatest (if still least known) catastrophes of British imperial history. Tropical disease killed the king's Redcoats in their thousands before they capitulated to the freed slaves. The defeat was the first time that a European army had surrendered to black troops. It inspired William Blake's abolitionist poem 'America: A Prophecy', dated 1793:

> Let the slave grinding at the mill run out into the field;
> Let him look up into the Heavens and laugh in the bright air

The Abolition Bill, long awaited, was thrilling to slaves and abolitionists alike. 'Well, Henry, what shall we abolish next?' Wilberforce asked a staunch Evangelist cousin. 'The lottery, I think,' came the reply. Abolition of the trade, however, did not mean emancipation of the slaves: Jamaica would have to wait another thirty years until its slaves were actually liberated by the 1834 Emancipation Bill. Even then, they had to serve a four- to six-year apprenticeship before becoming quite free.

Dissenting voices were heard long before Wilberforce. In 1752, a full half-century before abolition, Samuel Johnson took on a freed black Jamaican slave as his valet. Francis Barber, a ten-year-old orphan, had been entrusted to Dr Johnson by an English planter with connections in Jamaica. By employing Barber, Dr Johnson could put into practice Britain's fundamental principle of liberty (as he saw it) and realise the idea of 'imperial trusteeship' for the betterment of so-called native societies. His hatred of slavery was genuine. Sugar-rich Jamaica, in Dr Johnson's formula, was 'a place of great wealth and dreadful wickedness', and slavery a stigma on the British national character. Earlier he had shocked a dinner party in Oxford by proposing a toast to 'the next insurrection of Negroes' (after Haiti) in the British Caribbean.

The Jamaican waited on Samuel Johnson at table, answered his door, and provided him with a distraction from his habitual low spirits, while Dr Johnson, for his part, indulged his West Indian charge in a way that few eighteenth-century Tories would have considered proper. He refused to let Barber buy fish for his cat as he did not want him to have to attend on an animal; he paid for his education and, after thirty years of service, made him the principal beneficiary of his will. In gratitude Barber named his first son Samuel, and later settled in Samuel Johnson's birthplace of Lichfield, where he achieved some note; his son became a Methodist minister. Incredibly, Barber's descendants still live in the Lichfield area – but they are all white now.

*

Denzil Johnston is a black Jamaican living in Hull. Each August on the anniversary of Wilberforce's birthday he visits the emancipator's house to pay his respects. Johnston had never imagined that he would end up in the abolitionist's home town. 'It's a strange irony, isn't it?' he said in his Jamaicanised east Yorkshire accent. 'Me being down the road from Wilberforce.'

In his front room off Beverley Road, among the tiny model Spitfires and the display of gold Victory medals, was a studio portrait taken of Denzil in royal blue RAF fatigues: 'Kingston, 1945', the caption reads. Many young Jamaicans had fought and suffered in the Second World War and witnessed death on an unusual scale. At the outbreak of the conflict, RAF trucks had driven round Kingston with the words 'Give Unto Britain and Britain Will Give You More' stencilled on the side.

As the war with Hitler approached, Jamaicans were exhorted to donate scrap metal to help build planes for Britain. Johnston's father spent a good deal of time listening to the short-wave radio broadcasts from England which brought news of the sinking of HMS *Hood,* then later of Dunkirk and the Battle of Britain. In Kingston there was constant patriotic activity of all kinds. But was it right for Jamaica to back a European war for democracy, when its own people had been denied the right to self-rule?

Every Jamaican family in Johnston's circle gave up kettles, colanders, zinc baths, clothes-hangers for the mother country. 'We did all we could to help keep Jamaica British and keep Britain out of Hitler's harm,' Johnston recalled; Jamaica, a subject country, was going to fight to the death for the freedom of Poland. At Barclays Bank in Kingston, the imperial administration set up an account under the name 'Jamaica Plane Fund': money poured in from the scrap metal sales, and with it Jamaica was able to buy a Spitfire for the Battle of Britain. Housewives were proud to imagine that it was *their* saucepan – the silver-melt of *their* cookware – that had made part of the Spitfire, recalled Johnston. 'We Jamaicans were Britishers at heart and it would have been incredible if we – if Britain – had lost the war.' To be an Anglophile and a Jamaican was not, for Johnston, a contradiction.

He was in Wiltshire for the VJ (Victory in Japan) Day celebrations. 'Women came up to kiss me – they were thanking me – *me!* – for my service to Britain.' After training with the RAF as an engine-fitter, Johnston's first job took him to Hull, where for three decades he worked for British Aerospace, 'cheering', as he put it, 'for Wilberforce'.

With his Guyanese wife, in the drab city on the Humber, he raised a family but as the years went by he began to feel let down by Britain. Johnston could not believe that Britain's drift into irrelevance as an imperial power was the reward for his and his comrades' sacrifice. Why had Jamaican airmen never been invited to march past the Cenotaph on Remembrance Sunday? Surely they could be allowed to lay a wreath. 'Back in my short-pant days,' said Johnston, 'I was proud to run round waving the Union Jack.' But the British lion must have become a minor power – bankrupt, played-out – to ignore his contribution and that of thousands of other black service personnel to the Allied war effort. 'It's like we've been forgotten,' Johnston concluded.

*

Self-government was not British policy in post-Second World War Jamaica. Yet the winds of change were blowing through Jamaica, as they were through swathes of red on the imperial map. As Greater Britain (the United Kingdom and its imperial domains) evolved from Empire to Commonwealth, it was obliged to consider self-determination for Jamaica.

In 1938 a firebrand politician emerged as the leader of a social revolution in Jamaica. Over six feet tall with a shock of unruly hair and flashing eyes, Alexander Bustamante exuded a Lincoln-like gravitas and (when not drunk or swinging revolvers) a gift for oratory. Rumoured to be illiterate ('I come from the gutter of poverty'), Bustamante was born in Jamaica in 1884 as Alexander Clarke; he changed his name to Bustamante apparently while in Spanish-speaking Cuba. On his return to Jamaica in 1932 he made himself champion of Jamaica's dispossessed: the lowly sweating out their lives on the cane fields, at the Kingston docks, in canneries and freighters, on banana farms, without rights, without tenure – Bustamante proclaimed himself their Messiah. He would lead these people out of colonial servitude and into nationhood.

Before long, all the British West Indies were fighting for their rightful independence. Between 1935 and 1938, in what the colonial administrators termed the 'somnolent Caribbean', a series of strikes in oilfields, cities and sugar plantations turned into island-wide riots. In Jamaica the riots were fuelled by anger at British neglect. The British Empire seemed to be unmindful of its poor, yet costly to administer, dependency. Most Jamaicans had no vote, no voice; they felt as impotent, politically, as their forebears had done under slavery. The riots were no sooner under way, however, than the British jailed Bustamante on sedition charges.

Racial tensions and unrest had long simmered in the western

parish of Westmoreland; it was there, in 1938, that the most serious Jamaican riots occurred. John McIntyre, a planter, was visiting friends on Masemure sugar estate there when it was set ablaze and looted. He spoke of the episode to me from his retirement home in Mandeville, not far from Kingston, a thin white Jamaican in his early nineties. 'We were very fearful,' he said in clipped tones. 'The rioters had gone mad, they were setting fire to the cane fields and burning the very thing that they depended on!' McIntyre recalled that he locked himself in the estate office and dialled for the police.

The police arrived and barricaded the office doors to protect the staff cowering inside. The strikers were now marching in their hundreds on the Masemure estate: McIntyre could see the dust rising from the long road to the office. The strikers first of all raided the rum storehouse, and 'got completely soused'. Then they threw the distillery manager, a Mr Saddler, into a ditch of black malodorous 'dunder' sludge (made of the lees of rum-still). The humiliated manager had to crawl out of that ditch in his soiled white suit. 'It was a disgrace,' McIntyre recalled. Elsewhere, managers were shot.

On day three of the Masemure riots, the British army arrived from Kingston in open touring cars – 'huge American things' – commandeered from motorists along the way. At the sight of the khaki-vested troops the strikers ran off into the cane fields, while their ringleader was marched off at bayonet-point to a waiting car and sped to Kingston. 'To this day we don't know what happened to him,' said McIntyre. Jamaica in 1938 was a dependency maintained by British bayonets.

Three weeks later, on 21 May, Kingston was brought to a standstill when stevedores went on strike along the wharves. The colonial government, fearing greater unrest, released Bustamante from jail. From that time dates the painful birth of modern Jamaica. Bustamante formed a trade union which he named the Bustamante Industrial Trade Union. His cousin Norman Washington Manley, a former Rhodes Scholar and Jamaica's most brilliant lawyer, simultaneously launched his People's National Party, or PNP. Through trade unionism and party politics, Bustamante and Manley sought to channel the grievances of the Jamaican poor, and they each advocated representative government.

Yet by temperament if not by birth (both Manley and Bustamante were of mixed race), the men could not have been more different. Manley was a man of measure and reason, whose soft sardonic smile was seen by his supporters as a tonic to 'Busta's' devilish allure and self-cultivated image of the pistol-packing *condottiere*. Manley's policies of extensive public ownership, industrial development, mass education and social welfare were influenced by the British Labour Party; Bustamante, more conservative, had a personal dynamic and a shrewd pragmatism lacking in his quieter opponent.

In the weeks following the riots, Bustamante and Manley travelled round Jamaica urging calm and were hailed as national leaders. Jamaica was poised to become the first British colony to achieve full adult suffrage: every Jamaican man and woman was to have the right to vote. Reform at last was on the way. In the build-up to the general elections of 1944, however, ideological differences between Manley and Bustamante emerged. Bustamante had founded his own political party, the Jamaica Labour Party, or JLP, which was by now effectively conservative.

Jamaica found itself in a halfway house of compromise, with a dilute form of self-government subject to 'fatherly dictation' from Whitehall. Ultimate power was still vested in the governor, who was answerable to His Britannic Majesty the King. A small black middle class was fortunately emerging, and it was in this class that the principles of nationalism and the desire for independence bit deepest. Michael Foot was one of several liberal-minded British politicians who were delighted by Jamaica's progress towards self-rule. When Foot first visited the island in December 1944, his brother Hugh 'Pussyfoot' Foot was about to become the island's colonial secretary.

As the 1944 elections drew to a close, Michael Foot witnessed the final exchanges between Bustamante and Manley on the Kingston hustings. 'Busta's party had pretty well cleansed itself of its socialist leanings by the time I arrived, and was championing a middle course,' Foot told me. 'Still, Busta was a most effective public speaker. I remember him swigging from a rum bottle while his supporters sang "If God Be With Us, Who Could Be Against Us?" Rousing stuff – Jamaicans can sing as well as anybody else in the world, you know.' The 1944 election was a consequence of the fatal damage that the Second World War had done to Britain's position as a great power; Jamaican nationalism was filling the void left by an increasingly moribund 'civilising mission'.

I was ushered into Foot's north London home by his housekeeper. 'Michael's waiting for you downstairs, sir,' she said with old-fashioned deference. Foot, an elfin-faced man in a threadbare jumper and creaky black shoes, had lost the sight in one eye, but my impression was of a man who was not unhappy to be in his ninety-sixth year. (His dog Dizzee had been named not, as I assumed, after the Victorian Disraeli but the London rapper Dizzee Rascal.) Foot's interest in Jamaica stemmed from his father, the Liberal Party MP Isaac Foot, who as chairman of the British Cromwell Society was interested in the Protector's conquest of Jamaica. The Foot family's last link with Jamaica was Oliver Foot (younger brother of the late campaigning journalist Paul Foot), who had been public relations officer for Air Jamaica until he died in 2008, at the age of sixty-one.

The erosion of Britain's will to occupy Jamaica, according to Michael Foot, was overshadowed by the prospect of administrative breakdown in the Raj. 'Jamaica and India – two countries coming out of British control at the same time,' he said. Inevitably the destiny of the two colonies was independence. Why? 'Because the British Empire was past it,' said Foot, and self-government was a 'natural adjunct' of imperial decadence. 'Unfortunately the Empire with its blinkered, unimaginative types was getting in the way all over the bloody place – preventing Manley and Busta from implementing their reforms.' Foot sighed: 'In some ways, Jamaica was too small to accommodate two leaders of such magnitude and such immense style.'

To Michael Foot's disappointment, Bustamante won the 1944 election decisively. Even then, independence did not come to Jamaica for another eighteen years, as Britain continued to deny Jamaicans a proper say in their own affairs. So freedom arrived late for Jamaica – fourteen years after India's. By the time it finally did come in 1962, Jamaica had lost much of its reformist zeal, the enthusiasm for change tempered by years of colonial prevarication.

'Now of course Jamaica has gone to the American camp, and it's partly our fault – we've abandoned Jamaica,' said Foot. The United States had not only superseded the British Empire, it had become (in Foot's view) a world-wide anti-revolutionary movement in defence of 'dollar-colonialism', 'coca-colanisation', and other sinister interests. 'Bloody Americans.' Foot rocked back and forth in his chair, raising his voice crossly. 'They're too powerful.'

President Obama may yet restore America's battered image abroad, but did Foot lament Greater Britain's fading into non-existence? 'Of course not!' he countered; it was only such a 'shame' that, as the British Empire passed away, so the United States began to practise its own *imperium,* subjugating peoples in the name of democracy. The Ronald Reagan administration of 1980–87 made Jamaica the fulcrum of its Caribbean Basin Initiative (CBI), loaning an average of US$125 million a year, money that Jamaica was unable to repay.

Foot was nostalgic then, not for Britain's colonial stewardship, but for 'all that was best' (as he construed it) about British public life. By which he meant free speech, good governance, faith in progress, liberalism; qualities which certainly exist in Jamaica today, but in attenuated form. In the four decades since independence, Jamaica presents a world of 'fear and distrust', said Foot, where each week a new crime of 'hideous proportions' makes the headlines. And that was partly due – Foot clarified his position – to a 'diminished British influence' in the years following inde-pendence. In the first years after the Union flag came down Jamaica seemed to be infused with a new glamour and a sense of purpose. 'Jamaicanisation' meant well-intentioned displays of pan-African national costume and post-colonial culture. And now? 'Now,' Michael Foot concluded, 'Jamaica's in a fix.'

*

In Westmoreland parish, where the 1938 riots had flared up, stands a former slave village called Bethel Town. A recluse known locally as 'Squire' Cooke was rumoured to live in the hills above it. Chester Castle, his home, was said to have gone wild, gone back to bush. There was no telephone. So if I wanted to visit I would have to do so unannounced.

Up the hill to the slave mansion the bamboo groves radiated a jewel-like lustre. Locals called this a wild place; a green light filtered eerily through the forest canopy and strange-looking thorns caught at my trousers. Before long I was standing outside a two-storey Jamaican merchant's house of the mid-1700s, built of cut stone, with an open veranda at one end. The house, with its trailing bougainvillea, was shuttered and silent in the afternoon heat. A Land Rover lay abandoned in the tractor yard, the chassis white with bird droppings.

I knocked on the door for some time until it was opened by an elderly black man in dungarees, who introduced himself as Mr Dixon. 'Master Cooke's asleep,' he announced. 'But I'm sure he'll be pleased to see you.' Dixon, whose diction echoed BBC received pronunciation, said he had been in Cooke's service for sixty years. 'The master soon come,' he reassured me, and with that he disappeared into Chester Castle, leaving me to wait outside. I knew I was in for a long wait. 'Soon come' is an expression which haunts Jamaican life and, to outsiders, epitomises the Jamaican soul. *Soon come*. You can fume and fuss all you like about Jamaican lack of punctuality, but you quickly learn to accept the relaxed Jamaican attitude to time; you have to.

For almost an hour I waited before Ian Cooke emerged from his slumbers. Until that happened I could hear Mr Dixon moving from room to room inside, opening windows, throwing back the shutters. Cooke, a thin man bent almost double with age, punted himself towards me with the aid of a bamboo pole. His face had the waxy pallor of white men who have lived long in the torrid zones. 'What brings you to Jamaicaaah?' he asked, the vowels peculiarly drawn-out. Though haggard and distrait, he was still every inch the buckra, or white Jamaican planter.

He gestured for me to sit down in a room panelled in dark timbers that smelled faintly of beeswax and lamp-paraffin. There was little furniture to speak of other than a couple of broken Windsor chairs and a leather-seated armchair visibly eaten by termites. Cooke said his daughter had come out from England the other day and, staking her claim to the family furniture, 'cleared out everything' with a removal van. Cooke added (apparently by way of apology) that she lived in Tunbridge Wells.

The Cookes had lived in Chester Castle since 1773, and no doubt, like many of Jamaica's long-settled English, they were impervious to and contemptuous of the slave culture in which they found themselves. Cooke was friendly, though, and his hospitality freely offered. He said he had been educated in England, but England must have seemed quite unreal to him now. Upstairs the rooms had collapsed; tubers and shoots were pushing up through the floorboards and broken windows. A mattress lay along one wall, next to a pail for collecting rain.

'I love this country very much' – Cooke laid a thin hand on my shoulder – 'but it's no use now. Good Lord, we're hell-bent on our own destruction.' He began to rail against the native propensity (as he perceived it) for idleness and skylarking. The Cooke family slaves had been 'awfully lazy', he complained; consequently Chester Castle estate had virtually collapsed. In the last ten years Cooke had sold just two cows, two calves and one bull cow. He added grimly, 'and that's about it'.

I asked Cooke, 'Do you like it in Chester Castle?'

'Of course I jolly well like it,' he grunted in answer. 'And it breaks my heart to have to depart this island which I love so.' He added, 'I'm ninety-six, you know. Good Lord, I'm so old that it's almost *senseless* for me to die. But die I must, very soon, and now that my furniture's gone, dying will be my final act of dispossession.' Six generations of Cookes lay buried in the Bethel Town churchyard, 'and I hope to join them before long'.

Cooke got up and, using his chair as a walking frame, propelled himself down the hall towards the veranda, which overlooked a green ocean of cane-fields, the cane spearheads like polished metal reflecting the sun's glare. 'This poor body of mine is no blinking good any more,' Cooke continued, his voice thick with emotion. 'When you get to my age you accumulate a lot of regrets and one of my chief regrets is that I was never able to paint this . . . magnificent view.' Away in the distance behind a curtain of fan palms a smudge of white indicated the Baptist church at Mount Carey, and close by, the grounds of Montpelier, a Cooke estate saved from the Jamaican slave uprising of 1831–2.

Cooke sat down and stared dolefully at the bright Eden spread out before us. 'It is simply not possible that there can be anywhere as beautiful as this,' he said. 'Oh, I've seen some extraordinary things here – I've seen the sky darken with butterflies, yes I have, the butterflies actually *kaleidoscoped* the sky. Now there are no more butterflies left.'

Would I care to hold a telescope to the view? 'Rose! Dixon!' Cooke called out. 'Where's my spyglass?' The servants looked, but no telescope could be found. 'It's gone the way of all flesh,' Cooke said, adding with another sigh, 'I don't know what's going to happen.' The world he had come from had been reduced to this: an old man in an abandoned house on a hill. Cooke was born here almost a century earlier, the last of his kind in Jamaica. And Chester Castle, like Cooke, was at the end of its existence. I left him in the home of his slave-owning forebears, oddly saddened by the encounter, and returned to the forest path as the sun sank over Jamaica.

6

I've Got to Go Back Home

After years of estrangement in a foreign land, what can Jamaicans expect to find on their return home? The remembered warmth and blazing beauty of Jamaica have remained with them, in some cases, for over half a century of British or North American exile. Yet a hundred changes will have occurred since they left. Long brooding over the loss of one's homeland can exaggerate its charm and sweetness. Should Jamaicans stay 'in foreign' or go home?

The ambivalence is understandable; their very decision to migrate had reflected Jamaica's perceived failure to succeed as a nation. If so many Jamaicans had left in the first place, why should any want to go back?

The first significant wave of migration occurred in the 1860s and 1870s, when Jamaican labourers left for Panama to work on the early French efforts to carve out the great canal. After nine years in the humid and pestilential Panamanian climate, some 20,000 workers had died, the majority of them Jamaican. Those who survived were left stranded in the squalid camps of Colón and Panama City; many never returned.

Thousands more Jamaicans migrated to Panama as a second bid to build the canal commenced at the beginning of the twentieth century. In the hope of earning their 'Panama Gold', they worked in the mud up to their knees. Landslides were terrifying and routine; work was always hazardous and sometimes fatal. The Jamaicans who returned, however, enjoyed the reputation of being rich, though they had been paid less than their white counterparts and were segregated from them. 'Colón Man', so named after the Panamanian city, became shorthand for the wealthy Jamaican returnee with gold in his teeth, gold rings on every finger, gold-capped walking sticks and waistcoats adorned with gold watches and chains. Every Jamaican village had its 'Colón Man'; conversely, parts of Panama today remain distinctly Jamaican in character.

Over a thousand Jamaicans are estimated to go back each year to live. The great reggae song 'I've Got To Go Back Home' by Bob Andy expresses their dreams of flight and migration; it is about Jamaicans searching for a better life – and failing to find it. Andy wrote and recorded it in 1966 four years after independence; by any standards an exquisite statement of homesickness, the song has a tremendously infectious brass section which rarely fails to move Jamaicans in the diaspora. According to Andy, Jamaicans display an almost unrivalled need to absorb into societies other than their own – 'going foreign' is like an instinct for them.

The Kingston suburb where Andy lived, Patrick City, stood in uneasy proximity to the Brooke Valley badlands prowled by dustbin dogs and thieves. Andy's car had been stolen the day I visited him, yet he took the theft with philosophic resignation. 'When life is hard,' he said to me, 'a man will do anything.' Andy is best known abroad for his duet with Marcia Griffiths, 'Young, Gifted and Black', written by Nina Simone, which reached the UK top twenty in 1970. In person, however, he is a more substantial and thoughtful man than that pop song might suggest. In his early sixties, with grizzled dreadlocks loose over a denim shirt, he radiated a composed dignity. Andy had spent long periods of his life in Ethiopia and would describe himself as 'Afrophile'.

Closing his eyes, he asked me what I wanted of him exactly. I asked if 'I've Got To Go Back Home' was a song about a Jamaican living in Britain, or about a Jamaican living in Jamaica, who wanted to go 'home' to Africa.

Andy nodded his understanding. The song was ambivalent. 'It could be about a homesick Jamaican in England but' – he went on evenly – 'it hints at repatriation to ancestral Ethiopia.' After independence, Andy had become interested in 'black race consciousness' and Rastafari notions of a return to Africa. 'We Jamaicans have a great continental hunger,' he went on. 'That's why we have such a huge diaspora – home is always somewhere else.' The Syrian in his Kingston haberdashery shop (Lebanese, in fact, but Jamaicans call all Arabs 'Syrian') might think of his home as Lebanon; the Chinese in his duty-free store might think of his home as Shanghai; and the British planter class might look longingly to England as its birthright.

In Andy's view Jamaica was not so much a British colonial outpost in the Caribbean as an *African* outpost in the Caribbean, or, better, an English-speaking African country in the Caribbean. 'You say you've been to Coronation Market. Well, it could easily be in Nigeria – the mannerisms, the attitudes, the rhythm of life there are of Gold Coast Africa, not of Britain.'

Another beautiful Bob Andy song, 'I Don't Want To See You Cry', had been given a bravura reading in 1965 by the Jamaican pop-reggae singer Ken Boothe. In many ways it was the obverse of the later, more famous song as it expressed the feelings of a young Jamaican as he prepares to leave for the 'faraway land' of England. The man in the song will think of himself as a 'Jamaican outside Jamaica' – a temporary guest of Her Majesty's government – and dream of the day he returns, said Andy.

*

'Mandeville! Mandeville!' I was in the Darling Street bus terminus in downtown Kingston surrounded by bus touts shouting 'Mandeville! Mandeville!' Jamaica's fifth-largest town, Mandeville is home to the island's wealthiest and most 'successful' returnees and is spoken of by Jamaicans in the diaspora as a sort of El Dorado. Mandeville was the place you came to when you had made it in the motherland.

I wheeled into the tight mob of bodies, aware that I was being observed, and headed for my chosen bus. I found a seat at the back. Slowly the bus filled up with passengers, the air inside thick with petrol fumes and a sour human smell. I sat thrust up against the window, my shoulder bag jammed in my lap. Cardboard had been slotted against the glass to keep out the heat, but my mouth was cotton-dry, and after an hour of waiting I was bursting for the lavatory. In discomfort I sat still, trying to work myself into a transcendent state of mind, fists clenched, as finally we lurched out of Kingston.

On the scruffy outskirts of May Pen, one hour later, the driver ordered a halt and I was quickly out of the bus and on to the roadside. With five other passengers I peed into a ditch. No longer bladder-wracked, back in the bus I sat staring in relief at the landscape of shacks and green hills. If poor Jamaicans have to rely on cramped, privately owned minibuses such as this one, it is because Jamaica no longer has a railway network. Kingston rail station (adjacent to the Darling Street bus terminus) has been out of service since 1992. Built by the British under Queen Victoria, its iron arches today are sprouting vegetation, with railway carriages mouldering in the sidings, their windows smashed. Once, higglers had used these trains to ferry their produce across the island; now they have to find alternative means of transport. Politicians in modern Jamaica have little regard for the state, and the responsibility for its maintenance. So ordinary Jamaicans have no decent public transport.

As we approached Mandeville, sixty miles west of Kingston, mansions of a Pharaonic grandeur loomed into view. With their cod-colonial columns and feudal-looking towers, they were like Hollywood dream castles, gaudy returnee havens. Many returnees hope that their grandchildren will occupy these houses; but their grandchildren are likely to be British-born Jamaicans, who cannot look forward to 'returning home' because Britain is their home. So, after a returnee's death, the big house may remain an empty, echoing chamber.

*

The Astra Country Inn, converted from a nursing home in the early 1970s, must have been the emptiest hotel in Mandeville as I was the only guest. At breakfast I was joined by Diana McIntyre-Pike, the manager, who also ran the local 'Returned Residents Association' which met once a month to discuss social events and crime prevention. An indomitable woman in her mid-fifties, in 1993 McIntyre-Pike had been wrongly accused (she volunteered the information) of poisoning her husband. Unsurprisingly business had suffered since. 'People thought they'd get poisoned here and they stopped coming,' she explained to me.

'And are guests still not coming?' I asked, glancing warily at the menu.

'We get a trickle,' she said, raising a severely plucked eyebrow.

For our tour of Mandeville, McIntyre-Pike had put on a leopardskin-print chiffon scarf and mascaraed her eyes like a burlesque queen. 'People can laugh at me all they want but they can't ignore me,' she said (no doubt accurately). She was so sure of herself that I was beginning to like her. 'Just don't call me a husband-poisoner,' she said, driving with the air-conditioning on so high that I could have done with an overcoat.

Mandeville is not much loved by the rest of Jamaica. William Sewell, a *New York Times* journalist, on visiting in 1860, was reminded of a 'newly located town in an American territory, for the houses did not look very old, nor were the streets out of repair.' Not much has changed. A dubious PNP politician and dancehall producer known as 'Skeng Don' had a stake in developing Mandeville's moneyed suburb of Ingleside, where starkly white houses with red-tiled roofs showed a Californian influence. Like much of Mandeville, Ingleside was a synthetic world of satellite dishes and parked Hummer wagons, a fantasy of Beverly Hills.

Elsewhere in Mandeville, however, the gentle rise and fall of the land, the mist and the verdancy, reminded me vaguely of England. I half expected to see browsing cows and weekend cricket matches. But the big, self-service plazas and US-style shopping marts dispelled that illusion. Mandeville, like the rest of Jamaica, had become the willing stepchild of a greater and more powerful nation. McIntyre-Pike, meanwhile, had arranged for me to visit Blake and Hyacinth Norwich, a married couple who had returned from England in 1995. Their house was an elaborately porticoed folly with electronically operated gates and outdoor kennels for four Alsatians. As I pushed the bell, electronic chimes sounded Frank Sinatra's 'I Did It My Way'.

Noiselessly the gates jerked open, and Mrs Norwich came to greet me. 'Do come in,' she said in a cordial voice, 'my husband will be with us shortly.' We passed through a gelid, marble-floored sitting room, and made our way up to the terrace, which over-looked the green hills and waving palms.

Hyacinth had trained as a nurse in England in 1963, at Derby City Hospital in the East Midlands. Her student quarters were cramped, she recalled, but people were mostly kind to her, 'as they are kind to strangers'. Her future husband, Blake Norwich, whom she met four years later, was working on the buses for Derby Transport. They married in Derby, then moved to Harrow in London, where he set up his own transport company, and she lectured on midwifery at a nursing college.

I asked her, 'Are you happy to be home again in Jamaica?'

Hyacinth replied, raising her arm in the direction of the green hills, 'We like it in Mandeville. There's a good hospital. Plenty of pharmacies. The cleanliness and cool climate get our top marks.' She put a hand to her throat. 'Most important, the gunmen don't come here – they'd be chased out.' She paused.

'That you, Blake?' Hyacinth called out at the sound of approaching steps. A tall man with a heavily thoughtful face appeared at the top of the stairs. Blake Norwich, her husband, regarded me curiously, and sat down while she went on speaking. 'You'd be surprised how quickly the locals can tell us returnees apart,' she said. 'I don't know what mark of the beast we have on us, but they seem to *know* we're returnees even before we've opened our mouths!' Her husband nodded assent. 'But we're more mannerly than the locals,' he said, 'and we're more disciplined. And we're proud to be that way. We say "please", we say "thank you" – simple expressions of good breeding, which the people here don't always use.'

'Or don't know how to use, Blake,' put in Hyacinth.

Marooned in their Mandeville fastness, Mr and Mrs Norwich struggled to interpret the modern Jamaica that had changed so much in their absence. 'It isn't easy for us here,' Hyacinth admitted. 'After all, we've come from a First World country to a Third World country.'

Blake Norwich, every inch the prosperous returnee in his white chinos and T-shirt, looked at me with a level gaze. 'If you aren't careful,' he said with concern in his voice, 'the locals will take *all* your hard-earned cash.' It was best not to make friends with them: nod hello to them in the market, maybe, but with little or no show of mateyness. One returnee I spoke to had referred to the locals as 'natives', a word almost colonial in its hauteur. The art of being a stranger to your neighbour had been imported to Jamaica, it seems, by returnees. The locals were involved in all sorts of gossip, skirmishes, backstabbing. They did not share the attachment to 'fair play' and 'punctuality' that apparently characterised the British life as practised in Mandeville by returnees. The locals rarely queued; they argued noisily and in public, and they were uneducated. By temperament, also, they were 'lazy' – a people who could live and die without understanding the meaning of hard work. But the main shortfall, from which all these other shortfalls stemmed, was lack of 'respect': lack of respect for one's elders and betters, lack of respect for the rule of law.

The most striking thing about the Norwich household was the complete absence of Jamaica. Other houses in the area had on display at least token West Indian or even West African *objets d'art*. But there was nothing in the furniture, manner or comments of Blake and Hyacinth Norwich to show that they had any interest in their birthplace or their African roots. 'I'm afraid we've fallen into a position where we don't trust Jamaicans, and that's quite sad,' said Mrs Norwich. 'You'll hear a lot of hard luck stories from returnees,' she went on, 'but it's those returnees who were foolish enough to trust the locals who got cheated.'

Her husband said with quiet satisfaction, 'We've seen returnees with tears in their eyes because they've allowed themselves to be tricked by builders, swindled out of their savings, or whatever – and they can't afford to stay on in Jamaica.' Others go back crestfallen to England, claiming that locals have robbed them, when in reality they have run out of money. Mrs Norwich put it another way: 'It's more respectable to say you've been robbed. I mean, it's a terrible admission of failure to have to go back because you've run out of money!'

A mountain cold had begun to invade the terrace. Hyacinth Norwich, gazing out at the darkening hills beyond, announced: 'Most nights we have to wear cardigans. And to think we shipped out all our duvets from England!'

'It's as if England brings all its coldness here,' said Blake.

'Yes – who'd have thought of wearing woollies in Jamaica?' said his wife.

With the hasty West Indian dark, fireflies had come out, blinking luminous round the terrace. Later, Blake gave me a lift back to my hotel.

*

In Brixton, south London, Pearl Willis had described herself to me as 'a failed returnee'. In 1996 she returned to her birthplace in Coleyville, near Mandeville, but was burgled there, and came back to Britain in disgust. Fortunately she had not sold her house in Ducie Street, a small Victorian terrace, where she had lived for forty years. A cloying fragrance of air-freshener hung in the corridor there and beyond that an aroma of boiled yams and fish indicated that Pearl, in her early sixties, had prepared a Jamaican supper for us. We had been introduced by a mutual friend.

Pearl's first few months in England were among the unhappiest she could remember. 'Everyone was shut away in their rooms and alone with themselves,' she said. It was 1953 and Elizabeth II had just been crowned queen. Gradually Pearl settled and her attitude to England changed. Though her romantic vision of the motherland had been shattered, she found she was loath to go home. She had even grown to like British roast beef and the rituals of empire. 'It was surprising how quick we subtropical folk got used to the cold,' she said, with an amused look.

'So what was it like – when you went back to Jamaica?'

'How could I forget?' Pearl let out a nervous laugh. 'My husband had just died, I felt I was ready to go home.'

For a while she believed she really was home. She built a new house on a hill in Coleyville and shipped out all her furniture and savings from Brixton. 'My gas cooker was there, my lovely dining set was there – everything I owned was there.' But her new life in Jamaica began to go wrong; the locals jeered at her: 'Miss Pearly!' or 'Miss England Lady!' Pearl had wanted to put a bit of style into her homecoming; she went to Coleyville market in a smart kilt she had bought at a Harrods sale for £95. But the kilt only excited envy. 'Give me your skirt when you go home,' the higglers shouted at her.

Pearl set down her glass and fetched a tray of yams from the oven. Plates of ackee (a Jamaican fruit) and sweet potatoes followed. 'Then one day in Coleyville,' she continued, 'I was broken into. The burglars stole everything – even my plumbed-in washing machine.' The police wanted money in return for catching the thieves. 'The police are the next corrupted ones.' Pearl pulled a face. 'All they want is bribes – big-talk buffoons.' She looked down, and her mouth was trembling. 'No, I'm sorry, I don't want anything more to do with those Jamaican people, I don't want anything more to do with those respecters of *nothing*.'

For weeks after the break-in, the sound of rustling leaves or a barking dog would terrify Pearl. *It's the burglar man come back.* She installed burglar bars and grilles, but she began to feel homesick for England. 'Yes, I was pining for the far-off shining cliffs of Dover.' She smiled indulgently. 'Then one mornin' I look up to God in heaven and tell Him: "Lord, I'm lockin' up, I'm leavin'." And that's what I did.' Pearl gave a sad laugh at the quaintness of life. 'It pains me to have to say this, but Jamaica is another country for me now – a country where I thought I'd be *murdered*. At least in Ducie Street you can live with your windows open.' Pearl's attachment to Jamaica, she now realised, was a child's attachment to the place she was from. She was not even sure that there was such a thing as a 'return': you leave one place, you arrive at another.

And now, in a strange reversal of the migrant life, Pearl was a boarding-house landlady, who took in lodgers from Latin America and the Baltic States. 'They're good, clean, quiet boys,' she said – but added sourly: 'Africans are different – oh Lord, don't let me have them Africans again.' Africans never paid the rent. They were noisy. They were dirty. Pearl referred to Africans as 'Negroes' (though probably not with a Garveyite capital 'N'). This was the old Jamaican fear of the continent of darkness, with its unwanted reminder of slavery and blackness.

*

Mandeville was as peaceful as it can get in Jamaica; I could see why returnees came here. The air this morning smelled of freshly cut grass, with a clove-like scent of carnations in bloom. Still, the typical tale of returnees in Mandeville involved robbery, even murder. So I was surprised to meet a Jamaican home-comer who despised not the 'locals' but fellow returnees. In her view, returnees were 'vulgar' people who were 'disfiguring' Mandeville with their mock plantation residences and their claims to high social ranking. Among other returnees such a view was almost unheard of. Dorothea Minott-Tait, a widow in her early seventies, took her stand on very high ground indeed.

A practising Methodist, she lived in the Mandeville garden suburb of Knock-Patrick. 'How are you, sir?' she greeted me in a poised contralto voice. This old-fashioned courtesy is not uncommon among older Jamaicans; for Minott-Tait the use of a Christian name instead of 'sir' with a perfect stranger was a tawdry example of the 'new American' way of doing things, and to be avoided. Tall and slightly stooped, with set grey hair and rouged cheeks, she looked quite regal. Her home had rugs on the linoleum floor and white organdie curtains at the windows. The trees in the garden were hung with a variety of New Age wind chimes. Desmond, her 'steward' (as she called him), was hovering by the entrance when I arrived.

All the furniture had been freighted out from England. Chandeliers and elaborate, high-backed reproduction antique chairs, nests of polished side tables, a crescent-shaped bar with a Formica top. A gas fire glowed orange with plastic coals as Minott-Tait, patting her hair into shape, said, 'People thought I was extravagant to spend so much money shipping out the furniture – but if you decide to do something, you must do it properly.' The only concession to Jamaican decor was the large canopied bed (visible through an open door) hung with mosquito nets. Otherwise the home was a shrine to suburban England.

Minott-Tait had arrived in England in 1961, on a spring day she now regards as one of the most exciting of her life. In every way she was unprepared to accept her English domicile as an 'immigration'. She had not, she was keen to stress, left Jamaica out of economic necessity; she had no need to. She had a good job in Kingston as an accountant. No, she was running away from an unhappy marriage. 'I had to go to England to sort out my emotional problems.'

And yet, like many Jamaican migrants, she saw England as a colonial opportunity, a golden land. Enoch Powell, as the Tory party's health minister, was encouraging Jamaicans and other citizens of the British Commonwealth to come and work in the understaffed NHS, and Minott-Taitt had responded. She trained as a nurse at Wanstead Hospital in east London. On 31 August 1962 she organised a party there to celebrate Jamaican independence. She was the only Jamaican nurse in Britain to do this, she claimed.

From a desk drawer she removed a dog-eared photograph of the occasion, which showed a beautiful young women cradling a bunch of cellophane-wrapped flowers. Seated next to Minott-Tait is Wanstead Hospital's white matron (unsmiling), and next to her, Mr Hosford Scott, the Jamaican High Commissioner (also unsmiling, also white).

At the time the photo was taken, Minott-Tait had thought of herself as an advertisement for West Indian assimilation. She was doing good works, organising gala parties and Jamaican diaspora events. Settling in Britain, in those days, was a lifetime commitment, she said, that required a degree of emotional separation from the 'old country'. But nowadays, she complained, there are simply too many people living in Britain who have no wish to become citizens. 'They let too many people in – not from Jamaica any more, but from Somalia, from Eastern Europe.' Immigrants today, with the internet, cheap flights and satellite TV, no longer see themselves as aspiring Britons but as members of a foreign culture, hosted by, but not emotionally attached to, Britain.

Minott-Tait (who was on this subject like a dog with a bone) thought that that was terrible. In her day, migrants from the British colonies tended to behave in a 'very proper and refined British way'. Indeed she found she spoke 'far better English' than most of Wanstead Hospital's British nursing staff. Even the Jamaicans working at the hospital did not come up to her elevated standards, so she chose not to socialise with them, but passed them in the corridors with a perfunctory side-glance.

Minott-Tait surveyed her tea table with approval. Hers seemed to be an exaggeratedly English idea of how a tea table might look: paper doilies, thin-cut cucumber sandwiches. At a given signal, her steward Desmond wheeled in a blackamoor butler, about two feet tall, made of painted wood, with a dinky bow tie and tails. Tiny glasses of sherry were balanced on the butler's outstretched tray. 'Thank you, Desmond, you may go now,' said Minott-Tait. 'Yes,

Mrs M-T,' he replied mechanically. My host was taking this bizarre ritual of English afternoon tea very seriously but, secretly, I despised it, and this made me uncomfortable.

Taking a seat, I told Minott-Tait, 'I'm being spoilt.'

Apparently pleased, she replied, 'I try to maintain civilised standards,' and handed me a glass of sherry, which unfortunately I spilled.

When Minott-Tait took the plunge in 1993 and returned to Jamaica, friends warned her not to trust anyone. She refused to heed them. 'You have to *live*,' she said to me, and I admired her for the attitude. She drank Jamaican tap water, ate the local food, and walked about at night. One could hardly live in a country in a state of constant preparedness for the worst. Moreover, she found the very label 'returnee' disagreeable. 'I'm a retired Jamaican lady, if you must, but a returnee? Never.' Returnees, in her view, were often insular types, who looked at Jamaica from a peculiarly isolated perspective.

Minott-Tait did not miss England much. 'England can be a very lonely place.' Yet Jamaicans, she reckoned, needed to go back to English standards (as she saw them) of decorum and civility. 'Look at our funerals – they've become awful! All that bling and vulgarity.' Yes, Jamaicans should take a leaf out of the 'English book', and be more private in their grief. 'All that noise. What right do they have?' she said with an ascetic, unforgiving air.

*

The day I left Mandeville a commotion broke out in the taxi compound. Two youths had been caught stealing goods from the SuperPlus Food Store across the way. The manager and four of his deputies had tied them up, and set their dogs on them. That part of Mandeville was in an uproar as bystanders cheered at the barbarities meted out to the shoplifters. In the absence of a credible justice system, acts of mob vengeance can proceed out of a sense of nothing, it seems. There is no justification for them. Thieves get hacked to death – 'chopped' – simply for stealing yams. And the police may tacitly approve such vigilante killings because they have no faith themselves in the justice system. The next day's edition of the *Gleaner* revealed that the Mandeville thieves had been bludgeoned with shovels and pick axes, as well as bitten by dogs; one of them was unable to walk after spinal injuries. Dear God. At such times Jamaica seemed to be a society in moral decomposition; a hating and hateful place.

*

Before reaching Kingston I made a detour to Watercourse. Watercourse is a village so insignificant that it fails to appear on any map of Jamaica. Even the name is misleading, as there are no watercourses in the area and, as far as anyone knows, there never have been. Thelma Smith, a Jamaican who coincidentally also lived on Ducie Street in Brixton, had urged me to visit. Thelma was born in Watercourse in 1923 and had relatives there; on the rare occasions when she visited Jamaica it was always to see her childhood friend Benita Hailey in Watercourse.

'Thelma sent you?' asked Miss B (her local name) and, taking my hand, she pointed me to a chair on the porch. 'OK, my love, seat yourself.' A neighbour pegging out the washing appraised us curiously. Watercourse, a hillside community of perhaps 800 people, was a poor village and seemingly without Uzis, AKs and Hummer cars. While elsewhere in Jamaica, the American influence is very prevalent, in Watercourse the villagers only have to please themselves. The result was a dignified place, situated at an altitude above Riversdale in the heart of orange-grove country.

Children's voices were raised in playful chatter while Miss B went inside to fetch some refreshment. She returned with a pitcher of coconut water and a plate of dry boiled shrimps. 'Up here is country,' she said, pouring me a glass, 'and we country people is a nice people who care for each other.' Back in her working days Miss B had been a higgler, taking supplies of yam and plantain by train from nearby Linstead to sell in Spanish Town. 'But there's no train running now. Yes, my dear, them was good days.'

Miss B took a thin wheezy breath. 'Why, we can't even get water now.' Her grandson has to fetch water from a standpipe in Riversdale four miles away. The world that Miss B had known as a girl was falling around her; Kingston represented a confusion beyond the reach of reason, a terrible place. 'But we're living in Jamaica, my dear, and we have to stay here now.' Sitting on that porch, the air cool with a faint smell of juniper and orange, I felt a surge of affection for Jamaica; in the present uncertainty and emptiness, surely there had to be some possibility of hope, maybe even of a new beginning?

'Come, my dear,' Miss B got up. She could walk only with the aid of a stick. 'Miss B not so strong like the first time.' She caught her breath. 'Miss B getting *old*.' She led me by the arm to a shaded plot of earth where, under an orange tree, the gravestones of Thelma Smith's parents stood alone in the fading light. Miss B reached up to the orange tree and pulled down one, two, then six oranges for me. 'When you get home to Brixton,' she said, dropping the fruit into my bag, 'tell Thelma that Miss B give you some oranges – and kiss up your children for me.'

That moment in Watercourse, with the sun descending over a secluded burying-place, and the green-lighted fireflies which had begun to dance over the graves of Mr and Mrs Smith, defined for me old Jamaica.

7

Forward Unto Zion

Jamaica is an island of bewildering mixed bloods and cultures. Chinese, 'Syrian', British, Spanish, aboriginal Taino Indian, have all intermarried to form an indecipherable blend and vitality of peoples. Jews were among the earliest arrivals. They arrived during the Spanish occupation, a century before Cromwell's invasion. Expelled from anti-Semitic Spain in the 1490s and 1500s, they were Iberian immigrants or Sephardim (after *Sefarad*, Hebrew for 'Spain') in search of a refuge. Officially they were not allowed to settle in Jamaica or anywhere else in the Spanish New World with its Catholic orthodoxies. Judaism, if it was practised at all in pre-British Jamaica, was practised in secret.

After England seized the island in 1655, however, a number of Jewish families began to migrate to Jamaica and were given the right to worship in synagogue, as well as own tracts of land. Gradually other Sephardi arrived from Brazil, Holland, England, Guyana and Surinam. By the 1770s, Jamaica had become a thriving outpost of Jewry in the West Indies, with infusions also of Ashkenazi Jews from northern Europe – Poland, Germany, the Baltic and parts of north-west Russia.

At first no love was lost between the Sephardi and Ashkenazi communities but over time they pooled their funds and, calling themselves the United Congregation of Israelites, in 1888 built a synagogue in downtown Kingston on Duke Street, where they agreed to worship as one.

One evening I attended a Sabbath service in Duke Street. The synagogue had a small garden with richly sculpted gravestones, the trilingual inscriptions in Hebrew, English and Portuguese. Within, the floor was strewn with sand, muffling one's tread in symbolic memory of the enforced silence Jews had had to keep under Spanish rule. The coolness of the temple's marble was enhanced by blue and orange pools of light refracted by the setting sun through a stained-glass window.

Sadly Jamaican Jews are more and more reluctant to worship here, as Duke Street stands on the edge of what is, effectively, a war zone. On Hanover Street round the corner, rival gangs shoot at each other from the rooftops, leaving behind spent cartridges and shattered concrete facades. The congregation this Friday at dusk numbered no more than thirty.

To my right an elderly white woman was squinting at her prayer book through a magnifying glass but I could tell she wanted to talk to me and I gave her some encouragement. 'My name is Myra Lindo, and what is yours?' Her face lit in a smile of pleasure when I commented on the serenity of the temple's vaguely Byzantine interior. The gilt capitals with their marble vinery and breadfruit and the coronet-style gas lamps suspended from the roof testified to a small, hard-working community of discreet wealth and middling social rank.

'Yes,' Myra Lindo turned to look at me again, 'in all my international travels I've never seen a synagogue so beautiful.' At either side of the Ark, two perpetual lights flickered red to symbolise the unity of the Sephardi and Ashkenazi communities; and in tall, golden letters across the Ark was the Old Testament injunction in Hebrew: 'Know Before Whom You Stand.' A place of wonder and reverence. 'But we're short of members,' the old woman continued, 'we're dying off.' Her voice, somnolent and weary-sounding, seemed to come from a long way off.

In the early 1960s, when Kingston briefly became a refuge for Cuban Jews fleeing Havana under Castro, Jamaica's Jewish community had grown to between 3,000 and 4,000. But now there were only 200, at most 300, practising Jews left in Jamaica. The young had left for the United States, for Canada or Britain. 'And they'll never come back,' said Myra Lindo. So many people in independent Jamaica had become exiles, or sought that status; why should they ever come back? Jamaica seemed to excel in all the negative indicators: lowest literacy, highest murder rate.

As Kingston today has no rabbi, the *Shabbes* (Sabbath) prayer was intoned by the community's 'spiritual leader', who swayed from side to side with both arms raised, chanting His words in antiphonal responses. After the service, the congregation retired for the ritual 'breaking of the bread'. In a brightly lit room at the back of the synagogue, braided loaves were piled on a table draped in a white cloth. Candles flickered as wine was sipped from *kiddush*-cups. Someone tendered me a plate of fish paste sandwiches. I took a couple, and after a moment a tall, bearded man came up to me.

'*Shabbat Shalom.*'

'*Shabbat Shalom,*' I said.

'Where you from?'

'England. London.'

'You are welcome.'

The man gave his name as Patrick Mudahy and, stroking his lion-like beard, said, 'My ancestors came to Jamaica from Palestine in 1734.' I was impressed. As a young man, Mudahy had drifted from his Jewish roots and became a Rastafarian. The Jewish experience of suffering and exile, he said, with its emphasis on deliverance and redemption, had much in common with the pseudo-Judaic sect of Rastafari (named after the holy Ethiopian oligarch and semi-divinity Haile Selassie's pre-coronation title of Ras Tafari Makonnen). Like Judaism, Rastafari observes strict dietary laws and indulges in hair-splitting or 'reasoning' of Old Testament scriptures. (Israel Vibration, one of the great reggae bands of 1970s Jamaica, was aptly named.)

Mudahy had even met Haile Selassie. 'It was in 1966,' he said. 'Kingston. State visit.'

For Mudahy, the Ethiopian ruler was then nothing less than a messianic manifestation of the one true God and a bulwark against 'Babylon' (in Rastafari iconography, the biblical whore of St John's Apocalypse; more loosely, oppressive colonial society). Was it possible that this diminutive Ethiopian, this Ras Tafari, was the Saviour whose coming had been foretold in the Old Testament? Repatriation to Ethiopia – the one true 'Zion' – seemed in 1966 not merely necessary but inevitable.

'And now?' I asked Mudahy.

'And now I'm a practising Jew again.'

Outside the synagogue, night had descended to usher in the Sabbath.

*

A damp Thursday morning in Kingston, April 1966. Over 100,000 Jamaicans – Rastafarians as well as merely interested bystanders – swarmed Palisadoes Airport in the hope of catching a glimpse of Haile Selassie. The Ethiopian ruler was due to stop in Kingston en route to visit François 'Papa Doc' Duvalier in Haiti. Banners showing the Ethiopian Lion of Judah rippled amid clouds of ganja smoke as drum-beating and chanting welled up alongside the motorcade's route into the city. Though it was raining, the Rastafarians reminded themselves: 'When God comes, the sun will come out.' Selassie was the first African head of state to visit Jamaica since independence; he offered, among other things, an alternative to the new 'white imperial overlordship' as represented by the United States or Britain.

Unfortunately the Ethiopian Airways flight was delayed by two hours. When the plane finally touched down, hundreds of restless Rastafarians crashed the VIP line of Cabinet ministers and Opposition leaders. Converging round the plane even as the propellers were still turning, they sang praise to the Ethiopian god in human form who had come to redeem his Jamaican people dispersed from Africa. As foretold, the sun came out. 'It was as if Kingston had been bathed in the light of Addis Ababa,' Patrick Mudahy recalled.

Selassie remained locked inside his private aircraft, but after half an hour, 'tearfully overwhelmed', said Mudahy (or maybe just frightened), he ventured down the steps to greet the crowds. Cheers erupted as he was whisked off under police escort, and from the roadside Rastafarians cried out to the royal motorcade: 'King of Kings! Lord of Lords! Prepare a place for me in thy kingdom!' Not since Marcus Garvey returned from New York in 1927 had there been such an overwhelming mass of well-wishers in the Jamaican capital.

That evening, at 10.30 p.m., a reception was held on the lawns of King's House. Count Ossie and the Mystic Revelation of Rastafari provided a drum recital, while schoolchildren chanted Jamaican folksongs. Selassie, decked with medals, watched in silence from an upstairs balcony as a dreadlocked Jamaican began a vociferous and unscheduled speech in praise of the royal visitor. The Jamaican was Mudahy; his exclamation was swiftly drowned out by a military brass band.

The next day, Haile Selassie laid a wreath in King George VI Memorial Park (now National Heroes Park), before visiting the prime minister's residence at Vale Royal. There he attended an African folk art exhibition which, by the pointed absence of the Union Jack and other trappings of colonialism, served to emphasise the threadbareness of imperial Britain. During the exhibition Mudahy shook Selassie's hand. 'The Roaring Lion was very quiet, very nice,' he recalled. Afterwards Selassie was shunted along Jamaica's (now defunct) railway to Montego Bay on the north coast. At all points along the line, police and military stood two deep with bayonets fixed. Rastafarians held up their babies to the royal coach's windows in the hope of a blessing.

The effect of Haile Selassie's four-day state visit would last for many years, inspiring Rastafari poems and songs (one of which, 'Rasta Shook Them Up', by Peter Tosh, contained introductory words in Amharic, the Ethiopian language which Selassie had used to address Rastafari elders in Kingston). Not only had Selassie's visit confirmed the place in Jamaica of Africa and African culture, it had provided an antidote to the 'defilement' of the British imperial period and regenerated hopes of black redemption.

The visit was judged a success (a *'roaring* success', joked Mudahy) even by the Jamaican authorities. Days prior to Selassie's arrival, graffiti had gone up on buildings in Kingston attacking Jews, Chinese and Lebanese as 'white oppressors'. The Jamaican government, alarmed by the rise of Black Power and Black Freedom Movements in the United States, had begun to deny entry visas to American black leaders and banned radical black literature. As confidence in Britain's power waned, so the 'spectre' of Black Power in Jamaica increased. With Selassie's official welcome, however, the authorities were able to appease the Back-to-Africa brethren and, by bringing them into King's House, lend them a respectability which previously they had been denied.

It may seem puzzling that present-day Ethiopia, with its political corruption, its poverty and famines, could ever have been revered as a land of milk and honey. Yet the idea of Ethiopia, with its place in the Old Testament and the romance of its imperial past, understandably exerts a hold on the imagination. In the mid 1950s, when Jamaican migration to Britain was at its peak, Ethiopia was not considered as a destination. Ten years later, however, Ethiopia was hailed as the country to deliver Jamaicans out of 'Babylon'.

*

Sixteen Jewish cemeteries are believed to lie scattered across Jamaica, most of them now either inaccessible or, in a few cases, desecrated. The oldest is situated off Spanish Town Road, in the depressed Hunts Bay area. Hundreds of Jews are said to have been buried there, unwept-for and disregarded since the seventeenth century, making it one of oldest Jewish cemeteries in the Western Hemisphere. I had to apply to the Red Stripe brewery for permission to visit as the cemetery stands on their land.

'We'll have to provide you with an armed guard,' company security told me on the telephone. 'It's Red Stripe policy.'

'Will just one escort be enough?' I asked.

'Should be – if not, we've got plenty more.'

Ainsley Henriques, a Jamaican Jewish historian, and his wife Marjorie Lamont accompanied me there. Like many Jamaican Jews, Henriques had contravened the Talmudic injunction against intermarriage. All the same, he could trace his Jamaican Jewish roots back to the 1740s. His scholarly, unworldly air was nevertheless deceptive; Henriques was a well read, well travelled, comfortable citizen of the world, with friends and interests in the United States, Britain and Israel.

With Henriques perspiring at the wheel of the car, we inched along the traffic-congested Spanish Town Road, stopping off to buy a litre of water in case we fainted. At the entrance to the Red Stripe brewery off Hunts Bay an armed guard came to greet us. 'Is that thing loaded?' Marjorie asked him, pointing at his pump-action. The guard answered 'Yes,' as he climbed in the car. After a few moments we arrived at a stretch of perimeter fencing nailed with placards declaring 'No Firearms Allowed'. Henriques drew in his breath; we were alone in the great silence of the marshy plain. There was no road.

'Careful, honey, there's all sorts of ditches here,' Marjorie warned her husband as we dipped and lurched through muddy water. Would the jolting set off the shotgun in the back? In the distance there emerged a collection of shacks with a sordid, desperate air; this was the squatter settlement of Backtu, sprawled out along Jamaica's long defunct railway line (the 'Back-to' of Damian Marley's 2006 dancehall reggae hit, 'Welcome to Jamrock').

We continued over rough ground until the land became too marshy for the car. Then we got out and walked. The guard was some distance ahead of us, shotgun at the ready. It seemed he was lost in some military fantasy of his own, but presumably there was a real risk of being of shot at – from Backtu. Red Stripe did not want a PR scandal on their hands.

The cemetery came into view on the far side of stagnant water, a moss-covered discontented place, the tombstones sweltering in the soupy light. Henriques began to photograph the strange-shaped stones that marked the graves, pointing out the Portuguese legend on one tomb: 'S.A.G.D.G', *Sua Alma Goze da Gloria*: May His Soul Enjoy Eternity. Other stones, cracked and fissured over the centuries, showed a mortuary symbolism of hourglasses, skulls and crossbones. The earliest decipherable inscription that we could find dated to 1672, seventeen years after Cromwell's invasion. Though the burial-ground was dilapidated, the many Europeans laid to rest here attested to the days when Kingston was a busy cosmopolitan port. But only an archaeologist could find beauty in this mutilated and hopeless-looking place. In a mood of anti-climax we drove back across the stinking, marshy plain to the Red Stripe brewery, where we dropped off the armed escort.

*

Hope Road (2004) is the account of a Jewish life spent first in England, later in Jamaica. Maurice Stoppi, the author, had grown up in London's Jewish East End in the 1930s. His Polish grandparents, Golda and Moishe Stupai, had settled in the 1880s in the Jewish community north of Whitechapel Road and anglicised the name Stupai to 'Stoppi'. Maurice Stoppi's London childhood –

pickled fish, Yiddish theatre – is recollected with affection and a regard for family. Every Friday before the Sabbath Maurice was taken by his father to the Hackney Baths on Mare Street for a steam sauna. Hackney was a step up, socially, from Whitechapel. At his school Stoppi shared a desk with a boy called Harold Pinter, later his friend.

How had a scion of East London's Jewish diaspora settled in Jamaica of all places – itself a land of polyglot confusion? In 1958, after a spell in Israel on a kibbutz, Stoppi was sent to the West Indies as a quantity surveyor. Pre-independence Jamaica, with its caste and colour rankings, struck him as a colonial extension of the Raj. Little had he imagined that the island would become his home. Strange Oxford-accented voices could be heard extolling the virtues of Oxo cubes and Cherry Blossom boot polish.

Officially there was no colour bar yet Stoppi noted that the Kingston tennis club – that Mecca of social life among the British upper crust – had no black members. Native-born Chinese, by virtue of their lighter skins, had made headway in this stratified society however. As a Jew, Stoppi found an affinity with this family-orientated, commercially minded minority. And in 1965, after seven years in Jamaica, he married a Jamaican Chinese. It was then that a strange counter-process began; in England his faith in Judaism had faded, but in Jamaica it revived.

'Why was that?'

'Good question,' Stoppi answered me. 'I'll have to have a think. You see, having survived the Hitlerite storm, we English Jews didn't *want* to be reminded of our Jewishness. I myself became a very buttoned-up sort of a Jew, ashamed of what had happened to my people – but in Jamaica . . . it was different.' To Stoppi's amazement, not only had Jamaican Jews survived, they had actually *thrived*. His Jamaican co-religionists were 'sunshine Jews', he said, who impressed him with their vitality and confidence. Ainsley Henriques had previously been married to the Jamaican Chinese actress Sheila Chong (star of the 1952 film *Island of Desire*). It was through Henriques that Stoppi became involved in Kingston's Jewish community and, in time, was made to feel part of an ancient New World Jewry.

The conservatory of Stoppi's house in the Kingston hills was clammy in the afternoon heat. Stoppi was in shirtsleeves and he looked worried, his face pale and serious (with a touch of Peter Sellers about it). He went over to the bar and poured out a jolt of soda and lime. 'I wouldn't leave Jamaica now for all the world,' he said. 'I love this place like it was my birthplace.'

Oddly, having lived in Jamaica for half a century, Stoppi bore no trace of a Jamaican accent. 'I wish I did! – then I could cuss up and play dominoes with the boys downtown.' Stoppi took out a handkerchief and wiped the palms of his hands. 'When I first came here I couldn't understand why Jamaicans spoke so *loudly*. Then I understood: the raised voices were connected to the ghetto. In the ghetto, see, competition for space is so fierce, the moment you're born you're competing to make yourself heard. Yes, Jamaicans can be aggressive,' Stoppi added, 'but there's a *need* for it – it's a form of self-defence, it's part of the jungle politics of reward and revenge.' *Jungle politics?* Jamaica was not, in Stoppi's view, a true democracy. 'If it *was*,' he said, 'we'd be ruled by the masses down there, but we aren't and probably never will be.'

Jamaica was now his journey's end. 'I've come a long way,' Stoppi said, peering at me through his thick-lensed glasses.

'But what, in the end, do you make of Jamaica?'

Stoppi smiled at the touch of pretension in my question. 'I'll tell you what I make of Jamaica. Jamaica's like an old heirloom that's been handed down by an uncle to a relative. Yes, the Jamaican people inherited a piece of real estate from Great Britain, good for sugar and bananas, but not for much else.' He had a clearer grasp of Jamaica's predicament, it seemed to me, than many politicians. Jamaica is no longer a chief player in the world sugar and banana markets. Instead tourism has become the mainstay of the island. But can tourism alone sustain the economy? Stoppi, for one, doubted it.

8

Maximum Black

Rastafarians have long been despised by the Jamaican establishment as work-shy, narcotically impaired troublemakers. They live in constant expectation of some punishment or hardship. A milestone in the Rastafari night of martyrdom was Mussolini's invasion of Ethiopia (then Abyssinia) in 1935. The plundering of Haile Selassie's sub-Saharan kingdom by Fascist Italy gave Jamaica's fledgling Rastafari movement impetus and a cause. The Fascist 'Babylon' was defeated by the British army and, in 1941, the Lion of Judah was allowed to return home to his throne in Ethiopia.

At the height of the Ethiopian war in 1935, news had reached Jamaica of a secret warrior organisation apparently headed by Selassie himself called Niyabingi ('death to the whites'). The organisation's avowed aim was to extinguish the Caucasian race, no less. The white Jamaican establishment received news of its existence with considerable satisfaction, as it provided justification for the continuing presence of the British in Jamaica.

The prospect of a race war seemed never more real in Jamaica than in 1968, when the young Guyanese historian Walter Rodney gave a series of lectures in praise of Rastafari and Black political militancy. The lectures, delivered off-campus to groups of the urban poor in Kingston, sparked the greatest upheaval in Jamaican society since independence in 1962. In his lectures, Rodney held up 'Syrians' and Jews as 'oppressors' and 'lackeys of imperialism'; but he concentrated his attack on Jamaica's Chinese who, unlike their brothers in the People's Republic of China heroically 'fighting against white imperialism', were merely part of the 'white West Indian social structure' intent on chaining black Jamaicans in a 'Babylonian captivity'. If the Chinese did not relinquish their privileges voluntarily (meaning their shops and businesses), they would have to be 'deprived' of them forcibly. Only then could they be re-integrated into a society 'where the black man walks in dignity', judged Rodney.

Rodney, as a Marxist, was hardly without bias, yet he was right to point out that the abolition of slavery had not led to a recognition of African culture and traditions in Jamaica (as it might have done), but to an intensification of European values and Anglo-Christian 'imperialism'. Rodney gave renewed voice to the dispossessed of Kingston and Spanish Town. His nine lectures (published in Britain in 1969 as *The Groundings with My Brothers*) constitute a landmark in Rastafari self-assertion; 'beauty is the very essence of black people', Rodney proclaimed. He was influenced by Stokely Carmichael and Charles V. Hamilton's book, *Black Power* (1967), which called for a recuperation of 'African consciousness' in the mind of the modern African American (a strategy that has evolved to its unsophisticated form in today's obsession with 'respect').

The lectures became a *cause célèbre* not just in Jamaica, but in all the West Indies. On 15 October 1968, after attending a Black Writers' Conference in Canada, Rodney was banned from re-entering Jamaica. Hugh Shearer, Jamaica's conservative prime minister, proclaimed the Guyanese historian *persona non grata*. In retaliation, students at the Jamaican campus of the University of the West Indies threatened to boycott lessons unless Rodney was allowed to return.

Rioting – the so-called Rodney Riots – broke out in Kingston over a period of two days. Rastafarians joined students in marches downtown, shouting 'Black Power!' Accusations of police brutality were levelled and the *Gleaner* newspaper building – symbol of Judaeo-Chinese-Syrian 'oppression' –- was besieged. One man was shot dead; cars were burned and overturned. Rodney decamped to Dar es Salaam in Tanzania, where he was welcomed by President Julius Nyerere. Twelve years later, in 1980, he was assassinated in his homeland of Guyana, of whose government he had been no less critical.

In hindsight, the 'Rodney Affair' served to unite Jamaicans of all backgrounds in an uptown–downtown alliance that called for an end to foreign investment and, even, the nationalisation of certain key industries. After the riots, the authorities came to embrace a dilute form of Black Power, and promoted Jamaican cultural 'self-awareness' on a national scale.

Yet, forty years on, Jamaica is still riddled with social distinctions. Everyone in Jamaica today (black, white, brown) prides themselves on their superiority, while at the same time everyone is uneasily aware that someone, somewhere (Chinese, Jewish, black), regards them as inferior.

*

I was back at PJ's when the telephone rang.

The voice at the other end of the line asked me: 'I take it that you're a Caucasian of British nationality?'

It belonged to Arthur Newland, a lecturer in religious anthropology at the University of the West Indies in Kingston.

'Yes,' I answered, a bit nettled, 'I'm a Caucasian. Of British nationality.' I had contacted Newland for permission to visit the Bobo Ashanti Rastafarians in their community situated due east of Kingston, in the volatile Nine Mile region of Bull Bay.

'And you're a journalist?' the voice went on severely. 'Well, we don't like journalists snooping around up there – poking fun.' A silence. 'What gives you the right to visit the community? *Why* do you want to visit?'

Of all the Rastafari offshoots, the Bobo are reckoned to be among the most ascetic and uncompromising. While most Rastafarians have integrated in varying degrees within Jamaican society, the Bobo are not interested in accommodating (still less in changing) that society, because they have effectively disowned it. As fundamentalists, they have withdrawn from the mainstream of island life and taken a Nazarene vow of poverty. In order to support themselves they sell brooms at traffic-lights in Kingston; the brooms are symbolic of the Bobo endeavour to 'sweep away' the filth of Babylon.

In recent years, thanks to the fiery, drum-driven chants of the Bobo adept Sizzla, membership of the cult has grown. Sizzla's dancehall reggae goes beyond the usual gangsta celebrations of Hennessy brandy and Nike trainers. *Woman & Child*, his extraordinary 1997 album, is a righteous hymn to 'black supremacy' and the suffering caused by colonialism. Sizzla sees himself, in his tight-wrapped turban and long flowing gown, as a chastiser of the wicked come to cauterise the human heart of sin. And, like many Bobo, he appears to advocate violence (even if only symbolic violence) as a vehicle of deliverance: his lyrics are full of an Old Testament outraged godliness and the words 'purify', 'burn', 'overthrow'.

Yet, despite his biblical image, in 2005 Sizzla was arrested at his home in Judgement Yard (outside Kingston) for suspected gun-running and incitement to gang violence. The Nine Mile community, rightly or wrongly, is seen by many ordinary Jamaicans as a hive of criminality.

Professor Newland was proving hard to persuade but, not wanting to be pushed into defeat, I told him: 'Look, it's not my intention to stare and make fun.'

'All right,' – his voice softened – 'ask for Anthony Morgan, a Bobo priest. Say I sent you.'

*

I had no idea of what a Rastafari community – a utopian community – was like. It was important to keep an open mind, I reminded myself, as we set off for Bull Bay in a taxi.

It was two o'clock in the afternoon and the sun blazed down out of a cloudless sky. Myrtha Desulmé, a Haitian friend who lived in Kingston, was in the taxi with me. Black and strikingly stylish, Myrtha had fled Papa Doc's tyrannous Haiti with her parents in the 1960s. I was sure she would impress the Bobo Ashanti. She had dressed for the occasion in a Kente print dress, madras scarf and gold hoop-earrings, and looked like an Ashanti princess strayed into the Caribbean. Along the way, she teased me for my avowed interest in Africa and Afro-Haitian animist cults.

'You *blancs* always like to hunt for the dark – for the black, the alternative.'

'Oh?'

'Yes,' Myrtha went on with a shrug, 'you always go on about Africa's supreme natural beauty – its capacity for intuition, spontaneity, the ancient wisdom of its customs and instincts.'

'Do we? And what about you? Do you believe in any of that?'

'Only a bit,' she said with a touch of coquetry.

We turned up a dirt track that lead to a squatter settlement, where the corrugated-iron fencing had been spray-gunned: 'Poor People Fed Up To How De System Set Up'. The squatters, in their cinder-block huts, lived just below the Bobo commune, and co-operated with the 'dreads' in harnessing water and other resources.

On foot we toiled up a steep path, too narrow for the taxi, that overlooked a dried-out river. Our spirits rose as we continued on up the hill. The first clear view of Bull Bay was unrepeatably dramatic; way below us the Caribbean Sea spread out a dark, deep blue. The Bobo hillside community commanded giddy views all round and was encircled by wooden palisades like a US cavalry fort. Over the entrance there was the painted sign: 'BLACK SOVEREIGN NATION'.

A Bobo priest came to greet us, arrayed in a green turban and a green cape. Pinned to his cape was an outsize badge of Haile Selassie and another, equally big, of Marcus Garvey, the Jamaican apostle of black liberation. The Bobo priest, assuming a grave hieratic manner, introduced himself as Anthony Morgan – my Newland contact. He greeted me warmly, if disconcertingly, as 'Lord', while to Myrtha he bowed smilingly and said: 'Blessed, my Empress.' These magnificently medieval titles are adopted by the Bobo in opposition to the bourgeois convention of 'Mr' and 'Mrs'.

If Myrtha was 'sick' (menstruating) she would not be allowed inside the commune. Women are rarely an elevated sex among Rastafarians and are viewed by the Bobo as virtual chattels or Delilah figures whose legs and arms must be covered in the presence of their 'Lords'. Once a month they must go into menstrual reclusion, when they are kept out of sight in a sickbay built for the purpose.

An elderly priestess approached us carrying a wall calendar. The calendar was to determine the extent of Myrtha's 'defilement'. Here my resolution to be open-minded was stretched. Was it humane to subject a woman to a test like this in public? While the crone consulted with Myrtha I turned my back and looked out over Bull Bay; minutes went by. Having passed the calendar test, Myrtha was allowed to accompany me into the guardhouse. There, into a cardboard box, went our mobile phones, credit cards, tape-recorders, pens and other trappings of 'Babylon'.

I looked around. On one wall was a brightly coloured relief map of Africa, on which the Ethiopian capital of Addis Ababa was symbolised by a huge, five-pointed Judaic-Rastafarian Star of David. Next to that were black-and-white photographs of Marcus Garvey and Haile Selassie. Though Selassie had been condemned by Garvey as a 'great coward' (for fleeing Mussolini's troops in 1935), the Bobo revere him as a breathing – for he is not really dead – divinity. Even Bobo children, mere saplings in His Imperial Majesty Selassie's vineyard, must answer to the authority of the Ethiopian Pope Almighty.

Bobo Ashanti, founded in the 1950s by the Jamaican mystic Prince Emmanuel Edwards, owes its blend of Black Power and Pan-Africanism chiefly to Marcus Garvey, one of the most bizarre and misunderstood figures in twentieth-century black history. Born in Jamaica in 1887 to freed slave parents, Garvey had grown up with a powerful sense of racial awareness and grievance. On leaving elementary school, he worked as a printer in Kingston and at an early age became involved in movements aimed at improving the lot of black people. In 1914, during his self-imposed exile in Harlem, New York, he founded the Universal Negro Improvement Association (UNIA), intended to 'regenerate' and encourage the English-speaking black diaspora to 'return' to Africa. By the end of the First World War, branches of the UNIA had been set up in several American cities; Garvey boasted a membership of six million.

By embracing blackness and black race-consciousness, Garvey would be revered one day in Jamaica as a prophet. (His given middle name, Mosiah, was a hybrid of Moses and Messiah.) His Black Star Line shipping company was launched in 1919 with the aim of linking black communities in the United States with those in the Caribbean, as well as transporting them (should they volunteer) to a 'Negro Empire' in Africa. Though the company eventually collapsed through unpaid debts, it gave an immense sense of pride to black people, not only in Jamaica, but in parts of Central America populated by Jamaican migrant workers.

Garvey's adopted Harlem remained the centre of UNIA activity.

One in five Harlemites was estimated to be West Indian; many were Jamaicans who had earned good money in Panama in the early 1900s when the United States took over construction of the canal. These were the energetic 'Colón Men' who brought a taste of the tropics to Harlem. Nowhere else came close to the 'hot syncopated fascination' of that part of New York, wrote the Jamaican novelist Claude McKay, later a leading light in the Harlem Renaissance during the 1920s.

Jamaicans blocked traffic to hear Garvey preach in Harlem, their numbers swelled by curious, impoverished African Americans. Before long the Garveyite ideal of black emancipation had fused with the 'Harlemania' that took hold in Lower Manhattan nightclubs, as wealthy white thrill-seekers danced to Duke Ellington hothouse stomps and bumped up against West Indian migrant mento and the ragtime of tin-pan pianos. Black folk heritage – so-called 'primitive' art and music – became the mainstay of the Harlem Renaissance and behind it lay a Jamaican's doctrine of black self-help and empowerment.

By the late 1920s, the Harlem Renaissance had tapered off. Orson Welles's 'voodoo' version of *Macbeth*, staged in Harlem in 1935, was the movement's last gasp. (Macduff had been made to resemble a cartoon Haile Selassie, while a troupe of West African dancers contorted luridly on stage amid live goats.) While it lasted, though, the Harlem Renaissance had provided an important link between Jamaica and the pre-civil rights United States, which endures as the numbers of Jamaicans living in America continues to swell.

In his day, however, Garvey invited a degree of ridicule. He dressed in martial regalia copied from European Fascist models, sumptuously plumed and braided. Zora Neale Hurston, the African American author and folklorist, visited Garvey at his home on 129th Street in Harlem: 'On the walls of his living room hung a large picture of Napoleon,' she wrote. 'On the opposite wall hung one, still larger, of himself.' Yet in lampooning Garvey for his 'narcissistic Bonapartism', Hurston and other Garvey-baiters rather missed the point. The Napoleonic hats and gowns were part of a master plan to create a parallel world equal to that of the white man. In his love of pomp and ceremony, Garvey may be said to have anticipated Mugabe, Amin, Bokassa, Kenyatta and other (originally well-intentioned) African leaders who ravaged Africa.

The line separating fantasy from reality was not always easy to draw with Garvey. Somewhere in his messianic notions of Africa and African redemption lurked a dubious race politics. In the March–April 1934 edition of his *Black Man* journal Garvey proclaimed Adolf Hitler a 'wonderful personality' and 'trailblazer' who (in Jamaican fashion) demanded 'respect'. Later, when it became clear to Garvey that European Jewry was under the Nazi threat of extermination, he revised his earlier opinion of Hitler. Had he not done so, Jamaica may have been less keen to make him – as it did in 1964 – the island's first National Hero. Even so, Garvey's canonisation in modern Jamaica contains a contradiction: it claims the island as a black nation, when in reality Garvey's birthplace is a multi-racial, many-coloured nation. 'Out of Many, One People' is the hopeful Jamaican motto, reminiscent of the first motto of the United States, *E Pluribus Unum* – One from Many.

Garvey was even accused by his critics of being a member of the Ku Klux Klan. Garvey denied the charge (ridiculous, in any case, since the Klan were intent on lynching black people). Yet Garvey did not deny that he had met, in Atlanta in 1922, the Klan's Imperial Wizard. The Klan, in Garvey's tolerant view, had no other desire 'than to preserve their race from suicide through miscegenation'. Union between black and white was for Garvey regrettable, as it threatened 'a wholesale bastardy of the race'. Black people could find no future in white or even mixed-race societies, no matter how socially advanced these might be. Mixed marriages were thus a 'social misfortune'. Since that time white supremacists have tried to show Garvey up as a crypto-racist. In 1960s and 1970s Britain, not uncommonly, conservatives depicted Garveyite Black Power movements as an equivalent, anti-white racism, 'Enoch Powellism in Reverse'. Needless to say, the analogy is absurd: people with white skin generally enjoy the liberty of not having to define themselves in terms of race.

In 1922 the United States imprisoned Marcus Garvey after a conviction for fraud; he was sentenced to five years' imprisonment – later mitigated to deportation. By the time Garvey died in London in

1940, at the age of fifty-two, black disaffection in his native Jamaica and the diaspora had become more militant by his example.

Jamaica's first preacher of Rastafari, Leonard Percival Howell, was a militant Garveyite. In 1934 he was sentenced to two years' hard labour for the 'crime' of selling picture-postcards of the lately crowned Haile Selassie. The act was judged to be seditious by the colonial courts as it showed disrespect for the British Crown. In 1940 Howell formed the Ethiopian Salvation Society, a forerunner of Bobo Ashanti, whose headquarters were in a ruinous, 1,300-acre sugar estate called Pinnacle, north-east of Spanish Town. Howell was hailed 'Gong' (or 'Prince Regent') by his followers, who, aided by quantities of ganja ('thou shalt eat the herb of the field . . .' Genesis 3:18), reasoned from the Bible. Howell alone meted out punishments which occasionally involved flogging.

At Pinnacle the Howellites practised a Bobo-like ideal of communal labour, looked to Selassie for salvation and began to wear their hair in dreadlocks in imitation of Kenya's anti-colonial Mau-Mau. In so doing, they struck a blow at Jamaican planter privilege and anticipated Walter Rodney's racial defiance two decades later. In 1955, however, the commune was finally dissolved by the Jamaican government.

'Howell wasn't a bad man,' Patrick Mudahy had told me, 'but maybe he was a *mad* one.' In Jamaica the distinction can be quite a fine one. For many Jamaicans, Howell was like the man in the padded cell who believes he is God.

*

I was peering at a photograph of Idi Amin on display in the Bobo guardhouse when a voice cut in on my thoughts. 'You know Amin Dada?' A young-looking Bobo priest was observing me. I said to him: 'Not *personally*. Why? Is Amin worshipped here?'

The priest gave me a glance of ironical enquiry. 'Amin is *respected* here.'

Amin is in fact believed by the Bobo to be a physical re-incarnation of Marcus Garvey. No theology is more fluid or more elusive than Rastafari. Without scriptures and ordained leadership, adepts are free to invent their own version of the creed and their own divinities, even if one of them is Idi Amin.

'Surely it would be better to *dis*-incarnate from Amin,' I said to the priest. The Ugandan president had inflicted a murderous racism on his country's Asian community.

The priest, ignoring the remark, said: 'All good men are Rasta,' and led me towards a wooden coffer at one end of the guardhouse. A hole in the top revealed it to be an offertory box. At his invitation, I put a couple of notes through the hole. 'Blessed, my Lord,' he said to me solemnly.

Next, Myrtha and I were invited to salute the Holy Trinity of the Bobo Ashanti, which consists of Selassie (King), Garvey (Prophet) and the sect's founder, Prince Emmanuel (Priest). As we did so, the Bobo priest held his hands together at crotch-level, displaying a triangle-shape between splayed fingers and thumbs. The gesture was symbolic of the Bobo 'Godhead triumvirate' and not intended to be sexually suggestive. It is said that Haile Selassie descended from the plane in Kingston with his hands held in this way; his supporters saw the gesture as highly significant.

Thus triply blessed, we set off under escort to the Bobo temple, passing on the way storerooms, a kitchen, a generating plant, and a field of gungu peas. At the entrance we were instructed to take off our shoes (which I was happy to do, it was so hot). There were virtually no windows in the bungalow-like building. Three Bobo elders sat in turbans at a long table in front of us like a tribunal. A personal computer rested on the table; to the right of the table stood a filing cabinet covered in stickers: 'I LOVE AFRICA'. A life-sized painting of Prince Emmanuel in imagined conversation with Haile Selassie hung on the wall behind the turbaned priests. Selassie, eagle-beaked, looked like a company executive; Emmanuel had the patriarchal mien of a Highland chieftain.

Myrtha and I were gestured to sit down. One of the priests nodded for us to speak. Bearded, he wore a blue turban and said his name was Harold Mitchell.

'Who are you?' Mitchell turned to me.

I was worried that I would not be welcome here. White people are the demons, the Pharisees, the Philistines, the Pharaoh people and, as such, potential emissaries of 'Babylon'. All the concentrated malignity of Satan – according to Sizzla – is to be found in the white man.

'I'm a writer,' I replied.

'Books? You are a writer of books? What kind of books? Please tell.'

It did not seem the appropriate place or time to embark on a literary discussion.

'I'm writing a book about Jamaica,' I said, evasively.

Harold Mitchell scrutinised me. 'Are you married? How many children have you? I sometimes think of visiting London. How much does it cost to spend the night there?'

'That depends,' I said, 'on what sort of night you want to spend.'

Prophet Mitchell smiled at his attendant patriarchs, before turning to Myrtha.

'Empress. Who are you? And where are you from?'

'Haiti.'

'The black nation?'

'Haiti was the world's *first* black republic.'

Harold Mitchell lowered his head in a small (very small: Myrtha was a woman) gesture of respect.

Myrtha, with assertiveness in her voice, now asked the priest why the Bobo did not simply 'get up' and go to Africa. Right now.

The Bobo replied evenly, 'We're ready to go back at any time. We're only waiting for the ship to come from Africa.'

'But why,' Myrtha persisted, 'has the ship not come yet? Where is Haile Selassie? Why are you not ready to ride the Lion to Zion?' For Myrtha, the dream of a return to Africa was just that – a dream. Jamaica, she confided to me later, needed to put its own house in order; Africa was a distraction.

'These things take time, black princess lady,' explained Harold Mitchell, visibly taken aback. There was no agreement as yet on the date of departure to Africa, and funds were a problem. The Garveyite agenda for repatriation required money – lots of it.

Harold Mitchell, with a touch of annoyance, continued, 'We are the exiled children of Ethiopia – we are sufferers.' Bobo Ashanti are quick to subscribe to the doctrine of 'exploitation' and 'victimhood'. Yet that word 'sufferer' – *sufferah*, in island patois – is bandied about by Jamaican academics and politicians as shorthand for 'righteous poor person'. William Beckford (father of the Gothic novelist of the same name who had tried but failed to visit Jamaica in 1787), in his *A Descriptive Account of the Island of Jamaica* (1790), had referred to 'sufferers', and Lady Nugent in her Jamaica diary of 1801–5 spoke of the 'poor sufferer's life' with the same assumption of superiority. The term, by conferring a victim status, implied a deficiency that cannot be overcome and seemed to me dubious.

There is the lure of Ethiopia, and there is the lure of another, equally unobtainable salvation. In 1834, according to a Jamaican legend, Queen Victoria had earmarked £120 million for the repatriation of her West Indian subjects to West Africa. The project was never carried out, yet the Bobo believe the money is still owed to them. Prophet Mitchell had done his mathematics. 'With accumulated interest, the figure now stands at £7,469,696, 470,000,' he told us.

Myrtha (who was beginning to embarrass me) said, 'What?'

'Seven trillion four hundred and sixty-nine billion, six hundred and ninety-six million, and four hundred and seventy thousand pounds sterling,' said the priest.

'That's what the British Crown owes?' I asked.

'That's right,' Mitchell said. As this madness (if one can call it that) had slavery at its heart, it demanded something more than mere amazement as a response. Jamaicans had not asked to come to Jamaica: 'imperialistic interlopers' – to use Walter Rodney's phrase – had brought them here. The British Crown had a responsibility to redeem and compensate them.

Yet did the Bobo really expect to find salvation in war-torn Ethiopia? Only the most romantic could claim that Ethiopians ever lived (still less, live today) in a state of prelapsarian grace. Marcus Garvey had described Haile Selassie as a 'feudal Monarch who looks down upon his slaves and serfs with contempt'.

The Bobo elders wanted to hear my view on slavery. I began carefully (disliking the tone of righteousness in my voice) to speak about the question of responsibility. Slavery – chattel servitude – had been a part of Selassie's Solomonic Empire, and in fact most African nation states (Dahomey, Oyo, the Niger city-states) had practised slavery. In 1817, the Ashanti nation had even asked Britain to allow them to *renew* the slave trade – a request from one aggressively imperialising, militaristic nation to another. The Bobo Ashanti had taken their name from the Ashanti (sometimes spelled Asante).

Cautiously I said, 'I'm not saying that Selassie was a slave-driver, only that there was a flourishing slave trade in Ethiopia under his rule.' I could feel myself stepping on dangerous territory.

After anxious consultation with each other, the Bobo elders asked me if I was Jewish. Why? Because only the black race are the 'true Israelites' – they, the blacks, are the true children of Israel, the Chosen People who have long been denied their earthly Zion. From this it followed that the Jews eradicated by Hitler were 'false Jews' merely. To brand those Jews as 'false' struck me as callous, even contemptible. The millenarian creed of Rastafari, I decided, was not something I could easily buy into, not just because of its illiberal traits (the nasty streak of misogyny) but because the absolutism of its blood-and-brimstone visions was temperamentally alien to the dilute Anglicanism in which I had been reared.

But, in spite of its spiritual ferocity, Rastafari has now penetrated every level of Jamaican society. At Kingston dinner parties it is not uncommon to meet guests who forbear to eat pork (pork is prohibited in Rastafari as it is in Judaism), as well as processed or canned foods and salt. Middle-class attitudes to Rastafari changed for the better two years prior to independence, when in 1960 the Jamaican government commissioned the University of the West Indies to compile a report on the movement's rituals and beliefs.

One of the authors of the report, Professor Roy Augier, is currently coordinator of the UNESCO *General History of the Caribbean* (a heroic project that has been under way since 1980). He met me in the courtyard of the Senior Common Room at the University of the West Indies in Kingston, where he teaches history. A year before the report came out, recalled Augier, Kingston had witnessed an extraordinary saga of 'muddled idealism, Millenarian delusions and plain trickery', when 15,000 Rastafarians were duped by a mystic clergyman, Claudius Henry, into buying 'Miraculous Repatriation' tickets to Ethiopia. For almost a week, Henry's supporters camped outside his Kingston church in expectation of proceeding from there to Haile Selassie's kingdom in Africa. No ship came, and riots broke out when police came to disperse the aggrieved 'ticket' holders. Henry was prosecuted and imprisoned.

One year later, in 1960, fear and distrust of Rastafari intensified when the Reverend Henry's son, Ronald Henry, made a hare-brained attempt to 'liberate' Jamaica from British rule. With a group of African American self-styled revolutionaries he set up a guerrilla base in the Red Hills district above Kingston. There, he and his Bronx-based Black Power militia units (called the First Africa Corps) trained some 500 Rastafarians in the art of urban warfare. Before they could launch an attack on government centres in Kingston, however, their base was stormed by Jamaican and British soldiers, accompanied by aircraft and mortars. The guerrillas were all captured, several were executed and two soldiers died in an ambush.

It was during these troubled times that the *Report on the Rastafari Movement in Kingston, Jamaica* was published. From the report's careful, expository tones, Rastafari emerges as the peaceable, law-abiding religion it generally is. After a generation in the wilderness, Rastafarians now had an audience. 'The report was very widely read,' Augier told me. 'A group of Rastas even bought cut-price copies from the University bookshop and photocopied them to sell at a profit downtown.' A slew of books on Rastafari followed, but none has ever equalled that report for its objectivity and sympathy. One of its recommendations – addressed directly to the Jamaican government – was that a mission should be sent to Ethiopia to investigate the possibility of settling Jamaicans there. During the 1950s and 1960s some 2,500 West Indian and African American Rastafarians went to live in the vicinity of Addis Ababa (in what is now Shashamane Village) but only 300 of their number are believed to remain today.

*

After my visit to the Bobo encampment, at a friend's house in Kingston I met a descendant of Haile Selassie, Bella Tekle-Hawariat. Bella was self-confessedly one of Addis Ababa's Amharic elite; a necklace of semi-precious stones glinted at her throat. She had been educated in Switzerland, and prided herself on having Ethiopian as well as European manners. Her father, Germachew Tekle-Hawariat, had been a government minister under Haile Selassie.

'You should go to Ethiopia one day,' Bella said to me. 'The landscape has a *wild* exhilaration. But,' she added, 'there is much corruption now.' The corruption was a legacy of the 'Red Terror' under President Mengistu and Ethiopia's murderous border dispute with Eritrea. In Jamaica she preferred to keep quiet about her descent from Haile Selassie. Once, in the Bob Marley Museum in Kingston, she got talking to a Rastafari member of staff. 'He knew *everything* about the Ethiopian royal family – its descent from King Solomon and the Queen of Sheba. Its ancient Semitic connections. He even corrected me on a point of *my* ancestry.' Yet Selassie was not the great man Rastafari would have him be, said Bella. With his unbending antipathy to any kind of social reform he became out of touch and indifferent to the suffering of his people. 'Selassie didn't want to be taken up by Rastafari, of course not!' said Bella with some irritation.

She added, 'Do not forget that we Ethiopians are a people with thousands of years of civilisation behind us, we have a profound sense of our identity – of who and what we were, of what we *are*.' Jamaica, by comparison, had no recorded ancient history, religion or civilisation of its own (other than a recent history of British cruelty). In the absence of an indigenous civilisation, American culture, for good and ill, has engulfed the shallow soil of Jamaica. America is there in the ubiquitous basketball courts, the inadequate public transport system, in the fat policemen in Kingston with their hands poised on bulging gun-holsters. 'All the same,' concluded Bella Tekle-Hawariat, 'it's odd that Jamaica has no Haile Selassie Street – Haiti does.'

Papa Doc Duvalier, the Haitian dictator, had revered Selassie as a crusader in the battle for black solidarity. Not only had he named a street after Selassie in the capital of Port-au-Prince, but in April 1966 he equipped the national palace with a special luxury bathroom to accommodate the Ethiopian ruler following his visit to Jamaica. I have seen the bathroom: the rim of the lavatory bowl is adorned with gold leaf.

9

Stranded on Death Row

While I was in Kingston I went to see Father Webb, a Canadian Jesuit operating from offices downtown. Jesuits are often regarded by other Catholics as not quite regular clergy (they refuse to be cloistered in a monastery) and Webb was no exception. He took his itinerant ministry to the people who needed it the most – the poorest of the Jamaican poor – and had been threatened with death for his trouble. To some branches of Rastafari, Jesuits are sinister self-publicists bent on disseminating 'Romish' propaganda. The pope is often 'burned' lyrically in reggae songs (Max Romeo's 'Fire Fi the Vatican' is a good example), because the Vatican had blessed the Fascist invasion of Ethiopia in 1935.

Father Webb, though, was devoted to an ideal of 'social justice' and, in this role, had set up rural cooperatives and campaigned to abolish Jamaica's death penalty. Catechising the poor with passages of scripture was of no interest to him. Any Jamaicans he had recruited to the Jesuit Order, he had done by 'gentle cajolery' (he allowed himself a smile) rather than by 'proselytising'.

We met at St George's Jesuit College on the sun-blistered South Camp Road. The school, founded in 1850, was set back from the main road amid banana groves and seemed peaceful. Father Webb, a tall, thin man in his mid-fifties, was the school principal; his job was to enrol and expel pupils, as well as adjudicate at exams. A sense of ordinary goodness surrounded him – his office was practical rather than pious, with bare wooden floors and filing cabinets. Only the pectoral cross round his neck betrayed his high rank as Jesuit Regional Superior for Jamaica; he wore lay sandals and a T-shirt.

Roman Catholics have lived in Jamaica since the Spanish period, he explained, and today they run some of the best secondary schools in the island. Even non-Catholic Jamaicans will tell you, 'I want my child to go to a Roman school,' meaning St George's. Pupil attendance has declined in recent years owing to levels of violence downtown; parents are increasingly frightened to appear at drop-off and collection. 'I can't even get a *pizza* delivered here,' said Father Webb, who was standing under a portrait of Saint Ignatius Loyola (founder in 1534 of the Jesuit movement). 'Jamaicans are, anyway, much more apprehensive these days – there's a general atmosphere of violence.' In the twenty-five years he had lived in Kingston, said Father Webb, most things had been affected by the corruption of politics. 'I've even had to root out corruption from St George's but, unfortunately, impunity rules. You might say there's a power in the land like that of the Mafia.'

Father Webb paused. 'Jamaica has more poverty now, more marginality, unemployment and crime than it did when I arrived in the 1980s. Every house is grilled and double-grilled – and you only have to look at all the guard dogs . . .' In the past Father Webb had not hesitated to give lifts to people in the countryside; now he never does. 'A man might come out of the shadows and then you're in for all kinds of trouble,' he explained. So he drives as twenty-first-century Jamaicans drive: his car doors locked, the windows up and the air-conditioning on.

Catholic priests are intermittently murdered in Jamaica in reprisal for their 'meddlesome' politics, or because they are perceived as being homosexual. In 1993, Ron Pieters, a Guyanese Jesuit priest, was found nailed to a post in Kingston's Jonestown ghetto, symbolically thorned and crucified. The following year, in 1994, Father Vincent Power, a sixty-two-year-old Irishman, was shot dead while at prayer in his church in Falmouth on the north coast.

The killings intensified in the mid-1990s, when imports of crack-cocaine fuelled a cold-blooded violence. In 2000, Father Howard Rochester was found murdered on an isolated road outside Kingston; his car and mobile phone had been stolen. In 2006, two trainee priests from the Philippines were killed in Kingston as a single bullet passed through both men while they washed up dishes in their missionary base.

All these priests had worked at the front line of the ghetto, and were not afraid to speak out for the voiceless. One murder in particular haunts Father Webb. In 2001 a forty-one-year-old Canadian Jesuit, Martin Royackers, was gunned down in the parish of St Mary, where he was a pastor. He had been shot at close range in the chest as he went to open his door. The case, entrusted to the local police, remains unsolved.

A fortnight prior to Royackers's murder, Father Webb had received death threats which the Jamaican police took seriously. The threats had to do with Jesuit attempts to redistribute land, and for eight months Webb was assigned a police bodyguard. Today Webb wants to carry on Royackers's work in rural cooperatives, and in particular his innovations in the Catholic liturgy. Royackers understood that the Catholic Church had to become more 'Jamaican' if it was to survive. So he rewrote the liturgy to incorporate Afro-Jamaican religious expression: drums, call-and-response rhythms sung like a mantra. 'It's the African element – the element of magic in all of our religions,' said Father Webb.

Not all Jesuit attempts to translate Christian concepts into local vernaculars have been successful – some Japanese converts to Jesuitism reportedly believe that Noah survived the flood in a canoe rather than an ark. Yet Royackers had brought non-Catholics to his services by making the Mass more lively and charismatic. As a good disciple of Loyola he even preached at Pentecostal and other evangelical gatherings. The Jamaican upper and middle classes, however, with their antipathy to Africa, prefer to worship at the Anglican Church, where Afro-Revivalism is not a part of the liturgy. Africa is a darkness – a void – to be circumvented, the continent of the tom-tom and the bush.

*

Next day I went to ten o'clock Mass in a red-brick church downtown dedicated to St Anne. The church, known as 'Annie's', had been rebuilt after the earthquake of 1907, which devastated Kingston, and stood on the sniper alley between the JLP-loyal Denham Town and PNP-loyal Hannah Town. During outbreaks of gang warfare the Catholics of Hannah Town guide their priest safely down back streets to his home. In this part of Kingston the violence had become so prevalent that the inhabitants regarded it almost as part of the social fabric. Death was far and away the most thriving trade on this political borderline; one street was lined with undertaker parlours. With their white Doric columns and pilasters, they were like a poor man's dream of heaven. Jamaicans, if they can afford it, will spend as much as US $30,000 for a Cadillac hearse.

Peter Mais, a Jamaican lawyer, had done much for the neighbourhood, taking time off work to help the poor. I felt a sense of patience and goodness in his company as we walked past a group of rough-looking types playing dominoes outside 'Annie's'. His patch included the slums of Jonestown, Denham Town, Tivoli Gardens and Rose Town, home to many deportees ('dips') or convicted Jamaican criminals who had been sent back from Britain, the United States or Canada. 'Sometimes as many as fifty deportees arrive in a single day,' Mais told me. 'They have no family, they don't speak patois, and they can be very, very violent.'

'All these guys will have held a gun at some point,' Mais went on, gesturing vaguely in their direction. One man was bare-backed and I was shocked to see a criss-cross of scars there such as a lashing might have caused. 'That's Cecil.' Mais pointed out an elderly man crouched on the street corner. 'Cecil's a convicted murderer.' I felt a tension: what was I – a privileged, detached, self-involved white man – doing here? It must have been obvious in my soft, educated face that I would never have to live the life these people were living. With a sigh Mais indicated the marks on the church façade, bullet-holes from a drive-by shooting a couple of weeks earlier. 'Oh my poor decaying city,' he said as we picked our way through Hannah Town and smelled the acrid smoke from the hospital crematorium. Narrow fox faces watched us over the tops of zinc fences.

Today was the Feast of Saint Joachim and the church was packed with the Catholic faithful. A North American priest, Peter McIsaac, was giving the service, energetically preaching forgiveness and an end to violence. 'Brothers and sisters!' His eyes roamed over the congregation. 'Picture it, the clouds of darkness over Kingston, and the people full of fear – unless we put away our guns.' It was an odd mixture of Revivalist-Catholic fervour, superstition and holiday. 'Does the Pope know about this?' I asked Peter Mais, who was by my side. 'I hope not,' he smiled. The congregants clapped and swayed in their pews as the organist twisted and turned on his bench, feet flying beneath him, and the drummer hit rim shots off his kit, reggae-style.

On this Sunday at least the parish felt safe and united in their Afro-Catholic fervour, hand-clapping and the elements of Pentecostal hymn and testimonial. Afterwards in the refectory loudspeakers blared adorations to the Almighty in a ragga beat, as Feast Day food was served at trestle tables. Paper cups of soup, slices of pink-and-yellow coloured cake: it was a small celebration. Peter Mais showed me a tiny garden – the Princess Peace Gardens – opposite the church which his wife had built for the people of Hannah Town. 'Vilma likes to come here and reflect on things,' he said to me, indicating a small stone bench. Two weeks after I met Peter, Vilma, dreadfully, was murdered. His wife had gone to pray in Stella Maris church in uptown Kingston when a youth approached demanding her handbag. She refused, and the man stabbed her. She tried to run but the man stabbed her again in the neck and the face. She died in hospital. The result of her murder on 8 March 2006 was an outburst of indignation across middle-class Kingston: did Vilma Mais, a sixty-two-year-old mother of three, deserve to die in this way? The Kingston police, typically, could do nothing, and the indignation was quickly spent.

*

At the time of writing, the death penalty still exists in Jamaica, though most capital punishments are overturned in London by the Privy Council, Jamaica's Court of Final Appeal. Thus an ancient British institution comprised of mostly white Law Lords has become the unlikely defender of human rights in Jamaica. A majority of Jamaicans – not just conservative, pro-monarchy Jamaicans – see hanging as the only effective deterrent to criminality: murderers must face death. Yet the British Law Lords, through the grace of Queen Elizabeth II, use their power to prevent executions. Such paradoxes are part of the West Indian confusion: Victorian moralities that have long disappeared in Britain linger on in Jamaica, where they are compounded by retrograde American attitudes to capital punishment.

I saw no reason why Jamaicans should not be allowed to make

their own legal decisions. It is true that an indigenous Jamaican court might usher in an American-style Death Row, where many criminals are executed each year. Yet the Privy Council, surely, is too far removed from the social realities of Jamaica to pass informed judgement. An indigenous jurisprudence might be thought necessary to Jamaica's self-esteem and its notion of autonomy.

Jamaica's failure to wrest a genuine independence from Britain – its failure to 'go it alone' – had been foreshadowed in the short-lived West Indian Federation of 1958 to 1962. The Federation aimed to foster economic and political union throughout the British Caribbean and nurture the emergence of a West Indian identity (virtually non-existent at the time). Regional cooperation, it was hoped, would lead to the establishment of, among other things, a British Caribbean Court of Justice, promoting a separate judiciary from that of the parent country.

Ten British Caribbean islands, Jamaica and Trinidad pre-eminent among them, agreed to merge. Personal rivalries and insular prejudices, however, soon frustrated the purpose of the federative scheme which was to give the islands 'Dominion Status' (full independence) within the British Commonwealth. Jamaica regarded its smaller neighbours with condescension, and began to question the benefits of a federal form of government. While some significant advances were made (the University College of the West Indies is a genuinely regional institution), divorce seemed imminent.

Alexander Bustamante, the opposition leader of the JLP party, forced a referendum on the matter and in September 1961 Jamaicans voted 'No' by a significant majority. Jamaica's departure brought the West Indian Federation to an end. In January 1962, seven months before independence, it was formally liquidated. The British authorities had no option now but to contemplate what the federation had been intended to avoid: the piecemeal 'inde-pendence' of its Caribbean colonies in the uncertain world of the Cold War and greater intrusiveness from the United States.

*

Outside Kingston's Supreme Court was the usual miscellany of supplicants and poor. I was frisked at the entrance and told to proceed to the Jurors' Clerk for permission to attend a trial. The clerk's office stood on the first floor of a building erected in the dying days of imperial rule. About half the benches were filled with people waiting, the anticipation of more waiting to come on their faces. The Jamaican justice system has been described as a lottery where the dice are loaded against those who cannot afford to sway the course of justice through bribes or other influences, such as, occasionally, sorcery: toads with lips sewn together are used to warn witnesses not to speak.

The Jurors' Clerk, Leslie Chamberlain, was sitting in his office doing the *Gleaner* newspaper crossword. He was a pale-skinned Jamaican with a strikingly officious manner. 'Introduce yourself,' he said to me petulantly. I was taken aback by his tone, but what could one expect? Chamberlain and his underlings only ever saw the failures and aberrations of Jamaica. But in these Empire-era offices with their sad, grave atmosphere of collapse, they could lord it over others. Leslie Chamberlain's authority proceeded from a formidable knowledge of the operations of the British judiciary.

'Introduce yourself,' he repeated. I handed him an official letter from my publishers; he frowned and picked up a pencil from his desk, tapping the letter with the sharp end.

'And who is Neil Belton?'

'It says there – Senior Editor,' I replied.

The clerk seemed a very fastidious, mincing man (what Jamaicans call *fenky-fenky*). 'So you think you have a pass from Favour and Favour? I'm afraid that's impossible,' he added flatly.

'Impossible? What's not possible?'

'It is not possible for you to attend a trial,' he went on peremptorily. 'For that you have to go to the Registrar's Chambers.'

'How can I gain access to the Registrar's Chambers?'

'Only through the Chief Court Assistant and Supervisor in the Criminal Registry,' he explained, with intensifying satisfaction.

'But that's you, isn't it?'

'Yes, but this letter will not do.' Already I could feel the deadly stranglehold of red tape, Jamaica's legal system clogged up at all ends with Victorian-era delays.

'Please take away your piece of paper.' Mr Chamberlain pointed to the letter and, putting on his best official voice, added casually,

'Anyway, you could never attend a trial. You are in jeans. You must wear a tie.'

'Why didn't you tell me that before?' (He himself was not wearing a tie, but affected an overweening imperiousness, I suspected, to make up for the chaos of his surroundings.) Angry, I turned to face the eight or so junior clerks in the office: 'Can anyone lend me a pair of trousers?' I asked. 'Or a tie?' The room, piled importantly with Jiffy bags, filled with an awkward silence; eyes shifted nervously as I walked out.

Downstairs I said to a policewoman, 'I'm inappropriately dressed for court. Where can I buy a pair of trousers? And a tie?' After a moment's hesitation she suggested Hanna's Betta Buy at 18–20 King Street. 'They stock a wide range of merchandise and' – she looked at me dubiously – 'and they should satisfy all your clothing needs.' I thanked her and set off. The store stood virtually opposite the Supreme Court on a street lined with Lebanese dry goods stores and Chinese jewellery outlets. I explained my predicament to the shop assistant. 'I'm inappropriately dressed for the Supreme Court. What's your cheapest pair of trousers? And tie?' Minutes later I emerged from a cubicle in a pair of sky-blue nylon trousers with 'IMAGINATION' picked out in sequins on the right buttock. My tie was a subdued pink with a daisy pattern. I could feel the nylon sticking hotly to my legs as I walked back to the Supreme Court. Had I taken leave of my senses?

Leslie Chamberlain squinted quizzically at the razor-sharp folds in my trousers. 'You should never have come to court looking the way you did,' he began. 'I don't know how things are done in England' – his voice had taken on the old note of stridency – 'but here you must dress with befitting decorum.' I persisted and eventually he relented. 'Go to Court Number One! It's a *criminal* court.'

The court was empty and a smell of old dust hung in the air. Occasionally an usher in a white tunic dropped by to see if anything was happening. Nothing was happening. Jamaica is a land of waiting. Lawyers go to court fully expecting delays and sometimes, where it suits a client, they may even delay justice themselves. After an hour of waiting I realised to my alarm that my wallet was missing. I must have left it in Hanna's Betta Buy. I hurried back to the shop. The staff, slow-moving in the afternoon heat, looked at me nonplussed as I pleaded, 'If you find my wallet, please bring it to Criminal Court Number One.' As I spoke I was aware that any authority I might have had was undermined by my clothing.

Back in Court Number One, the accused was brought in by an usher who held him from behind by his trouser belt. This was another way to show who pulled rank. David Evans, thirty-four, had been driven from Death Row in the Spanish Town jail, and was dressed for his court appearance in a pair of spotless jeans and spotless 'puss-boots' (sneakers). The Privy Council had upheld his execution; his case was under review. Neither the judge nor Mr Evans's defender could be found, however, and to the assembled personnel the bailiff announced unnecessarily, 'There has been a delay.' The accused stood in the dock looking uncomprehending and resigned. How many times had he been reprieved from the gallows? Once? Twice? The slowness of Jamaica's judicial process seemed inhumane to me.

At last the judge came in, wearing a wig slightly askew, and scarlet robes. We all stood up. 'Evans, rise and face the bench,' the Clerk of Courts intoned in his best Gray's Inn accent. 'David Evans,' the judge sighed and hitched his robe (he pronounced the name 'E-vans'). 'I'm afraid the woman defending you is on duties elsewhere. In fact,' he looked at the clerk, 'I believe she's on holiday.' The judge manifested a slight impatience as he went on, 'We'll bring you back to court in two months' time, Mr E-vans. On the fourteenth of September. Is that clear?' The accused stirred himself slightly, nodded his understanding, and the judge concluded self-importantly, 'We shall now adjourn for luncheon.'

Everyone rose, and in the emptying courtroom I was startled by the appearance of the policewoman, who said my wallet had been recovered from Hanna's Betta Buy. Impressively it had been returned to me with its contents untouched. There seemed to be more ordinary human decency in that gesture than in the courtroom I had just left. Gratefully I returned the wallet to my (sequined) trouser pocket. On leaving the court I bumped into the unwavering Leslie Chamberlain. 'I see you aren't wearing a tie,' I said to him, pathetically vindicated. He gave no answer.

*

The death penalty has been on the Jamaican Statute Books since 1864, but it is rarely imposed these days, and the signs are that hanging will soon be reserved for particularly 'scandalous' cases only (serial killers or multiple child murderers).

Brian Massie, a Canadian Catholic priest, had served as Death Row chaplain in Jamaica for eight years. During that time, from 1986 to 1994, he accompanied a total of sixteen men to their execution in Spanish Town's District Prison. From his current home in Winnipeg, Canada, he spoke to me about those days. The prison death block, known colloquially as 'Gibraltar', contained fifty cells each measuring five feet by eight feet. Only those who were about to be executed had their own pail in which to defecate, said Massie; the rest had to use a communal latrine. At 8.15 a.m. on the morning of any given hanging, a group of prison guards would arrive to tie the condemned man's hands behind his back with a leather strap. As Father Massie walked with the prisoner to the gallows he would recite hymns in order to fill the silence. 'No one had the courage to look the condemned man in the eyes,' he told me.

In the death chamber different nooses hung over the trapdoor; the length best suited to the size and weight of the prisoner was selected. Nothing was said; the following ritual took place in silence. The man was positioned on the trapdoor: a hood was put over his head and the noose round his neck. Beneath the gallows was a concrete pit with a drain to collect the body waste. At 8.30 a.m. precisely the prison superintendent would give the signal and the hangman pulled the lever. The man vanished through the trapdoor and the noose snapped his neck. 'Oddly,' Father Massie said, 'it was often easier to kill younger men – older men died slowly and noisily.'

In the priest's view, the death penalty was a 'social sin', whose abolition would be a triumph over the 'darkness and moral confusion' of twenty-first-century Jamaica. Death Row merely added to the island's unnecessary suffering. 'I may be a bleeding heart, but to me the human species is redeemable – redemption is part of the mystery of man,' Father Massie said. One would have to have a heart of stone to disagree.

10

The Negotiator

Garfield Ellis, a Jamaican writer in his late forties, is part of what his publishers call the 'new wave of island prose'. In his fast-paced novel *For Nothing At All* (2005), Ellis tells the story of a group of school friends whose lives are torn apart by the gun culture and urban turf wars that erupted in Jamaica in the 1970s. Wesley, the narrator, is a bright boy determined to succeed at his school in Central Village, near Spanish Town. When a schoolmate, Skin, shows him a gun he has picked up, Wesley is horrified. Skin, for his part, can act out long-nurtured fantasies of cowboy-style vengeance (spaghetti westerns were all the rage then in Jamaica). Disastrously, however, a local thug named Danny Bruck Foot steals the gun; overnight, Central Village moves from a 'playground to a field of death' as Wesley and his friends become prey to Danny and his homicidal brethren.

The novel is interspersed with scenes from Wesley's childhood spent around Spanish Town; joyous bouts of truancy ('sculling'), a time of rural innocence. These passages, heavy with nostalgia for 'better days', serve as a counterpoint to the chapters set in the 1970s, when public life in Jamaica soured under the influence of a murderous, politically sponsored greed. Wesley, finally corrupted by local drug barons, shoots Danny Bruck Foot dead, and is jailed. His friends by now are either all dead or in prison like him.

When I met Garfield Ellis in New Kingston, the city's midtown business sector, I told him how much I admired *For Nothing at All*.

'I see the book's been well received. Yet you paint a very bleak picture of Jamaica.'

'And it's getting worse,' Ellis replied. 'I'm worried, really worried. Yes, it's gonna be bad. Bad for us all.' According to Ellis, the decade following independence was a turning point when, in the space of just a few years, Jamaica lived through an accelerated cycle of political temptation and folly. 'The Seventies demystified authority,' Ellis claimed. 'Now anything with any status is under fire. There's no regard any more, no respect for people, or for the past.'

There was something in the Jamaican people that '*required* them' to have an autocratic foreign hand, Ellis believed. Having gone through the euphoria of post-imperialism Jamaica had now gone back to a stage where it had to be run by outsiders. More than eighty American firms now operate in Jamaica, with a total US investment estimated at more than $3 billion. 'Our banks, corporations, airlines, the judiciary, hotels – they're all foreign-run.' Submission to foreign (chiefly, American) interests may be the price Jamaicans have to pay for failing to make it on their own after independence, said Ellis. 'History's repeating itself. We're perpetuating another kind of imperial colonialism,' he judged.

At Sligoville, a village in the hills above Spanish Town, Garfield Ellis's bitterness was echoed more despairingly by Monsignor Richard Albert, a straight-talking Jewish convert to Catholicism, originally from the Bronx in New York. 'Right now there's anarchy in Spanish Town,' he said to me. 'And the kids don't care if they die today, the next day, the next week: they don't care because they're *already* dying.' The monsignor's job, as he saw it, was to prevent the almost-dead from dying.

Albert knew the gang-infested ghettos of Spanish Town better than anyone. He spoke out fearlessly against the politicians and drug barons who manipulated the poor for their own ends, and saw himself (or so he intimated to me) as a tower of common sense and decency amid the 'moral bewilderment' of modern Jamaica. The poor revered Albert: 'The Negotiator', they called him, after the film of that title starring Samuel L. Jackson. Albert's speciality was to negotiate between the police and the ghetto dons involved in narcotics trafficking. This lent him a reputation for extraordinary courage, as the police rarely venture into Spanish Town's 'zinc communities'. In addition, the monsignor had been able to persuade wealthy Jamaicans to donate money to Catholic-run schools, training schemes, libraries, soup kitchens and counselling services.

'I exhort and I badger the wealthy,' Albert said to me. 'I tell them, "If you don't see to the needs of the poor today, you'll face an even greater social peril tomorrow." '

His signal achievement to date remains Saint Patrick's Foundation, which seeks to feed and provide education for the Jamaican poor, as well as provide a sanctuary for lepers, drug addicts and those infected with HIV. The Foundation does not give handouts merely, but provides skills to help the young escape from the cycle of poverty and violence. Kindness alone would feed few mouths and save no lives. 'The last thing Jamaica needs is charity,' Albert said.

I stayed a couple of nights at his Sligoville residence. A heavily built man in his early sixties, Albert had a pugilist's face and alert blue eyes. In his mouth smouldered the cigar which he was rarely without (except when saying Mass and, presumably, when asleep); he was a man of appetites, I could see, who liked his food and drink. His earthy good humour, however, belied his seriousness and the bravery he had shown as an inner-city priest. 'When I first came to Jamaica in 1976 I had a lot more hair,' he said, removing his baseball cap to reveal an entirely bald head. 'I lost it owing to the trials of living and working in the slums.'

He inhaled a lungful of cigar smoke. 'In some ways you've come at an awkward time, Ian. My grandmother's dying as we speak.' The cigar went back in. 'She's ninety-nine and the phone's been ringing all day.' Jamaicans say of the dying that they are 'travelling' – travelling on to a better world.

The house was illuminated by hurricane lamps, as rats had eaten through the electrical wiring. 'Sorry about that,' Albert said in his tough New York accent. He led me down a corridor lined with photographs of Mother Teresa and the late Pope John Paul II. A brass plate on his office door proclaimed him '*Servitor Pacis* – Servant of the Peace'. Albert was not averse to pontifical finery. Twice a year he travels to Rome to meet the 'the Big Guy', as he called the Pope.

He opened the door to a bedroom with blinds drawn and a fluorescent ceiling lamp now flickering back to life. I stowed my bag under the bed, doused myself with cold water, and took a nap. I was awoken by a fluttering sound and a shrill voice that seemed to say, '*Holy Father! Holy Father!*' From a cage in the corner of the adjoining room an angry green parrot stared at me. 'Hello', I said. The bird let out a screech. '*Holy Father!*'

*

'I hear you've met Albert,' Monsignor Albert said to me.

'Your parrot's called Albert?'

'Yes. Albert's a gift from an admirer.'

'He's a pretty big polly,' I said, trying to be clever, and took a seat on the veranda.

Below us the plain of St Catherine was spread out in pin-points of yellow light. An exhilarating view, I had to agree. 'When you're sitting up here, it's like the suffering below doesn't exist,' said Albert. He poured himself a whisky, and sat in his rocking chair. Three dogs, Taliban, Champ and Sligo, slavered on the teakwood planking in front of us as Albert spoke. 'You can't remain indifferent to the suffering if you've got a heart,' he said. 'The violence, the abandonment here is terrible.' In Spanish Town, nearly every household was involved in some kind of criminal activity, large or small. Car thieves, cooks and cleaners, musicians, tailors, squeegee men: they all made their money under the table. 'How could they not?' said Monsignor Albert. 'We have extremely high levels of unemployment here, not to mention illiteracy and teenage pregnancy.' His blue eyes were searching my face intelligently. 'Poverty breeds rage, and still the killings go on.'

Albert rolled the Scotch on his tongue as the hurricane lamps burned amber in the Sligoville night. The telephone rang and he got up to answer it. 'What's that?' I heard him say. 'Yes, yes. Give thanks and praise. And plenty love to you, too.' As he came back and sat down I enquired after his grandmother. 'Still travelling?' 'Still travelling,' he said, and lit up another cigar. 'Sorry, would you like one? They're Dominican,' he specified, holding a lit match up in his podgy fingers. He belched discreetly. 'Pardon me, I'm none too artistic.'

Albert's first Jamaica posting was to Riverton City in Kingston, a community of some 5,000 people not far from the Red Stripe brewery, who subsist on scraps recycled from municipal rubbish dumps. The experience seems to have exacerbated Albert's religious sensibility – as well as his fear of violence. 'People were shooting each other in the yard outside my house night and day. Have you ever heard an M16 fired? Trust me, it's terrifying!' The monsignor's eyes, full of fun and laughter before, were suddenly haggard as he recalled the bodies found in his yard. 'One of them had a *pickaxe* in its back.'

Even worse was when the police called the monsignor out to a murder scene. 'You'd never think a body could contain so much blood,' he said. 'It's so bad, the blood, your sneakers, they get all sticky from the blood.' He put another match to the cigar and watched the smoke for a moment. As a precaution, a 'Rapid Response' security team occasionally drops by to let the local bad men know who is in charge. Once, the monsignor persuaded them to loose off a round of ammunition over his balcony. Having lived in Jamaica for over thirty years he felt entitled. 'Some Jamaicans think I *am* Jamaican. Well, I think I've paid my dues by now.'

He rubbed the back of his hand across his mouth, belched. 'Ian, let me go to the men's room – I need to take a crap.' And with those unholy words he took himself down the corridor to the lavatory.

He had scarcely returned when a sudden noise altered him. 'That you, Henry?' His voice was edged with anxiety. 'Yes, Father,' came the reply from far off. Henry was the nightwatchman, a boy of about sixteen, who now approached us soft-footed carrying an electric torch. Soon after Henry had disappeared a car alarm went off. 'Henry!' Albert gave me a quick impatient look and poured himself another whisky. 'Henry! Our car's being t'iefed!' No answer; he thumped the arms of his chair with the heels of his hands. 'Henry! The dogs! They're barking! Check it out!' Albert blew out cigar smoke and said through it, 'Nobody's clean in Jamaica, I been around. You have to be on your guard – watch your back.' After a while Henry emerged again with his flashlight. Everything was fine, though Taliban and the other dogs continued to listen, ears pricked, through the darkness.

Soon the monsignor announced it was time for his bed. He called out to his nightwatchman: 'Henry! My nightcap!' Henry replied that a whisky was waiting by his bedside. 'Good,' Albert said and dropped his cigar stub on the floor and stamped on it.

I stayed behind with Henry and asked him, out of curiosity, how much it would cost to buy a handgun in Spanish Town.

'A Beretta? A Glock?' Henry asked. 'On the illegal market you mean?' He paused a fraction. 'About 100,000 Jamaican dollars.' (Roughly £700 – not cheap.)

'An M16 rifle?'

'Double that,' Henry said without hesitation.

'A British passport?'

'A quarter of a million.'

'Jamaican?'

'Jamaican.' (That is, £1,730, a great deal of money.)

I thanked Henry for his time and he shrugged; I went off to bed.

*

A cock crowed beneath my window while another answered it from the yard next door. Six o'clock; I got out of bed to find Richard Albert seated in the garden, reading from the Bible. Looking up, he said, 'Morning.'

'Good morning,' I replied but it didn't seem like a good morning really. A thick mist was rolling in from the hills and a wind was agitating the palm trees. Albert closed his Bible and announced, 'I love this early morning Sligoville mist – kinda chilly. Down in Spanish Town it's already stoking up stinking hot.'

Breakfast was served to us by a seventy-year-old Jamaican woman called Pearl. Nothing 'sweeted' Pearl more than a religious man, and no man was more religious (to her) than the Rt Rev. Msgr Albert. Pearl liked to cook for him, fill his belly with food, make his bed, and hear him at prayer. Each day she made the long journey from Spanish Town where she lived. 'Sligoville,' she said to me, 'is a piece of heaven fallen upon earth,' a place where one could meditate and take stock. The only drawback was the occasional racket of dancehall music from clubs nearby. 'Dancehall is a betrayal of England and our English heritage,' Pearl declared to me sternly. Monsignor Albert was masticating slowly, pontifically, with a slightly amused expression.

'Where's your fun, Pearl?' he said in between mouthfuls of bacon. 'Lord Jesus, lighten up.'

'Don't vain the name of the Lord,' Pearl upbraided the monsignor.

'Don't humbug me, Pearl,' the monsignor returned, half-jokingly.

As we drove that morning into Spanish Town, passers-by waved at Albert from the roadside. 'I can't go anywhere in Jamaica without being recognised,' he complained. On the outskirts of Spanish Town Albert stopped the car, put on a clean dog-collar, swigged from a bottle of Listerine, gargled the mouth wash, spat it out of the window, then lit another cigar. This was his daily routine before venturing into the ghetto; a preparation, almost, for war.

But first Albert called in at the Spanish Town police station. 'Morning, Constable Ross,' he greeted an off-duty policeman dressed in shiny sports clothes. 'Meet Ian Thomson, an English writer who's looking at Jamaica.' Ross grinned and looked me over, while the monsignor, blowing smoke from the corner of his mouth, said, 'All right, constable, how's the night been?' The policeman spoke without looking up. 'Just a few killings,' he said. 'Three bodies – buckshot in them – looks like a twelve-gauge sawed-off job.'

'That all?' Albert asked.

The policeman raised his eyebrows. 'Only happened about two hours ago, monsignor. What did you expect, a war?'

Armed with this good news (three bodies: almost nothing), Albert judged that it was safe for us to proceed. On leaving the police station, we passed a row of parked squad cars with a 'vision statement' stencilled on their sides – 'We Serve. We Protect. We Reassure'. The monsignor chortled, 'Ain't that a stitch? Jamaican cops do the opposite of all those things. Reassure? Are you kidding me?'

In Ellerslie Pen (one of Spanish Town's eighty-two slum shanties) Monsignor Albert was welcomed enthusiastically. 'Hey, pinkhead!' the inhabitants called out to him (his bald head, pink from over-exposure to the sun, had earned him that nickname). 'Morning, blackies,' he repaid the compliment, with a very Jamaican disregard for political correctness. 'Things quiet?' he asked. 'No shooting – everything level,' came the answer. On we drove to Railway Pen, a PNP stronghold: dingy shacks of zinc and board, congested, filthy streets with piles of decomposing matter, animal and vegetable. A man on a bicycle was busy collecting money from the taxi drivers parked by the disused railway line. 'Extortion's a multi-million dollar racket here,' commented Albert. The air was hazy with smoke: charcoal fires, burning tyres.

'You know Jamaicans hate each other,' Albert went on as we lurched uncomfortably over potholes. 'What's more, they're fearful of each other. Yes, the wealthy have locked themselves away – psychologically, physically – from the poor.' Could you blame them? The firepower of the dons is superior to that of the police; few middle-class people would like to rub shoulders with 'Bun Man' Hope, the don who ran the Tawes Pen shanty of Spanish Town, where we were now headed.

For half an hour we drove round unsuccessfully looking for the don's Honda Civic. Shiny rims, bright paint job. 'You can't miss it,' said Albert. 'You're a friend of his?' I asked the monsignor. He replied, waving his cigar, 'In my business you have to get on with everyone.' Bun Man, a master of crack-selling and protection rackets, controlled the pro-JLP 'One Order' gang. He died in 2006 shortly after my second visit to Jamaica. From photographs then in the newspapers he was a tall, high-shouldered youth, with braided hair and sombre eyes. He was wanted for killing a policeman. However, a rival gang had shot him through the window of his stationary Civic. In crazed reprisal, his supporters had set fire to the Spanish Town courthouse, hurling rocks and other missiles at the firemen who tried to save the Georgian building. The caretaker was shot dead and his body thrown into the conflagration, after refrigerators and other electrical equipment had been looted.

*

The Saint Monica Home for lepers – another of Richard Albert's projects – stood midway between Central Village and Windsor Heights (re-named by local politicians 'Sufferers Heights'). Of the thirty patients in the leprosarium, ten had Hansard's disease or leprosy (yaws, a variant of leprosy, widespread in slavery-era Jamaica, no longer exists). The other patients were terminally ill with AIDS. At the entrance we met Lloydie, a forty-eight-year-old who looked twice that age. He held out a claw-hand for me to shake. I took it – leprosy is not particularly contagious – and felt how thin and enervated it was in my own. 'Still chasing after the ladies, are we, Lloydie?' the monsignor joshed him. Lloydie beamed delightedly.

Within, nurses in starched aprons were going about the morning's ministry. A deportee from Philadelphia lay motionless on a bunk with AIDS and dementia, his eyes sunk like stones. Was he in pain? No, said the nurse, he would be comfortably medicated until the end. The atmosphere, in spite of the pall-like heat, seemed to be something like joy. James Clive, a seventy-four-year-old with leprosy, lay on his bed next to his electric guitar, his eyelids palsied. 'Everything's everything?' Albert asked him. 'Peace and love,' Clive replied, adding with a smile, 'Stay alive, Father.'

Any suspicion I might have had that Monsignor Albert had a charlatan streak – his kow-towing to the wealthy, his susceptibility to papal finery – was diminished after my visit to Saint Monica's. 'We do our best to make lives a little more comfortable,' he said to me as we left. 'It's a kind of balm yard, a place of soothing.' Saint Monica's provided palliative care for the dying, so they could leave this world with dignity, and a refuge for those unable to return to society.

11

Blood and Fire

Before leaving Kingston for the east coast I went to Cinchona Gardens, surely one of the most beautiful places in the West Indies. To previous generations of Jamaica-hands, Cinchona had been a botanical station of remarkable charm. Situated 5,000 feet up in the Blue Mountains, the gardens had begun life in the 1860s as an experimental quinine station. The cinchona plants had provided quinine as an antidote against malaria, one of the most debilitating and often deadly diseases in the British Empire. But poor roads into the mountains, together with competition from cinchona cultivated in imperial India, undermined the project and, a decade later in 1874, the Kew gardener William Nock turned Cinchona into a botanic station and haven for orchid-fanciers. He introduced monsoonal and other varieties of orchids. Visitors came after dark to see the night-flowering shrubs in the glass palm-houses.

A Swiss-German botanist, Andreas Oberli, wanted to see how the gardens had fared after the assaults of the recent hurricane. An authority on Jamaican flora, Oberli had been associated with Cinchona since 1982, when he was appointed the gardens' project manager, his brief being to restore the botanical 'Sleeping Beauty' to its Victorian state. At the same time he had transformed his own garden in Irish Town near Kingston, planting it with hundreds of exotic palms from across the world. When I visited him at his home, Oberli pointed out fan palms from Mauritius and hurricane palms from the Maldives. The palms did not grow from a random, chaotic jumble; a stern Swiss-German logic underlay their efflorescence. But the effect was beautiful. Oberli used efficient scholar-botanist explanations to explain the ideas behind the layout.

A self-confessed communer with plants (rather than with people), Oberli was a difficult man to warm to. He liked Jamaican women well enough and had a Jamaican daughter who had recently spent a year in the Bernese Alps milking cows. ('She's completely black but the Swiss loved her!' he said, apparently in some amazement.) Yet Jamaican men, possibly because they associated his love of plants with an effeminate nature, abused him. 'Depending on where I go, they call me a white pussyhole or a white batty man. Well, it's disgusting.' Tall and rangy, with razor-cropped hair, Oberli took refuge in an acrid, bitter irony. Jamaican men, as far as he was concerned, were 'totally fucked'. He let the significance of his words sink in. 'I only like the landscape and the plants, not the menfolk.'

He added, 'You don't believe me? Only foreigners can like this place. Jamaican men are miserable and also they are depressed.' Oberli's experience of Jamaica was certainly very different from mine, though it is true that only foreigners refer to Jamaica as a 'paradise'.

Before setting off for Cinchona we weighted Oberli's pick-up with cement blocks for balance: the road to the gardens was not good, he said, and the ballast would help reduce the risk of skidding. By midday the nose of the concrete-heavy Mitsubishi was pointing permanently skywards. The road edged along vaporous ravines while swirls of mist eddied round us. Along the way, Oberli pointed out which plants were native and which invasive species. The rolling greenness was broken by the occasional red flare of an African tulip. The same shrubbery, the same perennials, typified the Italian regions of Switzerland, Oberli said.

For the first time Jamaica struck me as beautiful. Waxy-leaved frangipani and outbursts of orange-white blossom enhanced the Blue Mountain road we were now on, a scene that cannot have changed since the 1680s when the Restoration collector-naturalist Sir Hans Sloane botanised his way across it. Sloane's heroic mapping of Jamaican plants and flowers (recorded in his *Catalogus Plantarum*) forms the core of the herbarium today in the Natural History Museum in London. And as we continued uphill to Cinchona I had a sense of the island's voluptuous over-ripeness, the lasciviousness, as captured by Sloane in his extraordinary and detailed drawings of the island's flora. 'If there was a worm-hole in the leaf or flower,' an American botanist based in Kingston (Dr George Proctor) had told me, 'Sloane put it in his drawing.'

Midway to Cinchona we stopped at a coffee farm called Green Hill. Oberli knew the owners, Alex and Dorothy Twyman. We parked the pick-up outside their hillside cottage, and made our way down a steep path to the entrance. Alex Twyman, a pale man with quizzical brown eyes, seemed pleased to see us. In his native London he had been a chartered surveyor. His wife, Dorothy, was Jamaican; her quiet voice contrasted with her husband's expansive talkativeness.

In 1997, the Twymans' son Mark had been killed at his home in the Blue Mountains. (Five bullets in his back, one close to his heart.) The Jamaican newspapers, made indifferent by the island's rising murder rate, devoted no more than fifty dry words to the incident, and to this day no arrests have been made. Aged thirty-five, Mark had got caught up in a meshwork of local corruption. His father suspects that men employed by the Jamaican Coffee Board, a government-run monopoly, had killed his son. For years the Board had obstructed Mark Twyman and his parents from obtaining an export licence.

Dorothy Twyman, absorbed and silent, asked if I would like to try some Green Hill coffee. When she returned she had also brought some dark beans for me to chew. Coffee cultivation had begun here in the early 1800s, when French planters from revolutionary Haiti brought their expertise to Jamaica. The coffee I was now drinking came from plantations laid out by those French settlers. Most of it is now exported to Japan, where the Blue Mountain brand is prized above all others.

As I drank my coffee, Alex led me to a window where I saw spread out before us a swathe of glistening green coffee bushes. We were at an altitude of 4,000 feet. The wattle-and-daub workers' huts were identical to those set up by the slaves after emancipation in 1834, said Alex. To my eye the huts looked timeless, an inheritance from Africa. Thirty-five Jamaicans worked on the Twyman estates. 'They've been picking coffee since they were two years old,' Alex said (as if that was something to be proud of). As well as coffee, the Twymans grew the cocoa plant *Theobroma cacao*, which Sloane had cultivated commercially in Jamaica and, on his return to England in 1688, used to manufacture blocks of 'Sir Hans Sloane's Milk Chocolate', thus introducing the delicacy to England.

'Did you enjoy your coffee?' Dorothy said to me, as she picked up the empty coffee tray. A solicitous woman, she made for the door with a self-effacing gesture.

*

As we drove towards the distant, violet-blue line of the Yallahs Valley the landscape was not so lush; a couple of bridges were down, and landslip had washed out parts of the road. Twice Oberli's pick-up got stuck in rough ground. 'Thank God it hasn't rained,' he said, 'otherwise all would be mud.' In these devastated surroundings, sweat-soaked and covered in roadside dirt, I caught my first glimpse of Cinchona Gardens. By the entrance was the melancholy spectacle of a North American tulip tree and a eucalyptus uprooted by the hurricane. Yet beyond the gate, Cinchona's beauty, with its lilac-coloured hydrangeas and rivers of blue azaleas, was overwhelming. The place appeared almost theatrical – the creation of some rhapsodising set-designer. Once inside I was aware of a hushed, almost private, atmosphere that felt remote from the world.

Oberli, camera slung round his neck, was taking photographs of Assam tea bushes; the cinchona trees had long since disappeared. Gold ferns – green on the outside, gold underneath – glinted exotically. At one point Oberli stumbled on a lone lily with an odd, crinkly bloom. 'Oh, you are a beauty,' he exclaimed and, crouching low to the specimen, he photographed it.

It had taken Oberli four years to restore the gardens to their present state. Nock's observatory house had been vandalised and his glass-houses, cottages and outbuildings had collapsed. In the mid-1980s, Jamaica's then prime minister, Edward Seaga, had wanted to develop Cinchona as his own private country club, complete with tennis courts and a helicopter landing-pad. Had Seaga got his way, the terraced rose gardens might now be decorated with stone winged cherubs, miniature obelisks and other 'big man' vulgarities. Oberli, to his credit, helped to block the project.

On one occasion Oberli witnessed the PNP politician Ronnie Thwaites ordering his servants to dig up beds of rare plants, bulbs and cuttings for him. No intervention was possible as the samples were hurriedly wrapped up for Thwaites to take home. Jamaica's politicians have long fed on public property, and it was no surprise to Oberli when Thwaites was later disgraced.

*

As the mountain mists cleared that afternoon, a cool bamboo scent reached into my lungs. Outside the observatory house, half a dozen Rasta plantsmen were lying about among the rose beds. They had been smoking ganja and, relaxed, were enjoying the beauty of this place.

'The more you smoke,' one of them announced to me, 'the more Babylon fall.' He took a long drag off his carrot-shaped cigarette and squinted at me through the smoke. The man next to him picked up a bottle of rum, tilted it to his mouth, and stood up unsteadily. He was Lloyd Stamp, keeper of the gardens since 1978, a big man whose belly hung off him like a dead weight. He began to complain bitterly of the Gardens Division of the Ministry of Agriculture, his employers in Kingston, who for the past thirty years had failed to provide him with adequate security.

'Thieves creep up here at night, Mr Oberli, and steal the Bermuda Ladies and orchids [*horchids*, Stamp said]. I need guard dogs, Mr Oberli, guard dogs is what I need.'

'Yah, dogs are good,' Oberli agreed. 'Dogs keep you alert – and they alert *you*. You need the dogs to patrol the botanical gardens of Cinchona, Mr Stamp.' There seemed little likelihood that he would get them.

Nothing, though, could tempt Stamp or his staff to work elsewhere, especially not Kingston. Far better to be isolated on top of this ridge of the Blue Mountains.

'The government can chat all the foolishness and all the poli*tricks* they like,' said Stamp, 'but up here we got all the vegetation and all the *meditation* we need.'

'Nock's beds still bloom up very nice,' Oberli said, as the garden staff puffed on their cigarettes in the great silence. I looked out across the valley to the Blue Mountain Peak in all its ethereal majesty and sapphire tinge. I felt lucky to be up here, enjoying the view. 'If life is fair,' Stamp looked at me, 'you will have to come and see us again.' I knew then that I would leave this place with sadness.

*

'Slow down, Prince. Don't drive so *fast*,' exclaimed Evelyn Matalon (née Mordecai). We were racing out of Kingston along the road east to Morant Bay. 'It's bad for your blood pressure.' Prince was doing his best to drive carefully, staying well under seventy miles an hour and keeping his eyes warily on the side roads for traffic police. 'As you can see, Mrs Mat,' he reassured Evelyn, 'I'm practising roadside courtesy and observing all road signs and applicable speed limits.'

'Well, keep up the good work, Princey,' Evelyn sighed, as he sounded a series of aggressive horn blasts at a passing lorry.

Evelyn turned to me with a weary look. 'Prince does love to toot his horn, but he's such a good driver.' Indeed, he was her chauffeur.

Elegantly dressed, Evelyn Matalon was a ninety-year-old Jamaican of fierce intelligence. The Matalons, a Jewish family, had run construction and food companies in Jamaica and worked at ministerial level for the PNP. But, with family deaths and divorces, they were no longer such a power in the land.

Evelyn lived just outside Morant Bay on an estate left to her by her second husband, Isaac 'Zaccie' Matalon. Isaac had been the Custos or chief magistrate of St Thomas parish, an arid area of the southeast, of which Morant Bay is the capital. No Jamaican town has a more fiery past. Morant Bay was the scene of the heroic popular uprising of 1865 known as the Morant Bay Rebellion. The colonial governor of Jamaica had suppressed the uprising with such ferocity that it became a *cause célèbre* in Britain, igniting an unprecedented debate about how an imperial power should conduct itself.

In 1934, at the age of eighteen, Evelyn Matalon had left Jamaica to study journalism in the United States. Having been raised in Jamaica by a Ukrainian-born Ashkenazi mother, she was barred by the white Anglo-Saxon students at Pennsylvania from membership of the undergraduate sorority. It was a cruel awakening, but pre-independence Jamaica was no less hostile. Her first husband,

Emanuel 'Manny' Henriques, was fortunate as a Jew not to be banned from the Morant Bay country club. 'All the same,' Evelyn said, touching the gold Star of David round her neck, 'Jamaica is a less prejudiced place these days for us Jews. The new Jews of Jamaica are the Chinese. They're envied for their wealth and sometimes even hated.'

It was a long ride from Kingston through the hot, humid morning to Morant Bay. We passed mile after mile of hurricane-damaged countryside. Eventually a sign to the right said 'STANTON ESTATES' and directed us through shrubs and spreading trees to a 1950s-era bungalow where Evelyn lived with a skeleton staff. A large man lumbered on to the drive at a blare from the car's horn. This was Peter, Evelyn's cook. Nodding to him, Prince pulled up beneath a portico with an iron-studded arched door, and I got out of the car.

The bungalow was very warm and quiet inside. Peter led me down the corridor to the room where I was to sleep. My bedroom was frowsy, with old mahogany furniture faintly sticky to the touch. A couple of towels lay folded on a chair. And in a cupboard were stacks of old knitting magazines. I turned off the big plastic 'Jamaica Wind' ceiling fan and opened the windows; moths and flying bugs trembled against the curtains. It would take some time to settle in here. After a shower I went out to find Evelyn sitting on the porch, listening to a recording of *The Sound of Music*.

Peter, the cook, emerged presently with a tray containing two silver goblets. 'Chilled egg nog – I used to drink it as a child,' explained Evelyn. 'It's wonderfully sustaining.' Peter, his eye-whites red (I guessed from ganja), ambled off back to the kitchen having delivered the drinks. The umbrella-shaped crown of a huge guango tree obstructed views of the lawn in front of us and, beyond that, there was a thick mass of green forest. Stanton was no longer a working estate – its 800 acres had been sold on Isaac Matalon's death in 1998 – and it had a forlorn air.

'Can you really sit here and think that Jamaica's such a violent country?' Evelyn asked me. 'It's so very peaceful.' I was admiring the view when Peter's rough voice announced: 'Lunch is ready, Mrs Mats.'

*

Jamaica loves a hero, and no Jamaican was more heroic than Paul Bogle, the Baptist preacher and reform agitator who led the Morant Bay uprising. The uprising was a defining moment in the decline of British imperial power. Bogle and his conspirators were protesting, not against their adored Queen Victoria and the empire she ruled from London, but against the plight of the half-starving black majority that was without work, without land or a future. By the 1860s – thirty years after emancipation – many Jamaican plantations had turned to scrub as the owners were unable to compete with the cheap sugar produced by Cuba and Brazil. Jamaica had become a patchwork of ramshackle, half-evacuated farmsteads, where rumours of re-enslavement (associated with the possibility of Jamaica joining the United States as a slave state) were rife.

Bogle's supporters had burned down the Morant Bay courthouse; a life-sized (but not very life-like) statue of Paul Bogle now stands at the foot of the courthouse rebuilt and re-opened in 1867. Beside it is a plaque that commemorates the 'patriots' of Morant Bay, whose 'sacrifices' paved the long way to independent Jamaica.

The uprising, far-reaching in its repercussions, led to the dissolution of Jamaica's local parliament – the planter-dominated House of Assembly – and the imposition of Crown Colony rule. Future governors of Jamaica were to be clad in the panoply of imperial power, but their paternalism was an improvement, at least, on rule by the reactionary local parliament. Crown rule brought Jamaica into line with the newly 'liberal' and 'enlightened' Britain. British money was invested in education, roads, electric telegraph lines; botanical gardens (notably, Cinchona) were built; and, most important, swathes of arable land were reclaimed from the post-emancipation wilderness and given over to former slaves. All this was largely in response to Bogle's 'West Indian Mutiny', as it became known to the British administration.

On 11 October 1865, after setting fire to the courthouse, Bogle and a group of black allies killed eighteen people, most of them white. Riots spread across St Thomas, with brutality on both sides of the widening racial divide. Planters and their families fled to the cane brakes or put out to sea. Eight years earlier the Sepoy Rebellion or Indian Mutiny (to use its British name) had resulted in a collapse of British law and order on the subcontinent. The governor of Jamaica, Edward Eyre, fearing an equivalent 'Jamaican Mutiny', decreed martial law and within a week the 'rebellion' (as he called it) was put down. In the months that passed before martial law expired, the British military indulged in shooting, flogging and more or less arbitrary executions. *Cornhill Magazine* put the number of deaths at 439 and the floggings at 600.

Governor Eyre's suppression provoked a scandal in Britain. The scandal was not about whether martial law should have been invoked (in the British public mind, it almost certainly should have been). Rather, it was about the unnecessary duration of Eyre's decree and the abuse of its powers. Eyre had personally called for the arrest of the mixed-race landowner George Gordon, one of the very few members of the (overwhelmingly white) House of Assembly to champion Bogle's cause. Eyre gave Gordon an instant trial without access to counsel and, on a trumped-up charge of treason, hanged him from the surviving arch of the charred Morant Bay courthouse.

Even by Victorian standards, the punishment was disproportionate to the emergency. To Eyre, however, Gordon was that dangerous thing: a rogue member of the land-owning elite, whose calls for social reform conflicted with planter interests. Eyre made an example first of him, then of Bogle – who was also hanged. Hundreds of arrests and further executions followed. The British press, keeping a close eye on events in the cane-cutting colony, agreed that Eyre had overreached himself, and should be relieved of his post. In August 1866, one year after the Morant Bay Rebellion, he was recalled home by the British government and stripped of his position. An embarrassment to the Colonial Office, Eyre retired to Devonshire, where he died in 1901.

Intellectuals in Victorian England were divided over what Eyre's fate should be. John Stuart Mill, Charles Darwin, Herbert Spencer and Thomas Huxley ('Darwin's Bulldog', grandfather of Aldous Huxley) believed that Eyre's was the worst case of political murder since Judge Jeffreys. Unless Eyre was prosecuted for murder, 'Britannia's robes' would be stained forever with blood. A Jamaica Committee was founded by these luminaries – all of them pro-Yankee in the American Civil War – with the aim of convicting Eyre and restoring the good name of Britain and Britain's fitness to rule over its colonial preserve.

A counter-committee, the Eyre Defence and Aid Fund, was set up by Thomas Carlyle (author of the *Occasional Discourse on the Nigger Question*) with the purpose of raising money for any legal action necessary on Eyre's behalf. Eyre had prevented a white bloodbath, a 'second Haiti', and moreover had protected Jamaica's 'tenderly nurtured women' from rape. Lurid sexual fantasies of 'black depravity' blended with the Fund's conviction that English law did not apply to a '*naturally* wild . . . inferior race'. Never mind the common law principle; it did not apply to black people. There was to be one law for the imperial nation and another for its subject peoples. 'Blacks' (as the pro-Eyre Fund construed them) were born to be mastered; civilisation depended on the *separation* of races, not on their harmonious integration. The old biblical belief that Africans and whites were members of one family had lost ground to race prejudice.

In the end, predictably, much of the British establishment sided with Eyre. Charles Dickens, Alfred Lord Tennyson and John Ruskin, old India hands with a memory of the 'Mutiny', as well as the Anglican canon and author of *The Water Babies*, Charles Kingsley, insisted that Eyre had saved the great British nation from the Haiti-like spectre of free and equal black rule. The majority of the British working class, on the other hand, was set against Eyre: the very goals for which Gordon and Bogle had died – an end to unjust tribunals and the denial of political rights – were the goals of the British workers, too. Eyre's effigy was burned in Hyde Park, but, partly because Queen Victoria deplored the un-Christian spirit of vengeance, he was never prosecuted.

*

Back at Stanton Estates I found Evelyn Matalon listening to a selection of Strauss waltzes. She looked up as I entered and asked how my Bogle research had gone.

'Well, I met quite a few Bogles.' One of them, Clovis Bogle, ran a shop selling satellite dishes on Queen Street; his smooth features and gentle bulging eyes uncannily resembled those of his namesake in the sepia photograph I had seen. He agreed, 'I have the Bogle looks.'

'Bogles are like Smiths round here,' Evelyn told me.

Paul Bogle's birthplace in the village of Stony Gut, a five-mile climb uphill from Morant Bay, was nevertheless a disappointment. A concrete memorial to the 'martyrs' of 1865 was crumbling and chipped. Bogle lay buried nearby, but his tomb also was uncared for. This level of neglect for a national hero would be unheard of in a more confident nation. Did it suggest a certain ambivalence still towards Bogle and his bid for equality and justice? Bogle was too black and too uppity. For years after the 1865 uprising the very name Bogle was synonymous with sedition and disapproved of by the British colonial class.

From outside Evelyn's house came the occasional sound of an owl and, closer to, intermittent plumbing noises. Evelyn got up to secure the windows. 'I have reason to be fearful,' she explained. In 1994 she and her husband had been held at gunpoint. Awoken by the barking of the dogs, the first thing Evelyn noticed was a smell. 'It was the gunmen's sweat – the smell of their own fear.' With the dogs barking outside, Evelyn crept out of bed and, unseen, felt her way along the corridor. She stopped halfway on seeing three masked men at one end attempting to cut the telephone wires. Still unseen, she crept back to the bedroom and told Isaac that men were in the house.

One of the intruders entered the bedroom, and put a pistol to Isaac's head, while another bound Evelyn's hands with rope to her husband's. For almost an hour Evelyn tried to talk the gunmen out of their 'madness' but one of them, his nerves starting to crack, snapped: 'Shut up! You chat too much – you chat too much and you don't say nothing!' They yanked off Evelyn's rings and bracelets, took all the electrical items they could find and, having found the car key, loaded their loot into Isaac's jeep and drove off into the night. The police, alerted by a neighbour, gave chase, but failed to catch the robbers. 'It was a nasty business, best forgotten,' Evelyn said to me.

Yet the intruders had showed an unexpected 'kindness', she added, in the care they took not to harm her or her husband. 'They put a gun to Zaccie's head and, yes, they hurt my hands with the rope, but I honestly don't think they would have killed us.'

'Violence would have been their last resort?' I asked.

'Yes,' Evelyn replied eventually. 'Violence and cruelty were their only weapons really.'

12

Revival Time

Paul Bogle was said to have beamed out with a Baptist-Revivalist light as he preached from his chapel in Stony Gut. Revival, one of the great religions of the Jamaican poor, incorporates elements of Low Church chant and hellfire hymnal with the spirit-possession and 'healing lore' of West African root doctors and shamans. An outpouring of the Holy Spirit is experienced by some adepts as they sob, gasp and shake in ecstatic trance-like states.

In the years after the First World War Bogle's example was adopted by Alexander Bedward, a Revival preacher who fired his followers with a hatred for their oppressed condition in British Jamaica. The Bedwardite Movement, as it came to be known, was based in the semi-ghetto of August Town (now a part of Greater Kingston) and foreshadowed Marcus Garvey and the militant wing of Rastafari in its attempts to combat imperial British rule. Pilgrims journeyed to August Town to receive the Reverend Bedward's healing ministrations and have their sins washed clean in Hope River nearby. Miracle cures were attributed to those waters.

A belief in miracles pervades the Afro-Jamaican mind, as it does the Roman Catholic mind. In 1920, Bedwardites gathered in August Town to witness the long-promised 'miracle' of their master's ascent to heaven. Addressing him by the Revival title of 'Shepherd', they crowded the Revivalist Church of Zion in anticipation of his flight. Bedward did not leave the ground ('Bedward Stick to the Earth', scoffed the establishment *Gleaner*.) The following year, in 1921, he marched 800 of his faithful on Kingston, stirring memories of the 1865 Morant Bay rebellion. He was arrested by police on sedition charges and died in a Kingston lunatic asylum in 1930, the fate of many religious Afro-Jamaicans. While the 'Lord of August Town' was alive, however, the colonial administration was powerless to disperse his immense following. Even quieter Revivalist brotherhoods were galvanised into action by his fiery example.

In August Town today the houses are broken down by poverty. I called on the last two surviving Bedwardites there. At first there was no answer when I rattled on their front door, so I rattled harder, again with no result. Eventually the door opened and a young woman appeared. I asked her if Esther Grant and Adaina Donnell were in.

The woman looked doubtful. 'I think they've gone to bed. I don't think you can see them.'

'It's about Alexander Bedward. Could you tell them that?'

At this point an elderly voice down the corridor piped up, 'I've not had a message from Bedward in a hundred years, I've got nothing to say.'

The young woman, turning her head, shouted back down the corridor, 'The man here says he's from England. He's a *traveller*.' The elderly voice replied, 'Tell him to come in.'

In the corridor a paraffin lamp burned dimly above a photograph of Bedward with the caption 'Shepherd of August Town'. I was shown into a gloomy bedroom filled with chintz and dilapidated furniture.

A woman was sitting in a chair with a card table in front of her. She was wearing a woollen hat and had been born, she said, in 1910. This was Adaina Donnell. Her sister, Esther Grant (born 1918), was lying in bed on the other side of the room, her head propped against a pillow. Mrs Donnell wiped her face with a pink hand towel, and began to talk about her life as a Bedwardite.

'I was a small child then but I remember when Bedward baptise enough people. Bedward said God give him the Hope River, and I've seen people who can't even *walk* get cured by him.' Women, hoping to become pregnant, drank Hope River water personally bottled and blessed by Bedward, said Mrs Donnell.

'Yes.' Mrs Grant was speaking now. 'Bedward was a *wonderful* healer. Even some Catholic people went there and got better by the water.'

The sisters asked me if I was baptised and when I said yes, they enquired, 'In a river?'

'No, in a church, probably.'

'Oh!' Mrs Donnell looked at her sister, then at me. 'In a river is much better, man.'

'When I was a baby girl,' Mrs Grant put in, 'my mother tell Bedward I'm sick, so he put some water in a basin and I'm bathed until the time I'm better. And since that time I don't get sick. Oh, I was a little stronger then than I am now, but I'm still quite hearty.' She had not been to the doctor since 1918.

'The year you were born?'

'Yes,' Mrs Grant said, 'when I did born.'

'But today it's not the same,' Mrs Donnell shook her head. 'They don't keep the church no good any more.' The Church of Zion had long ago lost its roof and been converted into a basketball court, the sisters said.

Mrs Grant said, 'All the good people have gone home [meaning they had died] and all of Bedward's relatives have gone home too. Yes, all of them dead out.' She paused. 'We don't even have his grandsons here now, all of them done away with and dead out.'

And did Bedward really attempt to fly? 'No, nothing happened like that, my dear,' said Mrs Grant. 'They jus' try to make the Bedward myth more sweeter, nice it up.' Who did? Why, the British government, Mrs Grant went on. Jamaican religious life is filled with mystic healers claiming descent variously from Abyssinian royalty, Jesus Christ or John the Baptist, and no doubt Bedward was prone to phantasmal visitations. According to another legend, he had attempted to fly with his followers to Africa. That yearning to 'fly back to Guinea' is characteristic of Neo-African possession cults, and it is one of the most pervasive themes in slave songs.

Each Sunday, the Bedwardite sisters take a taxi to the Church of Christ (not a Bedward church) to attend morning service.

'You don't fly there?' I teased.

'No, we don't fly there,' they replied crossly. 'Is a taxi we take.'

*

St Thomas is the poorest parish of Jamaica, from where the poorest Jamaicans had left for Britain and the United States. Working as kitchen-hands, road-sweepers or lavatory attendants, they experienced foreign city life at its rawest and most exploitative. In their darkest hours some of them took comfort in the Afro-Christian beliefs that had transformed their lives back home. At night in the St Thomas countryside funerary rituals still take place, designed to keep the dead safely in their graves through a drum and dance rhythm called Kumina.

Over the years, Kumina has merged into the more common Nine Night ceremony (the name for the nine-day period of mourning held to ensure a 'good' departure from this world for the deceased). A Nine Night, in turn, may absorb elements from other Afro-Caribbean religious cults such as Pocomania, Revival and the older Native Baptism.

The dwindling belief in an afterlife – the consolation that we might join our loved ones in heaven – has made Jamaicans less respectful of such Revival-inspired mortuary rituals. These days Jamaicans may prefer to rely on the commercial funeral home, though this often leaves them with funeral expenses they can ill afford to repay. In urban areas especially, the consolation afforded by a Nine Night has been replaced by a hankering after a gold-encrusted casket. Now even death wears bling.

In remote St Thomas, however, the bereaved still face the mystery of the end of life in Kumina. The corpse can be kept on ice for up to two weeks while relatives gather from all parts of the diaspora to pay their respects. In St Thomas returnees attend more and more Kumina rituals as the friends and family they had left behind in the 1950s and 1960s age and die.

A Nine Night was due to take place this evening in Leith Hall, ten miles east of Morant Bay. The deceased had been repatriated from New York and was now awaiting burial. If I wished to attend, I was to mention the name of a friend to one of the mourners.

For nine nights the body remains in the deceased person's home or 'dead yard'. During this time, mourners gather to propitiate the 'duppy' (restless spirit) of the deceased through song, dance and offerings of drink and cooked food. The individual is not considered to be fully dead until his or her duppy has been appeased and 'successful' entombment taken place. (As they say in Jamaica: 'No call man dead till you bury him.') If the dead person is not properly buried, his or her spirit may return to 'ride' (as in a nightmare) the living, haunt familiar places and people, avenge enemies and generally make mischief. Even more so than Rastafari, Kumina represents the most obvious rejection in Jamaica of Anglican orthodoxy and High Church instruction; as in West African and West Central African non-Christian belief, the living must be protected from the dead.

Again, as in Africa today, a variety of ruses are adopted to prevent the soul's unwanted departure. Care is taken, for example, to ensure that no parts of a corpse – hair, fingernails – remain above ground, otherwise they might be put to magic use. On the ninth and final night (known as the 'set-up') the duppy is invited to leave the dead yard and not come back.

Middle-class Jamaicans object that fussing over a corpse in this way is uncivilised. *Jamaica Superstitions* (1894), by the Anglican Reverend T. Banbury, condemned the Nine Night as 'Satanic' and tainted by obeahism (belief in sorcery) and other Neo-African 'devilry'. But in Jamaica, good and evil are not always antithetical. Magic designed to harm white planters occupied a nebulous area between good and bad. In 1831, Nine Nights were outlawed by the Jamaican government as being insufficiently 'Christian'. The ban was impossible to enforce, however, as the dead in Jamaica are too powerfully allied to the living.

*

I went to Leith Hall with Peter, Evelyn Matalon's cook, and her driver Prince. They were familiar with the variants of Revival and happy to accompany me to the Nine Night. By about ten o'clock we were deep in Kumina country. Prince, one hand on the steering wheel, ripped open a packet of Black Cat cigarettes with his finger-nail, lit one and said to me, 'Should be some good Revival tonight, Mr Ian.' He blew out a cloud of high-tar smoke and watched it whip out of the window.

'Spliff?' Peter asked from the back of the car; he reached for his stash of collie weed under the seat and began to roll a paper. 'Herb like fruit,' he added with a grunt, 'keep you healthy, keep you mind clear, a-true, Princey?'

'A-true, Petes,' said Prince. The ganja would be resinous, rich-tasting and very strong. Too much of it, and one would be seeing double and across time. Best to leave it alone. As Prince accelerated on through Lyssons and Prospect Point, a hot, oily smell came from the engine. I leaned out of the window for some fresh air and, in the huge darkness above us the stars hung low, burning steadily. The moon was the colour of a blood orange.

About a mile before Leith Hall the road petered out among shacks. Here the land had been 'captured' from the government by the rural poor and squatted on. After five minutes we saw a fleet of cars parked at a crossroads. 'This is it,' said Prince, slowing down. 'This have to be it.' Our headlamps disclosed a milling of people outside the dead yard. Prince dowsed the headlamps, and stopped the car. A stench of rubbish came in sweet and heavy through the moon-illuminated night.

We left the car and walked towards the house, a low concrete building with striped metal awnings. There were voices, the slap of dominoes on a backyard table and a dog set up a terrific barking. The noise quickened the pounding of my heart. At the entrance to the dead yard a woman stopped us. I mentioned the friend's name, and the woman let us in. At the back, a crowd of mourners was gathered on a concrete terrace, some of them standing, others seated on folding metal chairs. A blue plastic tarpaulin was stretched across the crowd to form a roof. We were outdoors and it might rain.

Nearby, in a cleared space, two Kumina drums stood unattended. This space was considered sacred and the drums were stuck round with lit candles. The audience, laughing and chatting sociably, were in most part drably dressed, though some appeared to be well off, with branded baseball caps, spiffy tracksuits or pressed jeans and glittery jewellery. I assumed they had flown in from the United States. The Jamaican population in America is even larger now than that in the United Kingdom (though Britain has a larger percentage of Jamaican people than America). Mine was the only white face in the audience, but, oddly, no one seemed to pay it any mind.

At intervals a musician ambled in to spray the drumheads with rum. Tonight was the third night of the Nine Night, when the spirit is believed actually to rise from the corpse. The body, apparently laid out on blocks of ice inside the house, was not something I cared to see. My father had just died, and the sight of his own body in the hospital mortuary stayed with me; he, too, had had to be 'repatriated' from abroad for burial.

A stout, middle-aged woman began to serve us cups of steaming 'mannish water' soup made of the entrails, testicles and head of a goat. (The risibly awful Rolling Stones album, *Goat's Head Soup*, had been part-recorded in Jamaica.) I looked into my cup and something peeped up at me through the steam. Chunks of hard-dough bread made the liquid's saltiness more palatable. 'Mannish water', so named for its apparent aphrodisiac properties, is a favourite at country weddings, as well as at funerals.

Amid a stir of interest, two drummers arrived and, in a sort of bene-diction, they sprinkled more rum over the immediate audience, made up (according to Prince) of the dead person's siblings, male and female. Chacha Beng, the chief drummer, wore a blue cassock, and many rings. A man of some importance, he was able to control the success, or otherwise, of the Kumina rhythms. As he straddled the *playing kyas* (the leading Kumina drum) he carefully tapped the stretched goatskin a couple of times. The younger man meanwhile took up a larger drum, the *kbandu*, likewise cylindrical and split-sided.

The drummers were now joined by five other musicians, also men, armed with shakers ('shak-shaks') and *catta* sticks (which make a 'rackling' sound against the drum's side). With a nod to the audience, they raised the percussion above their heads, much as a Vodoun priest might raise a sacrificial dove in Haiti. The drama of the moment was heightened for me by a rumble of the *kyas*, which settled into a low, rapid thrumming, as both drummers began to beat out a rhythm with their hands. The beat spread out, reached a pitch of strong, rapid strokes. An African call-and-response – a low hurrying beat – was ringing out now. And round the Kumina orchestra a group of men and women had begun to dance.

They started a slow, counter-clockwise shuffle, the jerky move-ment of their arms oddly resembling those of ska dance routines. Alternately bending forward and straightening up in rhythmic sequence, the dancers took an intake of breath, and released it with a James Brown-like 'huh'. Revivalists call this form of respiration 'trumping' – a form of hyperventilation. The percussionists with

149

their chattering beat kept the dancers in a continuous whirl, until cheekbones and foreheads took on a polish of sweat. One of the men had gone into a swinging, hip-thrusting dance of his own, clearing a space in the crowd. He was a Leith Hall cop, I was told, and his pistol was protruding nastily from his waistband; the safety catch was on, I hoped.

Then a woman began to shake, threw back her head and gyrated her arms in rapid circles. The duppy had entered her and seemingly put her in a semi-hypnoidal state. She stood up, staggered forward from her chair, her body colliding hot against mine, whirling away. Now she swayed a little towards Chacha Beng. Her eyes were closed, her lips were slightly parted and her breath was coming and going in little spasms. The audience stood calmly by, strangely unmoved by the display, though not for long. Three women dashed after the possessed woman, as she was now swirling away towards the entrance by the road. The crowds parted to let her through; she fell down, stood up again, did a spinning turn with her arms extended and began to tear away her blouse. The women coaxed her back into it and, mindful of her decency, replaced a stray strap.

The helpers now prevented the woman from dancing blindly out into passing traffic. They placed sprigs of herbs in her cleavage as a ward against 'unwanted' ancestor spirits. And they staved off men who wanted only to bump and grind drunkenly against her. I breathed in the hot body heat of the dead yard, closed my eyes and let a memory intrude of my father in that cold, unforgiving mortuary overseas. His body had been brought up to me from underground storage and lay in unremitting stillness under a shroud. I could not believe that this was my real father, in a real hospital mortuary. That freezing place, with its hum of refrigerators, contrasted starkly with the human heat of the dead yard.

Peter had been apprenticed in Kumina rhythms by his father and, after a lull in the drumming, he played the *kbandu* at Chacha Beng's invitation. Cheered on by Prince, Peter rode the rhythms so hard that he raised the mood in the dead yard to an ecstasy. 'Yes!' Peter shouted encouragement. 'Is it!' The woman now lay motionless on the ground for perhaps half a minute, until she stirred, signifying that she was conscious enough to stand. Quietened down, she was led back to her chair by the helpers, where she sat slumped and spent. At this point Peter and the musicians cut off their rhythms so abruptly that they seemed to hang there in the air for seconds afterwards. During this break more alcohol was smeared on the drumheads and poured down throats. The night was not yet over.

*

I was hardly disposed to like Edward Seaga; behind his courting of Jamaica's Revivalist poor there was a cool brain combined with a canny political finesse. For all his popular appeal, Seaga had a reputation for vindictiveness, violence, and scything his path to power. In 1974 he became the leader of the JLP and, in 1980, prime minister. Along the way, he exploited Afro-Jamaican religions and Pan-Africanist ideology for his own ends. In 1964, for example, he personally arranged for Marcus Garvey's remains to be repatriated from London, thus forging a quasi-Rastafari association with the man they called the Black Moses. After that, Seaga began to incorporate black Revivalist symbols and elements of Afro-Jamaican music into his election campaigns. He was thus able to win the support from swathes of Jamaican society that the leftist PNP had previously called their own. To his enemies, this was mere cynical opportunism or 'voodoo politics'.

All the same, Seaga's knowledge of Afro-Christianity, its music and beliefs, is impressive. In 1969, having graduated in social studies from Harvard University, he published in *Jamaica Journal* an article, 'Revival Cults in Jamaica', which provided the first mainstream account of the island's Afro-Caribbean wakes and burial rites. With a view to preserving Jamaica's indigenous black music, moreover, Seaga had founded West Indies Records Ltd, which issued vinyl recordings of Kumina drumming and Revivalist-inspired ska, the music of his crowded downtown constituency. He understood, as few Jamaican politicians have since, that the best way to reach the Jamaican people was through the music.

'I'll happily talk to you about Revivalism,' Seaga had told me on the telephone, 'but not about politics.' (Seaga had been misquoted enough times by journalists.) We met at his office in the University of West Indies in Kingston, where he had been a Distinguished Fellow since retiring from politics in 2005. The office was cluttered with display cabinets full of academic awards and diplomas picked up round the world. I was struck first of all by Seaga's extraordinary whiteness and restless manner. Throughout our conversation, a nerve in his face twitched with a tic.

Seaga had conducted the bulk of his doctoral investigations in St Thomas. Why? 'Because St Thomas is *the* Kumina parish – the Anglican church never got much of a foothold there, it's too remote.' Seaga added, 'Kumina comes out of the Angola region – West Central Africa – and it's survived in St Thomas as a largely *African* ceremony, one where the ancestral dead have the power to influence us from beyond the grave.'

His fieldwork was indebted to the black American folklorist Zora Neale Hurston (a luminary of the Harlem Renaissance) who, in 1936, had set out to explore Jamaica's Africa-derived religions. In *Tell My Horse* (1938), her magnificent ethnographic account of Jamaican (and Haitian) animist practice, Hurston concluded that Jamaica was a 'seething Africa under its British exterior'. The book remains a key work in the literature of Caribbean folk life, and the Seaga version of Revivalism drew on it.

'True,' he said, when I put this to him, 'Hurston was an influence. Mark you, it can't have been easy for a foreigner – and a woman, at that – to infiltrate Revival. Hurston must have had nerves of steel.'

'And you?'

'And me?' The tic in Seaga's right eye had stopped. 'Well, my mother was a Seventh Day Adventist and extremely apprehensive about my living with the sufferers.' That word again. Like many middle-class Jamaicans, she took a dim view of Afro-animist cults and her son's penetration of the Jamaican world of so-called superstition. Kumina and Revival, far from being inspired by the Holy Spirit, were regarded by Seaga's Adventist mother as undisciplined, even animal beliefs. She was mortified when, in the early 1960s, as the JLP's minister of development and welfare ('minister of devilment and warfare'), her son decided to live among the urban poor in Kingston's Back-o-Wall ghetto. Seaga then became intimate with Revivalist 'shepherds' – as well as port-workers, higglers, domestic servants. For a scion of a Jamaican Lebanese merchant family, this was considered unseemly.

In the 1950s and 1960s, Seaga made a series of reel-to-reel recordings of music in Back-o-Wall and St Thomas. These are deposited in the library of the Institute of Jamaica in Kingston, and I went there to listen to them. The recordings, interrupted by background murmurs, *sotto voce* remarks and the voice of Seaga himself ('Cut eight – spool one'), reveal percussive African beats with high-pitched hallelujahs and a repetitious Kumina rhythm vaguely reminiscent of Steve Reich's minimalism. Coming through the headphones was an ancient, Africa-derived music of mass-participation aimed at inducing spirit possession. Most religions in Jamaica formally reject possession (or *'myal'*, possibly from the Hausa tribe word *maye*, 'intoxication'), yet Baptists and Methodists may sometimes quietly and unobtrusively become entranced in church. Rastafari, despite its claim to be the most Africa-oriented of all Jamaican religions, affects to despise Revival as mere animist worship. Yet even Rastas may on occasion call down the spirit of Haile Selassie through collie weed intoxication.

For all that I knew about Seaga, ours had been an enjoyable conversation. 'Go to St Thomas – that's where you'll feel the hypnotic sway of Revival,' he had assured me.

*

It was close to four in the morning when we left the dead yard, and the stars were putting out one by one. Prince, driving away from Leith Hall, looked at me in the rear-view mirror. 'Well, Mr Ian, good show, no?'

'Good show,' I agreed. My face was blotched with insect bites.

'Nuh worry, Mr Ian,' said Peter, sitting next to me. 'Everything smooth an' cool.'

Back at Stanton Estates I bolted the jalousies in my room, and watched a lizard suction-fix itself to the ceiling. Revival seemed to offer a very comforting cosmology, where the ancestral dead are always close to the living. As the Jamaican anthropologist Jean Besson had told me, 'All those ancestors in one's back yard!' After her father died in 1986, Revival had helped her through 'a very difficult time'. Still I could not sleep off the hot Revivalist night, but lay restless in bed, waiting for daybreak.

13

Don't Call Us Immigrants

Linval Cousins, a Jamaican enthusiast for Queen and country, was born in St Thomas in 1933 but had lived in north London now for over a quarter of a century. On Dowsett Road – his Tottenham address – the only reminder of his native Jamaica was a West Indian takeaway: Peppers and Spice. Otherwise, Cousins complained, his street had gone 'all foreign', by which he meant 'East European'. It annoyed him that Poles and other immigrants from the former Soviet bloc were allowed to travel and work freely in Britain. 'They can't sing a word of the national anthem, can they? They're immigrants, that's why.'

Perhaps the Poles reminded him too painfully of what he used to be like. Perhaps abusing the next wave of immigrants is how earlier waves seek to prove their assimilation. 'I know all my British hymns,' Cousins protested. 'That's as British as you can get.'

'Define British,' I asked him.

'British? Well . . . Just don't call us immigrants.'

Cousins had left St Thomas in 1955 – the year Jamaica 'celebrated' three centuries of British rule. He was full of hope for a better future and felt secure in his British citizenship. But seven years into his London life, in 1962, the British government passed the Commonwealth Immigrants Act. By imposing tough new restrictions on entry into the UK (only migrants who had employment contracts or specific skills or who were the dependants of immigrants who had already settled in Britain were allowed in), the Act discriminated heavily against 'coloured' Commonwealth citizens. It was a humiliation for Cousins to have to provide re-newed evidence of his British citizenship. He thought of going back to Jamaica but reckoned it was too late for that. 'I felt I was marooned in England,' he said, permitting himself a note of despair. The more his life was lived in Britain, the more his ties to and involvement with Britain – despite the existence of organisations like the British Ku Klux Klan, the English Rights Association and the Racial Preservation Society – bound him to it. Gradually it dawned on him (as it did on many British West Indians) that the dream of return was just that: he was here to stay. 'Not that we older folk wanted to go back to what we'd once been in Jamaica – it wasn't much.' The one time Cousins did return to Jamaica, in the early 1980s, he found the island had changed utterly. 'The old sense of community had gone – everyone's an individual now.'

He leaned back in his chair, and contemplated the damp patch on the ceiling. 'Jamaica needs Britain to be strong again – we need the British to take care of us.' A lifetime ago, perhaps, that might have been possible; but the British Empire was long dead, and Cousins was better off now that Greater Britain had dissolved. Still, it would take more than the collapse of the Empire to undermine his relationship with Britain. The idea of Mother Africa and the Rastafari movement emerging in Jamaica following the Empire's demise was anathema to Cousins. Africa, far from being the cradle of mankind, was for him almost a place of ancestral shame.

His older brother, Lorenzo 'Larry' Cousins, was a Justice of the Peace in the unfrequented uplands of St Thomas. Richmond Gap (formerly Wilson Gap), the village where Larry lived, was not marked on my map of Jamaica, but at the Morant Bay courthouse I was able to negotiate the fee for a taxi there. Four other passengers accompanied me, all of them women. One was a security guard, the others, higglers.

At Bottom Pen we rattled over a bridge where the river was roaring white beneath us. Rainfall is ordinarily sparse in St Thomas, the riverbeds cracked and dry, but Hurricane Dennis had caused cars to vanish in mudslides and graves to be uprooted in torrents of water. Beyond Trinityville the river had pushed houses off a gully bank. Landslips had inundated an ackee-canning factory and even a dairy farm. The female security guard, surveying the devastation, announced, 'I'll get out of Jamaica if it's in a suitcase. Don't know when, but before I dead I do it.' The sight of drowned trees and collapsed houses drew gloomy comments from the higglers, too. 'God strike me dead if I don't migrate to 'Merica.' At this the security guard laughed; fat chance, she probably thought.

Larry Cousins was waiting for me at the police station in Cedar Valley, not far from Richmond Gap. Inside the wood-frame bungalow, painted a constabulary blue and white, a woman officer was talking to a tall thin man in his eighties. He looked up as I walked in. 'Mr Cousins?' I asked, and he replied, 'Call me Larry.' I followed Larry to his old Land Rover parked outside. Round his midriff he wore a leather truss. Two years earlier his car had slipped over the roadside and somersaulted three times down a ravine, coming to rest against a tree. 'It's a miracle I survived,' he commented, apparently unruffled by the memory.

As we drove uphill through old slaveholding estates, the landscape was increasingly forbidding. St Thomas, at around 5,500 feet, looked like a massive rock outcrop, with here and there a clump of green jungle like rampant broccoli. Along the road, farmers called out 'Justice!' to Larry in deference to his JP status. To these people of the interior, Larry was a well-liked man, their first link with the government and the wider world. Here in rural St Thomas it seemed a respect for elders persisted, and I was pleased it did. Larry was everything the locals expected: kind, gentle, humorous, as well as a little melancholy.

After an hour we arrived at a shed-like structure on the edge of an abandoned coffee field. 'Welcome to my shop,' Larry said. We parked in a strip of garden desultorily planted with grapefruit trees, the fruit mottled green and, according to Larry, 'bee-sucked'. Inside, shelves were lined with tins of fruit juice, lengths of dried cod, packets of Black Cat cigarettes and half-bottles of rum – the stock-in-trade of the Jamaican country trader. Life in Richmond Gap, a settlement of perhaps twenty families, was tough. Most of Larry's sixty acres of land were lying idle. Farming was considered 'slave's work', Larry explained; it was linked with backwardness and degradation. The young had therefore left for Kingston: anything to break free of sugar cane.

Outside the shop, I saw a gaunt-looking man approach, machete in hand.

'Phensic!' Larry called out to him (as in the headache pill 'Phensic').

The men embraced, and with a jolt I realised that I had met Phensic's father in Brixton, south London, some months earlier. Over drinks in the Paulet Arms, Cedric Wilson had told me he had six or seven children, 'give or take one or two', and that one of them lived in Richmond Gap. I asked Phensic if his father was Cedric and he looked at me with astonishment. But I soon fell silent as the present moment of heat, dust and poverty returned. Phensic cultivated a few bananas and carrots to sell on Fridays in Morant Bay market. He knew this land the way a dog knows a bone, a land fissured and strewn with stones, and given over to neglect, where men like Phensic each day faced destitution.

*

Another mile or so of driving brought us to Larry's house, which commanded spectacular views all round of the parish. 'What do you think?' Larry asked me, his arms extended in a sweep that embraced the St Thomas hills and the glittering sea beyond. We were at the highest point in the parish. 'I think it's amazing,' I said, truthfully. This land, with its unruly natural beauty, was associated with the Jamaican outlaw Three-Fingered-Jack who, having lost two fingers in a fight, was eventually ambushed and killed by Redcoats in St Thomas in 1781. *Obi: or, Three-Fingered-Jack*, was staged in London in 1880 to wild cheering crowds. A pantomime, it equated runaway slaves with black magicians or obeahmen from Africa and confirmed the British public's view of West Indian field-hands as devil-worshippers. A similar prejudice and Uncle Tom minstrelsy ('See the Lawd Gawd dere!') is evident in such Jamaican novels as *A Quality of Violence* (1959) by Andrew Salkey, an account of religious oblivion and rum-fuelled Revivalist devilry in turn-of-the-century St Thomas.

Larry unlocked the front door and we went into his kitchen with a single barred window high up on one wall. He poured two glasses of fruit juice for us and led me through mosquito-screened doors into another room, where we made ourselves comfortable in facing chairs.

Larry wanted to tell me about Britain at the war's end, when small, inter-racial communities had begun to evolve in the rooming-house sections of London, and writers and academics were starting to explore the attitude of British whites towards West Indians. Kenneth Little's *Negroes in Britain,* published in 1948, had concluded hopefully that a 'great deal of latent friendliness underlies the surface appearance of . . . prejudice in a large number of cases'. In Brixton, where Larry had settled in 1946, a number of well-intentioned societies had sprung up with the aim of bringing white and black citizens together. The Racial Unity Club, founded by Mary Attlee (sister of the British Prime Minister Clement Attlee), appointed Larry to its committee, while another brotherhood that claimed his attention at this time was the Black and White Social Club, founded in a Brixton church hall in 1947.

These societies were mostly run by white middle-class philanthropists with contacts in the National Council for Civil Liberties and the Institute for Race Relations. Larry was especially fond of Molly Huggins, wife of a governor of Jamaica, Sir John Huggins, who in 1945 had set up the Mass Marriage Movement in Jamaica. The movement aimed to halt the spread of 'promiscuity' and premarital sex in the island by encouraging couples to marry and stay married. It did not meet with much success. Lady Huggins had also set up, in south London, the Metropolitan Coloured People's Housing Association, which provided low-cost accommodation for Commonwealth citizens newly arrived in Britain. 'Molly was among the best women Jamaica had,' Larry remembered. 'You could call her up any time – she wouldn't mind.'

But, as the 1950s gave way to the 1960s, Larry decided he wanted no part of the nascent multi-cultural, Afro-Asian Britain. He was even, I understood, a reluctant supporter of the 1962 Commonwealth Immigrants Act, which, by restricting the flow of West Indians into Britain, ensured that Jamaicans already resident in Britain had more time to settle and improve themselves without fear of overcrowding and competition. 'I could see that Britain was going to be racially mixed up, that there was even a future in being mixed up,' Larry said to me, 'but in the end I came to believe that Jamaicans belong in Jamaica, not in Britain, or anywhere else.' So, in 1973, after thirty years of exile in Britain, he went home. Today he prefers to think of himself as a Jamaican who had never left Jamaica. 'I don't feel I was ever *really* out of the Yard,' he said.

*

The Jamaican author Evan Jones, for his part, seemed impatient of race distinctions. 'As a child,' he told me, 'I grew up with white Jamaican family members and black Jamaican family members, so I could be with one uncle who was black, and with another who was white; it made no difference to me.' Jones's novel *Stone Haven* (1993) is key, I think, to understanding the life and politics of Jamaica today. The novel filters five decades of island history through the life of a single Jamaican family in Portland parish: the semi-fictional Newtons. Grace, a Quaker missionary from America's Midwest, has defied her family by marrying a 'coloured' Portland planter, Stanley Newton. Stone Haven, the name of the house which Stanley builds for Grace on their marriage in 1920, becomes the focus of the Newton dynasty's increasingly clamorous sexual and political improprieties. Along the way, Jones charts the turbulent years of Jamaica as it struggled for independence up to and beyond the 1970s.

I met Jones, a tall man in his mid-seventies, at his home in south-west London. The study upstairs was cluttered with mementoes from his career as a scriptwriter for Joseph Losey and for BBC television (one of his BBC plays, *The Madhouse on Castle Street*, starred a young Bob Dylan in 1962). When I asked Jones about his mixed race background he replied that he had only encountered colour prejudice, in its legalised form, in America in 1945, when the United States still had 'White' and 'Coloured' signs in railway stations. 'When I first saw those signs I didn't know which waiting room to go into. Black? White?' In the end he just stood on the platform. As the calypsonian Lord Beginner put it in 1952: 'You can never get away from the fact, if you not white, you considered black.' Much the same point is made by Barack Obama in his memoir, *Dreams from My Father*.

In America at that time, Jones would have been described as 'yellow'; in Jamaica, as 'red'; in England, as 'half-caste'. The colour bar in the United States shocked Jamaicans who settled there during the war to work as farm labourers (though it was often seen as preferable to the subterranean, furtive racism of Britain). America nevertheless offered Jamaicans the possibility of employment, as well as a chance to improve their education.

Since his experience of America, however, Evan Jones vowed to see the Jamaican people, not as Black Power or White Power, but as who they are. The greatest honour one can confer on Jamaicans, he said, is to see them as people with 'individual backgrounds and realities', who exist in 'various colours' and in 'separate and different ways'.

I guessed it was easy for Jones to say that. It was only with the help of the 'white' half of his ancestry that he could afford to ignore the Third World notions of 'Blackness' and Pan-Africanism that swept Jamaica in the 1970s. The quest for 'identity' and 'roots' that animated many other Jamaican writers held little or no interest for Jones; he had become as British as his Anglican great-grandfather, who arrived in Jamaica from Wales in 1842 to serve as a church missionary.

In 1952, as befitted his class and colour, Jones came to England in some style. He and a Jamaican friend stowed on a banana boat (no *Windrush* 'immigrant' transport) destined for the London docks. Jones was about to read English at Oxford University and with the money he and his friend won at poker during the voyage they were able to pay for a taxi from London all the way to Oxford. 'Oxford,' they told the cab-driver at the dockside, and the driver said, 'Oxford Street. What number?'

At Oxford, Jones befriended the Jamaican poet and fellow Rhodes scholar Neville Dawes. In a pub one night Jones announced to Dawes that what Jamaica needed now was a literature of its own that would be accessible to the British tradition (Shakespeare, Chaucer), yet rooted in Jamaican patois or *patwa*. Like the Jamaican novelist Claude McKay before him, Jones saw the need for a parallel literary tradition in Jamaica, which would complement the BBC English of 'high culture'. English was officially the language of Jamaica, but it was not the language of most Jamaicans, who spoke (still speak) *patwa,* a vernacular with a folk strength that contains elements of English, Spanish, East Indian and Chinese, as well as words from West Coast Africa. Only by writing in this Caribbean tongue, Jones believed, could he celebrate the Jamaican people in their proper humour, hopefulness, fortitude and worship of God. 'Do it,' Dawes challenged him.

The result was the epic poem 'The Song of the Banana Man'. From the first stanza it was clear that Jones had captured a Jamaican 'back-a-yard' free of the gracious suavities of standard English. A tourist accosts a banana-seller in a market in Portland parish:

> Touris, white man, wipin his face,
> Met me in Golden Grove market place.
> He looked at m'ol clothes brown wid stain,
> An soaked right through wid de Portlan rain,
> He cas his eye, turn up his nose,
> He says, 'You're a beggar man, I suppose?'
> He says, 'Boy, get some occupation,
> Be of some value to your nation.'
> I said, 'By God and dis big right han
> You mus recognize a banana man.

The poem, first broadcast on BBC radio in 1953 and today much anthologised, influenced Linton Kwesi Johnson and other Jamaican 'dub' poets of the 1970s, among them Mutabaruka and the late, great, Michael 'Mikey' Smith. Johnson, who uses a London-sited Jamaican Creole as a weapon of resistance and political protest, told Jones he revered 'Banana Man' as a chant and mantra style verse that 'told it like it was'. In Jamaica, Jones is perhaps better known for his 1975 television documentary, *The Fight Against Slavery*, transmitted each year on Independence Day on 6 August.

Portland parish, where Evan Jones was born in 1927, is a damp and mountainous terrain adjacent to St Thomas. The writer's younger brother, Richard Jones, a vet by training, currently runs the family estates there. At one time these had covered 10,000 acres, but now they were part of the increasingly barren Portland countryside, and drifting towards impoverishment.

*

The house sounded empty when I entered through the front door, and except for a dog, it was. Darlingford, the Jones residence in

Portland parish, had thin-slatted jalousies, mahogany rockers and louvred windows that suggested the peace and serenity of a Victorian-era retreat. After calling out Richard Jones's name, and hearing silence, I wandered down corridors past glass hurricane lamps and white-painted wicker chairs. On a walnut table was a leather-bound visitors' book signed in 1975 – I noted with interest – by Bob Andy. Andy, whom I had met in Patrick Town, Kingston, had married into the Jones family; he is the model for the reggae singer Hungry Man in *Stone Haven*. On another table was a note from Richard: 'Make yourself at home.'

Darlingford, arrived at by obscure bushland paths, had been built in 1910 on a giddy clifftop above the Caribbean Sea half a mile off the road from Morant Bay. The silence in my room was broken by the crash of seawater on the rocks below. I took a shower, then set out on foot for Manchioneal, where the Reverend Jones had built his missionary church in the 1840s.

Once a prosperous port run by the United Fruit Company, Manchioneal survives today through fishing and, occasionally, drugs. Bales of cocaine dumped by Colombian dealers as they try to evade the US Coast Guard get washed up against the Manchioneal coast and are picked up by fishermen. Under cover of dark the fishermen take the bales, weighing up to 300 kilos, to neighbouring Haiti, where they can exchange them for money or guns. They reach Haiti by dead reckoning – without the aid of stars or navigational instruments: a hazardous business.

Manchioneal, when I got there, lay stifling and somnolent across a horseshoe bay. Hard by the Victorian Anglican church a group of Rastafarians was pushing a boat out to sea and on a ribbon of sand at the sea's edge a John Crow (vulture) spread its wings over a piece of carrion. Just beyond Manchioneal was a village called Hector's River, where a Quaker meeting was about to begin. My uncertain religious instincts made me uneasy about trespassing on the meeting, yet I admired the Quakers. From the 1780s onwards, the pacific and democratically minded Quakers had been at the forefront of abolition. The 'Inner Light' of God's revelation shone equally on all human beings, they believed, regardless of their race or class. However, the all-important sense of guilt at the heart of

Quaker missionary endeavour, and the attendant prohibitions of drink and extra-marital sex, had not greatly appealed to the freed slaves.

Instead, the bulk of Quaker converts in Jamaica was made up of contract labourers from India known as 'coolies' (a Chinese term for lowly manual labourer). Evan Jones's mother, an American Quaker from the Midwest, had converted so many Indians to Quakerism that her Portland parish meeting house became the 'coolie church'. It was of no concern to Mrs Jones that Indians already had their own religious faith, and she made no distinction between any of India's vast range of cultures and religions: Hindus, Sikhs, Buddhists, Muslims, Jains – all alike were heathen and ripe for salvation in her eyes.

*

At Hector's River the Seaside Friends Meeting House was a solemn concrete building with stained glass windows. A woman in church-going white greeted me: 'Friend, you look like a stranger.'

'I *am* a stranger.'

'So where you from? From distant parts?'

'England.'

'But I *know* your country!' Her daughter, she said, lived in Tottenham ('Tottenham N17', she specified). The woman held up a thick black book, and smiled. 'Thank you for coming to Seaside, my dear, and take time off to be holy.'

The service was given by Dr Horace Hall, a lay preacher of Indian descent, whom I had met earlier in Morant Bay. Hall had gone to Quaker school in Portland parish in the 1960s, and retained (he said) a very Quaker morality. The stern injunctions on his surgery walls – 'Smoking Is Dangerous', 'Do Not Abuse Alcohol' – suggested as much. Jamaicans can be very moralistic, yet the Quaker movement now has no more than 400 registered members in all Jamaica. The rise of Pentecostalism – what Dr Hall called 'the more emotional sort of Church' – had contributed to the decline in numbers. Quakerism's silent inward address to God, together with its disciplined pietism, contrasts unexcitingly with Pentecostalism's good-time effervescence.

Quaker hymns, especially, had lost their appeal to the young.

'What's needed is a livelier tempo,' said Dr Hall, and with this in mind he had made efforts to incorporate 'up-beat sounds' into Quaker prayer meetings. 'But the traditionalists, the old-time people, they don't want the hand-clapping and the tambourines.'

Dr Hall smiled brightly, neatly. 'We ask for simplicity in dress – we don't believe in ritual: no baptisms, no other extravagances. We practise what I call social living and a life of committed social service.' The early British Quakers, with their loud public prophesying and rejection of conventional society, in some ways foreshadowed Rastafari. *Social Living* was the title of a reggae album by Burning Spear. Dr Hall paused for emphasis. 'Like I say, we practise Christian togetherness, and we do so in deference to God.' But he concluded doubtfully: 'We Quakers *have* to change, otherwise we'll die out. And I'm sure we *will* continue to exist, in some form or other.'

*

Dr Hall arrived at the Sunday meeting in a brown suit and matching tie. 'Morning, Doc,' the Quakers greeted him. 'Morning, friends,' he said. Fifty strong, the congregation was made up of women and children of Indian or part-Indian ancestry. Dressed in blues and pinks, the children wriggled uncomfortably on the oak pews while an elderly woman rose to speak from an improvised pulpit. Her voice increased in volume as she began to fulminate against the sinful life. 'The devil is smart, oh very SMART. My friends, is he not smart?' Nobody answered. In a hushed but still emphatic voice she went on: 'Oh Lord, send us the old-time POWER because we're stepping out into the light . . .' Here was the Pentecostal influence of which Dr Hall had spoken, the evangelical fulminations against rum and punnani ('pussy').

The sermon over, Dr Hall announced: 'Today we have a very special guest – a warm Quaker welcome, friends, to Ian from England.' Oh no. 'Please stand up, Ian, so that we may see thee.' I got up and smiled, mindful of my dirty, sweat-charged clothes. 'Ian's writing a book on Jamaica,' Dr Hall went on. 'And you can hardly write a book on Jamaica *without* taking into account the Quakers.' This was said lightly, as Dr Hall was anxious that it should not be taken as a church sermon. The ceiling fans whirred and clacked, while we filed out to the strains of 'He Who Would Valiant Be' by the Non-Conformist John Bunyan. Pray for Jamaica. Pray for all those souls out there in the dark. Oh Lord.

*

When I got back to Darlingford a dreadlocked man was leading a horse by the reins across the lawn. 'How you?' he called out as I approached. 'Okay,' I shouted back. Three other horses stood cropping the grass. The Rastafarian, as I knew from Evan Jones, trained horses for the Kingston racetrack. 'You were admiring my arses,' he said. It sounded like a statement, not a question.

'Arses?'

'Yeah, man,' he gestured to one of the chestnut mares. 'The *arses* them.'

'Oh them!' I replied. 'Nice, nice.'

The man blinked. 'Name's Winston Bernard, but everybody call me Bobcat. I look after the '*orses*,' he said in an amused tone. 'You know Mr Jones?'

'I've met Evan, but not his brother Richard.'

'Richard's the boss.' Bobcat flicked his cigarette accurately into a watering can on the lawn. 'Richard call the shots.'

Bobcat was forty-four but, with his somewhat long curling lashes, looked younger. When not training horses he scratched a living in Manchioneal as a fisherman.

'You've worked a long time for Richard?'

'Oh, a good likkle time now,' Bobcat said, grinning strangely. He seemed to like Richard because Richard never 'acted the Massa'. Not all Jamaican landowners were known for their even-handedness.

*

Back in my room, the windows thrown open to catch the salt air, I sensed a pre-storm sultriness. Darkness was less than an hour away, something chaotic was stirring.

The cook, Hopeton Patterson, emerged from the kitchen, stopped to say hello to me then went to the veranda where he laid the table. As he did so, I watched the sun disappear into a bank of rain clouds over Portland parish. Visitors to Jamaica often remark on the sadness that falls on the island after sunset. There is scarcely any twilight in

Jamaica; when the sun sets, it is dark, finally and completely.

Hopeton did not permit himself to smile much. Years of deference had obliged him to be blank-faced. He knew 'The Song of the Banana Man' from school and was amazed, years later, to wait on its author, Evan Jones. There was no bitterness in Hopeton's voice (more like pride, if anything) as he described his impoverished childhood in nearby Cedar Valley, where he had grown up as one of fifteen children. Kingston, to his mind, was a loveless place, where there was more 'scoundrel', more 'thief', more 'whore' and 'murderer' than anywhere else in Jamaica. His wife came from Kingston, and Hopeton was estranged from her. The one, all-shadowing trouble of Hopeton's life seemed to be his three-year-old daughter: who should take care of her? Tonight, Alicia was content to be with her father, and in the kitchen, amid a rattle of crockery, she looked up at me curiously as Hopeton poured her a cup of brown-sugar lemonade. In a land of absent fathers, Hopeton defied the stereotype.

As I ate on the veranda the storm welled up with real violence. To right and left of me, high winds lashed the trees, sending grit and sand flying in whirls. Under the awning I stayed dry but on the rocks down below the sea waves were mounting, and a hard rain was slanting now against the palms. A rainy night in Portland. But, just as suddenly as the storm had begun, it ended. The abruptness of the Jamaican weather, like the abruptness of the Jamaican temper, can leave you feeling disorientated.

*

'This land used to be an Eden on earth,' Richard Jones said to me as we stopped off for coffee in Manchioneal, 'but it's been abandoned now.' In the familiar story, migration had sent everybody packing to Kingston. Jamaica had *become*, in a sense, Kingston. And while Richard struggled to cultivate coconuts and bananas, leaf-spot disease and bad weather had forced him to rely on Jamaica's oldest and most bitter crop: sugar. He was agonised by financial worries; Jamaica appeared to be drifting towards disaster on a tide of American imports. These included not only clothes, cars, guns and electrical goods, but sugar. Today, after a generation of 'development' since independence in 1962, Jamaica was neither the industrialised country it had wanted to be, nor the agricultural country it once was. According to Jamaican trade statistics released in 2003, 55 per cent of Jamaica's goods are imported from the United States.

We drove through the Jones family estates, passing mile after mile of unused, unredeemed land, once flourishing but now given over to wild growth; in legal parlance, *in ruinate*. Most of the villagers worked on Jones properties. In the sugar season from January to July they cut the cane and transported it to the sugar factory at Duckenfield. The factory workers proudly called themselves 'engineers' and commanded a certain respect locally. During this slack time of year, however, when the cane required little attention, time hung heavy on the Duckenfield machinists and fieldhands alike. Petty thieving and drunkenness increased. And with the rum-drinking, sometimes, came violence.

Richard could not afford to be discountenanced by these human dramas. Earlier that morning Hopeton and Bobcat had been found siphoning off vodka from the Darlingford drinks cabinet; Richard had had words with them, but no more than that. On his estates he had men and women of all ages who respected and even loved him; it would have been pointless to fall out with them over a quantity of missing vodka. As the last-born of the Jones children (what Jamaicans call the 'wash-belly' child), Richard anyway belonged to a less strict generation.

*

On a chequerboard plain of cattle settlements and grazing pens, Hordley village came to view. Matthew 'Monk' Lewis, the English Gothic novelist, had owned estates on the St Thomas–Portland border, one of which was Hordley. I was curious to see what (if anything) remained of it. Lewis had visited Hordley for the first time in 1818 during his last and, it turned out, fatal voyage to Jamaica. Expecting Hordley estate to be 'a perfect paradise', instead he found it a 'perfect hell'. The overseer had created his own fief-dom, like a prototype Kurtz, and subjected his slaves to white-man violence. Lewis made two trips to Jamaica during the last three years of his life but he wanted no part of slave-driving. His *Journal of a West India Proprietor* (1834), published a full sixteen years after his death, flickers with the shadowy Gothic imagery of his youthful fiction yet it also brilliantly captured that uncertain period in Jamaican history between slavery's abolition in 1807 and emancipation twenty-seven years later.

Nothing since Lewis's debut Gothic novel, *The Monk*, was as good as the Jamaican journal he kept intermittently between 1815 and 1818. It opens in England: Lewis, determined to improve the conditions of his Jamaican slaves, is about to sail from Gravesend laden with trinkets, beads and other gifts for them. Arriving first at his 1,600-acre estate in the west of Jamaica, he sets up a lying-in hospital for the slaves and abolishes the lash. These innovations came a quarter of century before the Crown government under Queen Victoria finally emancipated slaves in the British dominions. By implementing them, Lewis played an honourable if small part in slavery's eventual eradication. For this he earned the respect of his slaves (some of whom later took his name: Lewis is now one of the most common surnames in Jamaica), as well as the contempt of his neighbours.

Yet Lewis's attitude to what he called 'the execrable slave trade' was ambivalent. Though benignly protective of his slaves, he feared (like Governor Eyre forty years after him in the 1865 Morant Bay rebellion) that too-hasty emancipation might lead to the expulsion, or worse, of Jamaica's minority white population.

In the summer of 1816, after his first visit to Jamaica, Lewis travelled to Switzerland to visit his friends the poet Percy Bysshe Shelley, his wife Mary and Lord Byron. At their villa overlooking Lake Geneva Lewis unsettled his guests with tales of 'zombification' and the brutalities he had witnessed first-hand in Jamaica. Incredulously his hosts learned that sugar cane was grown in Jamaica. Sugar cane! The uprooter and enslaver of men! Cultivated and reaped by Lewis! One year later, on 5 November 1817, Lewis returned to Jamaica, this time having altered the beneficiaries of his will to include his slaves.

He stayed at Hordley for just five days, but that was enough for him to see how his slaves had been 'maltreated with absolute impunity' by their overseer. Lewis dismissed and demoted the staff responsible, and on 4 May 1818 he left for England. To his mother he wrote from shipboard, 'You see I am still alive, which is strange enough, for I have been doing everything that makes other people die outright here.'

Lewis had in fact developed Yellow Fever. During his homeward voyage to England he managed to scrawl in his journal, 'It is a matter of perfect indifference to me what becomes of this little ugly husk of mine.' Those were to be virtually his last recorded words. He died on 16 May and was buried at sea, but his coffin was seen to bob up and drift back across the Gulf of Florida towards Jamaica. He had never married, but a relative reported that he 'provided very liberally for his beloved Mother, who mourned his loss'. Byron, on hearing of his friend's death, wrote:

> I would give many a sugar cane
> Matt Lewis were alive again.

*

On the outskirts of Hordley the road climbed above banana groves, dark green amid the lighter green of sugar canes. Hector's River flowed to our left and wisps of smoke coiled off the riverside fields. The road – made of Barber-Greene asphalt – was named the Ken Jones Highway after the JLP minister and brother of Evan and Richard Jones, who died after falling drunk off a hotel balcony in Jamaica in 1964. (Ken Jones is portrayed in *Stone Haven*, not very flatteringly, as the alcoholic politician John Newton.)

At Hordley works yard a group of Rastafarians was busy repairing cane carts. Smoking lung-scorching Lion Pride cigarettes (imported from India), they nodded a laconic greeting as we arrived. Nearby a man in a hard hat was consulting a clipboard. Seeing Richard, he hailed him with an uplifted hand and came over to greet us.

'Morning, Mr Jones, sir.'

'Morning, boss,' said Jones.

Courtesy of this sort is quite common in rural Jamaica.

The man in the hard hat shook my hand with both of his and smiled in welcome. He introduced himself as Henry Gray, the Boiling House Superintendent of the Duckenfield sugar factory. Richard asked him to show me round Hordley great house and he laughed softly at the request. 'Hordley great house? How come I never heard of it?' This was because the property lay concealed in vegetation; battered by the hurricane in 1988, it had been left to rack.

Hordley, situated not far from the works yard, was, sure enough, smothered by greenery. Accompanied by Gray I forced my way inside. The remains of a double stairway emerged from the undergrowth and, where the roof had been, light leaked through a lattice of vegetation. In the green-tinged light we could make out a stone 'cooler' window and the remains of a stone porch, its brickwork spangled with flowering plants. Surreally, a fig tree had taken root in the window ledge and spread down the side like Daliesque chocolate. Hornets were flying round the ledge with a low drone. Gray confessed he was afraid of them.

He was born in Golden Grove – the sugar cane shanty of 'The Song of the Banana Man' – in 1957. His Hindu parents were descended from labourers imported from the British Raj to meet the labour shortage following emancipation in 1834. His father's name of Lal had been changed to 'Gray' by an ignorant Scottish overseer, who was unable to pronounce it. Henry Gray himself seemed to care little for his Indian ancestry. What caste his grandparents were, where in India they came from, was only of academic interest to him. Quakers had converted his parents to Christianity and his parents in turn had extinguished all traditional Indian practice from their home. Henry later rebelled against their new-found militant Christianity. 'And I'm *still* rebelling,' he said, as 'My Boy Lollipop' (certainly not a Quaker hymn) blasted from his car radio.

Holland Bay, flat and as dream-like as a Dutch painting, had been irrigated in Matthew 'Monk' Lewis's day by a network of canals which, though now overgrown, still showed in the odd cut-stone bank. Scottish engineers had harnessed river-water to flow down the canals; the canals not only powered the water mills, but floated barge-loads of sugar out to the sea. 'Man! The amount of planning and engineering that went into making this place work!' Henry exclaimed. From the Lewis family, ownership of Holland Bay had devolved to the British planter-politician Simon Taylor, 'the richest proprietor in the island', who died in 1813 in Jamaica. Almost two centuries later, in 1987, villagers descended on his tomb in St Thomas and demolished it with pickaxes, leaving slabs of funerary marble lying broken in the grass. A rumour had circulated that a stash of gold was hidden in the tomb; nothing of any value was found.

The desecration of the Taylor tomb might well exemplify rural Jamaica's reputation for superstition combined with violence. Plantation lands, with their history of brutality and romantic air of neglect had fascinated Matthew Lewis. 'Nothing can be imagined more sublime or more beautiful than this scenery,' he noted in his journal. A strain of 'Jamaican Gothic' runs through many other British accounts of the island. William Beckford, in his *Descriptive Account of the Island of Jamaica* (1790), described a place of otherworldly beauty and fascination, 'truly sublime', yet also 'with some degree of pleasing horror'. Two centuries later in *The Wide Sargasso Sea* (1966), Jean Rhys wrote of a comparably strange landscape. Even Ian Fleming, in his Jamaican novels *Dr No* and *The Man with the Golden Gun*, offered glowing sketches of a 'sublime' landscape in the pre-Romantic Gothic vein of Beckford and Lewis.

A more recent novel, *John Crow's Devil* (2005), by the Kingston author Marlon James, took the Gothic element in 'Monk' Lewis to an extreme. The novel recounts a tale of Jamaican religious mania that occurred in 1957 five years before independence, in the fictitious village of Gibbeah somewhere in the Revivalist heartlands of St Thomas. A spirit of witchcraft descends on Gibbeah, while the inhabitants are plagued by John Crows and other devilish omens. The novel, thrillingly macabre, seems to encourage the view of countryside Jamaica as a place overrun by devilry, pillage and extortion, where tombs are broken open and villagers stoned to death in attempts to exorcise the 'kingdom of Satan'.

*

Continuing our tour, Henry Gray was now standing by a stone humpbacked bridge in front of a ruined Georgian great house. 'Man, it's beautiful here,' he said, smiling. '*Beautiful.*' The rowing boat he used for fishing was moored in the canal beneath us. Using shrimp for bait, Gray pulls in mudfish, jack, snook, drummer and sometimes also crab. Upstream, he said, the canal broadened into a lake among mangroves, where the water's surface was broken by lilies and floating coconut limbs.

Suddenly a bird flapped squawking from the riverbank and Gray was on the alert. 'Crocodile,' he said. Six years ago, beneath this very bridge, a boy had been killed by a crocodile. His family had gone hunting for the reptile but it was never found. A little later, some friends of Gray's visiting from Guyana had wrestled a crocodile out of the canal, killed it and cooked it for supper. 'The tail was a bit gamey,' recalled Gray.

'Was it *the* crocodile?' I asked him.

'Mos' def.'

Next, we took a side road heading for Morant Point, where a lighthouse was said to mark the easternmost point of Jamaica – a 'miracle of British engineering', Gray called it. On the way we passed Golden Grove, Gray's birthplace, where the cane-cutter hovels were pervaded by the aroma of clarified butter and curry, a heavy and overbearing smell that Gray said he associates with colonialism and the British Raj. 'Anyone living in the cane belt is poor,' he remarked.

Beyond Golden Grove, a 'lethal yellowing' disease had invaded the cane fields and taken the heads off the coconut trees. A tangle of prehistoric aerial roots announced a mangrove swamp on our left. 'A little tang of hydrogen sulphide in there,' said Gray, noting the swamp's rotten egg stench. In the autumn months he likes to drive down here to watch the ducks fly in from North America and skim the swamp's brackish waters.

We were now at the eastern extremity of Jamaica. Frigate birds hung motionless in the air, their long beaks angled down like hornet stings. At the end of a dirt track a wire-mesh fence impeded our way. A notice cautioned: 'PORT AUTHORITY. TRESPASSERS WILL BE PROSECUTED'. The fence marked the end of the Jones family properties and the beginning of government land. Gray drove on through a gap in the fence. 'It's like the end of the world down here,' he said. The beach, alternately rocky and sandy, was littered with plastic bottles and other detritus dumped from Panamanian and Colombian tankers.

The lighthouse, painted red and white like a candy-striped barber's pole, stood in a wilderness of thatch palms and salt-scorched trees. According to the plaque, Kru tribesmen transported from Africa had built it in 1842. It had been cast in England at a time when the Empire was still spread in swathes of red across the world. But the Kru tribesmen – had they settled in Portland parish? Or had the great Portland emptiness closed in about them, extinguishing all traces?

A tall thin man was approaching us now, followed by four undernourished-looking children. On reaching us, he said he was the lighthouse keeper, shook a cigarette out of a pack, lit it, and added that he had worked in this bleak station for fifteen years and, yes, those were his four children. 'Does your wife live here too?' Gray asked, making conversation. The keeper studied the lighted end of his cigarette before answering that he did not have a wife, and did not want one, either.

Saying this, he unlocked a door at the base of the lighthouse, and invited us to follow him up the spiral stairway. As we pulled on the stair's brass handrail we passed cast-iron wall panels stamped 'Charles Robinson Late Bramah Engineer, London'; the same panels, riveted and stamped 'Charles Robinson', line the inside of the engine house of the Battersea Waterworks in south London. In the light-room 100 feet up, the air was hot and fuggy, with a reek of engine oil. Twilight was dimming the skies but we could just make out Morant Cays reef, once feared by sailors. Haiti lay 100 miles due east of the reef.

In spite of the light-room's reassuring beacon-code – dark, light-light, dark – ships continue to be wrecked. One day in 2004 the keeper had watched in horror through his binoculars as a tanker swayed on high seas, with a small craft huddled against it. The craft had gone under, and not reappeared. The keeper assumed the passengers were Haitian refugees. If Haitians stray any distance east of Morant Point they will be swept down towards Panama and, most likely, be drowned. Wooden sail-boats had been found 'mashed up' on the shore, with no sign of their crew.

In 2004, an estimated 600 Haitians were swept up on Jamaica's east coast. They arrived in flotillas of sail-boats, dehydrated and starving, at points between Morant Bay and Port Antonio. The majority had intended to sail to Miami, but the north-east trade winds had taken them to Jamaica. They were, most of them, supporters of the Haitian President Jean-Bertrand Aristide, who had been ousted in an American-sponsored coup earlier that year. (His outspoken advocacy of the poor had made him a red bogeyman to Washington.) People in Manchioneal went out of their way to help the Haitians, bringing them what food and clothes they could; they had been at sea, some of them, for up to five days. Having been 'processed' by immigration authorities in Manchioneal, the Haitians were taken to detention centres on the north coast. A lucky few escaped, but most were repatriated to an uncertain future in Haiti.

It was getting dark now and the air, not yet cool, had a tired end-of-the-day smell of damp sand. 'All right, gentlemen,' the lighthouse keeper said to us as the beach turned monochrome in the setting sun, 'twice blessed and good night.' This was a sad place in which to leave the keeper and his ragamuffin children. People mostly avoided Morant Point. Even the beach fishermen, who were no strangers to solitude, kept away from the godforsaken loneliness of this outpost.

14

English Upbringing, Background Caribbean

Port Antonio, capital of Portland parish, radiated a torrid, hothouse decay. The streets were lined with old warehouses and wooden tailor's shops; matchbox buildings, easy come, easy go. At night a damp inshore breeze reached me in my hotel, smelling faintly of muddy water and bananas. It was the sweetish, salty breeze that corroded the metal fittings in people's homes, and bred damp-rot in their clothes. Port Antonio in the period 1880 to 1920 had been Jamaica's chief banana port, shipping out three million bunches of 'green gold' on average a year. A Boston sea merchant, Lorenzo Dow Baker, had introduced banana shipping to the area; his business became the United Fruit Company.

When Port Antonio was booming, American tourists began to arrive, and before long Hollywood had discovered this drowsy 'paradise'. In 1946 Errol Flynn bought a small island here. The British government, worried by the American influence, created the Fyffes banana company in 1913 to rival Dow Baker's, but it ran into financial difficulties and was taken over by United Fruit. My immediate interest in Port Antonio, however, was the sizeable Indian community hereabouts. Indians, referred to in the West Indies as 'East Indians', make up the largest ethnic minority in Jamaica today: between 1.3 and 3.5 per cent of the population. Their migration had been sponsored by the British Colonial Office in 1845, in order to supply post-emancipation Jamaica with plantation labour. It continued for eight decades until just after the First World War. During that time an estimated 38,000 Indians, most of them Hindu, settled in Jamaica from Uttar Pradesh and Bihar, the Punjab and the North-West Frontier province, Assam, Bengal, Orissa and Rajasthan.

Poverty had driven them from their homeland and condemned them to a bonded (usually five-year) contract. Poorly paid, the East Indians lived in overcrowded barracks that offered little privacy to married couples; rape, alcoholism and even murder were not uncommon. The statistics for East Indian fatalities in Jamaica are numbing (as statistics so often are in Jamaica). Out of the 5,500 'coolie' labourers who arrived in 1848, over 1,500 died of malaria or hookworm infestation.

After their five-year term had expired, some 12,000 East Indians went home. (The indenture agreement provided for their return ticket.) Many of them never got beyond the Calcutta docks, and lived out their days as city paupers. The majority stayed behind in Jamaica, where they reverted to their ancestral trades of farming, fishing, jewellery-making and money-lending.

*

De Montevin Lodge, with its barley-sugar columns, pepper-pot roof and gingerbread veranda, had an atmosphere of the spittoon and pot plant. It had once been a United Fruit executive's home. Errol Flynn had planned to turn it into a New Orleans-style brothel but ran out of funds. Port Antonio had everything that Flynn wanted: a warm climate, sailing, rum – and the people spoke English. 'This must be the Paradise written about in the Bible,' the film star announced on his arrival. Swollen with alcohol, and fleeing a statutory rape charge, Flynn launched the tourist's pastime of river-rafting on the Rio Grande and a sexploitation of Jamaican girls that endures to this day. The locals spoke of 'Flynn Fever'.

But Flynn was long dead and De Montevin Lodge (to judge by the alien pubic hair in my bed) had become the lowest type of cheap-rent rooming house. The armchairs in the reception area had been covered in protective see-through plastic, with attendant leopardskin rugs and bouquets of ghetto-fabulous plastic flowers. An elderly woman in high-heeled gold shoes showed me to my room. The walls did not quite meet the ceiling, so I could hear everything next door, usually a Bible television programme turned up to full volume, with the preacher ranting boringly. On my first night I lay on my bed under the lamp's glow and looked up at a picture on the wall of Jesus walking on the water.

*

In Kingston, earlier, I had met a doctor from mainland India, Ajai Mansingh, who had come to Jamaica in 1973 to lecture in entomology at the university. Nowhere in the world, Mansingh believed, had Indian culture been so neglected as in Jamaica. In 1999, hoping to remedy this deficiency, he and his wife wrote and published a book, *Home Away from Home*: *150 Years of Indian Presence in Jamaica 1845–1995*, which charted the iniquities of the British indentureship scheme and the plight of Hindi-speakers in general on the island. Above all, Laxmi and Ajai Mansingh wanted to show how much Jamaican culture was influenced by Indian culture. Rastafari (in their Indocentric opinion) had borrowed not only the 'sacramental practice' of ganja-smoking from Hindu holy men, but also the art of 'meditation' and 'cultivation of dreadlocks'.

'Alas, Mr Thomson, after all these years, we *still* find that Indo-Jamaicans are very ignorant and uninformed about themselves,' said Professor Mansingh. We were sitting in his spacious garden off Bamboo Avenue, midtown, sipping iced tea. He went on: 'Still, I do not regret leaving India, in fact I feel a great happiness to be in Jamaica.' He was keen for me to meet a learned Hindu man or pundit called Nathan Sharma. 'Nathan is Jamaican-born. But he is the man you should see for information on Indo-Jamaican culture,' Mansingh assured me. 'Each week he is going with his offerings to the temple. I will call him now.' He dialled a number on his mobile. Bollywood music banged and wailed from his home as he did so.

'I have successfully contacted the pundit,' the professor said eventually. 'He will be joining us presently. Another cup of tea?'

'No thank you, but the food smells delicious.' A smell of curry was wafting from the kitchen.

'It is curried potato.' Mansingh made a temple of his fingertips. 'And it is excellent.' While we waited for Pundit Nathan to arrive, we had a conversation about Jamaican food and the unreliability (as Mansingh saw it) of Jamaican 'servants'. Until recently, six Jamaican staff had cooked and cleaned for the professor and his wife, but they stole the food (even the grandchildren's milk) from the fridge, as well as, oddly, the plastic models of the Hindu deities. The professor sacked them and employed servants from Mumbai (Bombay) instead. 'Indians don't have this chip that they're being discriminated against – as Jamaicans do,' the professor explained.

He went on, unstoppably, to say that the Indian influence on Jamaica's cuisine was not confined to curried goat. 'All green vegetables in Jamaica – roti, callaloo (what you are calling spinach) – are Indian. In fact,' – Mansingh sniffed the evening's cooking – 'callaloo really developed wings in the 1980s, when it became a regular breakfast option on Air Jamaica. Neither must we forget rice. There was no rice in Jamaica before the Indians came. Only cassava. Only yams. Rice is now the national dish of Jamaica.'

'And ganja?'

'One moment please while I continue with the foodstuffs. Mango, jackfruit, tamarind: all are Indian. And now for ganja. Many Jamaicans have reason to regret its importation, everyone is telling you something different about ganja.'

'What's your view?'

'My view? I am believing that ganja has beneficial effects when taken in moderation.' Mansingh raised his eyebrows. 'It has been used in India as a euphoriant and as a medicine for over 5,000 years. In Jamaica it has been used for 150 years (not a long time, but long enough). Ganja can create serenity of a high order, and this the Rasta Man also has learned from the Hindu.'

'But ganja does not always promote serenity,' I pointed out, pompously. 'Ganja can, in unpropitious circumstances, promote paranoia.'

Mansingh, glancing irritably at his watch, said, 'This also the Rasta Man has learned from the Hindu.'

Pundit Nathan was forty minutes late. It would not do to keep the professor waiting. The Jamaicans' fabled relaxedness was not at all to Mansingh's liking. 'Jamaicans have two speeds,' he told me gruffly, 'dead slow and stop.'

Mansingh emptied his tea cup, held it upside down a moment, and gazed at the cricket bat 'Made in India' resting on his knees. 'Cricket is also an Indian invention,' he was saying, just as Nathan Sharma arrived. The pundit got out of his Mercedes and came over to greet us. He was in his mid-fifties, not very tall, and dressed in white trousers and white shoes. A knife scar ran jagged down one cheek and his hair was sculpted into a high-pomaded, Nat King

Cole pompadour. I got up to shake his hand. 'I'm shockingly late,' he said.

'Oh sit down, pundit,' Professor Mansingh said to him irritably. I sensed India's complex caste separations at work in the way Mansingh had addressed the latecomer. New World Indians like Pundit Nathan – Jamaican by birth – were no longer, in Mansingh's view, of Asia. Their temples existed, all right, but their languages and rituals had decayed long ago. Pointedly, Mansingh did not offer Sharma a drink.

Instead he said to him, 'Mr Thomson here would like to hear you talk.' Sharma ran a finger down the side of his good cheek, looked at me, smiled warily. 'What you want to know?' He had a watch-fulness that contrasted with Mansingh's loquaciousness. The pundit explained that he was a government-registered Hindu priest; his grandfather had been a pundit also. From his grandfather he had learned about Hindu ritual and was taught some Sanskrit.

'Have you never wanted to live in India?' I asked him.

The pundit shook his head. 'India is so different. We Jamaican Indians have moved on – but Indians have not. Indian Indians are very, very poor.' By leaving India, Sharma had reformed but the old country, it seemed to him, had stayed just as it was. The idea of Jamaica – more precisely, Kingston – excited the pundit more than ancestral India. He explained why: 'Most of us Jamaican Indians have made money and done well for ourselves. You won't find us sitting lazy on street corners like the blacks.' The pundit looked nervously at Professor Mansingh, who was glancing at his wristwatch again.

The pundit, like Mansingh, was careful to make a distinction between himself and Jamaica's black majority.

'You can easily distinguish us Indians from the blacks,' he went on. 'We have finer features and finer manners than they do. Yes, we're more . . . mannersable.'

Black Jamaicans were characterised by dullness, 'uncuriousness' and apathy; they made poor businessmen, and they smoked too much weed. To top it all, they were less 'progressive', less 'ambitious' and less 'refined' than East Indians (as well as presumably Indians). It is well known that Indians living outside

India can be rather racist when it comes to other people of 'colour', I reminded myself.

*

At number 114 Hagley Park Road, amid the second-hand Japanese-car dealers, stands Kingston's Hindu Temple. The temple is a small, hangar-like structure set back from the beep and brake of traffic as it crawls on its way to Tinson Pen domestic airport. A Sunday morning *pooja*, or Hindu prayer ceremony, was about to begin. The temple was empty except for a Brahmin (high caste) priest in a Nehru-shirt who was sitting cross-legged on the marble floor, lighting incense sticks. Looking up, he seemed surprised to see me.

'You are coming from – ?'

'England.'

'But you don't look particularly Indian.'

'I'm not Indian.'

I took off my shoes and, at the priest's invitation, sat down on the prayer mat in front of him. Ranged on a dais behind him were statuettes of the blue-skinned Krishna and the all-destroying Shiva.

'England,' he continued, touching the sandalwood caste-mark on his forehead, 'and you are in Jamaica?'

'Yes – I flew in.'

'Heathrow?' His eyes, bird-bright behind spectacles, seemed to dance. 'I have been to Heathrow.' The Brahmin excused himself a moment later to continue with his *pooja* directives. I left him in peace, while his voice settled into a drone and he began to sprinkle water round a tiny, sacrificial flame.

At this point Pundit Nathan turned up. 'You made it!' he said to me with a smile and, removing his white shoes, sat down on the mat by my side. We watched the Brahmin priest, Dinesh Maraj, continue his recital of prayers to the Hindu divinities. The pundit whispered to me, 'Mr Maraj is now scooping out ghee to make a flame to represent the human being.' His cardamom breath was hot on my face. 'Yunnerstand?' The roar of an aeroplane coming in to land muted my reply.

The Brahmin, turning his attention to me, now offered a brief history of the British indenture system by way of background information for my book. 'Your countrymen sent us to Jamaica as paid slaves. We fitted in. We were good agriculturalists. But the blacks were not. They were envious of our cleverness and our financial know-how. They could not build houses for themselves and they could not recite lofty spiritual poetry. And' – his brown eyes were steady on me – 'after all these years the blacks *still* squat on Crown land.'

Incense fumes – a sweet suffocating presence – wafted through the temple as six or seven worshippers, barefoot, arrived to take part in the morning's invocations and debate. 'One thing that we'd like you to know, Mr Thomson,' the Brahmin went on, 'is that we Indians are a very thrifty people – we save up our moneys. At the same time we generously gave the blacks *roti* to eat, did we not?' ('*Roti*' was used here in the colloquial Indian sense, I imagined, of 'dinner', not just bread.)

The priest, speaking now to Nathan Sharma, said: 'Play something for us, pundit. You have done many great deeds in uplifting Hinduism for this island. Play us something for *pooja*.' The pundit, nodding gratefully, unpacked the portable harmonium he had brought with him. Soon his fingers were dancing over the keyboard, the harmonium moaning, as he played a devotional hymn, or *bhajan*, to Ganesh the elephant god. But the Brahmin brusquely interrupted him. 'I'm sorry – could somebody please plug in the fan to ease the heat?' A woman in a green sari went over to the free-standing fan, and switched it on. The pundit, visibly miffed, continued his oration to Ganesh.

A boy banged a gong, the signal for the green-dressed woman to bring out trays of saffron-coloured sweetmeats stowed in a cupboard. She began to serve these to the worshippers on paper plates. She did not wait for the men to eat first (that was a thing of the Asian past), but washed the food down with a Jamaican version of *faluda* milkshake made of Carnation milk mixed with apple juice. Outside on Hagley Park Road, meanwhile, the traffic roared, and the heated air grew hotter, as I took myself back uptown to PJ's.

*

Portland parish, a muggy day in 2007. A spillage of shacks and hutments, with little fenced-off gardens, sheltered the East Indians who had lived in Tom's Hope village since the nineteenth century. Banana trees, planted three-deep, bordered the village paths. The steamy heat released yeasty vapours: I was in the lush Rio Grande Valley and the morning sun had come up, spreading a lemon glow over the semi-jungle. A far-off concussion of hammers indicated that tinkering was a trade still practised here. Small as it was, Tom's Hope was celebrated locally for its organic farm, Tamarind Hill, run by Vincent Slimfort and his wife Joanna.

Vincent Slimfort was approaching sixty but he had jet-black hair and plenty of it, with a dark handsome face – a face that was alive. Born in Tom's Hope in 1943 under his Indian name of Sital-Singh, Vincent had grown up in conditions of near poverty. Child marriage was a commonplace misery for East Indian Jamaicans at the time; it was a world Slimfort knew only too well. His mother, a Hindu, had been married at the age of twelve to Vincent's future father, a Sikh, then a mere thirteen. As a result Vincent took a very dim view of matters such as child brides, the dowry system, caste, and the abolition òf inequalities from which all Jamaican women (not just East Indian women) suffered and continue to suffer.

Above all, Slimfort despaired of the routine degradation of teenage girls in rural Jamaica. 'Sex is the most powerful currency here,' he said to me. 'Older men offer girls food, then go into their houses in return for sex. The girls have a lot of children when they're young – it's not good.'

Slimfort's wife Joanna said, with a concerned expression, 'It's the only way these girls have of showing the world – showing themselves – that they're worth something, that they can *do* something.' The more children a girl can bring into the world, the more potent the man feels. For, just as the girl is only considered 'really' a woman after she has borne a child, so the proof of the man's virility is in making her pregnant. An egregious example of this priapism is Aston 'Family Man' Barrett, formerly the bassist with Bob Marley and the Wailers, who claims to have fathered fifty-two children. (In 2006 Barrett was expunged from the official Marley website after claiming in court that he was owed £60 million in unpaid royalties.) In Kingston I had heard rumours that some Chinese and Lebanese store owners gave girls free food and household items in exchange for sex. Some residents were very upset at the practice, but most others said that it had been happening like that for centuries. Preying on the bodies of girls had indeed been a characteristic of Jamaican slavery. Planters (in the words of one contemporary) preferred 'goatish embraces' with their young slaves to the 'pure and lawful bliss' of married love. Thus a train of 'adulterated beings' – mixed-race Jamaicans – was brought into the world.

'It's a really terrible problem,' Vincent Slimfort continued, 'and it's prevalent right across Jamaica.' Abuse of girls, made worse by its private nature, remains a shameful and buried phenomenon in Jamaica. The collusive silence round the issue protects the abuser and allows the practice to continue. Seeking help from the police is often seen as an act of betrayal; Jamaican girls are *expected* to bear their abuse. 'It's how people do things round there,' said Joanna. And though it does not necessarily imply abuse, she added, eight out of ten Jamaican children are born out of wedlock.

Slimfort's grandparents had come to Jamaica in 1913 during the last years of the British labour scheme. At the recruiting depot in Calcutta they had been full of dreams of the easy wealth to be made in Jamaica. On arrival, however, they were forced into a rural hard slog that came close to a definition of slavery: nine hours a day, six days a week, weeding and cutting in the sugar fields.

Religion offered at least some comfort. The Shiite Muslim minority in Tom's Hope celebrated a dead yard observance called Hosay (or Hussay). For nine days the mortuary rituals went on; Hosay provided an opportunity for an intermingling of faiths and skin colours and cultures, as black Jamaican onlookers were invited to join in with the dancing and drinking. Slimfort is quite moved when he thinks about Hosay today. 'Where else in Jamaica could you find such tolerance, the old-timers getting up to entertain the young, the Hindus helping the Muslims, and the black Jamaicans united with them?' Sadly Hosay has all but vanished from the island.

Slimfort's life-story offered a curious assortment of social self-improvement, ambition and immense love. As soon as they could afford it, Slimfort's parents had gone to London. Their aim was to make enough money there to pay for their son's education at a good London school. They were able to put a deposit on a house in Willesden, north-west London, and two years later, in 1955, young Vincent was summoned to join them. He had scarcely berthed at Liverpool when his father died. He was fifty-seven. 'Every life,' Slimfort stated axiomatically, 'is marked by tragedy.' His mother, alone in the Willesden semi-detached house, was more than ever determined to do right by her son: social self-improvement was her ambition. At Ebury Technical School in Victoria, then at Westminster Grammar, Vincent excelled in maths.

Bullying and racist slights were frequent, but Slimfort gave as good as he got. 'Don't forget – I was physically fit from my childhood in Tom's Hope, swinging from the banana trees.' (That, of course, was what his tormentors said of West Indians: they were 'monkeys' up the trees.) Laughter, said Slimfort, kept him sane in those far away, trying times in 1950s London; that, and study. Hoping to develop a 'top-carat' public school accent, he attended night classes and learned all there was to learn about dukes and lords and princes. He changed his name from Sital-Singh to Slimfort and considered himself a genuine colonial, striving towards metropolitan 'sophistication' and a certain image of England.

Vincent could not suppress a smile at the memory. 'I had this . . . avid yearning for knowledge.' Kilburn Library was 'ransacked' by him. Etiquette books. Social case histories. 'All kinds of stuff.' His East Indian background, he explained, encouraged a desire for social betterment. 'I was planning to be a very intellectual and progressive person. I didn't allow myself to take even *one day* off studies.' He taught himself Latin and he lifted weights like a man who will never be strong enough – body-building night and day. After school he got a job as a laboratory technician in the Cancer Centre at Hammersmith Hospital, mixing doses of radioactive Strontium 90 for £16 a week.

Coming from a British dependency, Vincent had always been fascinated by the British armed forces. In 1961 he began a three-year course in guided Bloodhound missiles at RAF Weston-super-Mare. The Cold War was on. The clock was running down fast on British rule in Jamaica and Slimfort believed he was guarding

British shores against Soviet attack. ('The Russians are Coming', Val Bennett's rocksteady interpretation of 'Take Five', is a classic of Jamaican Cold War phobia from the 1960s.) In Slimfort's mind, Britain's technological pre-eminence coincided with her greatness as a nation, and in 1964 he enrolled at an Officers' Training College in Bedfordshire, where he arrived equipped with his primers on English etiquette. Not surprisingly he was viewed with suspicion by the other West Indian trainees.

'They thought I was a swot,' Slimfort recalled. 'Yes, a swot. But the Jamaicans, they didn't have too much brain. Always bragging they were, always womanising.' Slimfort was seen by his compatriots as an 'honorary white'; each night they threw firecrackers under his bed. Having discharged himself from the army, Slimfort got a job for Burroughs in data processing in London. He installed the Police National Computer Unit and, more prosaically, he computerised the Spiller's dog-food factory in Catford. His secret ambition, though, was to retire to the West Indies in comfort.

In 1983 he opened a hotel in the British Leeward Island of Nevis, and invested in properties there. After eight years on Nevis he met his future wife Joanna Bulova, who was there on holiday. Born in England of Austrian refugee parents, she was a scion of the Bulova jewellery firm. For her, England was the West End of London, a world far removed from East Indian Jamaica. She and Slimfort could not be more different: he, a talkative, twinkling man; she, poised and reserved, with just the wraith of a smile.

Slimfort took Joanna back to Jamaica where in 1990 they got married. Born at the war's end in a 'bamboo hut' in Portland parish, he had come home as a man 're-made' in England. A very West Indian story, this, in its racial and social admixture, and its collision and cohering of roots and cultures. I wondered, did Slimfort think of himself as Asian Jamaican? Indian or British? 'None of those,' he said. He saw himself as beyond and above them, a new kind of fusion. Imperial Britain had given Slimfort an education in Shakespeare and Tennyson, Clive of India, *Kennedy's Latin Primer* and the Anglican Lord's Prayer, and he was grateful for it. Yet he said he was less beholden these days to the idea of England. The British monarchy only served to maintain the delusion about

Britain's great place in the world. 'It's a bit of a con, really,' said Slimfort, with rapidly blinking brown eyes. 'But I bear no grudge. I'm the man who would be English.'

Saying this, Slimfort gave a sudden start, and half rose from his chair. 'Whoa! Here comes the rain!' From far off came a whooshing sound made by fat raindrops as they pelted down on the banana leaves. Moving inexorably towards us, the sound grew louder. 'You get a five-minute warning before the rain falls right on your head,' said Slimfort, with a laugh. Soon the rain was hammering on the roof of the house, and then it was absolutely roaring. But just as suddenly it was quiet again, and the insects were back to whirring round our faces.

*

The Trident Hotel, a Disney-like folly on the Port Antonio seafront, was owned by Earl Levy, a white Jamaican who had been very much a part of Portland's *demi-monde*. The hotel was spookily empty when I arrived, with a recording of Richard Clayderman piped into the forlorn-looking bar.

'Yes sir?' There was nothing on the hotel barman's face, apparently, but boredom.

'Is Earl Levy in?'

'I'll check for you – can I get you a drink?'

He poured me a soda, then spoke into a phone at the end of the bar. When he came back he told me that Earl Levy was away in Vienna with Errol Flynn's widow; he would be happy to see me on his return.

My impression, as I carried the soda over to the dining room, was that I was in a re-make of *The Shining*, where the hotel is alive with unseen ghosts. The dining room, quite empty, was decorated with vases of peacock feathers and bowls of potpourri. Camp? I should say so. The bright red, frilly table cloths looked like coffin linings. I took a seat. Twenty minutes went by and the piped Clayderman coming though a mock-Greek archway had changed tempo without my noticing it.

Truly vibrant tourism in Jamaica only exists in the north coast resorts of Negril and Montego Bay. They present a white man's fantasy of a 'paradise', one in which Jamaicans are vendors of coconuts and coloured beads, their native calypso-reggae 'pulsing' exotically behind them. In Negril especially, you feel you are in a Disneyfied version of Jamaica. On the day I visited, life-size Sesame Street puppets wobbled up and down the beach, dispensing beer and hot dogs to groups of Americans too scared to leave the environs of their hotel.

There was no one to leave the Trident Hotel, however, because the Trident Hotel was empty. I had brought along my book, *Slaves Who Abolished Slavery* (1985), by the Jamaican historian Richard Hart, about Jamaica's runaway slaves or Maroons. I was reading the introduction when a shadow fell across my table. 'Tonight the chef is recommending fish fingers,' the waiter announced as he handed me a menu decorated like an illuminated manuscript.

'Fish fingers?'

'I am sorry' – he corrected himself – 'on this night we have soup and a curried goat.'

'Sounds good. But tell, me is the Trident always this empty?'

'These days, yes. We really could do with some business.' The waiter's string vest showed through his white shirt.

I went back to reading my book and was halfway through the chapter 'The Beginning of Black Resistance' when the waiter announced at my elbow, 'Your bread roll, sir'; and, lifting the lid of an aluminium salver, transferred the roll to my plate with a pair of tongs. 'Water, sir?' I said yes but immediately wished I had not. A too enthusiastic measure was poured and ice cubes plopped from the jug on to my lap. With an apology the waiter began to remove the cubes with his white-gloved hands (though not, I am glad to say, with the tongs). The atmosphere in the dining room was now more *Carry On* than *Shining*. Having successfully disposed of the ice cubes, the waiter continued to hover, his brow creased in a troubled smile, at my table.

The mulligatawny, when it arrived, was garnished with a whorl of stiff cream substitute. I waited in apprehension for the curried goat. As I ate the goat the dining-room lights went out one by one, and by the time the coffee had arrived I was in semi-darkness. A fingerbowl was the final gracious touch to what had been an unusual evening. Outside, the early moon lay quiet on the hotel lawn, and the Trident's façade was bone-white in its glow. A romantic night, but I had a damp patch at my groin where the ice had been.

*

Earl Levy was dressed in a poplin shirt and white loafers with gold buckles; but he looked discontented. In its heyday the Trident had been patronised by a handful of royalty and epicureans of independent means. Princess Margaret, inevitably, languished there beneath the palms, lost in a haze of Famous Grouse and tranquillisers. Since then the Trident had been prinked, re-staffed and re-furbished several times but still nobody came. Tourists preferred the all-inclusive resorts on the north coast. 'The only way to bring this hotel back to life is to have the English nobility back here again, but there's no longer any demand for marvellous things, I'm afraid,' said Levy. 'The English have all gone to Barbados.' He lowered his voice on the word 'Barbados' with a suggestion of disapproval.

Earl Levy's Sephardic Judaism had been abandoned for Anglicanism long ago – officially there was now no Jewish blood in his parentage and, I suspected, he would flinch from the very idea. 'Did you know Princess Margaret?' he enquired. 'No? Sarah Churchill? *Surely* you've met her. No? Oh dear.'

Levy moved uneasily in his seat. 'I am a prominent and I may say an *influential* member of Jamaica's aristocracy. Indeed I am an Earl!' He laughed at his own humour, and added self-deprecatingly, 'One of my ancestors was an Irish sea captain – that was back in the days of the potato famine.' I suspected this was fantasy; fantasy was what animated Earl Levy.

For all his fine 'English' manners, Earl Levy had a foul temper. We were watching peacocks on the hotel lawn beyond the French windows when he said with sudden rage: 'One of my staff – the stupid bitch! – pulled out *four* of that peacock's feathers. Said she'd picked them off the grass, but the tips were bloody, anyone could see that.' He threw up his hands and brought them down thwack on his knees. 'Oh, I could've whipped her. I sacked her.' I was too startled to say anything. A little later a wedding party arrived at the hotel and assembled on the lawn. The party was black and, it seemed, not to Levy's taste. 'Oh, they're just unsophisticated little people,' he said in a tone that admitted no argument. Jamaica's old class rankings and race barriers were firmly in place.

Occasionally, to Levy's delight, an English aristocrat turns up at the Trident. In 2000 the twelfth Earl of Portland (the actor Tim Bentinck) arrived in the hope of exploring the Jamaican parish which had been named after the Duke of Portland, governor of Jamaica from 1723. On his return to England, the Englishman invited Earl Levy to stay with him in his house. 'I was so excited, I couldn't sleep,' Levy said to me. The earl took him to see the House of Lords and Buckingham Palace; and so, after a fashion, his craving for social acceptance was gratified.

'But now, my dear sir,' Levy said with a sigh, 'the Trident's dying and I can't even afford to pay the electricity bills. And do you know,' sinking his voice into a conspiratorial whisper, 'I'm tired of Jamaica. I never thought I'd say that – *tired of Jamaica*, but it's true.' In 2007, shortly after my third visit to Jamaica, the Trident was bought by a Jamaican Chinese businessman, Michael Lee Chin. Its future is uncertain.

15

Everything Crash

In 1968, when the Ethiopians released 'Everything Crash', Jamaica was convulsed by industrial strikes and go-slows. The JLP government under Prime Minister Hugh Shearer, one of the most repressive that the island has known, had failed woefully to improve the social and civic rights of the poor majority, as it had pledged to do. While a number of reforms were made (the provision, for example, of hundreds of primary schools), this JLP party had by now abandoned its trade-union roots and, just six years after independence, served merely to aggravate social inequalities and tensions.

In Jamaica, as elsewhere in the English-speaking West Indies, what the Colonial Office called the 'orderly transition' to self-government had been deceptive. Beyond the clarion-call of decolonisation simmered a volatile mixture of nationalist pride, Black Power activism and racial resentment. 'Everything Crash', with its litany of woes, became a best-selling record of 1968:

> What go bad a morning
> Can't come good a evening
> Everyday carry bucket to the well
> One day the bottom must drop out
> Everything crash

The song (affectionately known as the alternative 'National Anthem') is still routinely broadcast on Jamaican radio in times of crisis.

I met Leonard 'Sparrow' Dillon, the lead singer of the (still existent) Ethiopians, in a bar adjacent to the Port Antonio police station. Immensely tall, he said he was descended from runaway slaves or Maroons. And, like many Maroons, he was very black, his blackness emphasised by a black baseball cap, black T-shirt and baggy black shorts. Dillon ordered a Campari mixed with Stones Ginger Wine (a classic Jamaican 'man's drink'), and said to me, 'Everybody did have a problem back in 1968. Yes, man, even in them days things a get from bad to worse.'

The Ethiopians, one of the great vocal groups of 1960s Jamaica, were among the first ska-reggae bands to play in England; their music, rooted in the calypso and Revival rhythms of Dillon's native Portland parish, was heard in a number of venues from the Ramjam in Brixton to the African Club in Sheffield. The audiences were usually mixed, and sometimes predominantly white. 'I worked some places in Kent and in the audience is just *one* black I see!' Dillon raised a be-ringed finger and reached for his tumbler of dilute Campari. 'Yes, in them days the English like my music very much.' But now his music had been superseded by dancehall, of which Dillon took a characteristically dour view. 'Dancehall is a different call,' he said; it reflected a 'darkness' at the heart of modern Jamaica.

The 'bottomless decline' of Jamaica, as Dillon went on to call it, was a subject I constantly heard discussed. Jamaica had apparently come crashing down in the 1970s under the left-wing premiership of Michael Manley, who served two terms in the 1970s and one towards the end of the 1980s. During his earlier 'populist' terms Manley had sought to instil self-respect in the Jamaican poor and rid them of the sense of servility ingrained by slavery. He died in 1997, at the age of seventy-three, almost convinced that he had achieved his goal.

To be called a 'Manleyite' in some quarters today is an insult; the implication is that Manley has become a byword for disaster. To his enemies, Manley was an insecure, rash-tempered man driven by a need to outshine his more capable (if rather less charming) father, the PNP founder Norman Washington Manley, who in the post-war years had helped to lead Jamaica towards independence. Michael Manley's speeches were deemed to be full of overheated meaningless phrases ('black redemption', 'social struggle') and dangerous enthusiasms elevated to the status of wisdom.

To his supporters, though, any attempt to examine Michael Manley's pretensions and failures is tantamount to heresy. Manley was a heroic individual who had rescued Jamaica from colonial dereliction. A myth has thus emerged of Manley as a Castro-like spokesman of the dispossessed.

Rachel Manley, in her memoir of her father, *In My Father's Shade* (2004), invites us to reflect on Michael Manley as a glamorous failure. In this work of filial devotion at least, Manley emerges as the man whose reformist vision of Jamaica as a nation without race hierarchies or colour prejudice was both timely and necessary. From an early age, Rachel had learned that the island was run by a small 'brown' elite made up of 'Syrian' (Lebanese), Asian, Chinese, white and near-white ('local white') British Jamaicans. Only black Jamaicans were desperately poor; white Jamaicans were not.

Manley was no sooner elected than he urged Jamaicans to abandon the streak of self-hatred and suspicion towards their own kind. In his Garvey-inspired vision, Jamaica's African heritage was the colonially induced dark area of self-denial in the national psyche. It was time to rehabilitate the notion of Mother Africa and, to that end, Manley established links with Jamaica's Rastafari communities and even allowed himself to be called Joshua. Like his Biblical namesake, he was a prophet come to rid the nation of the corrupt 'Pharaoh' – Hugh Shearer of the ruling JLP. Manley promised to beat Shearer with the 'Rod of Correction', a cane given to him in 1970 reportedly by Haile Selassie himself.

Though Manley adopted rhetoric from the Black Power and Civil Rights movements of the 1950s, 1960s and 1970s, he was a light-skinned Jamaican of the middle classes. His forebears were a variety of English tradesmen and Methodist priests who had married into Kingston's European and mixed-race families. Proud upholders of the British Empire, they formed part of the island's small professional class whose job was to ensure that, as Rachel Manley puts it, 'colonial life ran smoothly'. So Michael Manley was both beholden to and in symbolic rebellion against his 'browning' ancestry, his partial 'whiteness', like that of Barack Obama after him, a mixed blessing.

After Manley's landslide victory in 1972, Jamaican politics

shifted decisively to the Left as he nationalised the foreign-owned electricity, telephone and public transport companies, as well as a number of North American sugar factories, mining firms and the British-run Barclays Bank. The expropriated foreign owners were compensated financially, but they harboured a hatred of Manley and his experiments in centralised socialism. While foreign capital leaked out of Jamaica, Manley aligned himself further with the ghetto and Rastafari communities. Not that he liked reggae much (his preferred music was bossa nova). Yet during this early, hopeful period, many reggae singers backed Manley. 'Better Must Come', by Delroy Wilson, had been co-opted by the PNP as their campaign song, while 'Press Along Joshua' and 'Let The Power Fall On I' were pro-Manley 45 rpm anthems by the great Max Romeo.

All kinds of Jamaicans, not just Rastafarians, supported the newly elected leader. Black, white, brown and yellow; Indian, Chinese, Jewish, rich and poor, working, middle and upper classes, vested interests, professionals, business people; all were joined in optimism about Jamaica's future and prepared to make a contribution and a sacrifice. 'Jamaicanisation' became the new watchword, and 'Jamaicanisation' extended to music, art, literature – even to fashion. Out went the tweeds and ties of the colonial British, and in came the loose-fitting bush jacket or Kareba. (No self-respecting PNP minister was without his Kareba; JLP activists, pointedly, continued to wear suits and ties.)

Key social reforms were pushed through, among them the adult literacy programme of 1973–4, which enabled poor Jamaicans to attend reading and writing classes. A feeling of pride and self-worth was instilled by the literacy (JAMAL) programme. In 1975 a national minimum wage was introduced after a radio call-in programme, *Public Eye,* exposed the scandalously low pay of Jamaican domestic servants. Maids and stewards began to call in to say how they had been locked in rooms without food or water as punishment for 'stealing'. Wealthier Jamaicans, feeling themselves under attack, proclaimed the programme's host, John Maxwell, a 'class traitor'. Shops in uptown Kingston meanwhile sold out of telephone padlocks which immobilised the dial phones used by maids who 'wanted to phone Maxwell'. In the end, PNP justice prevailed, and the minimum wage was fixed at US $20 a week. Jamaicans in socially degrading occupations became aware for the first time of their political potential.

John Maxwell, a burly man with a hip-jive patter, had stood against Edward Seaga in the 1972 general election and saw then how the JLP was dispensing guns in return for votes. Later he campaigned, fruitlessly, on *Public Eye* for a nationwide ban on firearms. By the mid 1970s, gangs on both sides of the JLP–PNP divide were killing each other senselessly and, it seemed, without restraint. For all his original good intentions, Manley came to preside over new heights of violence as fears intensified that he was planning to adopt, not just a 'third way' between capitalism and socialism, but the Cuban model of communism.

Manley's admiration for Castro, genuine enough, was not unqualified. He could see that Cubans were suffering the indignity of police surveillance and rationed food. Yet it was hard for his party to quibble with the improvements made in Cuba to health and literacy. Before the nationalist-communist *revolución* of 1959, almost half of Cuba's rural population was illiterate. By the time Manley was elected in 1972, only 2 per cent of Cuban adults were unable to read and write. Manley visited Castro for the first time in 1975; afterwards he said that he would 'walk with Castro to the mountaintop'. Such public declarations did not go down well with wealthier Jamaicans, who began to transfer their capital out of Jamaica to the United States and Canada. Increasingly, skilled workers, managers and professionals packed their bags for Miami and Toronto; many of them never came back.

At one point it seemed that Manley was even encouraging Jamaicans to leave. 'For anyone who wants to become a millionaire,' he is reported to have said on his return from Cuba in 1975, 'we have five flights a day to Miami.' The remark, made half in jest, was picked up by the pro-Seaga *Gleaner* newspaper. The next day, and for months afterwards, flights to Miami were booked solid.

Throughout the 1970s, as well-off Jamaicans continued to migrate, it became apparent that Manley was no longer able to take the middle classes with him. He had attempted too much too soon, and now he had run out of funds. Edward Seaga, the opposition

JLP leader since 1974, saw a conspiracy at work in his rival's regard for Cuba. Though Manley had not advocated armed struggle (as the Cuban revolutionaries had), in his speeches he pledged to make Jamaica's foreign policy less subservient to Washington and seemed to endorse Castro's ideological aversion to the United States. Washington bullets wanted Castro dead: well then, Manley wanted nothing to do with Washington.

All this displeased Seaga, who perceived Manley as anti-Western and anti-capitalist. In fact, Manley's government had been careful to allow private enterprise to flourish, but that was not enough for Seaga. In the mid-1970s the Americans (and, to a lesser extent, the Canadians) embarked on a campaign to discredit Manley and the PNP. New class wars were prophesied with a final catastrophic crumbling of Jamaica's post-colonial society. Marxist sugar co-operatives were about to infest Jamaica! Kingston was about to have its own Red Square! 'Don't let the comrades Castro-ate you,' warned the JLP; Manley was suffering from 'Castro-enteritis'.

Manley's 'anti-capitalist' cause was not helped by the increasingly repressive measures he adopted against crime. In 1974, in a bid to curb the political violence, he set up the Gun Court detention centre in Kingston. The centre, today encased in barbed wire with laager-like watchtowers, was used to isolate anyone found in possession of an unlicensed firearm or just ammunition. Now Jamaicans could not only be arrested, tried and sentenced all on the same day, they could be detained indefinitely. Manley was determined to put Jamaica 'under heavy manners' and make an example of wrong-doers. Even films that 'depended on violence for their theme' were banned and scenes with gun-play edited out.

As the killings began to ratchet up, neither the PNP nor the JLP was prepared to take responsibility. It was far easier to blame the ubiquitous (but conveniently nameless) 'gunmen' than the corrupted politicians. By now the PNP were doling out guns quite as generously as the JLP. The party of rectitude and reform was becoming tainted by the corruption it had decried.

Manley, it was clear, had not materially improved life for poor Jamaicans as he had promised. In the depressed areas of Kingston the inhabitants were getting hungrier and more angry. Manley and the PNP were now seen as traitors. 'All of them a Judas, can't you see,' sang the wild-eyed reggae star Junior Byles. The economics failed to add up; the PNP could no longer afford to pay for its social policies. Washington began to withdraw aid and investments. In 1971, Jamaica had received $23 million from the United States; by 1975, that amount was down to $4 million.

Ironically, Michael Manley's growing stature as a Third World spokesman made him increasingly important to US policy-makers. Henry Kissinger, visiting Kingston in 1975 as Secretary of State for America's post-Nixon government, tried to persuade Manley into withdrawing his support for Cuba's intervention against South Africa in Angola. Manley refused: Jamaica, he reminded Kissinger, had been the first country to break off diplomatic relations with the apartheid regime and back the African National Congress.

In July the following year, a bomb exploded in a suitcase at Kingston airport as it was being loaded on to an Air Cubana plane. Four months later, an Air Cubana fight en route to Jamaica exploded in mid-air; all seventy-eight passengers were killed. Anti-Castro groups in Miami claimed responsibility for the attacks. Fears of an imminent civil war – PNP versus JLP – were now heightened by an extraordinary reggae song, 'Two Sevens Clash', by Culture, which invoked a prophecy uttered decades earlier by Marcus Garvey, that apocalyptic violence would erupt on 7 July 1977. The song's predictive wail was heard on radios across Jamaica as another general election loomed.

Steel-helmeted soldiers began to patrol the political borderlines downtown. And in August 1976, as the killings multiplied in the build up to the election, Manley declared a State of Emergency. He had come to suspect (rightly, it turned out) the existence of a JLP–Seaga–CIA-backed campaign to destabilise him and his government. In spite of the opposition, Manley won the election. Visitors to Kingston at this time – among them Joe Strummer and Mick Jones of the Clash – reported a frightening place on the edge of bloodshed. ('Yes, i'd stay an' be a tourist but i can't take the gunplay,' Strummer sang on 'Safe European Home', an oblique comment on mid-1970s Jamaica.)

Seaga, brooding over his electoral defeat, claimed that Manley was turning Kingston into the 'subversion capital of the Caribbean'. Cuban doctors, nurses and construction workers were increasingly a presence (if scarcely a political influence) in the Jamaican capital, with the Cuban Embassy seen as a hotbed of indoctrination. While Fidel's Cuba actually had very little bearing on PNP policy, fears of a red insurgency only encouraged Washington to see Jamaica in terms of East–West, Cold War prescriptions.

Most American citizens living in Jamaica endorsed the American campaign to discredit Manley. Among them was Errol Flynn's former wife, the much younger screen actress Patrice Wymore. In Wymore's estimation, Manley was a dangerous radical bent on leading Jamaica into the Red Bloc. In particular she feared his socialist ideas about the rationalisation of land ownership. On Errol Flynn's death in 1959 she had inherited over 1,600 acres of farmland on the outskirts of Port Antonio. Locals claim that Flynn obtained the land in the most underhand way, by inviting Portland farmers on board his yacht and plying them with so much rum that they signed away their tenures for a pittance. The story of the matinee idol's chicanery was told to me by an intimate of the Flynn circle in Port Antonio. Whether it is true or not (a tincture of exaggeration is allowed), it has become part of local legend.

As most of Flynn's land lay unused, the Manley government understandably had plans to make use of it (it would not have done so otherwise). Project Land Lease was launched by the PNP in 1975 with the purpose of leasing out idle land such as Flynn's for peasant cultivation. No Manley reform was more contentious. Land tenure was – still is – highly inequitable in Jamaica. In 1961, the year before independence, 10 per cent of the population owned 64 per cent of the land; today the imbalance may be even greater. The Manley government failed to make any significant expropriations. Patrice Wymore refused to loan out even a portion of the Errol Flynn Estate. In 2000 the *Wall Street Journal* listed the Estate for an asking price of US $50 million. The rumour is that the Errol Flynn International airport will be built on the property.

*

I met Errol Flynn's ex-wife at her ranch-office outside Port Antonio. Considered to be a difficult and withdrawn person, her life in

Jamaica (apart from the few details she cared to volunteer) could only be guessed at, and I was a bit nervous about meeting her. The Errol Flynn Estate, a vast expanse of pampas rolling to the sea, looked unkempt as I made my way across it one hot afternoon. The grass was sere and grazed by tired-looking cattle: Jamaica Reds, Jamaica Blacks. A notice by a cattle trough announced: 'STRAY GOATS WILL BE SHOT'. Feeling like an extra from *The Magnificent Seven* I went up to the door, where a tethered horse dozed.

'Haven't we met before?' Patrice Wymore said to me as I walked in after knocking. 'You remind me of somebody I know.'

She was a gaunt woman in a pair of pink skinny jeans, her reddish-blonde hair concealed beneath a scarf, Bette Davis-style.

'I don't think so,' I said warily, taking in the riding crops and spurs hanging on the wall.

'Oh,' she said, lighting a cigarette. Patrice Wymore was eighty-four but looked younger, her eyes a cornflower-blue like a china doll's. After eight years of marriage, in 1958 she had divorced Flynn, who died the following year at the age of fifty having more or less boozed himself into the grave. Since then, she has denied rumours that Flynn enjoyed sex with men ('Errol, *gay*? Don't you think that I would have noticed?'). However, by the time she co-starred with him in the movie *King's Rhapsody* (1955), his sexual philandering and drinking had become so bad that he was having to *play* sexually philandering drunkards. (By Wymore's admission the film was 'quite dreadful'.)

By good fortune, Wymore had not been cut out of Flynn's will, and when she returned to Jamaica after his death to inherit paintings and jewellery, she also took on 800 head of cattle and the Port Antonio estates, which she began to manage in 1968. 'That was no easy thing,' Wymore said, fixing me with a baby-eyed stare, 'especially not in those Manley years.' Almost every week in the 1970s thieves threatened to steal (and in fact did steal) her cattle. 'There was nothing I could do,' Wymore pulled a face. Manley was inciting the 'rabble' to racial hatred and vengeance. As a wealthy white woman in a poor black country, Wymore claimed she was despised.

She lit another Benson and Hedges, exhaled elegantly. 'You don't believe me? I tell you, the poor were out to butcher what remained of the middle classes.' Listening to Patrice Wymore, it occurred to me that politics under Manley were no longer a question of Left and Right, but black and white. Politics had shifted to a form of post-colonial nationalism in which 'colour' increasingly determined whose side you were on. In 1978, during Manley's second term, gangs of farmhands began to squat on the Errol Flynn Estate and glared murderously at the white woman as she drove past them on her way to the office. 'I was cussed and verbally assaulted,' Wymore recalled.

The PNP's 'race ideology' was motivated chiefly by envy, she insisted. 'Envy's the number one problem in Jamaica.' Did Wymore mean black Jamaican 'envy' of white privilege? 'No,' she said, 'it would be the same if I were black, the envy would still be there. I mean, look at Bob Marley – Jamaicans *hated* Marley in the beginning, oh yes they did, he was hated and he was envied.' Jamaicans generous? Rubbish: Jamaicans are a 'shiftless, shady, jealous kind of people [quoting the title, unwittingly or not, of an O'Jays song]. Yes, jealous, and always have been.' Wymore was a harsh judge. 'Jamaicans feel a tremendous envy and suspicion towards their own successful children,' she said.

*

At the dawn of the 1980s, it was literally a fight to the death between PNP and JLP. Even Jamaicans of moderation and decency were tempted to commit grotesque acts of political violence. The violence was exacerbated at this point by the spectre of national bankruptcy. Between 1975 and 1980, Jamaica's foreign debt had doubled to reach US $2 billion – the equivalent of 90 per cent of the gross domestic product. The worldwide oil crisis had hit the Jamaican dollar hard, and Manley agreed, reluctantly, to accept emergency relief from the International Monetary Fund (IMF). A combination of financial mismanagement and muddle-headed ideology had obliged him to reverse his anti-capitalist course. Manley's revolutionary spirit, it seemed, was giving out amid more strikes, walkouts, and ever higher rates of inflation.

A minority of PNP activists, feeling betrayed by Manley's sudden reliance on foreign loans, veered further to the left. A Marxist-Leninist offshoot of the PNP, the Workers Party of Jamaica, began to send brigades of Jamaican youth to Cuba for military training. The PNP's covert alliance with this pro-Moscow splinter faction was later denounced by Manley who (in spite of his anti-imperialist rhetoric) had come to realise the risks he ran in alienating the business sector. Officially the Kingston–Havana PNP *Brigadista* programme was intended to train Jamaicans in construction skills (some 1,400 were indeed sent to Cuba for that purpose). Training Jamaicans in guerrilla tactics was not endorsed by the mainstream PNP.

Horace Jackson, in his early sixties now, still had something of the former Workers Party of Jamaica activist in his studious, concentrated expression. In his thirties he had had contributed articles to the WPJ journal *The Struggle*; I liked him, he had believed in something. Yet he seemed uncomfortable, embarrassed even, to talk of his experiences under a Cuban sun in 1980, when he had received instructions in how to infiltrate and deploy troops. Cuba had been an experiment he would never quite recover from, a kind of 'political folly', he called it.

We were speaking in his office at the Jamaica Bauxite Institute in Kingston, where he had worked these thirty years. Of the twenty *brigadistas* flown out with Jackson to Cuba, only three were known to him. All were under strict instructions not to discuss their activities with anyone outside the group. On arrival in Havana the Jamaicans still did not know the purpose of their visit. A truck drove them to an 'undisclosed location' in 'hilly terrain', recalled Jackson, about ten miles from the Cuban capital. The camp, when they got there, had barrack-sheds, bunkbeds and lecture halls; the Cuban instructors, didactic to the last, had chalked diagrams of guns and grenades on the blackboard. A photograph of Che Guevara with saintly eyes and straggly black hair hung above the door. Che had been dead for thirteen years, but the Jamaican *brigadistas* worshipped him still.

At thirty-eight, Jackson was the oldest of the Jamaicans in the group, too old, he says now, for 'Third World revolutionary stuff'. He had never handled a gun and accidentally almost killed one of the instructors with a grenade. 'I wasn't properly in control of that grenade,' Jackson told me, adding, 'I wasn't properly in control of anything.' He was taught how to dismantle rifles and dress correctly in olive-green fatigues. He went into woods, he waged mock war and, armed with M16s, Uzis and SLRs, crawled on his belly across semi-swampland. By the end of his two-week course, Jackson said he was ready to kill, but he added in mitigation: 'The Cold War had frozen our ability to think – it had killed off interesting thoughts, interesting people, interesting ideas.' Worse, Manley's Cold War rhetoric of 'US and Them' served to draw a line in the sand, which one crossed at mortal risk. Nevertheless there was something about the conflict that 'got your blood going', Jackson remembered.

Back in Jamaica, meanwhile, events were occurring that terrified him: PNP activists were being killed in their sleep. Seaga was about to overthrow Manley in a CIA-sponsored coup, it was believed. Practically anyone could get hit at any time. 'Seaga was – is – a very scary man, who surrounded himself with very scary, dangerous types,' said Jackson. 'My recollection is that Jamaica was on the brink of anarchy.' He looked at me intently and shook his head. 'Anarchy, I say, anarchy.'

On his return to Kingston, Jackson began to research CIA suspects living in the city, took photographs of their houses, and borrowed an automatic rifle from WPJ headquarters. The rifle was 'necessary' to protect himself, his mother (with whom he lived) and her house, 'because any day someone could come for both of us,' Jackson explained.

In the summer of 1980, with ten other WPJ activists, he got the order from high up to storm a pro-Seaga radio station in Kingston. The saboteurs waited, their M16s cocked, in their bandanas and fatigues; but the signal for attack never came. 'We were taking on something much bigger than ourselves – and that made us very, very dangerous,' Jackson recalled. 'Yes, we were arrogant – full of the *possibility* of power.' As it happened, the JLP won the October 1980 election, gaining a landslide fifty-one of the sixty seats in Parliament. Seaga was set to govern by rejecting all that Manley had stood for, or so it seemed.

The reality is more complicated. Though Seaga is often seen as the man of the establishment and Manley as the renegade leftist, both views are misleading. It was Seaga who had written scholarly papers on the Afro-Christian religions of the ghetto and was one of the early producers of reggae, while Manley, the son of the nation's revered founding father, had published a 600-page history of the West Indian cricket team. Nevertheless, Seaga was able to please the Reagan White House and the IMF by preaching free enterprise and selling off the industries that Manley had nationalised. Yet Seaga's administration during the eight and a half years that followed Manley's was no more successful. His unthinking reliance on the goodwill of the Washington administration – his blinkered faith in Regan's free market – was to leave Jamaica even more violent and poverty-stricken. By accepting International Monetary Fund loans in excess of US $ 2,000 million, moreover, Seaga helped to double Jamaica's external debt.

Jackson, for his part, continued to wear a Lenin badge to the Bauxite Institute but was prompted to renounce violence when, in February 1985, three WPJ activists were killed in a shoot-out with the police in the Redhills district of Kingston. The men were known personally to Jackson. 'SLAIN THREE HAD COMMUNIST HISTORY' reported the *Gleaner*. Jolted into reality, Jackson returned his rifle to the WPJ headquarters and washed his hands of his old militancy.

Not that a Castro-style communism was ever going to happen in Jamaica. Cuba, a hybrid of Hispanic and African cultures, remains quite distinct from its 'British' neighbour. Jamaicans, by virtue of their fierce individualism and gift for self-assertiveness, are more prone to see the state as an evil to be kept at bay than as a saviour. Jackson put it another way: 'There's not much of a tradition in Jamaica of mutual cooperation. Socialism in Jamaica would have meant *total* war.' He went on, 'We Jamaicans can't agree on anything. Put us round a conference table, we'll only end up fighting.' In their decisions and actions, Jackson concluded, the 'I' is often more apparent in Jamaicans than the 'We'.

*

When Michael Manley was returned to power for the third time in 1989, incredibly, he sided with a Ronald Reagan-like capitalism. If nothing else, his political about-turn indicated a continued hunger for power. Manley had changed allegiances with the same enthusiasm, untempered by pragmatism or caution, with which he embraced his earlier nationalist-socialism. The Reagan market model, unfettered and deregulated, pro-IMF, was once more unleashed on a society of gross inequalities. 'You just can't improve on Adam Smith,' Manley is said to have remarked. By now the PNP was virtually indistinguishable from the JLP. And, as the erosion of the 'old time' values of service, decency and respect for others continued apace, so a murderous anti-social behaviour was fomented at all levels of Jamaican society.

With the abandonment of Michael Manley's 'Third World' ideology, at least tourism picked up again. The prevailing anti-white mood in the 1970s had been a calamity for a country whose livelihood depended in part on the hotel business. By the early 1990s, hordes of Britons and North Americans were flocking back to the West Indian 'paradise' for its promise of oblivion, reggae, rum, sun and cheap sex. Patrice Wymore organised 'Errol Flynn Tours' of her estates, but so many tourists turned up unannounced that she called a halt and, for good measure, removed 'Flynn, Errol' from the Port Antonio telephone directory.

Now, as the dream of Third World revolution has unravelled (except, perhaps, in Bolivia and Venezuela), one can see to what a ruinous state Jamaica had been brought in the 1970s and 1980s. In the election year of 1980 alone, a shocking 900 Jamaicans died in episodes of political violence. Manley's policies had begun to hurt those whom the PNP sought to help the most – the poor – and alienated the residue of the middle class.

*

Yet, for all his faults, the half-thought thoughts and rash designs, Michael Manley had urged Jamaicans to take pride in their country, and for a while it looked as if he could lead them into the radiant future of his promises. Many of his projects contributed beneficially to welfare in education (free secondary and higher education), health, equal pay for women, and the empowerment of other disenfranchised groups, among them young people and domestic servants. Impressively, too, Manley helped to create a black entrepreneurial class and enabled a black managerial group of mostly women to prosper in the growing financial sectors of New Kingston.

But something else needs to be said. Manley, a tall, back-slapping man's man, was fortunate to possess the (not unusual) facility for mixing sex with politics. He had a reputation as a philanderer, and this earned him the honorific nickname 'Housewife's Choice' (the title of a popular Jamaican song of the 1960s). He married five times, moreover, across the Jamaican race spectrum, from black to white to mixed-race to Chinese. All this counted for much in a country where a sector of the electorate is illiterate.

Until his re-election in 1989 Manley remained faithful to the ideology of the party, the PNP, which his father had founded four decades earlier in 1938. His fall from grace, in part the result of mismanagement and political naivety, was all the harder for his followers to take because, in the early 1970s, there had been a genuine popular support and a willingness to make sacrifices. Michael Manley, the voice of impatient reform, remains for many Jamaicans a revered figure.

Curiously, his political experiment had been foreseen sixty years earlier by the playwright George Bernard Shaw who, invited to Jamaica in 1911 by the British Governor General (a fellow Fabian, Sir Sydney Olivier), complained to the *Gleaner* newspaper:

> What is wrong in Jamaica is that you produce a sort of man who is only a colonial . . . If a Jamaican wishes his son to be a fully civilized man of the world in the best sense – to belong to a great intellectual and artistic culture – he has to send him to Europe. Now that's not a necessary state of things. On the contrary, it ought to be far easier to build up a Jamaican culture than it is to civilize a Camberwell Cockney. Jamaica for the Jamaicans, say I.

Well said: *Jamaica for the Jamaicans*. 'The politics of participation', Michael Manley had called it. Such was his dream, a dream of almost universal goodwill. And what Manley had hoped to offer by this dream was not merely a Jamaica fully independent, but a Jamaica governed by the people *for* the people. It was a model of self-reliance now, sadly, gone sour.

16

Nanny Knew Best

Much romantic nonsense has been written about the Maroons, or runaway slaves, of Jamaica. In the 1970s during Michael Manley's socialist experiment, Maroons were hailed as forerunners of Black Power, and the world's first black freedom fighters. Even today, descent from Maroons is regarded by some Jamaicans as a mark of noble background. Marcus Garvey claimed Maroon ancestry as has, more recently, the British Jamaican hip-hop celebrity Ms Dynamite.

The truth is, Maroons fought only for their own liberty, not for the overall liberty of enslaved Africans in Jamaica. As a condition of their freedom (and in return for land and other privileges), they had to agree to return other fugitive slaves to the imperial British and even help quell slave revolts. Infamously, Maroons had helped to put down the Morant Bay uprising of 1865, acting as bounty-hunters for Her Majesty's murderous Governor Eyre. Thus the surviving Maroons in Jamaica are left with an ambivalent legacy as both heroes of, and traitors to, black freedom.

The mountains and waterfalls east of Port Antonio provided an ideal refuge for the Maroons and their descendants who, on first encounter, seem to look and live much like the Jamaican majority. Unlike most Jamaicans, however, Maroons have conserved a unique subculture of African language, music, divination and spirit animism. The African lore has been handed down the generations by the Maroons' Ashanti (Asante) and Fanti slave ancestors. These tribes, the Ashanti and Fanti, were called 'Coromantees' by the British after the slave forts which held them captive on the Koramantine coast of Africa prior to their deportation to the West Indies. A minority of Maroons can still speak the Asante-Twi and Fanti languages of what is today Ghana.

During the Maroon Wars of Jamaica, which lasted from 1673 to 1796, the most repressive measures were taken to crush a people whom the British regarded as on a level with 'savages'. Cuban mastiffs trained for manhunting were unleashed on the runaways in the west of Jamaica. In 1796, 600 of them were herded on to ships for Nova Scotia in present-day Canada for re-settlement. The transportees who survived the harsh North American winters were later transferred to the 'experimental' free colony of Sierra Leone in West Africa, where they formed the nucleus of a tribal elite whose descendants still dominate that country.

Maroons have existed throughout the Caribbean, notably in the English settlement of Surinam, ceded in 1667 to the Netherlands. Tall and athletic, their name derives from the Spanish *cimarrón*, meaning 'wild', originally applied to cattle in the wilds of Hispaniola or present-day Haiti. In Portland parish they were led by a 'Coromantee' tribeswoman known as Nanny, who fended off British troops (according to the – possibly Jamaican – legend) by catching bullets in the cleft of her buttocks. Even today, the idea that this Boudicca figure used her rear (or, according to another tradition, her vagina) to catch enemy bullets is offensive to some Jamaicans. In all likelihood, the bullet-catching legend was contrived by agents of British colonialism with the intent to ridicule. It is just as likely that Nanny, in the folklore of Jamaica, lifted her skirts to moon at the Redcoats – a gesture of extreme contempt, signifying 'batty man'.

Nanny – 'Grandy Nanny' – is now a Jamaican national hero; and although no contemporary images of her survive, her imagined likeness appears on the JA $500 banknote ('Give me a Nanny!' street beggars implore). In 1994, her regal status was enhanced when the *patwa* words 'Nanny a fi we Queen' (Nanny for our Queen) were found spray-gunned on to the entrance of the university campus in Kingston, shortly before Queen Elizabeth II was due to visit. The graffito, the work of anti-royalist Jamaicans, was hastily removed.

Some theorists see Jamaica's Maroon history as interwoven with the island's mountainous landscape and with the 'defiant' Jamaican character itself. Among them is the Guyanese author and publisher

Eric Huntley. When Huntley first came to England in 1956, it was the Jamaicans who by their defiance and willingness to confront authority dominated West Indian expatriate life and urged Huntley to 'stand up' for his rights. 'Jamaicans had this *grit*, this cussedness that really was like a Maroon rebelliousness,' Huntley told me. In Huntley's view, the Maroons were 'the first true anti-colonials'.

Parts of Portland parish are backed by fantastic mountain shapes. 'You should take a look,' Huntley urged me. 'All those mountain ridges misted and aloof – a proper setting for guerrilla strikes!' The terrain certainly offered scope for resistance. 'In Guyana, though, we have no mountains to speak of, so we don't have much of a runaway slave culture either.' In 1968, taking a leaf out of the Maroon book, Huntley set up the Bogle–L'Ouverture Press in west London, named after the freedom fighters Paul Bogle of Jamaica and Toussaint L'Ouverture of Haiti. One of its earliest authors was the British-Jamaican poet Linton Kwesi Johnson, whose irate protests against the British authorities ('Inglan is a Bitch') Huntley saw as an inheritance variously of Maroon culture, Rastafari militancy and the Black Power ideology of Walter Rodney (another Bogle–L'Ouverture author).

*

Moore Town is home to one of Jamaica's four existing Maroon communities and is accessible by bus from Port Antonio. As I waited at the bus stop on Williams Street (opposite the blowsy-looking Top Hat nightclub), Vic Taylor's sorrowful 1969 song 'Heartaches' welled up from a taxi radio. Moved by it, I watched a promenade of locals on their way to Sunday morning church as a group of higglers meanwhile gathered by my side.

'How long before the bus comes?' I asked one of them.

'Nine and a half hours,' came the reply.

After a careful pause I said, 'Things don't move fast in Jamaica.'

'No, my dear,' she agreed, 'they don't move at-all at-all.'

After a couple of hours the bus arrived. It had a slogan painted on the side: 'SMILE – IT INCREASE YOUR FACE VALUE', which I had seen on a Revivalist church in Haringey, north London. The bus was driven by a young East Indian with a miniature gold imitation revolver hanging from a necklace. The higglers hailed him 'Coolie

Bwoy!' and I sat in the passenger seat next to him. He turned out to be a deportee from the United States and, with unabashed relish, he explained to me how his deportee status had arisen.

'I went down for aggravated felony in Miami, 1991,' he said, as we creaked and crunched out of Port Antonio. That year saw a crack epidemic in the big US cities and 'Coolie Bwoy' spent two years in a Miami jail for selling the stuff. Air Jamaica flew him home. Apart from the detectives to whom he was handcuffed at the back of the plane, only the stewardesses knew he was a criminal. On his return to Port Antonio, 'Coolie Bwoy' felt nothing but shame: the mere sight of him was offensive to the police. 'Everybody saw me as a failure – and motherfuckin' right I was a failure! I'd been to the richest country in the world and come back a dip [deportee].' His eyes swept quickly across the road. 'To be a dip in Jamaica is to lose face.'

After months of searching for a job he was taken on as a bus driver and was now grudgingly accepted by his family who had come over from Calcutta in 1912 on the same day the White Star liner RMS *Titanic* went down. Each year an average of 3,600 Jamaican nationals are deported from the United States, Canada and, increasingly, Britain. Many are flown back for non-violent offences and not considered a threat. Into this category fall drug couriers and 'overstayers' – Jamaicans working abroad without a permit. A handful of deportees are extremely dangerous.

The most notorious in recent years was the Jamaican boxing champion Trevor Berbick. Convicted in the United States for sexual assault, theft and burglary, in 2006 Berbick was deported to his birthplace in Portland parish, only to be murdered there by members of his own family over a land dispute. Deportees with gangland connections can cause local crime rates to soar, the more so if drugs are involved. Invariably each new import of narcotics into a community coincides with a run of the sales on the cocktail cabinets and widescreen televisions at the local, yellow-painted Courts furniture store that dominates every Jamaican town.

*

After eight miles of driving we pulled up in front of a roadside bar called the Monte Carlo Club; passengers got out to empty their bladders, quench their thirst or smoke a cigarette. Below us were the slow-moving waters of the Rio Grande where Errol Flynn had gone rafting. Here, British Redcoats had been tracked by armies of invisible opponents, who laid pit-traps concealed by branches and hid out in 'back-o-water' caves. The eerie wail of the *abeng*, a ram's horn used by Maroons to communicate over distances, warned the British that a marauding party was on the way to plunder plantations – they were easily ambushed, outwitted by the Maroon scout networks.

Betrayal was a constant danger in the Maroon Wars and even today Moore Town's 2,000-odd inhabitants remain suspicious of outsiders or *obroni* as they are known in Asante-Twi. 'Trust no shadow after dark,' cautions a Jamaican proverb; a Maroon might add, 'Trust no one, ever'. Every five years Maroons elect a new colonel to arbitrate in land disputes, minor court cases, disputes over taxes and even marriage, as well as guard against the incursions of *obroni*. In spite of their secretiveness, Maroon settlements have been infiltrated by anthropologists, chief among them Kenneth M. Bilby, an American, who arrived in Moore Town in 1977.

At first Bilby was taken for a CIA agent. Those were the fear-ridden months of Michael Manley's second term, when the United States (or right-wing forces operating within Washington) seemed intent on destabilising Manley and the PNP. Eventually Bilby, having won the trust of the local colonel, was given free passage through Maroon territories in the east of the island. His book, *True-Born Maroons* (2005), based on hundreds of taped interviews, provides an extraordinary oral history of Afro-Atlantic slave custom. For Bilby, the Maroons were not 'traitors' to black freedom, but representatives of a defiant New World blackness, who dealt a lasting blow to the British Empire and British rule in the West Indies. *True-Born Maroons*, a record of a fast-vanishing culture, has a valedictory tone that moved me. While in London I had contacted Bilby, who provided me with an address in Moore Town where I could stay.

*

Moore Town was a beautiful, shabby place under the high peaks of the John Crow range of the Blue Mountains. I got off the bus on the far side of a river. A cluster of shacks emerged from the morning haze, and then I heard my name. An old man was calling it, gesturing at me from a porch. 'Ian!' He was hollering now. 'Oyea!' He turned out to be Leonard Pryce, a tall man of about sixty, my Bilby contact.

He welcomed me into his house, a concrete bungalow built in 1975, and by local standards spacious, with four bedrooms leading off a white-painted corridor. The remains of old Maroon shacks with galvanised zinc roofs stood nearby, unoccupied. Leonard introduced me to his wife, Gene, a reticent presence. I was to have a room at the back that belonged to one of her three sons, all of them making a decent wage for themselves now in London, she said.

The walls were covered with posters of jacked-up American cars with gold wheel rims and one of Al Pacino as Tony ('white powder') Montana in *Scarface*. I had to remind myself that I was in the house of 'true-born Maroons': Nanny's children were drifting from their ancestral moorings. Above the bed was a photograph of Gene's sons standing outside the *Guardian* newspaper on Farringdon Road: gold earrings, high-tech puss boots, black Nehru jackets.

After a shower I made my way down the corridor to the kitchen stacked with cooking utensils left and right, including a pot of something Gene had prepared for lunch. 'Tripe,' she explained, 'with garlic.' While I ate, she and her husband pottered round the kitchen, chatting.

'Things used to be lovely here in Moore Town,' Gene said to me as I picked at the tripe. 'Now it's gone rotten.' When old-time Jamaicans survey post-independent Jamaica, often they see nothing but chaos and ruins. 'You right, Gene. You is so right,' her husband agreed. 'PNP fight JLP. Kingston poli*tricks* have come to Moore Town. Well, it was never like that.'

'Is it really that bad?' I asked.

Leonard nodded. The Jamaican capital, with its gangland murders, its vitriol-throwing, its rapes, used to be considered the reverse of Maroon territories, where you could walk from village to village without fear. All that changed in the late 1990s, apparently, when a kind of undeclared war broke out between Moore Town's PNP and JLP factions.

Matters deteriorated further in November 2003, when UNESCO donated US $1 million to help Moore Town preserve its African culture and African language. Much of that money, according to the Pryces, was stolen. 'Moore Town is becoming just as bad as the city. Slowly but surely', said Leonard.

*

Isaac Bernard, a *fete-man* or Maroon elder, lived in Castle Comfort village three miles distant from Moore Town. Apparently he could speak the 'secret' African language of Asante-Twi and had the power to cure sickness or bring about evil.

Next morning along the trail to Castle Comfort, Maroon settlements drifted into sight through the morning river mist. A smell of earth rose heady from the rain-soaked land, and not for the first time, the beauty of rural Jamaica exhilarated me. The Rio Grande was out of sight, but the slopes of its great jungle-like valley, its green hillocks and scattered groves of palms were caught in brief brush-strokes of lilac, green and grey. At Alligator Church a swing-bridge took me across the river dashing white over rocks a hundred feet below. From somewhere in the hills Tenor Saw's dancehall anthem of 1985, 'Ring the Alarm', welled up like a Maroon war cry. *Hey, woah, ring the alarm. Another sound is dying . . .*

The high, forested cliffs of the John Crow Mountain showed in the distance and, closer to, wide acres of ripe cane. I had to pass through Cornwall Barracks village, an old Redcoat outpost. Here the sun glowed red in a clear sky, the air burning hot against my skin. The barracks were little more than a crumbled stone wall choked by weeds. The British troops stationed here were believed to have had children by Maroon women, and brown-skinned Jamaicans inhabit the village today. Half-Maroons are known in patois as *waitamigls*, or 'white-a-middles'.

A buzzard flapped heavily through the air as I approached Castle Comfort, my destination. On the outskirts a man was lolling coolly against a tree. He called out to me in the voice of a plantation overseer, 'Bwoy! Come here!' He added, 'What's up, bwoy, you have some business here?'

I asked him if that was a question.

'It's a question. What mission are you on?'

'I'm looking for Isaac Bernard.'

'Who is Isaac Bernard?'

'Isaac Bernard? He's a *fete-man*.'

'You sure of that?'

I knew Jamaican hostility but this felt like open aggression. Actually, as I later found out, the stand-off was a Maroon tactic designed to confuse or ward off outsiders. Runaway slaves had used *jijifo* – an Asante-Twi-derived word meaning 'evasive manoeuvres' – to mislead and trap the Redcoats. This verbal sparring was intended to wrong-foot *obroni* like me.

'Anyone with you?' the man went on.

'No – not exactly.'

'What does that mean, not exactly? Either someone's with you or you're alone. Are you alone?' The man's voice sounded throaty, vibrant with triumph.

After more questions back and forth we parted amicably enough. 'No harm – was jus' conversin',' said the man. 'Go through!' He stepped aside and, with a friendly air, pointed out Isaac Bernard's house to me on a hilltop.

When I got to the house, a thin, long-legged man was seated on the veranda, polishing a pair of shoes: stout, churchgoing ones. He sat looking at me with puckered eyes.

'Who sent you?' (Here we go.)

'Colonel Sterling.' (The recently elected colonel of Moore Town.)

'Who do you represent?'

'Represent?'

'You're with somebody. Tell me who.'

I identified myself.

Bernard Isaac, the *fete-man*, said to me, 'You shall come in,' and, waving his left hand at a chair, added, 'You may sit down.' Like many older Jamaicans he seemed to be afflicted with English *politesse*. I moved over to the indicated chair, and sat. Isaac poured a libation of rum over the side of the veranda, then drank some. He did this with his eyes closed and muttering an invocation in (I guessed) Asante-Twi.

'What do you think of that, mister?' he said, with the air of a showman exhibiting a trick.

'It looks ceremonial.'

'It *is* ceremonial,' he said. Rum trickled down his chin like tarry sweat. To my astonishment, Maroon scouts had been watching me walk up from Moore Town. 'All *obroni* have to be checked out and foundated with us,' explained Isaac. 'You might be a spy. You might be here on bad business.'

I was about to say something but he put his finger to his lips for silence.

'Maroons always a tricky people – plenty *obroni* have died and plenty sick and can't cure because they try and fight us. Yes, them die for it. Or Nanny *cuss* them off. But hear me now, we Maroon people is a *well-meaning* people. Yes, a friendly people. We don't move among strangers, but still and all we don't attack *obroni* unless they attack us. The spirit ancestors – them throw the bad people out.'

He laughed, then scowled. 'Is the hand of God that throw them out.' Isaac, like many Maroons, practised an evangelical Christianity combined with an African-derived ancestor-worship which involved the 'science' of telepathy and a belief in the paranormal. 'I am foundated with Jesus, definitely so.' From his wallet he removed a membership card for the United Holy Church of God. 'But I also receive messages from the spirit world far, far away. And when I cut loose [meaning 'die'], I fly up, go to Africa. Because all Maroon come from Africa. Yes, my foreparents them come from Africa. And,' Isaac went on, with his eyes to the veranda roof, 'you have met Colonel Sterling?'

'Not yet.'

'Colonel Sterling is a brown-skin man,' said Isaac, with a hint maybe of disapproval. 'Most of us Maroons is black.'

'Is that a problem?'

No – a Maroon community would accept anyone irrespective of pigmentation or ethnicity. 'All the same, is mostly *black* we have up here – no Chinee or coolie people.' He added, 'Jamaica don't have enough trouble as it is with coolie Hindians, but now we must have slant eye too!' It was as if, having discovered his proud African 'voice', Isaac attributed a lack of authenticity to other Jamaicans. Maroons, in Isaac's formulation, were a chosen people, an African elect. 'Anyway Chinyman no good at domino or making Maroon food,' he concluded gruffly.

He stood up, staggered slightly, then disappeared a moment down a hall to fetch an *abeng*. 'I use it for bugling,' he explained, lifting it to his lips. 'I use it to summon folks to meetings, as a call to arms and to make jollification at Christmas time.' Through the *abeng* he blew three long, foghorn-like notes and, pausing for breath, stopped. 'No one learn me how to blow – all my bugling is self-taught.' He demonstrated an array of *abeng* signals – long and complicated Morse codes to communicate a warning, or summon help. 'If you drop dead from a tree, I can blow this horn to announce as much. Or if you gets lost in the bush, I give a long–short–long message like this . . .' He blew again, and the notes rang out mournful across the foothills of the Blue Mountains.

Before I left, he asked me for a sum of money – what he called, in Asanti-Twi, *takefa*. The elder was poor, with few extenuating circumstances. We regarded each other for a moment as I took out a couple of Jamaican $500 'Nanny' notes (about £10). The transaction made me feel dirty – as though I was buying Maroon knowledge and had obliged the *fete-man* to sell it to me. He flattened the notes on his knee and then, bizarrely, pressed them against his eyelids for a second.

'Why do that?'

'Because we call money "eyesight" in Maroon tongue,' Isaac answered cryptically. (Back home, I could find no explanation for why money should be referred to as 'eyesight'.) I did not touch on the missing UNESCO grant, but instead asked Isaac about the trip he had made in 2003 to Surinam in what used to be the Netherlands West Indies. 'Surinam!' He echoed excitedly. The Maroons of Surinam were kin to Jamaica's and even spoke a Creole language, Saramacan, cognate with Jamaican patois. Yes, the Surinamers used the *abeng* too. 'Only their gears are more fashionable than our gears – they wear wrap-skirts and waist ties like sashes.' Jamaican Maroons wear no such tribesman finery.

As Isaac spoke, his eyes seemed to be looking far into the future, or perhaps into the past. I found him inscrutable and, in some way, sinister. He was a powerful person, with a confident and slightly haughty manner, and was said to be a good community leader. He was convinced, he told me (with the kind of smile that usually goes with a wink) that Maroon culture would survive modern times. For how long? In 1946 the African American dancer Katherine Dunham had come to Jamaica in search of 'wild exotic Maroon music' but at first could find only radio broadcasts of Duke Ellington and Cab Calloway.

*

At about 6.30 p.m. the sun went down in a haze of dust particles, and by the time I got back to Moore Town it was dark. A full moon was forming on the edge of the sky and I stood outside my room watching the moon riding, careering, through the clouds. Gene Pryce invited me to join her in a game of dominoes on the porch. (Every Jamaican village has its domino expert, who does little else but 'play domino'; a domino could feature on the national flag.)

Gene set the domino tiles out on the table.

'Come, Lenny,' she called out to her husband, who had also been gazing up at the moon. 'Sit down for domino.'

'All right, Gene.'

'And come, Ian, you too.'

'Soon come,' I said, throwing Gene a newly acquired phrase.

A bat swooped round the lamp's uncertain light above the table. 'Double 6' was a new game to me. I banged down the bone pieces hard. A bottle of rum rested between me and Lenny, and Lenny was drinking tots of the stuff. 'Thought you had me trapped there, Lenny, my dear,' said Gene, celebrating a domino victory over her husband. A neighbour called Michael ('Come, Mikey') presently joined us for a round. He sat at the table with his eyes modestly lowered, and remained silent throughout. One by one, other domino hotshots followed Michael to the game of 'Double 6'. The players sat packed in tight under the lamp, chatting. A group of children, lured perhaps by the presence of the *obroni* (or the sound of concentrated chatter), stood on tiptoe peeking over shoulders. I looked up at the spangled night sky: life here was not so bad.

*

'What's your job?' Colonel Sterling asked me – the question so sudden, I had to think before answering it.

'Well, I write.'

'A writer, you say?' the colonel replied with a degree of Maroon stateliness. 'Well then, you can write how we Maroons are at the crossroads now. Yes, any kind of development – a new school, a new church – will come at the cost of having something of our old ways eroded.' The colonel laughed mirthlessly. 'It was hoped – it was *expected* – that Maroon families would pass on African culture to their children, but this has not happened.' In order to safeguard what might soon be lost, Sterling was planning to open a Maroon Cultural Centre.

'With the UNESCO money?'

'With *some* of it.' He looked at me cautiously.

'A sort of museum?'

'A sort of museum,' he agreed.

Though Colonel Sterling was, comparatively speaking, a newcomer to Moore Town (having been raised in Cornwall Barracks in the 1950s), the attention he paid to his adopted town – its history, its people – was impressive. The controversy surrounding the UNESCO grant was part of a quarrel that had been simmering for decades. The trouble started, said the colonel, because of petty political jealousies. Moore Town's JLP faction, led by one Charles Aarons, and others of his political persuasion had long prevented Sterling and his PNP allies from obtaining their rightful share of local power. Now Charles Aarons of the JLP was spreading wild rumours about the colonel's financial improprieties. 'If only Aarons would simmer down,' Sterling said, as we sat talking in the muggy, rain-washed morning, 'Moore Town would not be so . . . troubled.' The remark carried a barb that would surely rankle with Aarons.

*

Aarons's house, a big, bland-looking concrete construction on the mountain path up to Cornwall Barracks, was planted round with white, green and red flags on tall bamboo poles. The flags indicated that the occupant was a 'science-man', one of those Jamaicans who mediated between the world of the living and the unseen world of the spirits (and was perhaps also a practitioner of 'anti-social magic', or witchcraft). According to the Pryces, when Aarons was in spirit possession (*myal*) he was able to perform such extraordinary physical feats as climbing coconut trees upside down, and devouring glass.

Aarons appraised me suspiciously: his ancestors had advised him not to talk to *obroni*. He was wearing dark glasses, which enhanced his mystic appearance. After the first flush of suspicion, he seemed prepared to talk. And what he wanted to talk about, above all, was Colonel Sterling.

'Me and Sterling, we used to be as close as batty and bench,' (the colloquial Jamaican expression sounded a ribald note) 'but now is knives we have in each other. Yes, I'm vex and I'm disillusioned.' Among the colonel's shortcomings, apparently, was his inability to speak Asante-Twi.

'Does he need to?'

'Yes!' Aarons retorted in a surprised voice: Asante-Twi was the language of the old people, of the custodians of Maroon life. The surviving traces of the language were guarded possessively by town elders such as Aarons, whose company Sterling (because he spoke no Asante-Twi) had no right to keep.

Aarons added, 'Moore Town's a sad place today.' He repeated, 'You don't find Moore Town a sad place, mister?'

'I haven't noticed any sadness.'

'But look at the state of our roads! Everything overgrown – Nanny's town's turned to bush! Is this what Nanny's children deserve?' Of the UNESCO donation he demanded to know: 'Where *is* it? What has been done with it? It need investigation!'

The quarrel went deeper than money or politics: it involved religion. Colonel Sterling, a Seventh Day Adventist, disapproved of Charles Aarons's practice of *obeah*. 'The colonel say I sup with the devil – that I oppose to goodness. Well, I just play my Maroon drums in reply to that.' Aarons was the devil – Sterling was the devil. Aarons hated Sterling, and he hated him with an intensity he was unable to mask. The thwarting of the colonel was a duty which Aarons felt compelled to fulfil – for the sake of Moore Town's 'salvation'.

Aarons removed his dark glasses. He had a cataract in one eye. A tall, narrow hand-drum called a *gumbay* stood by his side, and on it he began to play a 'Coromantee' war dance rhythm designed to bring destruction on enemies. (I did not ask who these enemies might be.) As Aarons played, the flowing, ever-changing syncopations sounded to me like Caribbean *mento* folksong overlaid with rhythms from Gold Coast Africa. But Aarons was playing something more ancient. This was Africa as it might have sounded in the sixteenth century, not the deep booming of a Revivalist or Salvation Army drum, but a sharp staccato beat struck off a tight-drawn goatskin.

Aarons rubbed his hands and said, 'The drumming was to your liking?' We might have been at a classical concert. For Aarons, too, had absorbed a colonial British emphasis on ceremony and formal correctness. Maroons might look reverentially to Africa yet, paradoxically, they had adopted the British military title of 'colonel'. Queen Elizabeth II remained for them the Great Ruler of the Universe, moreover, associated in the Maroon mind with a benevolent and fair rule. In 1796, at the end of the Maroon Wars, the British Crown became the guarantor of Maroon laws and the Maroons' special 'treaty status'.

Understandably for some black nationalists the 'Britishness' adopted by Maroons signals a lack of ideological purity, even a covert loyalty to imperialism. Is that fair? In spite of their anglophile insistence on pomp, Maroons have always taken a great pride in their African identity. And this identity has not been acquired at a distance from an autocratic Ethiopian monarch – Haile Selassie – but was passed down the generations and still lives in the 'Coromantee' spirit of Moore Town. I felt privileged to have stayed, if only for a few days, amid the runaways of eastern Jamaica.

17

The Killing of a Chinese Shopkeeper

I had come to Annotto Bay, a dank coastal outpost of St Mary parish, by bus from Port Antonio. Mosquito-infested and poor, the town had warped jetties and boats upended on marshland, and exuded a sense of things rotting. The grocery shops, many of them, were owned by Chinese who had settled here in the 1840s as contract labourers. The Chinese residents were not always liked. They tended to live apart, venturing into Annotto Bay only on market days to buy supplies. To some Jamaicans, they were 'economic oppressors', an easy target for resentment.

In 2004, an inexplicable (or at least still unexplained) murder took place, of a Chinese couple, Ilene and Winston Chin, at their home in Highgate near Annotto Bay. Their shop, 'Chin & Co', was empty now and the windows still boarded against looters.

Annotto Bay also has another unfortunate association. As I related earlier, Father Martin Royackers, a Canadian Jesuit, had been gunned down outside the Catholic rectory in this broken and marginalised parish of St Mary on the evening of 20 June 2001. According to the police, nobody had heard the gunman's shot, at any rate nobody had come forward yet.

I rang the bell to the rectory and the door was opened by Jim Webb, whom I had met earlier in Kingston. His pale face and slightly reticent manner still spoke of an absorbing melancholy.

Along a dark, earth-smelling corridor Webb led me to a terrace overlooking the sea, where a lunch of fried pork awaited us. 'I hope pork's to your liking?' He asked the question with some trepidation: 'I thought you might be vegetarian.' Beneath us the Caribbean Sea brought in a scummy-looking tide where a group of children was fishing hopefully for snapper and other food, feeding out their lines.

'They never catch anything,' Father Webb commented dolefully. 'Nobody ever does.' A couple of birds circled on a high thermal out to sea, like black wreaths.

Watched by the children, we sat down to eat. In the uncertain light the scene looked bleak enough. Most of the children slept four to a bed, said Father Webb. They sailed paper ships in the gutter, rolled hoops across rubbish-strewn beaches (as some were doing now), and failed their exams: but by twelve they had learned to shoot guns, and by twenty, if they had migrated to Kingston, were dead. Martin Royackers's death remained a 'great trial' to Webb. Police files had been checked, suspects considered, resulting in nothing. 'Martin was ready to die, I believe, though what exactly provoked his death I'm not sure.' A contract hit? Many have suggested as much. 'Martin's assassination was political,' Webb agreed. It was the best he could surmise.

Prior to his murder Royackers had managed to re-assign sixty acres of idle land to St Mary farmers. This had offended local business interests. Very little land in Jamaica is under church or government control; it remains either in the hands of the plantocracy or giant (usually foreign) business corporations. With Father Webb's help, however, Royackers had returned a portion of land to the peasantry and encouraged small-scale cultivators to set up cooperatives. The Jesuit-run St Mary Rural Development Project had helped to transform the hillside communities of the parish.

However, Royackers's confrontational personality could make him prickly and hostile in the presence of authority. 'We priests are human,' Webb explained, 'we share some of the prejudices of our backgrounds and upbringing – and maybe Martin was pugnacious by . . . circumstance.' From rural Ontario, Royackers cared little for social niceties. Even Jesuits found his attempts to reconcile Christianity with communism peculiar. 'Martin was a curious mix of Opus Dei and Arthur Scargill,' a Canadian friend of his, Richard Greene (incidentally, the editor of Graham Greene's letters), told me. 'Very right wing theologically, but very left wing politically – a combination that's not that all rare among Catholic priests in the Third World.'

On that fateful day in 2004, a Jesuit deacon had risen early to find Royackers's supper uneaten and the refectory lights still on. The priest was discovered lying face down and his body plugged with a single bullet, powder burns at the entry indicating that the killer had been less than five feet away. 'I may not be comfortable in Jamaica,' Royackers had written in a letter home, 'but, like the morning's first drag on a cigarette, the noise and heat and insect bites remind me that I am alive.' The Klondike sleaze of Annotto Bay appealed to him.

Father Webb offered to take me to see the effects of Royackers's land redistribution project. In Jamaica, where everything waits for the government (and is often corrupted by politicians seeking 'fish head' – bribes) a private scheme such as St Mary Rural Development was new and encouraging. We would go in a week's time.

*

Travel in rural Jamaica, away from the great tourist tracks, is difficult, and Green Castle agricultural estate was not easy to find. I went there on foot from Annotto Bay, using as my landmark a stone windmill tower that stood, like an imperious beehive, on a hilltop. From the tower I was able to find my way to Robin Crum-Ewing's house, where I was to spend a couple of nights. A Taino Indian village had been excavated on Green Castle in 1999, and Crum-Ewing had found funds to develop it into a 'heritage site'. Meanwhile, he was an exception among Jamaica's landowners, as Green Castle was run by him as a non-profit-making organisation, in which any surplus is shared by the employees. He recognised that the Jamaican agricultural system, with its age-old inequalities and iniquities, was in need of reform.

I found Crum-Ewing at work in a cattle pen branding heifers. He looked like a Wild West rancher in his wide-brim hat yet he was a physically slight man, with pale skin mottled red with sun spots. 'Very good,' he said, emerging dusty from the pen, 'come with me.' We got into a van and drove past fields of sleepy-looking horned Brahman cattle.

During the 1960s, Crum-Ewing had worked at management level for Jamaica's bauxite industry. Bauxite, the raw material from which aluminium is made, is abundant in Jamaica's rust-red soil and by the mid-1960s, Jamaica was producing over 20 per cent of the world's supply. Most of it was mined by foreign multinationals such as Alcan, Reynolds and Alcoa. A few top-ranking Jamaicans, Crum-Ewing among them, profited handsomely. But in the real world, down in the ghetto, the new money had not reached the poor. Jamaican outrage at foreign business concerns was well founded. The bauxite companies were not paying Jamaica anything for the raw material they were taking. In 1974, therefore, Michael Manley subjected the bauxite industry to government regulation, with levies imposed on production.

Crum-Ewing was a privileged Jamaican by marriage only, having married a descendant of the Scarletts, wealthy landowners in Jamaica since Oliver Cromwell's time. He wanted to take me to see the strange beehive-like windmill tower, a family inheritance on his wife's side. It was reached along a rough path leading to Robin's Bay (where the British painter Augustus John had stayed in 1937). A smell of salt and seaweed irradiated the lukewarm air; the scene was beautifully calm. From a distance the stone tower seemed to be honeycombed with holes. On closer inspection the holes were filled with rotted mahogany beams, which had served as scaffolding. The slave-owning English had used the mill to power cane-crushing machines.

The mahogany was salvaged, most likely, from a dismantled Spanish vessel or other timber re-used from the time of Christopher Columbus's first landfall off Jamaica in 1494. It has been radiocarbon-dated to the fifteenth century. Made of coralstone, the windmill tower was unique in Jamaica for its wall-piercings and quaint shape. Chunks of Cornish stone used as ballast on the slave ships had been built into the brickwork. Today the beehive tower is home to nesting owls. Eighty-two bird species had been identified by Crum-Ewing as native to Green Castle. That figure, he conceded, was probably reduced now, as pollution and deforestation had taken their toll.

This saddened him, as he identified strongly with Jamaica and had developed a relaxed attitude to life with an inclination to do a minimum of work which, he claimed, was Jamaican. 'It's like this,' he explained. 'We Jamaicans live on a very rich island, but we don't always get rich from it. We don't really know *how* to and we're too lazy.' (This was a well-worn chestnut, I thought, about Jamaicans.)

'We're hopelessly and irretrievably lazy – lazy *and* ill-disciplined. Why should we work? We don't *need* to work. We don't need to save money for winter coats for the children – because it's always warm here.' In Green Castle, a quiet, slow-moving place, food grew in abundance. 'And it's God's own food ripe for the picking.' Jamaica's natural wealth was so great that 'no one need starve', he concluded. In the Taino Indian language Jamaica – *Xamaica* – meant a country abounding in springs; every green valley had its stream, every crag its cascade.

In this Eden, Crum-Ewing grew orchids for Jamaica's Chinese market, the flowers cultivated under rows of tunnel cloches. Decorative orchids are displayed by every Chinese business: they are emblematic of fertility and, in the popular Jamaican mind, Chinese aloofness and clannishness. Traditionally Jamaican Chinese have not cared to 'marry out', and their perceived standoffishness has helped to stoke riots against them. In 1918 and again, more seriously, in 1965, Jamaica was shaken when 'Chiney' shops and 'Chiney' homes were looted and set ablaze. At this time of growing 'black consciousness', the Chinese, having little involvement in the movement, were seen as a foreign, exploitative people.

*

At 176 Old Hope Road, near the Bob Marley Museum in uptown Kingston, is a pagoda-like building with stone lions at the entrance. This is the headquarters of the Chinese Benevolent Society, founded in Kingston in 1891 to oversee Chinese interests in the island. Dalton Yap, the president, asked me cautiously at the entrance, 'So, why you come here see Yap? You want talk, right?' He was a thin man with high cheekbones and skin the colour of cork. I followed him downstairs, where he unlocked a door which opened on to a room crammed with jade objects, paper fans, china dolls and items of furniture upholstered in pale green fabric. 'Good,' Yap announced, looking around the Chinese museum. 'Everything good.' He flicked a switch on the wall and the sound of a stringed instrument plucking a Chinese melody (to my ears, a weird, quarter-tone wail) filled the room. 'That's a recording of an *ehru* guitar,' Yap said. 'Oh, it make a terrible melancholy sound.' The notes hovered in the air like ice crystals.

On the wall hung an anatomy chart for acupuncture, along with advertisements for Kung Fu lessons and conversational Mandarin. The first Chinese to arrive in Jamaica came from south-east China in the 1840s and spoke Hakka (not Mandarin or Cantonese). They were mostly young, unmarried men. By the end of their sixteen-week sea journey to the West Indies, many of them had died, some of opium withdrawal. The journey had taken them round India with a brief respite in Java to the Cape of Good Hope and on up the western coast of Africa across the Atlantic to Jamaica.

Unlike their Hindi-speaking counterparts, the Chinese quickly escaped the indignity of plantation labour and set up shops in countryside villages. The Chinese were seen as less lowly (because more 'white') by the British authorities who gave them opportunities not available to the East Indians. Chinese shops, redolent of pickled fish and kerosene, offered credit or sold by barter, and were a boon to Jamaicans in the interior without access to provisions. By the early 1890s, almost every Jamaican village had its 'Chiney shop' where customers could exchange plantation crops (pimento and ginger) for butter, flour, salted fish and other groceries.

The fear – then as now – was that the Chinese would monopolise Jamaica's retail business. From the mid 1920s, as the rate of arrivals increased, Chinese were required by Jamaican law to deposit £30 on arrival and demonstrate a written ability with fifty words in English, as well as submit to a physical examination. Still the 'Children of the Dragon' continued to arrive and eventually they moved to downtown Kingston, where they set up betting parlours, laundries, fortune-telling shops, tattoo parlours, supermarkets, bakeries. Barry Street served as the east–west spine of Chinatown, with Hakka restaurants and Hakka shops that sold lychee ice cream, oysters and booby (sea bird) eggs.

Tensions developed between the Chinese and their black neighbours. The Chinese were 'dog-eaters' or 'bananas' (Oriental yellow on the outside, white colonialist on the inside). Mixed marriages were frowned on by both sides, with black Chinese mockingly referred to by the Hakka community as 'Eleven o'clock People' (*Ship Yit Tiam*): not quite twelve o'clock, they were not quite complete. Ian Fleming's sixth 007 novel, *Dr No* (1957), is coloured by its disgusted (to the modern reader, perhaps disgusting) portrayal of Jamaica's half-Chinese community as a 'hideous' yellow-black race. Fleming, like many Englishmen of his class, was repelled by the notion of hybridity and in *Dr No* he wrote with ill-concealed antipathy of 'Chigroes'.

China Town disappeared when Kingston's railway station was closed in the early 1990s. Far fewer Chinese businesses operate downtown now, the old shops are boarded up or else they serve as crack dens. The Chinese still have their own athletic club, though, as well as their own newspaper (*The Pagoda*) and their own free-mason societies, called *Tongs*. The *Tongs* control many of the nightclubs, brothels and illegal betting dens across Jamaica. Most Chinese restaurants in Kingston (notably, the Mandarin on the city's North Side Plaza) operate a backroom gaming parlour. At Foxy's International, a nightclub on the north coast, groups of half-Chinese and, increasingly, Russian prostitutes in cheongsams (the high-necked, slit-skirted Chinese dress) talk to customers round the hot centre of the dance floor. When I visited, a couple of middle-aged white women in search of 'big bamboo' lay slouched against the bar, plainly drunk or stoned. Another nightclub, the Gemini in Kingston's Halfway Tree Road, has a raised platform for dancing, a bar and, at the rear, a number of cubicle-like rooms, decorated with orchids, for paid sex. One of the women was visibly bruised, apparently from a pistol-whipping by a Colombian or Russian customer. One word out of line here and you get your 'cranium cracked', she told me. What she wanted above all (apart from money) was a bottle of 'Dom P' (Dom Perignon), the Jamaican gangster's preferred drink.

In the 1960s and 1970s, a number of Chinese record producers operated in Kingston, among them Vincent 'Randy' Chin, Leslie Kong, the late Byron Lee and Justin Yap (related to Dalton Yap), who in 1964 signed the Skatalites to his Top Deck label. They have all, at various stages, been accused of 'Chiney man' exploitation of ghetto music. Byron Lee sanitised ska for an uptown clientele, adapting it for more affluent white tastes much as Elvis had done with rhythm and blues, or João Gilberto in Brazil with bossa nova, the dance music fashioned out of African samba.

Byron Lee died in November 2008 at the age of seventy-three, not long after I met him at his home in the Stony Hill suburb of Kingston. It was the aftermath of Hurricane Dennis, and the windows, blown out by the storm, had been replaced with temporary plywood. As I got out of the taxi Lee, a stout man in a track suit, rose from his chair on the porch and gave a bob of greeting. 'We have a crisis situation – hurricane waters – the house is flooded.' Inside, stacks of vinyl records, mattresses and a wardrobe spewing clothes had been dragged out into the corridors to dry. The house was airless and sticky – the fans were immobilised – with mosquitoes biting and whining thinly. Lee, a courteous man, apologised for the lack of air-conditioning.

On the shelves in his office were sepia photographs of Chinese relatives. Lee's supposedly privileged status as a Chinese belied the fact that his mother was a black (or near black) Jamaican, who instilled in him a love of Afro-Jamaican Revivalist and Kumina music. His father had arrived in Jamaica from Kowloon in the 1920s and spoke no English. 'Whether they call me a half-Chiney or a Chiney-Royal or an Eleven o'Clock,' Lee said to me, 'it make no difference. First of all I'm Jamaican.'

In 1957, when Byron Lee founded the Dragonaires, Jamaica had no popular music to call its own, but a new sound was evolving in Edward Seaga's Back-o-Wall constituency. It was called ska, and it was uniquely Jamaican. With Seaga's financial backing, the Dragonaires put a dance spin on the rackety, 'hop, skip and jump' downtown sound, and transformed it into a slick, show-band confection with elements of calypso and traditional Trinidad *soca*. It lacked the grit and drive of ghetto ska, and Byron Lee was criticised for making money out of a black music not his own. (He later produced Eric Clapton's sanitised version of Bob Marley's 'I Shot the Sheriff'.) Byron Lee was not a ska originator, and his professional association with Edward '*Ska*-aga', a white JLP politician of Lebanese descent, looked like commercial opportunism. 'People can say what they like,' Lee protested to me, 'but until Seaga came along we Jamaican Chinese were not considered part of the music scene.' Chinese record producers were 'like garbage', said Lee, 'like lower-class'. Lee later purchased Seaga's

West Indies Records company based in Kingston, and renamed it Dynamic Sounds.

Most controversial was Seaga's decision to send the Dragonaires to New York in 1964 to represent Jamaica at the World's Fair. Ska's true originators, the Skatalites, were not chosen. Why? Their zingy, post-independence music drew from a variety of sources, among them news headlines ('Christine Keeler' celebrated the call girl who had helped to bring down the Harold Macmillan government), film themes ('Third Man Ska', 'Exodus'), swing, bebop, Ellingtonian jazz-inflected Chinoiserie and R & B. In these magpie borrowings, surely, there was something for everyone. The bland *ska-lyp-so* as purveyed by the Dragonaires was hardly Jamaica's National Sound. Byron Lee's beaming, mixed-race band wore shiny dinner jackets and Lee himself, like an Ed Sullivan show host, played electric Fender bass. The sound they made was hotel-circuit clean.

In hindsight, however, Seaga's was a sensible choice: the Skatalites, insufficiently disciplined, were not to be relied on to provide entertainment for an international trade convention. Their erratic trombone genius, Don Drummond, was probably schizophrenic (indeed, he would soon murder his girlfriend).

The Dragonaires for their part had already contributed to the soundtrack of the first 007 movie, *Dr No* (shot in Jamaica in 1962), and introduced tourists to basic ska dance steps such as the 'Kingston Head Roll' (done 'to relax and cool off') and the more energetic 'Rowing'. Unfortunately for the money-conscious Seaga, the Dragonaires failed to make an impression in America. Their single 'Oil in My Lamp' flopped after just one week in the US charts (at number ninety-eight). In Britain, where Millie Small had triumphed with 'My Boy Lollipop' (with Rod Stewart on harmonica), it was a different story. The Mods were listening to ska; and so were Jamaicans.

*

Everyone in Morant Bay seemed to appreciate the Chong Sangs – a likeably high-spirited, hard-working Chinese family. George Chong Sang, the father, owned a hardware store and wholesale outlet on Main Street near the Paul Bogle statue. Business, with the ever-increasing numbers of returnees, had never been so good. 'We have five truck and five truck driver. No-stop trucking!' George said to me. Busy, busy. In the delivery yard George's four grown-up children were taking stock, clipboards and calculators in hand. They were beautiful and I told George as much. 'Mix Chinese *are* beautiful,' he said proudly. 'We have all kind of mix people in Morant Bay. Black and brown and Chiney and Hindian. Even chestnut man!' At the age of three, George was sent to Canton to be educated and *learn manners*. The school was 'very strict and harsh', he recalled, with classes in 'etiquette correction'. But that was not the worst of it.

When Japan invaded China in 1937, George was told he might never return home. Emperor Hirohito's troops – the Asian master race – began to press-gang Chinese into forced labour; street executions were not uncommon. In the Nanking Massacre some 150,000 Chinese civilians were bestially slaughtered. For a long time afterwards George could not look at a Japanese. ('I *hated* them.') Not until 1948, eighteen years into his Chinese exile, was he finally able to sail home to Jamaica. In Morant Bay, he took over his father's hardware business and was elected president of a local *Tong*.

Like many Jamaican Chinese, the Chong Sangs were Buddhist converts to Catholicism. George explained, with an awkward smile, that the Catholic Church was 'less dominated by black people'; Baptist and Revivalists, for his taste, were a little 'too black'. Listening to him, I could see how the Chinese might have given rise to the notion that they were in business solely to exploit black Jamaicans. In the summer of 1965, after a rumour had spread that a black woman had been beaten by a Chinese baker in Spanish Town, anti-Chinese riots flared in the Jamaican capital.

Significantly, the riots came just days after the 'Negro Disturbances' (as the Jamaican *Gleaner* called them) had erupted in the Watts ghetto of Los Angeles. Until 1992, these were the worst urban riots in the United States. In downtown Kingston, as in Los Angeles, Chinese were seen as the nearest approximation to white people. Their shops and houses were burned down and looted, the owners verbally abused and even 'chopped' – attacked with machetes. The Jamaican establishment showed little sympathy. In an editorial of 31 August 1965 ('Girls and Mice') the *Gleaner* upbraided the 'Chinamen' of Kingston for their 'timidity' and 'panicky' reaction in shutting down shops and homes. 'It is a pity', the newspaper lectured, 'that so many [Chinese] business people lent greater point to the trouble by locking their doors, thus attracting the ribald notice of ragamuffins.' The language is that of the British country club bar; John Chinaman seen as the slant-eyed coward.

In 1975, fearing a communist revolution under Manley, George Chong Sang fled with his family to Toronto. For five years they lived in that earnest, multicultural metropolis. George finally returned in October 1980, the month Seaga won the general election, fifteen years ahead of his children. He could not believe Jamaica's transformation. 'The traffic! The crowds!' Some 400 Jamaican Chinese were now living in Morant Bay. Outwardly, relations between them and the black majority were much better. 'If we treat Jamaicans good,' George said to me, 'they come buy from me. We are *glad* to serve them!' However, the fact that George had referred to the black community as 'Jamaicans' and his own people as 'Chinese' suggested a gulf still to be crossed.

*

Business is a hard game in Jamaica, and Gloria Palomino (born Lyn Ah Ping), is reckoned to be one of the toughest and most successful financial powers in the land. She owns a diesel haulage company on Marcus Garvey Drive, as well as restaurants and a café in the Blue Mountains. Her home, barred against burglars, is situated in the aptly named Armour Heights area of the Kingston hills. The sitting room with high white walls was adorned with Jamaican art; sticks of incense burned on the balcony. A wide expanse of glass allowed guests to see the port beyond and the shanties sprawling at the sea's mouth.

In 1988, Palomino's sister was killed by intruders, who broke into her store in St Mary parish. The murder prompted Palomino to go to China for the first time in search of her family roots. To her surprise her father's birthplace in Guangdong province was full of elderly 'black' Chinese who had been sent from Jamaica in the early 1900s to receive a Chinese education. The outbreak of the Sino-Japanese war had prevented their return home, and they had stayed ever since. Palomino might well have been among them. In 1937, with a suitcase full of clothes and toys, she was in a group of Jamaican Chinese children awaiting transportation to China for schooling. In straight lines the children waited in silence to board the ship moored in Kingston docks. Finally the ship's captain strode down the gangplank with a megaphone to announce that China had been invaded by Japan and that departure was to be postponed indefinitely. In tears of relief Gloria was escorted back to her parents' house in Kingston; her true home, she knew then, was Jamaica, and always would be.

Today, as the economy and population of the People's Republic of China strengthens, hundreds of mainland Chinese have been allowed to set up in business in Jamaica. A rivalry has developed between the newcomers and the established Jamaican Chinese. 'We consider the mainlanders rather common,' Palomino explained, with a quick, deprecating laugh. Oh, she was loath to let these Mandarin-speakers get anywhere near her financial empire. 'They wouldn't *dare* interfere – I'm too much competition!' she said, meaning it. In 2005, Jamaica opened a new embassy in Beijing, while the Chinese Embassy in Kingston, a huge modern complex off Sea View Avenue, mills at all hours with Mao-suited officials.

*

I returned to Father Webb for my long-held appointment to visit a cooperative farm. The farm was a short distance away by car. Rain and mist hung over the sea-coast sprawl of St Mary parish. Most of the neighbouring countryside was owned by businessmen, minor politicians and gunmen who were operated by the bigger politicians in Kingston. Little could be done locally without these men, said Webb; they had become the law. The farmers, some too poor to own even agricultural implements, were obliged to plough with machetes and use their fingers to remove stones from the earth. But, thanks to the St Mary Rural Development Project, a handful had their own land, and with this had come a sense of achievement and hope. In one field we passed, plastic pipes laid by Martin Royackers brought water down from the mountain rivers and streams. Irrigated fields and space for crops were what the farmers of St Mary needed.

By midday the sky had turned a robin's-egg blue and the shanties east of Annotto Bay looked less forlorn. We arrived at the farm, Georgia, where a sturdily built man was wielding his hoe with slow, laboured movements. He watched us get out of the car and walked towards us. 'Morning, Father.' There was real enthusiasm in his greeting. Father Webb seemed to provide encouragement as he advised the farmer on what sold well in Annotto Bay market ('Dasheen – you should plant more dasheen'), quoting market prices for pumpkin and sweet pepper. The farmer's cassava plants were doing well (though rats kept eating the pumpkin seeds).

Georgia might have been an image of agricultural barrenness. Yet it offered hope: the dedicated Jesuit priest who was encouraging the cooperative farmer to think of irrigation and crop rotation, who patiently advised, and listened. It lifted the heart, to think that something solid and beneficial was being built here.

By 2008 the Jesuit-run farms were able to compete with the market produce in Annotto Bay, much of it controlled by the Chinese and imported from the United States. For all their continued hardship, the St Mary farmers were among the lucky ones. In Annotto Bay, at least, the liberation theology of the Jesuits had gone hand in hand with a new sympathy and respect for the poor.

18

007 (Shanty Town)

'Tell me', Blanche Blackwell said to me, 'have you ever been to Jamaica?'

'I've just come *back* from Jamaica.'

'Oh tell me!' she exclaimed airily. 'What was it like?'

'Well . . .'

'You know I could *never* go back to Jamaica.' Mrs Blackwell waved her handkerchief expressively. 'Jamaica is getting too . . . *pronounced*. All those sex and machete fights! Dear, oh dear.' Ever since her house in Kingston was burgled for a third time in 2003 alone she had vowed never to go back. 'I'm going to stay put in Europe. Anyway,' she reflected, 'to Jamaica from Europe is really too much of a journey. Would you care for some lunch?'

She turned to one of her Jamaican maids. 'Rosie, what's for lunch?'

'Roast lamb, Miss Blanche.'

'Oh *good-o*.'

Blanche Blackwell was half sitting, half reclining, in her flat off Lowndes Square in Knightsbridge, west London. Known to friends as 'Birdie', she was, at ninety-five, legally blind, but one would not have known it. Of Jamaican Jewish ancestry, she wore her white hair bobbed round an animated face. She was the mother of Chris Blackwell, the founder and former owner of Island Records who, back in the 1970s, 'discovered' the rock-reggae of Bob Marley. Mrs Blackwell's life, until she decamped to London, had been one of island entertainments and literary friendships.

Born in Kingston in 1912 as Blanche Lindo, she had married Captain Joseph Blackwell of the Irish Guards and heir to Crosse and Blackwell foods. However, she was not happy in the marriage. Errol Flynn ('a gorgeous god', she called him) became one of her lovers, as, later, did Ian Fleming. By the time of her divorce in 1949 she had moved to Jamaica's north coast to a house equidistant between Noel Coward's and Fleming's. 'Noel became a special pal of mine,' Mrs Blackwell said to me, adding, 'Of course, we all knew he had latent . . . proclivities.' Ian Fleming was to write all thirteen of his 007 novels in Jamaica, though only three (*Dr No*, *Live and Let Die*, *The Man with the Golden Gun*) were set partly on the island.

Impishly, Fleming included sketches of his friends (and enemies) in his fiction. Blanche Blackwell was supposedly a model for the Sapphic aeroplane pilot and martial arts expert, Pussy Galore, in *Goldfinger*. Fleming, with his tall, alcohol-swollen frame, adored 'Birdie' Blackwell and her darting, kingfisher mind. And Blanche, in her turn, considered Fleming a 'charming, handsome, gifted man', but plagued by self-doubt and even self-hate. 'Ian was an *angel*,' she told me (though at first she had thought him the rudest of men). 'Errol was another angel. Both lovely men – both exceptionally manly and definitely *not* for domesticating!' Sightlessly she stretched out a hand towards a full-blown pink rose. 'Not that I should complain. I've had a marvellous life. Do smell my pink rose.' It was part of Mrs Blackwell's style, I suspected, to ask men to smell her roses.

I asked her, 'So Jamaica's lost its charm for you?'

'Oh absolutely. It's not so much the *violence* that I object to – I've lived long enough not to be afraid of violence. No, it's the change in the *people*. The corruption. And the lack of respect is totally dreadful.' (Mrs Blackwell seemed inclined to faint.) A gulf of privilege separated her from other Jamaicans, yet she shared in their complaint about 'declining standards'.

'But surely Jamaica is a fairer society today?' I persisted.

'My dear young man! Jamaica is now so disgracefully managed, one hardly knows to whom to complain. Independence was the *worst* thing that could have happened to Jamaicans – they were simply not ready for it.'

A Jamaican maid tinkled a bell to signal that lunch was ready; she was one of three, pink-aproned black women who tended to Mrs Blackwell. 'Thank you, little dear,' she said to the maid as she served the lamb.

I glanced round the flat. Dresden figurines and porcelain monkey musicians stood on a Georgian table by the window; it was a well-appointed property. Blanche Lindo had grown up in Jamaica in scarcely less rarefied surroundings. The Lindos, Sephardi Jews hailing from western Europe (possibly Bordeaux), had settled in Kingston in the second half of the eighteenth century. One of them, the rum merchant Alexandre Lindo, loaned £60,000 to Napoleon to help him re-instate slavery in Saint Domingue, subsequently Haiti. Like many European Jews of the Napoleonic era, Lindo was sympathetic to Bonaparte and the new French Republic. However, after Napoleon had been defeated by the freed Haitian slaves, the French government stinted on repayment of the loan. Lindo ended his days in poverty in a house in Finsbury Square, north London, and, in 1812, was buried in the Jewish cemetery off Mile End Road. In 1833 his grandson, Louis Lindo, married Fanny Brawne, formerly the fiancée of the poet John Keats.

'It's quite a saga, isn't it?' said Mrs Blackwell and, addressing a third maid, exquisitely reminiscent of the plantocracy, 'Would you please bring in the toffee-treacle pudding?'

*

Ian Fleming died of a heart attack in 1964, at the age of fifty-six. The new Labour government under Harold Wilson (anathema to the Tory Fleming) had been sworn in and Bond mania was about to take off with the premiere of the film of *Goldfinger*. Although the novels have been praised for their style and wit – in 1960 Fleming had met an admiring John F. Kennedy in Washington – the films would become ever more gadget-ridden and fantastic. Yet four decades on, Ian Fleming's endearingly absurd creation, James Bond, shows no sign of flagging. The centenary of Fleming's birth in 2008 saw a pastiche Bond novel and an 007 exhibition at the Imperial War Museum in London. Surprisingly, little attention was paid to Jamaica, yet to understand the birth of Agent 007 one has to look at the country which Fleming made his home for over eighteen years. Without Jamaica, it is safe to say, there would have been no James Bond.

Fleming's Jamaican retreat, Goldeneye (named after the Carson McCullers novel *Reflections in a Golden Eye* and dubbed

'Goldeneye, nose and throat' by Noel Coward), stands above the old banana port of Oracabessa, due east of Annotto Bay. The visitors' book reads like a who's who of English letters and privilege in the post-war years. Evelyn Waugh, Stephen Spender, Cecil Beaton, the *London Magazine* editor Alan Ross (Commander Ross of *The Man with the Golden Gun*), Anthony Eden and Graham Greene all stayed. Chris Blackwell and his mother Blanche now own Goldeneye as part of a prohibitively expensive '007' hotel complex frequented by Sting and other dreary rock 'ristos' (as they say in Jamaica).

In that sun-warmed pocket of the British Empire, Fleming could savour his remoteness from cold, drab Britain and delude himself that he had risen above the ignominy of his country's imperial demise. He had long wanted to be a writer but felt that he lived in the shadow of his older brother, Peter, a successful travel journalist. Jamaica seems to have provided the space, time and leisure for the novelist in him to flourish. In pre-independence Jamaica, moreover, the Britain of Fleming's youth, with its class-bound social order, was better preserved than in austere post-war Britain, where, as we read in *Dr No*, 'people streamed miserably to work, their legs whipped by the wet hems of their macintoshes'.

What Fleming loved about Jamaica, apart from its antique social hierarchy, was its physical beauty. The fireflies and the melancholy of the tropical dusk seduced him. Fleming married Ann Charteris (previously the wife of Viscount Rothermere) in Jamaica in 1952, with Coward as his witness. In January of that year he had begun his first 007 novel, *Casino Royale*. The name for his action hero was taken from an ornithological classic dear to Fleming, *Field Guide to the Birds of the West Indies,* a standard reference published in 1947, by James Bond.

Fleming wrote his 007 extravaganzas with the jalousies at Goldeneye closed so that he would not be disturbed by the sunlight and birdlife. Even so, Jamaica is a presence in virtually all the Bond plots. In *Casino Royale*, Bond passes himself off as a 'Jamaican plantocrat'. *Dr No*, the sixth in the 007 series, alludes to the Jamaican Governor General Sir Hugh Foot. Some of the stories in *For Your Eyes Only* and *Octopussy* have Jamaican locales, but after the first five incomparably stylish novels, the prose became tired; and then came the disappointment of *The Man with the Golden Gun*, published posthumously in 1965. At Goldeneye, Fleming's creativity had become enfeebled though vodka and cigarettes – like 007, he smoked seventy a day; unlike 007, they took a toll on him.

One cannot imagine Fleming dancing to 'Lively Up Yourself' by Bob Marley (his long-suffering wife Ann Fleming complained of Jamaica's 'ganja-happy Negroes'); but Blanche Blackwell did, frequently, after her son Chris had helped to transform Bob into a semi-divine rock star for a (mostly white) international audience.

Mrs Blackwell, sweetly, will not hear a bad word about her son. 'His career has been an exquisite example to Jamaicans every-where,' she told me, her tone suddenly stern. Actually Chris Blackwell is greatly admired in Jamaica as a businessman, if not as a reggae studio man. Mrs Blackwell became more amenable when the pudding arrived. 'Now come *on*, Mrs B!' she said to herself. 'None of this crossness!' The 'most silly things' amused her now, bingo, for instance. Each week her chauffeur takes her to the Cricklewood Mecca to play bingo. In Kingston she had liked to bet on the horses, but London bingo (even played in braille) was not without its thrills. 'Cricklewood might seem a little dull to you,' Mrs Blackwell smiled. 'It isn't really. I could sit for hours in the Mecca. The tension as your number comes up. Bing-bing-bingo!'

It was late afternoon when I left Lowndes Square. 'I'm afraid the sunset will be a failure,' Mrs Blackwell said to me as she asked a maid to draw the curtains over the Knightsbridge view. 'It always is in London.' Only in 007's Jamaica is the sun such a bright 'blood-orange' red, as Ian Fleming would put it.

Mrs Blackwell rose as I made to leave.

'Don't forget to send me a copy of your book, will you?'

Tough and good-humoured, Blanche Blackwell disliked what had happened to Jamaica today. She hoarded her memories of old Jamaica like a squirrel, taking them out as she needed.

*

Ocho Rios, a cruise-ship destination near Goldeneye, is dominated by the 'Island Village' shopping mall owned by Chris Blackwell, where tourists can buy Bob Marley CDs and bottles of 'reggae' skin moisturiser extracted from 'Bob Marley' cannabis fibre oil. According to the poet Benjamin Zephaniah, a kind of political correctness dictates that one should not be too unkind to Bob Marley, who died of cancer in 1981 aged thirty-six. Yet much of his loping, mid-tempo music (with the exception of the early Lee 'Scratch' Perry productions: 'Duppy Conqueror', 'Soul Rebel') sounds slightly vapid to my ears. For many non-Jamaicans, Bob Marley *is* reggae; he remains an international Rasta celebrity, honoured with a waxwork at Madame Tussaud's as well as a Jamaican Order of Merit (the third-highest honour in the Jamaican honours system), an induction to the Rock and Roll Hall of Fame and a Bob Marley restaurant at Disney World in Orlando. Each year the Bob Marley Museum in Kingston attracts thousands of cruise-ship tourists, among them dreadlocked Japanese.

Oddly, during the 1970s when Marley's was the best-known name in Jamaican music, he was actually very much removed from the music scene. The first Bob Marley and the Wailers album to be produced by Chris Blackwell, *Catch a Fire* (1972), was an accomplished Jamaican-American hybrid, whose hard-driving Kingston rhythms were overlaid in London with rock guitar solos and even the brittle clavinet sound made famous by Stevie Wonder on 'Superstition'. (The original drum-and-bass mixes completed by the Wailers in Kingston – released for the first time in 2002 – have a raw simplicity and directness that even Blackwell, years later, said he preferred.)

It was Blackwell's, not Marley's, idea to aim the music at a rock audience. The end product, while it was a great rock-reggae album, seemed quite detached from Jamaican ghetto culture with its paraphernalia of sound systems and deejay-toasters. *Catch a Fire* was largely ignored by Britain's black reggae crowd (to whom the Harrow-educated Chris Blackwell was Chris 'Whiteworst'). The album sounded too much like 'reggae for people who don't really like reggae'. The sequel Wailers album, *Burnin'*, released within twelve months of its predecessor, offered a less adulterated, more dread-heavy sound, but still it bore the imprint of session rock musicians, and was directed mainly at the white middle classes, for whom Marley was now the King of Reggae.

Marley's domestic influence was at its peak in 1978 when he brought (if only for a moment) Michael Manley and Edward Seaga together onstage in a symbolic act of reconciliation during the famous 'One Love' peace concert in Kingston on 22 April (the date was chosen to coincide with the twelfth anniversary of Haile Selassie's visit to Kingston). Blanche Blackwell watched the concert on television. Bob Marley's international success may have been due, at least in part, to his mixed parentage. With a Caucasian father (Captain Norval Marley, a quartermaster attached to the British West Indian Regiment), he would have found it easier to deal with the world at large – that is, white people. Marley's fair complexion and aquiline features lent him an acceptable 'uptown' look.

Today, Bob Marley is the reason why so many tourists come to Jamaica. In Ocho Rios the wealthier among them stay at Jamaica Inn, reckoned to be among the most stylish hotels in the West Indies, whose manicured lawns and planter's punch ambience have attracted, among others, Winston Churchill, Marilyn Monroe, John Major and, latterly, Mick Jagger ('Mick Jaguar' to my taxi driver). Guests are offered indulgently soporific beachside massages and then bussed to an equestrian farm which specialises in Bob Marley-branded 'jungle treks'. Afterwards, to the accompaniment of canned Marley, a candle-lit dinner is served by a waiter who claims to remember both Noel Coward and Ian Fleming.

My publisher's advance would not stretch to such an establishment, so I checked into a guest house with plastic poolside chairs and (inevitably) framed photographs of Bob Marley.

The house belonged to Leeroy James Campbell, since 1990 a self-appointed 'Scientific Ganja Researcher' to the Jamaican nation. At seventy-five, Brother Leeroy (as he insisted I address him) looked well preserved in his swimming briefs and silver arm-bracelets. He was a dreadlocked Reborn Christian for whom marijuana and the rituals of smoking it were holy.

We were relaxing by his pool when he said to me, 'Brother Ian, may I ask you a personal question?'

'Please do.'

'Do you like to blow bush-tea?'

Smiling, Brother Leeroy began to roll and lick cigarette papers into a spliff. He plugged one end with a cardboard filter, lit the spliff, puffed on it, coughed, exhaled, and passed it to me. 'Brother Ian, it give you spiritual upliftment,' he said in a small, tearful-sounding voice. I drew on his King Size creation and waited for the visionary moment to come; nothing happened. Instead I watched smoke leak like treacle from Bother Leeroy's nostrils. Janice, his Canadian-born wife, was smoking an even larger cigarette on a sunlounger, her roach-box open and her legs wide apart. In her early sixties, very white, she had on a silver cannabis leaf neck-chain such as a rapper might wear.

'Well, my adorable honeybaby,' – she was addressing her husband – 'how you feel?'

'I'm good,' he said.

'How good?'

'Real good. Fulla vibes.'

Marijuana is illegal in Jamaica, yet Jamaicans smoke it, cook with it, drink it as a tea, grow it, pass it to their friends, sell it to tourists, and praise it in music and poetry. The Ethiopian Coptic Church of Zion, of which Bob Marley was a member, sanctions ganja consumption during services as a sort of Host. After tourism, narcotics are without doubt the single most important contribution to the Jamaican economy. Eight thousand marijuana plantations are said to exist across the island. Yet those found in possession of ganja can expect a hefty fine or jail sentence.

Earlier I had visited a ganja dealer who was on a murder charge in St Catherine's jail in Spanish Town. A crude facility built by the British in 1898, St Catherine's is Jamaica's principal prison, designed to hold 600 inmates but now holding twice that number. It had high, mustard-coloured walls surmounted by barbed wire and watchtowers. Guards in green fatigues stood watching me, swagger-sticks twitching in a study in nonchalant authority.

I met the youth, still in his teens, in the prison church where he was attending a Friday morning service with his mother. She had come with supplies of soap, towels, T-shirts and above all religious manuals. Through an open door of the church I could see prisoners gathering in a courtyard for their daily exercise. Many of them, also mere teenagers, were kicking a football and arguing. Washing hung everywhere in the midday sun: underwear, shorts, tattered shirts marked 'A.C.C.' (Adult Correctional Centre) pinned to the high, mesh-wire fencing. A couple of white prisoners could be seen among the black faces. Europeans doing time for ganja?

'Coolie Thief' (as he was known to inmates) chewed his lower lip as his mother pulled out an expensive-looking shirt for him from a brown paper bag. Once, the youth's status as a ganja dealer had made him big among men, but here he had become a ghost of himself, a lost child. During the church service the prisoners seemed to be very quiet until one of them began to make a shrill racket, which rose gradually to a wail. As we left the church the boy's mother spoke to me of the iniquities of the Jamaican justice system. Her son had been wrongly accused of murder. Yet the judge had spoken of his 'callous display of deliberate, prolonged, deadly gun-fire'.

*

'I think you're going to find me a very interesting person, Brother Ian.' Brother Leeroy squinted at me though his marijuana smoke. 'I may not be college-educated, but I have a pretty reasonable acquaintance with general knowledge of all descriptions.' As a 'Ganja Guru', he promoted marijuana as a medicine for migraine, clinical depression, anorexia, Aids wasting syndrome, as well as the chronic pain of MS.

Janice was now quite wreathed in smoke while I was beginning to experience feelings of confusion, if not incipient paranoia. Had Janice not noticed? The aroma of her smoke alone seemed to loft me giddily upwards. Now she was offering me a slice of pumpkin pie from a plate. 'It'll take the edge off your hunger,' she explained, leaning rather too close. The pie – was it pharmaceutically active? Brother Leeroy's dreadlocks had begun to wave slightly before my eyes. I must have laughed.

Brothers and sisters, I have smoked grass. But the potent, Special Brew varieties of marijuana currently available in Jamaica and Britain were unfamiliar to me. After smoking the whole of one of Brother Leeroy's collie weed joints, and while halfway through another, I had begun to feel unpleasantly unusual. The weed was causing me to lose control of the muscles round my mouth: a creeping hilarity was taking hold. Had Brother Leeroy not noticed?

Apparently not. He vanished to return moments later with a pamphlet on ganja, *Grow Jamaica*, which he and his wife had written and issued in 2002. Reading it later, I could see that it was indebted to the work of Lambros Comitas and Vera Rubin, American anthropologists who in 1975 had published their research on the role of marijuana in Jamaican life in a treatise, 'The Social Nexus of Ganja in Jamaica'. Controversially, Comitas and Rubin insisted that poor Jamaicans worked harder (not less hard) if they were heavy ganja-smokers. Leeroy Campbell regarded the Comitas–Rubin findings as sacrosanct since they had provided an antidote to received ideas about the drug and brought a connoisseur's nose to the subject. Victorians – Brother Leeroy was telling me now – had smoked cannabis as relief from lung disorders. By the 1880s most London tobacconists sold marijuana cigarettes at 1s. 9d. a packet. Ganja had arrived in Britain from the British Empire – India and, to a lesser extent, Jamaica. 'But,' said Brother Leeroy, grinning beatifically, 'it was only classified as a dangerous drug in Britain in 1925, whereupon it was illegalised.'

Moral panic did not flare up until the early 1950s, when West Indians were accused of spreading 'reefer madness' from Soho jazz dives and Notting Hill basement 'shebeens'. Soon the camelhair-coated Kray brothers were peddling (and possibly also puffing) the outlawed weed. Ironically, the first draft of the American Declaration of Independence had been written on hemp. 'So in some ways,' Brother Leeroy concluded sagely, 'ganja's as American as apple pie.'

'Only it's a whole lot better for you,' put in Janice, whose voice had gone very low.

Holy smoke. I felt I needed to ask if cannabis could cause (or at least aggravate) mental illness. Brother Leeroy gave a start of surprise at the question. 'Brother Ian!' He shook his head sadly. 'Ganja helps to create a serene state of mind.' Really? 'Oh yes,' the voice went on, 'you must learn to combine ganja and the Lord's Prayer.' Did he – *could* he – really believe what he was saying? Far from giving me a fruitful mystical experience, the collie weed was taking me to a far continent of anxiety. What horrible stuff it was. How right the Jamaican government was to ban it. I began to rehearse a little speech on the matter. But then I remembered that Brother Leeroy had been a policeman – my arguments would be familiar to him. Incredibly he had served in the Jamaica Constabulary, admittedly a long time ago – 1949 – but still it seemed odd.

'Did you make any arrests?' I asked him.

'One – for sheep rustling.' Sheep? In Jamaica? The grey-bearded face nodded. Sheep. Definitely sheep. In those days the Jamaica Constabulary had been entirely British-run and indeed almost British-paramilitary in its use of drills, arms and barrack-room discipline. Leeroy had loved every moment of it. 'The police used to be feared and respected,' he explained, 'now the police is just feared.' Little clouds of blue smoke were swirling round the ex-policeman. His life-story sounded to my ears more and more bizarre.

In Philadelphia, where he had settled in the 1970s, he had been diagnosed with prostate cancer and believed his end had come. He asked God for His help. 'I needed something with Biblical in it,' Leeroy said to me. 'Something with "shalt" and "thou", something deep.' Needless to say he found it in ganja. 'And Brother Ian, from the moment I took my first puff I *knew* there was something in it for me.' Ganja had given him a vision of the Eternal One, no less, and he began to experience God's life in *his* life. 'And the more I smoked, the more I knew I had to spiritualise myself up.' He and Janice began to smoke marijuana, lots of it; at the same time they tried every far-out fad available to them in 1970s Philadelphia. Parapsychology. Integral massage. Vedanta Hinduism. L. Ron Hubbard's dianetics. The yogis of increased awareness.

'But weren't these exercises in pure and applied pointlessness?' I heard myself asking. The herb had emboldened me dangerously.

'No, Brother Ian!' Brother Leeroy sucked his teeth sharply. 'Ganja gave us a necessary *benediction*, man, a breathing space.'

Janice looked at me through slow lazy eyes. 'Ian, every seed-bearing pod became our friend,' she said. 'We looked upon those pods as our truth-and-beauty pills.' Nothing seemed to matter any more to Janice and Leeroy but ganja, the giant Rizlas which they filled daily with Jamaican lamb's breath, the only variety of marijuana that had Brother Leeroy's sanction. They began to grow cannabis plants in their flat and hoped to save the planet by smoking them.

Brother Leeroy was now a shimmering mass of pointillist particles. What to do? On the pretext of feeling tired I went to my room, a thin-walled cubicle hard by the swimming pool. I lay on the bed there fully dressed, pretty confused, with the blinds pulled down. My idea had been to take a nap, but I remained fully awake and actually rigid with fear. From the direction of the pool I could hear Brother Leeroy wheezing and coughing. I caught the word 'spy', and wondered whether I should get up and confront the suspicion that I was a government nark when to my relief I overheard Janice say, 'It's strange how these cicadas suddenly get *really* loud, then quiet again.'

'They're communicating, man,' Brother Leeroy said to her.

'Yes,' replied Janice, 'but communicating *what*?'

After a long pause Brother Leeroy answered, 'Right. It isn't as if there's any *danger* to communicate.'

'There might be!' said Janice, adding, 'How do you know there's no danger?'

'Meaning?' Leeroy asked, the word both a question and (I thought) a veiled threat to me.

But before he could speak further, Janice said, 'Meaning? Meaning there might be a rat in the house.'

Now I could hear them laughing; but I could not tell if they were laughing about me, only that they were laughing. I thought about running but if I was seen to leave now (especially if I was seen to leave at great speed) it would look like an admission of guilt. The situation had really become quite bad.

*

Two hours later I was back by the poolside, feeling bright and beatifically attuned.

'How you feel?' Janice asked me.

'I feel all right,' I said.

'How all right?'

'All right all right.'

'Brother man, tell me *exactly* how you feel,' Brother Leeroy was asking me now.

'Good,' I said. 'Fulla vibes.'

'Jamaican collie make you jolly,' Brother Leeroy added (quoting the great London-born Jamaican deejay Lone Ranger).

A Jamaican friend of his, Lloyd Cummings, had joined us on a visit from Philadelphia. He too liked to smoke enormous quantities of marijuana. Why not? Everything was absolutely tip-top. 'You and me is bredda,' Lloyd commented as he looked at me through bloodshot eyes.

Janice was busy again with her expert chemistry of cigarette papers and little packets extracted from her roach-box. Did she never stop? Puffs. Inhalations. Exhalations. By the time Leeroy had loaded his kutchie pipe the sun had dropped below the horizon and now a blazing three-quarter moon hung over Ocho Rios. There was enough moonlight for us to see each other in the dark and, looking at Leeroy's grizzled braids, I thought of the Lee Perry song 'Dreadlocks in Moonlight' when, yawning, Janice announced to her husband: 'Ganja plants would make a beautiful aromatic addition around our swimming pool, Leeroy.'

'So true, Janice, so true,' said the ex-policeman, with a sincere Christian smile.

'Fi real, Breddaroy!' Lloyd Cummings agreed, sleepily, before nodding off. Close by, the cicadas had recommenced their chorus of chirping. Or were they communicating?

Up until now I had been convinced that Bob Marley's pseudo-hippie 'One Love' vibe had died a death in Jamaica: there was too much violence for soft, kindly idealists like Brother Leeroy, who interested themselves in universal love and ate nut cutlets. But Leeroy, I decided, was the incarnation of a Christian-Rastafari ethos that Westerners with their noses to the grindstone would find impossible to understand. He was a man who meant well, even if he had gone, if not quite to pot, then awry. I liked him.

*

Noel Coward's home, Firefly, stands on a coastal road ten miles from Ian Fleming's. It has been left almost intact since Coward died there in 1973 not long after his appearance in *The Italian Job* as a monarchy-loving gangster. Tins of beef suet and granulated gravy lie unopened in a dust-caked kitchen; a pair of Fortnum & Mason pyjamas hang, slightly stained, in a wardrobe. And in the main room the table is still set as it had been for a luncheon visit by Queen Elizabeth the Queen Mother in 1965. Parts of the north coast – Firefly is a good example – still live off a trumpery notion of their Englishness, where the 'long-settled' (or not so long-settled) white (or near white) inhabitants tend to see themselves as the descendants of English planters or even English royalty.

The Faceys, comfortable in their assumption of privilege, live in the pastoral uplands of St Ann parish in a great house called Bellevue, not far from Firefly. Situated amid 2,000 acres of land, Bellevue had been built in the 1750s by a British Redcoat army officer, Captain John Davis, but over the years it had passed to a number of Jamaican planter families related either by blood or by marriage. In 1980 Maurice and Valerie Facey – he, a mixed-race Jamaican; she, a white American of Irish–Polish Jewish extraction – bought the property and refurbished it with mahogany floors, Hepplewhite chairs imported from England and bookshelves conspicuously crammed with gilt bindings. Jamaican society journals had run photographs (which I had seen) of the house, with its lawns like green velvet, and bouquets of tropical flowers in the morning and retiring rooms. A portrait above the fireplace painted in 1964 by the fine Jamaican artist Barrington Watson showed Valerie Facey as a handsome woman in her early thirties.

I was driven to the property by the Facey family's chauffeur, Mr Chattersingh, an East Indian without any teeth; his car without any suspension was a 'charabanc', he told me. Painfully we advanced through parched savannah with herds of cattle grazing on tussocks of grass. Eventually we passed the long brick walls of the Bellevue kitchen gardens, before reaching a stone gate emblazoned with the Facey coat of arms on a background of lions rampant. A sign bearing the words 'Bellevue Great House' struck an equally grand note. Under the high trees by the yard gate, the array of Range Rovers and Land Rovers was almost as numerous as the odd-job men at work in the industrial-sized kitchen. They were busy decapitating and gutting a quantity of birds which Maurice Facey, his family and friends had shot earlier that morning on the estate. It was a muggy afternoon in August, the season when bald pate and other doves may be hunted lawfully in Jamaica. However, the hunting season was coming to an end, and when I arrived the Faceys had not yet succeeded in killing that many birds. There was a family tradition that a minimum of twenty birds – the government quota – should be bagged each day.

Maurice and Valerie Facey are, among other things, venture capitalists, conservationists, publishers, social climbers and extremely generous hosts. Laura Facey Cooper, Valerie and Maurice Facey's daughter, is well known in Jamaica as a sculptor. Her eleven-foot 'Redemption Song' monument (named after the Bob Marley song) was unveiled in Kingston in 2003 to terrific controversy. The monument consists of two massive nude slave figures, male and female, with startlingly large breasts and genitals. At the time it was objected that the pale-skinned Facey Cooper had 'disrespected' the island's black majority by presenting them without clothes. Shortly after the unveiling a woman was seen to gyrate lewdly in front of the monument dressed only in her underwear; she was removed to Bellevue psychiatric hospital (not to be confused with Bellevue great house), many felt unfairly.

Once through the mansion gates, Mr Chattersingh handed me over to the butler, Lloyd Codner, who showed me to the Strawberry Room where I was to sleep. Alone in the vast shuttered chamber the sound of gunshot reached me as birds continued to be blasted across the moors above Ocho Rios. A towel-rack with mono-grammed Facey towels and a collection of towelling robes with other heraldic devices encouraged the idea of a venerable aristo-cracy. In spite of their high social standing, the Faceys' had not been an easy marriage. Valerie's mother, Julia Rypinski, had objected to her daughter's betrothal to a non-white Jamaican and, in 1952, she even asked the island's governor to block the marriage. He refused and the wedding went ahead.

*

Maurice Facey, worn out by the day's shooting, joined me for pre-dinner drinks dressed in monogrammed burgundy slippers and a pair of sharply pleated tartan trousers. (I was reminded of Sir Hugo

Drax, 007's opponent in *Moonraker*, in his 'plum-coloured smoking jacket' – for the patrician Ian Fleming clearly the height of sartorial vulgarity, like a pink trilby or red socks.) Copies of *Country Life* and *Shooting and Conservation* lay displayed on the coffee table before me. I did not want to come across as a sulky house guest, so refrained from making any untoward remarks.

'Good evening, sir,' the Hon. Facey said to me as he poured himself a measure of Talisker malt whisky. In manner he was very welcoming but I daresay he could afford to be. Bellevue is a great parkland where animals are introduced as hunting targets and the land and everything on it is owned by one single family. Families like the Faceys are a phenomenon of Jamaican rural life hardly changed since the eighteenth century. As chairman of the PanJam group of companies, Maurice has a substantial stake in Jamaica's economy: investment, banking, life insurance, food manufacturing, agriculture and tourism. ('I have even taken a patriotic dip in sugar – a very sticky business,' he said.)

'Do you fish?' he asked me, his eyebrows raised a fraction in enquiry. 'I've always wanted to fish – for salmon. On the Spey.'

'The River Spey? In Scotland?'

'Indeed, sir.'

I was not surprised that he should want to fish in faraway Scotland. Maurice Facey, who came of quite ordinary origins, had worked his way up from sales representative (Jamaican Floral Exports), and was just twenty-five when he became managing director of his father's property development company. His financial interests in food manufacturing (bottled hot sauces, pickled relish) had made him a tidy fortune, too, so he was now ready to crown his ascent into the highest social spheres (as he saw them) by fishing among grandees on the River Spey.

Maurice was a tall, handsome man with much-permed white hair; a very un-English English gentleman. He appeared to preside over his family like a Victorian-era patriarch, by turns stern and indulgent. His daughter Laura, the sculptor, sat demurely in a corner of the drawing room, talking to her mother Valerie, who looked regal in primrose trailing skirts. In awed tones Valerie was telling Laura of my presence at a Kumina ceremony. (Nothing encourages the middle-class Jamaican view of the countryside as a place of Afro-Jamaican devilry more than Kumina.) The insight Kumina had afforded me into the 'dark, secret lives' of countryfolk lent me (I felt) an aura.

Valerie's son, Stephen, an architect, sat silently reading a copy of *The Field*; he was wearing a batik-patterned sarong and was married to a talkative, dark-haired woman, who said she came from New Zealand.

Supper consisted of plates of bald pate dove, the birds' tiny bones delicious to suck if occasionally chewy with 12-bore shot. 'Bald pate love to eat pimento berries,' Maurice Facey was saying to me. 'The flesh, I think you'll find, has a peppery tang – from the pimento.' The dinner-table conversation proceeded in this stilted fashion even as the subject of Jamaican crime came up. The Faceys did not seem too concerned by the violence; they exchanged a few generalities with me about the 'dreadfulness' of the Kingston ghetto, then declared that it was time for bed. The hospitality shown to me had been munificent, though the affectations of baronial splendour made me somehow uneasy. We were in the Caribbean, not Balmoral. Early the next morning I was awoken by the sound of yet more gunshot. The Faceys would be riding to hounds, I thought, if foxes existed in Jamaica.

*

The title song of Horace Andy's magnificent reggae album *In the Light* (1977) bewails the teaching Jamaicans had received in pre-independence days when history meant the history of British imperial endeavour, exemplified by Mungo Park, David Livingstone and Cecil Rhodes. Little or no mention was made of Jamaican history – the slave system and its abolition, the Maroon Wars, Paul Bogle or Marcus Garvey.

> When I was a little child
> I didn't know my culture
> when I was a little child
> I didn't know my foreparents were from Africa
> all the things they used to teach I
> was about England Canada and America

but now
I'm in the light I'm in the light
and it's shining bright . . .

In Jamaica, schools were the Empire's most important agency in moulding loyal imperial subjects; they were intended to create an educated Anglican elite that was necessarily alienated from the Jamaican environment. It was only after independence that Jamaicans were provided with a history of their own country. The curricular change was part of a nationalist agenda of 'Jamaicanising Jamaica' – the development of a true history of the island and its people.

The British Empire was already moribund when, in 1945, Sheila Duncker was interviewed in London at a government institution called the Overseas Settlement of British Women that found and filled teaching and other posts abroad. 'There's nothing for you in Rhodesia, dearie,' Duncker was told, 'but we do have a vacancy in Jamaica.' Duncker accepted. For the next twenty years she taught history at Wolmer's Girls School in Kingston.

Everything about the stolid, red-brick school struck her as extraordinarily imperial, not least the headmistress, Evelyn 'Skay' Skempton, an immaculately coiffed Yorkshirewoman who did not approve of athletics for girls as it was unseemly for them to run (they could, however, walk briskly). Instead girls were to be instructed in Posture and Elocution (with an annual Elocution contest). Only then could they develop into 'proper English ladies', suitable for marriage to proper Jamaican gentlemen.

What schoolgirl born on Jamaican soil to Jamaican parents could possibly hope to become truly British? The British teachers (and they mostly were British) at Wolmer's displayed an almost mystical belief in the Empire as an 'uplifter of subject peoples'. Not surprisingly Duncker had her misgivings about the school's Empire-bound etiquette. Yet from the moment she set foot in Jamaica, she was in love. 'I felt I was in paradise – Jamaica in the 1940s was like the Britain of fifty years before, an antique, time-locked place.' Both of her children (one of them the novelist Patricia Duncker) were born in Jamaica.

A sympathetic woman, Duncker was speaking to me in her basement flat in Primrose Hill, north-west London. It was a cold afternoon in February, and the room was correspondingly dark, crammed with yellowed books on Jamaican history. One of the books, *The World Before Britain*, Duncker had used as a history primer at Wolmer's. Determinedly Anglophile, it had colour-plate illustrations of Gladstone and Disraeli, and placed a very Victorian emphasis on enunciation and syntax. Its unstated purpose, said Duncker, was to consolidate the Anglicisation of Jamaica and promote loyalty to the British Empire.

The notion that learning could – or should – be 'fun' did not exist during Duncker's time in Jamaica, any more than it did elsewhere in the world. Children were submitted to the altruistic dedication of sympathetic if unimaginative white people who saw themselves as instruments of Anglican enlightenment. ('A' was for apple; 'B' for book.) One day, she recalled, a school inspector in rural Jamaica asked a group of children, 'How many feet has a cat got?' The question was put in strenuously clipped Queen's English, any departure from which was considered 'bushman talk'. A long bewildered silence followed until a Jamaican teacher re-phrased the question in patois: 'How much foot have puss?' A forest of hands went up.

At Wolmer's, that calm, sunlit institution within easy reach of so many mild satisfactions (Lawn Tennis, Posture classes), it seemed impossible to Sheila Duncker that danger might be lurking. In August 1962, however, on the eve of independence a man was found hacked to death outside the school gates. Duncker decided to go home. By the time she eventually left in 1964 a groundbreaking primer had been published for use in Jamaican secondary schools. Compiled by four academics with Caribbean connections (one of them, Mary Turner, had taught at Wolmer's Boys School), *The Making of the West Indies* seemed partially to fulfil Marcus Garvey's call for the black majority to 'affirm your ancestry, claim your history'.

The book was strikingly different in kind from all other school histories of the Caribbean. Instead of focusing on 'imperial' concerns – sugar production, Henry Morgan, Lord Nelson – it narrated events as they had affected the West Indian people, from the Taino Indians to the Morant Bay rebellion of 1865. Published in London in 1960 by Longmans, the primer filled a need in Jamaican schools.

Some teachers, British and Jamaican-born alike, considered *The Making of the West Indies* uneducated and anti-British in its iconoclasm and reforming mission. There was a minority of Jamaican teachers who disclaimed their West African ancestry and, in their Anglophile bias, chose not to be informed about (or interested in) Jamaica. However, the book influenced a generation of post-independence Jamaicans dissatisfied by the old, closed imperial view of their past. It grew out of earlier attempts in the 1950s to form a Federated West Indies and, further back, to the nationalist sentiments that flared up in the late 1930s with Jamaica's anti-imperialist riots. In its small way, the book helped to promote psychological independence from Britain, and even now, half a century on, its success is spoken of as something extraordinary.

Incredibly, the history of the British Empire is still taught in some Jamaican schools in the interior. In Coleyville I visited the oddly named 'Butt-Up Basic School', where the children were trained to rattle off key dates from the Industrial Revolution and the Battle of Trafalgar. The headmistress, Madge Allen, did not seem to encourage questioning from her pupils: tuition was blackboard-driven and done largely by rote. Up on the classroom wall was a photograph of Denzil Johnston, the Jamaican ex-RAF serviceman I had met six months earlier in Hull. Impressively, Johnston had returned to his birthplace of Coleyville fifteen times since he left in 1945, and each time he had brought with him a suitcase of pencils, sweets, sports gear and books for the children.

The class, as I entered, stood to attention and chorused loudly: 'Good evening, Mr Johnston.' (I did not bother to correct them.) They had been busy memorising the British national anthem. To swot and cram by rote encouraged a properly British habit of 'discipline' and 'ordered thinking', Madge Allen said to me. And, as one, her pupils placed their hands on their hearts preparatory to singing. How much of the anthem were the five-year-olds able to understand? Throughout the recital I heard a small child being beaten somewhere in the school; it wailed loudly, dramatising its misery. Physical punishment is part of Jamaican culture. God save the Queen. God save Jamaica.

19

Sitting in Limbo

You see, he feels like Ivan
Born under the Brixton sun
His game is called survivin'
At the end of the harder they come
                    'Guns of Brixton', the Clash

I was sitting in front of a roaring log fire in Bellevue great house, a tin of mango juice in one hand, while the rain lashed down. There was still no sign of Perry Henzell, the Jamaican film-director and novelist, and a wet afternoon was rapidly turning into a dismal evening. Five hours earlier Perry had telephoned to say that he was on his way from Kingston: I was looking forward to seeing him again. Had he got lost? *The Harder They Come*, his debut film, had depicted Kingston's cut-throat music business at a time when Jamaica was struggling to define its post-colonial identity. Released in 1972, it remains a landmark in world cinema (in 2008 it enjoyed a successful run in London's West End as a musical).

For the moment I was on my own in this neo-Georgian country retreat. Maurice and Valerie Facey had left that morning for Montego Bay, leaving me in the care of their butler, Lloyd Codner, a restless man with a lot of questions for me. 'So you like jazz?' I had put on a recording of Ernest Ranglin, a hero of mine. No one plays jazz-reggae guitar like Ranglin, so precise and understated. He had first performed in London in December 1963 at Ronnie Scott's jazz club, where he jammed alongside Sonny Stitt and members of the Ray Charles band. 'Anyone who wants to come to London from the West Indies,' Ronnie Scott had introduced the Jamaican guitarist, 'is of course stone raving mad.' Listening to those recordings now in Bellevue I was struck by how un-Jamaican they sounded. Only 'Soul D'Ern', a blues-calypso composition, hinted at the ska hits that Ranglin was to cut for Studio One in Kingston.

Jazz was Ranglin's first love; in his earliest Jamaican recordings one can hear all jazz guitar from Charlie Christian (who died in 1942 after pioneering the electrically amplified six-string) to Wes Montgomery. Only later would Ranglin evolve a uniquely Jamaican sound. In the 1950s, after hustling in Kingston, he joined a Jamaican swing combo, the Eric Dean's Orchestra, which routinely toured Latin America, and by the end of the decade he was playing at the Kingston cricket clubs and hotels frequented by Ian Fleming and other tropical voluptuaries. His virtuosity in a number of guitar styles from bolero to blues to Mississippi washboard rhythms endeared him to wealthier Jamaicans, who did not want too much of Africa in their music. In 1958, after triumphing at the Half Moon Hotel in Montego Bay Ranglin was approached by a young Chris Blackwell, who signed him to his fledgling Island Records label in London.

Blackwell had had considerable success distributing hot-from-yard singles to the eager Jamaican record-buying community in Britain. Now he instructed Ranglin to explore the Jamaican ska scene as it was unfolding in London's black quarter – its boundaries enclosing the Arch (Marble Arch), the Water (Bayswater), the Gate (Notting Hill) and the Grove (Ladbroke). During his nine-month residency at Ronnie Scott's, Ranglin did just that, and his explorations paid off. In 1964, with Blackwell at the controls, Ranglin recorded guitar for the novelty ska version of the R & B jolly-up, 'My Boy Lollipop'. The song became the seventh best-selling single that year, ahead of the Beatles and the Rolling Stones.

Even then, in the mid-1960s, at the culmination of British imperialism in the West Indies, Ernest Ranglin had been grateful to be a citizen of the Colonies and to have had the freedom to enter and remain in the United Kingdom. It was one of the special benefits enjoyed by British subjects, Ranglin said. Things were different now. 'London's not what it used to be. The police – they have to walk with guns and thing. Yes, it used to be a lot more relaxed in London town.' If Ranglin had stayed on in London he would have become an immense star; instead, lured by Studio One, he went back to Kingston.

We were sitting in the garden of Ranglin's bungalow-residence on the outskirts of Ocho Rios. 'How about a Red Stripe?' he asked me, getting up. He went off to fetch two cans, pulled off the ring-tabs, wiped the lip of my can with a towel (a fastidious man, I could see) and poured a little beer into our glasses. He brought his glass to his lips and, after tasting the beer, said, 'You know, Jamaica's a better place than it used to be. Oh yes, more opportunities, more social mobility.' Jamaica falling down? On the contrary, Jamaica was *looking up*. Ranglin was not interested in perpetuating a nostalgic legend. 'A lot of old-time Jamaicans spend their time living in a pastime paradise,' he said, quoting the Stevie Wonder song, 'glorifying days long gone behind. Well, that's not for me.'

Ranglin looked at me and sighed. That was the problem with this whole island, he went on. People forget. They make themselves forget the bad things about the past. 'But,' he added with a look of grieved amazement, 'there's a kind of foolishness in seeking happiness in the past, not so?' The sun, sunk low over James Bond Beach, was reflected in Ranglin's still and serene face. His expressions of hope had taken me by surprise; it was a rare Jamaican that showed such optimism for his country. The Ranglin version of Jamaica allowed for greater hope than I had thought possible.

*

The butler, having come back to light the fire, went off on some ill-defined errand down the long, oak-panelled hall, just as a proper storm welled up, turning the room dark and the air inside muggy. Where was Perry Henzell?

When I first met Perry it was a winter's day in London, and the rain had turned to snow. With a rush of icy air Perry had walked into the Soho club, wearing a wool skullcap and a camel-coloured wool overcoat. Heads turned as he greeted me with an accent that was hard to place. Irish? With his long beard and flowing white hair, he suggested a smaller-statured Walt Whitman. He was good company: genial, with a lopsided smile.

Over a bottle of red I asked Perry what his parents made of *The Harder They Come*.

'My parents? They'd disowned me long before the film came out,' Perry smiled and laughed. 'I was a drop-out.'

'A drop-out?'

'Yes. I never mixed with the 007 set in Ocho Rios, if that's what you mean. I'm a first-generation Jamaican – so I was never part of Jamaica's old plantocracy.' He spoke, with a measure of guarded fondness, of white Jamaicans. 'I've got nothing against them' – he himself was the son of a white Trinidad planter.

By Perry's own account, the idea for *The Harder They Come* had occurred to him while at his boarding school in England in 1948. That year, Kingston was terrorised by the antics of a Jamaican outlaw called Vincent 'Ivanhoe' Martin, who in the course of armed hold-ups killed three people and wounded four others. Like a Caribbean Ned Kelly, Martin seemed to model himself on the film stars: Jimmy Cagney, perhaps. After a six-week manhunt the police shot him dead on Lime Cay, near Kingston. 'Thus ended the bullet-scarred career of a man who thought he could out-wit the police,' hurrahed the *Gleaner* of 11 October 1948.

To Perry's schoolboy imagination, Martin was like the West African spider-hero Anansi, a trickster figure who eluded capture even as he taunted the authorities. 'Getting away with it' – a much-valued skill in Jamaica – would be the great unstated theme of *The Harder They Come*. In those days before television, Anansi stories were told at dusk on Jamaican front porches and continued a West African (specifically, Guinean) tradition of the *griots* or praise-singers who could hold a village spellbound with their tales. Anansi, a spider with human attributes, seemed to Perry to personify those qualities of survival which the enslaved Africans, torn from their homelands, must have found appealing. (In Ashanti lore, the great spider symbolises wisdom and is comparable to the Legba divinity of Haitian Vodoun.) With his disreputable, indomitable humanity, agility and cunning, 'Ivanhoe' Martin was the very embodiment of 'Anancyism' – clever rascality – as he fought the law; ultimately the law won.

In 1968, twenty years after 'Ivanhoe' Martin's death, Perry decided to update the story to contemporary Kingston, and turn it into a film about a country boy who comes to the big city to try his luck as a singer. He fails, but he goes out in a blaze of glory; in his journey from rural parish to concrete jungle one might see a metaphoric journey of the newly freed Jamaican nation into modernity. In the outlaw's story Perry also saw the plight of the little man crushed by authority; a sense of doomed failure.

The singer Jimmy Cliff was chosen to play the part of Ivan O. Martin (as the outlaw was now renamed) and he brought a touch of rude boy swagger to the role. Filming was funded partly by Perry's wealthy relatives. It began in 1969 but dragged on for two years as money ran out and some cast members even died. Jimmy Cliff's own song, 'The Harder They Come', provided Perry with his title, and also captured, as few Jamaican songs since then have, the desperation of Kingston youth fighting for survival in the post-imperial city:

> So as sure as the sun will shine
> I'm gonna get my share now, what's mine
> And the harder they come, the harder they fall
> One and all

Perry's interest was not just in the Jamaican music business; he wanted to dissect the morally ambivalent world of Kingston under Michael Manley in the early 1970s, the city's murky underground, where the police were in cahoots with the politicians, and where murder was a consequence of all this corruption. *The Harder They Come* is, among other things, a documentary, bleakly fixed in the ganja-yards and urban alleys of western Kingston. Nobody before Perry Henzell had brought such a raw energy to Jamaican cinema; it remains Jamaica's first home-grown film and still its finest.

The soundtrack, put together by Perry in less than a week, was superb ('The best week's work I ever did,' he told me) and it effectively introduced reggae to white British audiences. Fashionable dinner parties in 1970s Britain often enjoyed a musical accompaniment of the Maytals' gospel-hot 'Pressure Drop' or Desmond Dekker's '007 (Shanty Town)'. Without the soundtrack album, it is fair to say, roots reggae would not have taken hold in 1970s Britain in the way it did.

Reggae had previously been given only minimal airplay on BBC radio, and the British music press was hardly enthusiastic. Reggae is 'black music being prostituted', *Melody Maker* reported Deep Purple and the Edgar Broughton Band as saying. In 1985, going one better, Morrissey of the Smiths announced: 'Reggae is vile.' One may detect in that remark a very British 'anti-immigrant' sentiment. In 1976, at his concert in Birmingham, Eric Clapton had even urged his audience to vote for Enoch Powell and stop Britain becoming a 'black colony'. Bizarrely, in October 2007, British Conservatives adopted 'The Harder They Come' as a Tory anthem, the party of law and order thus endorsing, if unwittingly, the crime habits of a Kingston outlaw.

At the premiere of *The Harder They Come* in Kingston in June 1972 the crush of people outside the cinema was so great that not even Jimmy Cliff could get in. Sally Henzell, Perry's wife, arriving in her gala finery, had to be hoisted up and passed over the heads of the waiting crowd towards the entrance. Inside, the audience packed every available space and, as the film began to roll, they hooted, howled and fired non-stop praise for over an hour. It was the first time that Jamaicans had seen themselves on screen and, for Sally Henzell (as she told me later), the 'most moving experience' of her life.

Overseas, the reception was more restrained. At the Cork International Film Festival an invited audience of media 'person-alities' (among them Peter Cushing of Hammer Horror) watched the film in silence. Perry and Sally Henzell feared a critical drubbing but, in fact, the Irish had loved the film. Its implied protest against life on the breadline and thoughtful portrayal of a rural boy gone bad had struck a chord. The Jamaican screen accents, moreover, were thought to approximate the Cork accent, and at the press confer-ences afterwards it was asked if 'Cork natives' had settled in large numbers in Jamaica. Perry was awarded the 'Editor's Prize': that was how much Cork had liked his film.

In England, however, the film looked set to fail. At the Classic Cinema in Brixton (now the Ritzy) the press screening was so poorly attended that Perry was reduced to handing out publicity flyers at the tube station. Understandably Britain's expatriate Jamaican community did not want to be reminded of the violence and the poverty they had left behind. Why should they pay good money to watch it? It was unsettling – a humiliation – to be reminded of their impoverished Jamaican years. They stayed away in droves.

It was not until the *Observer*'s film critic, the late George Melly, got on his bicycle and rode down to the 'Frontline' of black London in Brixton to review the film that the middle classes began to take notice. Melly had loved *The Harder They Come*. Before long the Classic was packed at every screening as word spread of a Jamaican triumph. The film went on to win a 'Best Young Cinema' award at the Venice Film Festival, where its indebtedness to the gritty 'newsreel' school of Italian neo-realism (such as *The Bicycle Thieves* and *Rome, Open City*) did not go unnoticed.

*

The clunk of a car door, the sound of approaching footsteps . . . Perry Henzell, damp and bedraggled from the rain, walked into Bellevue great house with his hands spread wide in apology: 'Ian! I'm late – the traffic . . .' We shook hands and I followed Perry across the gravel drive to his car.

The foul weather returned as we drove on past Drax Hall (the sugar estate owned by the father of the eighteenth-century Gothic novelist William Beckford which had given its name to the dastardly Hugo Drax in Fleming's *Moonraker*). Clouds hid the mountains to our right and rain pattered against the windscreen. 'God!' Perry said. 'It's worse than England!' We stopped at a Chinese restaurant, where Perry ordered a bowl of sweet-and-sour. He looked thinner, more worn, than when I had seen him last, and in fact, unknown to me, was seriously ill.

It was midnight when we arrived at Itopia, the Henzells' home. This was a Cromwell-era stone house surrounded by jungle creeper not far from Ocho Rios. At this hour Itopia seemed to be full of ghosts. The shuttered rooms smelled peppery, like the inside of a cigar box, and moonlight leaked in through a crack in the roof. The house had served as an overseer's residence for a Roundhead family, the Blagroves, signatories to the execution of Charles I. For taking part in the regicide, Cromwell had rewarded the Blagroves with eight square miles of land in Jamaica. After the Restoration of Charles II in 1660, many of the other signatories were beheaded, but the Blagroves had fled to Jamaica and escaped. They were eventually pardoned and there is now a Blagrove Road in Notting Hill Gate, London. In 1974, when the Henzells bought Itopia, it had been a mildewed place under threat of demolition by a bauxite company. 'Goats were living in the kitchen,' Perry said to me, as he rolled himself a cigarette.

'Want one?' he asked eventually. 'We have Babylonian spliffs and Ital spliffs.'

I considered what I was being asked. 'What's the difference?'

'Babylonian is mixed with tobacco – Ital is pure grass.'

'Thanks,' I said, 'I'd better not.'

Perry said goodnight and I made my way across the garden to the annexe. His wife, Sally, was recovering from flu and fast asleep in the main house. On a bed hung with mosquito nets I put down my bag and got undressed. There was a Burmese-lacquer box on a bedside table stuffed with collie weed for use, I imagined, by more adventurous guests. The bathroom walls, encrusted with shells and shards of coloured glass, gave the impression of a fairy grotto; everything was at once antique and enchanted.

*

Sally Henzell, feeling better, came to greet me the following morning. 'Rudes will be down shortly,' she said, meaning 'rude boy' Perry (who was far from rude). A breakfast of papaya and grapefruit was brought to us by Euphemia, a Jamaican who had worked at Itopia for fifteen years. Sally, vivacious and with a radiant, sunbeaten face, might have been (and had been) a Jamaican flower child with hippy virtues. Her father, born to British tea planters in Ceylon, had met her British mother (born in China) in Jamaica in 1929. They married and never moved. Something set Sally apart from her class and kind, however. She had on camouflage-pattern hot pants and a T-shirt advertising the Calabash Literary Festival held each year in Jamaica and organised by Sally's daughter, Justine Henzell. Sally was not in the least stuffy. If the old colonial world had been divided between the 'natives' on the one side and those in power on the other, she seemed to blur the distinction and was equally at home with Jamaica's old colonialist bourgeoisie and the roots-reggae world of Afro-Jamaica.

Perry, joining us at the breakfast table, tore open a sachet of powder, stirred the powder into a glass of water, and drained it one long gulp. 'Medicine,' he said with a grimace, adding cryptically, 'The beast has come back.'

He ate a mouthful of papaya and said to me, 'This is not such a bad place, you know.' I heard the note of affection in his voice: Itopia had become a haven for Perry in his sickness. He had cancer; but he could at least enjoy the quiet shelter of this place deep in the Jamaican interior. As we ate a rose-red bird pursued a blue one across the overgrown lawn. 'Parakeets,' said Perry, matter-of-fact. In the bedroom next door to us, a psychedelic mural done by Joni Mitchell in the 1970s added to the strangeness of the morning for me.

At midday Sally came to take me on a tour of the area. First we visited a stretch of greensward nearby which served as a local grave-yard. We went there by car, the air warm and fragrant with a smell of wood smoke. Eventually we arrived at the graveyard: 'This is where Perry will be buried when his time comes,' Sally said. (He died at the end of November 2006, aged seventy.) Small flowers bloomed in the grass of the burial ground; in a tangle of foliage at one end four gravestones were hemmed in by iron Victorian palings. The stone inscriptions were so worn, they had to be traced by finger like Braille. We cleared away dead and rotting roots and saw that one inscription read: 'Here Lies Ian Thomson'. (Not yet surely!) Another commemorated a Blagrove who had died at Cardiff Hall in 1812, a property owned years later by the film actor Peter Finch.

For two centuries the Blagroves had run Cardiff Hall as an English bastion, complete with slaves, servants, race horses (some of them exported to the United States) and polo ponies. In 1950 John Minton, the British Neo-Romantic painter, had stayed there as a guest of Captain Peter Blagrove and his wife, Alice. Though Minton disliked many of the Jamaican landowners he met, the Blagroves were hospitable to him, and allowed him to site himself on their land. Minton's paintings from that time conjure Jamaica's potential for violence as well as the sadness that lies beneath the travel-brochure romanticism. Britain's 'importance' in the world was surely now at an end, and in his Jamaican canvases Minton captured the moment of imperial retreat.

We headed west out of Runaway Bay along the coastal road to the old shipping port of Rio Bueno. In 1964 the port had served as a set for the film of *A High Wind in Jamaica*, based on Richard Hughes's great 1929 novel of the same name. Like the film of *Dr No* shot in Jamaica three years earlier, *A High Wind in Jamaica* lingered indulgently over the island's semi-tropic beauty and did not venture into the Kingston shack dumps, as *The Harder They Come* would do. Poverty and violence had no place in these Kodachrome fantasias of Caribbean island life. By the time *A High Wind in Jamaica* was released in 1965, no amount of patriotic sentiment could have hoisted the Union flag over the island again. Yet the film, with its jolly Jack Tar pirates and scenes of British Navy derring-do, helped to maintain the illusion of a still marvellous imperial colony and a last breath of British self-confidence in the West Indies.

On the way to Rio Bueno Sally Henzell, her eyes on the road, gave me a sidelong glance and said, 'You know I'm dead squeamish about you turning your gaze on Jamaica, Ian. You're going to unravel all kinds of murder and mayhem, aren't you? Then you're going to contrast it with poor old whitey here leading the life of Riley.' I watched Sally as she said this: teasing me, was she? She went on, 'You're going to say the petrol Miss Sally puts in her car for a week would feed one hundred thousand million people for three *months*. You're going to say that while people are gunning each other down in Kingston, Miss Sally is having tea and playing polo on Saturdays. Aren't you?' In fact, Sally was a businesswoman who ran a hotel on the south coast (Jakes) and was a significant employer, no lady of leisure.

We had crossed over into Trelawney parish when she concluded with a laugh, 'You know I don't trust you one jot! You sly mongoose. You ole rass, you.'

I said to Sally, 'Writers are a low, creeping breed.'

Rio Bueno was destitute with the remains of a Redcoat fort called Fort Dundas overlooking the sea. Fustic (the dye used for yellow 'khaki') had been exported from Rio Bueno, as well as logwood flower honey; no longer. Rio Bueno had acquired a decrepit appearance: formless, unkempt, deserted and a little sinister. All the same it was a pleasingly anomalous sort of place, which had managed to escape some of the developments of post-colonial Jamaica: beach-ringed hotels and golf courses for tourists.

Sally drove back to Itopia to be with Perry, while I stayed on in Rio Bueno. The Anglican church, set at the sea's edge in a walled garden, had a pretty cemetery with a stone path easily recognisable from *A High Wind in Jamaica*. A lizard crawled under a tomb which belonged to John Minton's hosts, Peter and Alice Blagrove. They had died within a year of each other in the mid-1960s, according to the inscription. Jamaica, in their day, had been a very British world of race meetings at the Kingston Racecourse, patriotic gatherings at the Embassy, elaborately formal dinner parties and much drunkenness. It could not be sustained.

On 29 June 1964, Anthony Quinn and James Coburn arrived at Rio Bueno and put up at the Runaway Bay Hotel, where apparently they began to drink heavily. Rio Bueno had not seen such excitement in years. From the revenues of 20th Century Fox the port began to prosper a little. Three hundred screen extras were employed on *A High Wind in Jamaica*, the parts filled by 'West Indians from Notting Hill Gate', reported the *Gleaner* – inaccurately; they were Rio Bueno locals.

Martin Amis (as he has often told us) had a bit-part in the film of the Hughes novel, a very British tale about the treacheries of the adult world which foreshadowed William Golding's *Lord of the Flies*, as well as J. G. Ballard's Crusoe-like parables of extremity and isolation. Few novels that I know of describe so vividly a rite of passage from childhood into the perils of the adult life, as pirates kidnap a group of schoolchildren in Jamaican waters, with shocking consequences.

I climbed a cindered pathway up to Fort Dundas, the sweat running warm between my shoulder blades. Below me stretched a crescent-shape of coast where two reproduction galleon-schooners were seen to float during filming. Five centuries earlier, in 1503, Christopher Columbus had careened his ships off the same coast during his fourth and last voyage to the New World. He was looking for a western passage to the Orient and its gold, silk and spices. However, storms, disease and desertions forced him to run aground in Jamaica. Two of his caravels – the *Capitana* and the

Santiago de Palos – are known to lie at a depth off St Ann's Bay near Rio Bueno. Soundings to dredge them began in the early 1990s but were halted during the five-hundredth anniversary of Columbus's arrival in the Americas in 1492. The Genoese navigator was seen by some Jamaicans as a rapacious imperialist, whose search for gold inevitably involved him in slavery. The wrecks have still not been recovered.

Fort Dundas was a Georgian ruin, its walls pierced with embrasures for cannon. Refuse scattered everywhere over the compact earthern floor was under investigation by a small, incontinent dog. A rank seaside smell reached me, the ruin abuzz with August flies.

*

Back at Itopia I found Perry in the sitting room staring out into the starlit garden. A pale silvery light filtered in though the window and an odour of paraffin and ganja dominated the gloom. 'Everything all right?' Perry asked me, expelling a plume of Ital spliff smoke. Jung Chang's biography of Mao Tse-Tung lay open on the table in front of him. I said everything was fine, and left Perry to his book. On reaching my bedroom in the annexe, I saw that a bright light was shining overhead. A star so brilliant, I knew, could only be Venus.

I closed my eyes and drifted into a half-sleep, as peenie-wallies (fireflies) flashed green above me inside the mosquito net. Pure grace, I thought, looking up at the luminous blink-a-blinks. When I awoke, however, a hot tension was in the room and I was extremely frightened. I felt in the skull, rather than heard, a faint scratching at the window as of tiny scrambling limbs. Something, I half-dreamed, half-thought, was trying to get into my room. The next moment it was climbing up the leg of my bed. Turning my head I caught a brief, out-of-focus glimpse of a white dwarf figure. I lay in the dark, shivering, breathing fast, my head under the sheets until daylight.

*

I smiled – attempted to: it had been a freakish night – as I joined the Henzells for breakfast. They seemed appalled when I told them I had seen something that spooked me. 'Oh *Ian*!' Sally cried. 'Why didn't you tell us?' I should never have puffed on the contents of that Burmese-lacquer box; it had put my night literally out of joint.

In spite of the ordeal, I was sorry to leave Itopia, and affectionately embraced Sally and Perry.

About two hours after leaving Itopia I was on a stretch of corn-coloured sand close to the seashore ruins of Seville Nueva. Seville Nueva, the first Spanish colony in Jamaica, had supplied cocoa, bread, meat, alcohol and other provisions to the Spanish armies operating in conquered Central and South America. Diego Columbus, the navigator's son, had made Seville Nueva his base in about 1510, having been appointed Spanish Governor of the Indies (which included Jamaica). After twenty years, however, the settlement was abandoned in favour of Villa de la Vega, or Spanish Town, the first capital of Spanish Jamaica, until it was destroyed in 1655 by looters in Cromwell's expedition. Some little way off, half buried amid a Caribbean type of sea blackthorn, were the remains of a water mill signposted as part of the 'Governor's Castle'.

Overlooking the archaeological site, cooled by breezes blowing in from the hills of St Ann's Bay, were the ruins of Seville great house, whose slave dwellings and sugar-grinding houses were still just standing. A flock of goats was cropping the grass by the former overseer's quarters. A figure moved behind a doorway – a Rastafarian, I guessed, from the Lion of Judah flag that fluttered from the roof.

I hailed the man as he emerged from the ruin. He was thin as a stick of sugar cane, with his hair, what was left of it, in locks and not too many (brown) teeth. We began to chat. How long had he been living here, in the overseer's quarters?

'Oh plenty time,' he replied to me, smiling, 'since eighteen, nineteen, maybe.'

'1819?'

'No, man, since I was eighteen or nineteen.'

'Oh – a long time.'

'Yeah, plenty long time.'

Did he not get scared at nights on his own here? The Rasta thought a moment. 'There's a very special *eerie* atmosphere,' he conceded. Duppies? 'No, I don't see them. The stillness here, it help me meditate.' The word 'meditate' seemed to remind him that lamb's breath was just now what he needed. He fetched some from a pocket and began to build a spliff. Oh God no. After what seemed an unconscionable time he gave the Rizlas a tender lick and a roll, lit the cigarette and handed it to me by the thin inhaling end, which I declined.

He drew on the smouldering stick, exhaled, drew, exhaled. 'A man can't work without a likkle weed in him belly,' he announced after a few minutes and, self-absorbed, smoked on. The Rasta, with his easy-going, brotherly communitarianism, had fetched up on an estate where (according to Lady Nugent's horrified description of 1802) slaves had slept rough on the floor amid their own filth. Only the other day Land Office officials had ordered him off the premises. 'And I *would* leave,' the Rasta said to me through tartared, gum-shrunk teeth, 'only I need proper warning, so I can take up my plants and banana trees and thing.' I saw a kind of justice in his occupying a slave-driver's property. As Jamaicans say: 'What serves too long, serves another man.'

*

On the road to Kingston, hard by the ruins of Seville Nueva, I waited for Hugh Dunphy to arrive. The sun above me was hot as a stove as the cars sped by. I had met Dunphy and his Jamaican wife, Ouida, at a party in Ocho Rios, where they offered to give me a lift back to Kingston. They ran an art gallery in midtown, called the Bolivar.

Hugh pulled up in a Japanese car with Ouida, poised and haughty-looking, seated in front. Dunphy was, there was no denying it, eccentric-looking. With his white hair worn long in a ponytail, he suggested an ageing rock musician or yoga teacher. Arthur Koestler, in his travel book *The Lotus and the Robot* (1960), mentions Dunphy as a young English dropout who has retreated to a Zen temple in Kyoto. His eccentric appearance was, I suspected, a form of self-protection: Jamaicans had been more friendly to him, he told me, since 'I've looked like a freak – Jamaicans *like* freaks'. Well, I got into the car.

The road to Kingston was narrow, and passed through spectacularly lovely waterfalls and lush hills. At one point we stopped and walked across a suspension bridge that swayed under our weight, the sound of water reaching us in a haze of spray. Along the way, Dunphy showed a keen eye for unusual shrubs ('My God! An Amhurstia!') and local curiosities of all kinds. At Castleton Junction he remarked of a woman standing by the roadside that her bottom was '*steatopygous*', and explained what he meant by that: 'Jamaican women have splendid posteriors but some of them can be quite alarming, sort of like shelves. Yes, *steatopygous*.' Oiuda, after a silence, expressed her displeasure at Hugh's sexist rudeness. 'You are horrible,' she said. 'I've a good mind to hit you with my yardstick.'

*

Herman van Asbroeck's house, situated near the nineteenth-century tourist attraction of Devon House, midtown, had razor wire over the main gates: nine times Herman had been burgled. Nowhere in Kingston seemed to be safe any more, he would say. Only the other day a youth had been shot dead in the neighbourhood as he tried to steal an orchid from a garden. Shot dead for a lousy orchid. But, the grimmer things became in Jamaica, the more Herman insisted on staying. 'My business is here in Jamaica.' He was unlikely ever to return to his native Belgium. He had been living in Jamaica since 1980: 'Herman the German', people nicknamed him.

I liked Herman. A lugubrious but good-humoured character, he managed to find a comedy in all aspects of island life. Jamaica had become for him a place that ridiculed analysis and took him beyond despair to a place of semi-comic bafflement. 'Absurdistan', he called the country, long before a novel about Russian immigrants in the USA, *Absurdistan*, appeared.

The door opened and Herman said to me absently, 'Welcome back, Ian,' then typically fell silent. I walked in with my bag. From loudspeakers upstairs wailed Ethiopian music of the 1970s by Mahmoud Ahmed. (Herman had a magnificent record collection.) His bearded, melancholic face, like that of a Degas absinthe drinker, regarded me blankly as I sat down. He had been eating supper with his partner Eunice, who looked up at me from the table as I walked in, and smiled in greeting. Eunice was from St Lucia in the eastern Caribbean and as strikingly black as Herman was white. Her cheerful manner contrasted with Herman's occasional gruffness. As a professional picture-framer Herman's reputation was for no-nonsense – even brutal – honesty. Difficult clients who did not mind getting 'barked at', as he put it, usually came back; Herman had the best rates in town.

The house, low-ceilinged and clammy, was filled with Congo fetishes and cabinets of African exotica and pre-Columbian Taino marvels. Herman's curiosity seemed to be unlimited. Bizarre, rainbow-bright paintings by the late 'Ras Dizzy' Livingstone, a Rastafarian artist whom Herman had long championed, hung from the walls. I climbed the stairs to a room off a landing lined with books on African art and tribal custom, and went to bed. I slept fitfully. That night a sound of gunfire reached me from nearby Kingsway. The gunfire put a strain on my nerves, as did the sporadic barking. A bout of barking would end in a high-pitched yelp of (possibly) pain followed by silence – then renewed barking as the dogs started to fight again. Such was life in Absurdistan.

20

Police and Thieves

Next morning I woke up in a room jammed with art catalogues and paintings. Above the door frame was a portrait of Herman as a bearded African Christ figure. He was planning to visit an artist acquaintance of his, Andy Jefferson, who lived in Newcastle, an hour's drive out of Kingston. Did I want to go? In Queen Victoria's day Newcastle had served as a British army hill station; Anthony Trollope, visiting in 1859, had commented on the trim lawn planted with Union Jacks.

We left sharp at six. To Herman, behind the wheel, there was something reposeful, even magical, about the heights round Newcastle. The scenery reminded him of earlier days in Jamaica, when he had gone to Newcastle to escape the heat-trap of Kingston. But violence was creeping up from Kingston even to these idyllic lands. At Red Light, once a brothel town for the British troops, a pack of kids glared at us as we drove past. Murder was on their minds, said Herman; murder and money.

When Herman first came to Jamaica, in 1980, he worked for the United Nations 'development' office in Kingston. For four years he was absorbed by UN conferences and seminars; the European experts, with their talk of 'moral responsibility' and 'intermediate technology', were going to help Jamaica. But Herman began to doubt it. On the eve of the 1980 general elections he witnessed from the window of his flat an American remonstrating loudly with two Jamaican men by his poolside. One of the men took out a knife. 'The guys then just walked away,' Herman said to me; they had cut the American's face from ear to ear.

Quickly, his idealism flattened into something like cynicism. He decried the American influence on Jamaica, with its emphasis on material comfort, disposable goods and gadgetry. And he spoke with exasperated disenchantment of Jamaica's murder rate, which by 2008 had reached an average of five killings a day. 'Something's gone wrong,' Herman would say. Fortunately he had found a new sense of purpose in collecting, cataloguing and promoting naïve or 'intuitive' Jamaican art. He became champion to self-taught Jamaican painters and sculptors, helping the poor 'develop' in more concrete ways.

*

Andy Jefferson's home, a bungalow-shack on bare earth, was part of an informal bus-stop area called Cedars, which looked out across green hills to the Newcastle barracks. Jefferson had been expecting us. 'Cup of tea?' he asked in his cockney-Jamaican (he came from Plymouth but had lived in London). 'Why not?' we said, and Jefferson went off to boil a kettle. Disconcertingly his head, shaved, was covered in hospital stitches where burglars had pistol-whipped him the other week. 'I thought I'd be safe up here near the barracks,' Jefferson explained, bringing in the tea. 'Not a bit of it.' The intruders – two men in ski masks – had tied him up and set about stealing his money, computer, camera and CD player. Blood was everywhere but Jefferson managed to drag himself into a room and lock the door, so protecting himself from further violence. One of the burglars he suspected as being the boy who tended the lawns at Newcastle. 'A *nasty* boy,' Jefferson said with emphasis (the boy was later prosecuted); but, incredibly, there was no hint of resentment or even hatred in his voice. A part of him, I guessed, had become inured to the violence.

As we sipped PG Tips we could hear, in the distance, the sound of the drums and cymbal-crashes of the Jamaica Defence Force beginning their morning drill. On a cream-coloured wall above the kitchen sink handprints showed where the burglars had prised open the window. Until the burglary Jefferson's life, except for the occasional visitor, had been extremely isolated. What could keep him in Jamaica?

Justice, or the lack of it, said Jefferson. In 1993, he and his brother Mark had been out driving for the day near Kingston when a road block forced them out of their car. The muggers shot Mark dead; Andy survived, without injury. The same judge who later acquitted his brother's killer also acquitted, the following year, a man who had 'car-jacked' Jefferson on the road to Kingston. 'So where's the justice in that?' he asked us. Yet Jefferson said he would have to stay in Jamaica. 'What else am I supposed to do?' His passion for Jamaica – its African-inspired art and music – was very great. The Kingston ghetto especially, with its underlying Afro-Revivalist customs, was fascinating to Jefferson. In a series of acrylics and prints done in the 1980s he depicted the rise of Jamaican dancehall fashion and music. The paintings – *The Don is Back*, *The Crack Den* – sold well: Jefferson became a name in Jamaican art circles.

But since then he had endured more humiliations and violence. The 'One Love' Jamaica he had once known (fast expiring even in the late 1970s) was now dead. 'Dead, I say, and it makes me so *effing* sad. The young blokes here, they don't have the old sweetness any more. Gone, all fuckin' gone.' Bob Marley was Jefferson's idol. But Jamaica had changed. Several of the original Wailers had died violent deaths. In September 1987 Peter Tosh was murdered; Carlton 'Carly' Barrett, the originator of the 'One Drop' style of drumming, was shot and killed that same year (apparently by his wife and her boyfriend). Twelve years later, in 1999, another original Wailer met a violent death: Junior Braithwaite was killed in Kingston by three armed men.

Jefferson's solemnity deepened. 'So I'm left with this love–hate relationship: I still love Jamaica, but I hate what's *happened* to Jamaica, and what happened to my brother. Well, it's a shame.' A frown appeared on his white face.

Over at Newcastle a peace had descended on the parade square after drill practice. 'I hope you're not a copper,' Jefferson said to me, half-joking, as he pointed to plastic pots of cannabis plant seedlings in a neighbour's garden.

*

I had an appointment with DCP Mark Shields, a senior Scotland Yard officer on secondment to the Jamaican police. His office, situated on the first floor of a modern building in New Kingston, stood stark and cheerless on Oxford Road. A frosted glass panel on the main door proclaimed, in gold leaf, JAMAICA CON-STABULARY FORCE.

In reception a duty officer, his burly figure encased in regulation blue, asked me if I was carrying any firearms. 'Sir, I have to ask you that for security reasons.'

'No,' I said.

'A knife?'

'No – no weapons at all.'

'Good. Are you from England? Here on business?' He was looking into my eyes, trying to read them.

'Sort of – I'm researching a book. On Jamaica.'

'It'll have to have a catchy title. How about *Everything Crash*?'

'Sounds a bit drastic,' I said.

'Well, Jamaica's a drastic kind of country.' He added banteringly, 'How about *Keep the Pressure Down*?'

I could see that he was the talkative sort.

He went on, 'Somebody once told me, he was a book-writer like you, he told me if you put the word *nurse* in a title, you're guaranteed a million-dollar sale.'

I said, '*Keep the Pressure Down, Nurse*, for example?'

*

According to a report in the *Gleaner* newspaper (26 June 2005), most Jamaican police suffer from 'clinical sleep pathologies' and other 'stress-related lifestyle diseases'. At any time, they 'may be as highly impaired by fatigue as if they were legally drunk'. In their depleted state, underpaid, overworked, it is hardly surprising that some policemen take bribes and rake-offs from rackets. This has only helped, of course, to make some areas of Jamaica even more violent and poverty-stricken.

Mark Shields was reckoned to be tough enough for Jamaica. He had served in both the anti-terrorism unit of Special Branch and Scotland Yard's Operation Trident, which investigates gun crime in London's black community. In March 2005 he was appointed director of Jamaica's counter-narcotics and 'major' crime force, Operation Kingfish. Many doubted he would last a week. He was not black, and while many Jamaicans, in their vaunted desire to re-institute 'British' law and order, were happy to submit to a British law enforcer, others understandably were not. In January 2006 this letter was featured in the *Jamaica Observer*:

> It is disturbing that four decades after gaining independence we have to call in a foreigner to help us catch our wrongdoers. Have our present-day policemen no pride in their profession?

All the same, 'Top Yard Man' Shields quickly became a Jamaican hero, a sort of Clint Eastwood figure. Once installed in his Oxford Road office he was inundated daily with telephone calls, not all of them yielding hoped-for criminal intelligence (Shields has many women admirers). He made international headlines in March 2007 when he was appointed chief investigator into the death in Kingston of the Pakistan cricket coach Bob Woolmer. Heart attack? Strangulation? Eight months later, in November 2007, the Woolmer inquest was closed by the coroner: murder had been overruled.

Shields was half an hour late – not bad considering the Kingston traffic. 'DCP Shields,' he said, extending his right hand and, passing the examination rooms with their wire-mesh windows, led me into his office. A detailed map of Kingston marked with coloured pins hung on one wall. He put down his takeaway cup of coffee on the desk, loosened his tie, said, 'It's hot today,' and looked up at the clock on the wall. Ten minutes past eleven; he had to be downtown by half past: we had twenty minutes in which to talk.

I got to the point and asked Shields if he had suffered antagonism as a white Deputy Commissioner of Police in Jamaica.

He replied, with an air of finality, 'No. None at all,' explaining, 'In a politically correct country like Britain we're acutely aware of racial problems. But these problems are simply not an issue in Jamaica. Ninety per cent of Jamaicans have embraced me.' But after a moment's hesitation he said, 'There's an element in the Force who *don't* want me here, but that's not because I'm white. It's because I pose a direct threat to their criminal activities.' The benefits of corruption are known to every working policeman in Jamaica. Shields was determined to deal with the problem. 'If a policeman's got a suspiciously big house, or a flash Escalade or Hummer car, but no *visible* means of income, we'll go after him.' In some parts of Kingston, the police control where and how openly a gang can operate; they can put just about anyone in jail.

Shields went on, 'People here are poor, they don't have jobs, and there are, I believe, *cultural* reasons why Jamaicans kill each other with such . . . frequency.' It will take more than police action to bring down crime rates. Traditions of vengeance have been handed down the generations like family silver. 'A murder might have occurred fifteen, twenty years ago,' Shields explained, 'and nothing happens until one day the dead man's son decides to exact retribution.' Jamaicans can be – increasingly, *are* – murdered for a trifle. 'I'll give you an illustration – the other week in Kingston a bloke lifted up a woman's skirt on the bus. This was seen as a major act of "disrespect". A tit-for-tat killing situation ensued.'

An entire family was 'rubbed out' in order to avenge the affront. (Often, if a person marked for murder is not available, his women and children get hit, never mind their innocence.) Why – I was curious to know – is this disregard for human life not found to the same degree elsewhere in the English-speaking West Indies? Was there a specifically Jamaican predisposition to gun crime? Or was that too narrow an assumption?

Shields looked at me intently. 'I really don't know how to answer that. I do say publicly that these levels of violence are peculiar to Jamaica, and Jamaicans aren't offended by that. I'm not going to be politically correct: I speak as I find.' Some see Jamaican assertiveness – an assertiveness which can easily spill over into violence – as a delayed response to the cruelty of plantation life; Shields had little time for such niceties: all the theory in the world means nothing if you can't read the street. 'I don't know about slavery, what I do know is that we've found all kinds of weaponry in Jamaica,' he said, glancing at the clock again. 'Rocket launchers. Grenades. Sophisticated stuff. Political? Well, the jury's still out on that.' In recent years, said Shields, the politicians have sought to *distance* themselves from the criminals. A new type of don – the narcotics don – has begun to dictate the terms to the politician, rather than the other way round. 'All the same, the link between politics and crime is still very pronounced in Jamaica. *Very*,' Shields concluded.

The political no-go areas of Kingston reminded Shields of Northern Ireland, only in Kingston the boundaries are not as clearly defined as in Belfast, which only made them 'more lethal'. In the 1970s, when he had served with the Met in north London's Stoke Newington, Shields had encountered Turkish-Cypriot gang warfare on Green Lanes. The problems he encountered then were not so different from the ones he was encountering each day in Jamaica. Only (Shields used the word again) they were more 'lethal'.

Jamaican police not infrequently die in the crossfire between rival gangs. 'They're doing some of the most dangerous police work in the world,' said Shields. One gang might try to take over a drug sales location that belonged to another gang. Or one gang might attempt a drive-by shooting in another gang's territory, hoping to scare off its customers. Shields was not worried by the small-fry Jamaican criminals – the Heathrow 'stuffers and the swallowers' who might do a couple of years in Holloway for cocaine smuggling. 'No, it's the big-time cocaine gangsters – the blood money men in Philadelphia, Manchester and London – that worry me.' Each day they pump more guns and money into their Kingston 'corner'. The deportee from Peckham will expect his 'corner' to have remained the same as when he left it. 'But,' Shields explained, 'another man's moved in – and that's when you have a turf war.'

Shields has pledged to bring Jamaica's murder rate down by 4 per cent. 'Not much, you might say, but I don't want to make promises I can't keep. If we reduce the killings by even *one* per cent, we're doing very well.' It is uncertain whether the government will consider appointing an outsider as Jamaican police deputy again. For the moment, it may not be irrelevant to point out that as a foreigner Mark Shields is not yet embroiled in, or compromised by, island corruption.

*

In Jamaica's catalogue of police and gangland brutality, Carolyn Gomes holds a special place. She is the director of Jamaicans for Justice, a human rights group she founded in 1999 with the aim of combating the abuse of state laws and capriciously wielded government authority. It offers legal instruction and assurance to the poor, and keeps a hawk-like eye on perversions of justice in both Kingston and the parishes. Though Jamaican police kill an average of 130 to 150 citizens a year, cases of police brutality make up only a small part of Gomes's work. Many police officers are happy to cooperate with her. 'We like Mark Shields,' she told me. 'He respects the Jamaican people – and you can always work with Jamaicans if you show them respect.' Shields, I assumed, was civil and courteous towards Jamaicans.

Gomes added, in her quiet, level voice, 'Jamaica's justice system has not moved on with the rest of the world's.' The dishonesty in Jamaican public life had made her wary of politicians and the machinery of the Jamaican state. Yet what I had not understood in all my months in Jamaica was the extent to which violence – and the threats of violence – had rendered the justice system inoperable. Failure of civic society had gone hand in hand with the failure of leadership. Pathologists are often too frightened to serve as observers at post-mortems. The post-mortem room at the Spanish Town Hospital has no refrigeration so what might serve as evidence disintegrates fast. 'Call the Hearse' by the reggae singer Bushman had articulated the problem:

Somebody call the hearse
Cause the body is getting stink
It needs to leave the turf
Make it quick because it's getting rather worse

'Have you been to the Spanish Town mortuary?' Gomes asked me. When I said yes, she frowned. Bodies are brought in by the commercial funeral homes in the early morning, and piled up in corners, often on top of each other. The pathologists don't get to the bodies until eleven – if at all. Usually they don't even weigh the organs – and the bullets are left in the bodies. Currently, Jamaican hospital forensic laboratories come under the control of the Ministry of National Security and Justice; therefore scope for corruption, as well as error, is ample.

Single-minded and tireless, in 2003 Gomes gave up her job as a paediatrician to work in the volatile Grants Pen area of Kingston. The neighbourhood encroaches on no less than four political boundaries. 'You don't cross them,' Gomes said to me. Murders and assaults occur often enough in Grants Pen, but only exceptional murders are reported in detail by the press. One such occurred in

1994, when the police executed a youth on the premises of Nuttall Hospital in Kingston, where Gomes was then working. She was in her office when the police ran past in pursuit of the youth who had found his way, terrified, into the maternity department. The police dragged him out, laid him face down on the floor, and shot him six times in the head (once was not enough). That same day Gomes went on national radio to condemn the execution and within two hours she had received death threats. Extrajudicial police killings are not, on the whole, seen as unlawful by Jamaicans, many of whom believe in instant remedies for crime: death by firing squad, death by mass beatings. Fundamentalist evangelical Christianity, with its calls for the hangman, is partly to blame for the harsh justice, as well as public lack of faith in an overworked and inadequate judiciary.

Gomes answered my next question – where do the guns come from? – with a slight weariness.

'We really don't know. Some say Haiti – as payment for drugs. Others say the Balkans. Maybe Manchester. Maybe Liverpool. Maybe even Northern Ireland.' Like any other globalised economy, in other words, the guns come from all over the world. They are cheap, and getting cheaper; and to the new breed of Jamaican criminals who use them, so is human life. Gomes is reluctant to attribute all gun crime to Jamaica's narcotics trade. The Jamaican police put the figure of drugs-related crime at only 30 per cent, a statistic which Gomes saw no reason to doubt. Social deprivation as well as the decline in 'family values' have helped to make Jamaica the country it now is. For Gomes, a committed Catholic, the 'ravaging' of Jamaican society by absent fathers is nothing short of a 'tragedy'. Fatherless Crew, a notorious Kingston gang, is typically made up of youths whose fathers are in jail, abroad or, most likely, dead.

But is Jamaica really the 'fatherless society' so often portrayed in the foreign press? Barry Chevannes, a social anthropologist based in Kingston, has devoted much energy to challenging the myth. Poor Jamaican men do not uniformly neglect their spousal and parental duties. The problem, as Chevannes sees it, is simply one of poverty. Fathers who can no longer provide are 'pressured out' of home and family; despised by their wives as 'wutliss' (worthless), they may well turn to crime. In 1991, with the aim of challenging the stereotype of the irresponsible Jamaican 'baby father', Chevannes set up a 'discussion and counselling' group in Kingston called Fathers Incorporated. Jamaican men, Chevannes said to me, must not be left 'burdened with the blame'. All the same, generations of Jamaican boys have grown up – are growing up – without fathers. No amount of counselling can detract from that.

I asked Carolyn Gomes whether the culture of 'respect' – and the gun violence that so often accompanies it – was an American import. ('Respect', on the revered rap album *Ready to Die,* by the Notorious B.I.G., glamorises violence in a way I had assumed to be narrowly American.)

'No,' Gomes replied emphatically. 'The business of dissing and respect is home-grown Jamaican. When your life's so degraded, you *need* people to respect you, you need a gun to stand out.' Notions of 'respect' have hatched in the absence of civic values, said Gomes, and encouraged Jamaican men to pursue power and money for their own sake. American rap culture has made spectacular inroads into Jamaican life. Customised wheel rims carrying Mafia-gangsta names like 'Soprano', 'Pistola' and 'Vendetta' are all the rage. The motor accessories, harmless enough, have become an important part of the braggadocio and notions of 'respect' among young Jamaican men. Along with Nike footwear and spiffy track bottoms, those rims are advertised in the pages of American King Magazine ('The Illest Men's Magazine Ever!') and on Black Entertainment Television. There are plenty of uptown cowboys, too, said Gomes, who pack guns and take drugs 'Everybody is *suffering* here,' she concluded.

*

Kingston, like Bogotá or São Paulo, Johannesburg or New Delhi, has a thriving industry in personal security. Security firms seem to make their biggest profits in those cities where the gap between rich and poor is greatest. Trevor Macmillan, a Sandhurst-educated Jamaican, runs a security advisory business off Hillcrest Avenue in uptown Kingston. The business, pervaded by the neutral smell and faint hum of air conditioning, specialises in security for the home as well as for automobiles (M16-proof windshields). Guard dogs are always to be recommended. Most of the dogs are imported from Britain because it takes too long to clear dogs through US quarantine. Black is the preferred colour as it is harder to see at night. 'Jamaicans have a special terror of dogs,' Macmillan permitted himself a grim laugh. 'If things get really rowdy at a cricket match, all the police have to do is bring on the dogs. The crowds go quiet. You should see it!'

Macmillan was one of those increasingly rare uptowners who did not carry a gun. 'I've got a licensed shotgun at home but I *never* carry a gun – it's too dangerous. Of course, for many Jamaicans, a gun is *the* symbol of authority. I mean, you can buy things with a gun – you can rent guns out.' Macmillan should know: between 1993 and 1996 he served as Commissioner of the Jamaican police.

Sandhurst, I supposed, had inculcated in Macmillan a love of Empire and England. He loved cricket. He loved the thick, wine-red carpets of the British colonial administration. His commercial empire, not unlike the British Empire, separated a handful of wealthy people from the rest and barricaded them inside fortresses. In Kingston, entire parts of the city had become fortified gated communities, surrounded by the 'have-nots' living in permanently excluded zones. Macmillan spoke of these Jamaicans as though they were a people apart, different from him. ('Jamaicans tend to be highly reactive'. 'Jamaicans are harder then the rest'.) A part of him, I suspected, wanted Jamaica to go back to the days of 'British law' and 'the London bobby' but, he said, 'There's this brutality in Jamaicans,' and, given the chance, they would be more repressive than British law would allow. 'Jamaicans want to bring back hanging. Jamaicans don't want softly-softly,' he said.

And DCP Shields?

'Shields is the great white hope for upper-class Jamaicans,' said Macmillan, 'but he isn't getting the resources and the help he needs from the Force.' Why was that? The police had become more biddable and corruptible in recent years, in Macmillan's view, and Shields stood in the way of vested interests. The corruption seemed to have a direct connection with police abuse and violence. Jamaican police were often in the national news for beating – sometimes even killing – people who had shown them insufficient 'respect'. But the culture of corruption had caused the lack of respect, and loss of self-respect.

Macmillan added, with a wave of the hand, 'What Jamaica needs is a *new* Force. The Force has to purge itself of all known – or merely suspected – corrupt policemen and put them on early pensions.' Arresting those who are merely 'suspected' of wrongdoing sounded a dubious, extra-legal note, surely. Macmillan would not be drawn, but sat for a moment in silence. Something close to chaos, he continued, could now be seen in the Jamaica Constabulary. Police Academy graduates find themselves at the mercy of their regional superiors, who tell them, 'Here we do it *our* way.'

The Constabulary itself is not respected as it should be by the government. A white foreign DCP drafted in to deal with corruption was obviously a political gesture. The entire Jamaican police force is understaffed and under-resourced, and in need of investment. Seventy per cent of police stations are in disrepair, the floors caving in, ceilings collapsed. Morale is low.

As I left, Macmillan asked me, 'Are you mobile?'

'Mobile?'

'Always carry a mobile phone with you in Jamaica. You never know when you may need it.' He took my hand and, holding it between both his hands, said: 'Be careful.' In 2008, shortly after I met him, Trevor Macmillan was appointed Jamaican minister of security. One year later, in the spring of 2009, Mark Shields resigned as DCP: he had had enough of Jamaica.

*

In the cool, rhododendron-rich heights above Kingston is a house signposted 'John Hearne'; John Hearne, the Jamaican novelist, had lived and died here after a period spent teaching in Leeds in England. Here, uptown, an undertone of fear can be felt on dark nights, when moonlight casts black shadows across the trim lawns, guard dogs bark and the house alarms go off. Hearne's widow, Leeta Hearne, was nevertheless still resident, an ironic, bright woman who had come to Jamaica from England as a teacher in 1953. Her sitting room was filled with tattered cane chairs and a brocade sofa. Leeta was seated on the sofa most evenings, pouring out tea; I went to visit her many times. ('I'm sorry,' she would say, handing me a cup of Darjeeling, 'you'll have to make do with a Christening spoon.') I enjoyed her company and the stories she had to tell – good and bad – of Jamaica.

Not long ago a man had come down off the roof, very drunk, demanding money and brandishing a machete ('cutlass' in Jamaican). The police shot him dead. Leeta's sensibilities, like those of many Kingstonians, had become blunted by the violence, yet she refused to be lured into any nostalgia for those ill-defined 'good times' when Jamaica apparently had no crime and the police were incorruptible. Some Jamaicans, she said, are wilfully detached from the present, and live in a cocoon of fond remembrance. Over the fifty years she had lived in Jamaica she had seen many changes but even in those 'charming' pre-independence days you could still feel threatened by a hint of violence in the air.

Leeta was prey to a language disorder called nominal aphasia, where periods of articulacy are sabotaged by what she called 'vocabulary amnesia'. Her forgetting was like a metaphor, she said half-jokingly, for Jamaica's own historical amnesia, where the past had been conveniently forgotten.

She had little difficulty, however, in speaking about her husband John Hearne. His first novel, *Voices Under the Window,* published in London in 1955, unfolded in a fictionalised West Indian island (in reality Jamaica) at a time of gross social inequalities on the eve of the Second World War. It was followed by four other novels set on the same imaginary island of Cayuna. While other Jamaican novelists were chronicling Kingston poverty and the rise of Rastafari, Hearne in the 1950s and 1960s chose to write instead about the Kingston bourgeoisie and the agricultural middle classes of which he was a part. His work irked some West Indian writers. George Lamming, the great Barbadian novelist, thought that Hearne had glorified 'a mythological, colonial squirearchy'. Yet Hearne's last novel, *The Sure Salvation* (1981), was set on a transatlantic slave ship during the early nineteenth century, and provides a powerful indictment of the 'Africa Trade'.

Initially pro-PNP, John Hearne had lambasted wealthier Kingstonians behind their burglar bars uptown, who lorded it over the 'Quashee' or black majority. In the mid-1970s at the height of Michael Manley's socialist experiment, Hearne commented:

> Look at those bastards up there. They live like kings and Trench Town is less than two miles away. It's a wonder they haven't all had their throats cut by now.

On his death in 1994, Hearne was virtually forgotten, though he had been 'widely read once', his widow said ruefully. Leeta Hearne, with her English tea service, seemed like a planter's wife in an Indian hill station in the 1940s, mindful of the country's past deficiencies and fearful of what was to come, yet unable or unwilling to leave. One evening as I was getting ready to go she glanced up at the roof, wary that someone might be up there again. In an hour, she said, it would be dark, more than enough darkness for us all.

21

Night Nurse

Down Orange Street past the Rockers International record shop (the reggae bass reverberating heavy in my gut), past the high-rise *Gleaner* building, I was back among the clacking of the domino players in the Parade, and back on to King's Street and its KFC and Burger King. Everywhere I went that day the voice of Wilmot 'Motty' Perkins could be heard chivvying callers on his radio chat show. 'Motty' is probably the most controversial political commentator at work today in the Anglophone West Indies. The whole of diaspora Jamaica – not just Jamaica – often seems to be engaged in either an attack on or a defence of some opinion Perkins has just aired on the radio.

His call-in show manages to inform, educate and often amuse with its litanies of doom and frequent settling of scores. Perkins must have a streak of sustained vindictiveness, as the unkindest things are said on the show. His greatest contempt is reserved for Michael Manley, in his view 'a good, charming, civilised man, but also a dimwit'. To his enemies 'Motty' is a tiresome, even quixotic figure who revels in controversy for its own sake. 'Perkins harks back to a time when Jamaicans spoke the Queen's English and when there was an assumption of British law and order,' said the Kingston-based historian Roy Augier (not, since Augier is an anti-imperialist, an endorsement).

Yet Perkins is so much more than merely a scourge of government corruption. He made his name in the early 1970s when, along with John Hearne, he was a sharp-shooting political journalist initially sympathetic to the PNP's black nationalist, Pan-African agenda. Gradually, however, as Michael Manley failed to provide career and investment opportunities, Perkins withdrew his support, and in his gossipy *Gleaner* column, 'Listening Post', he portrayed an increasingly autocratic and high-handed leader. Under Manley, Perkins claimed, state security had begun to hunt down and murder opponents, acting like vigilantes. In 1978, five opposition JLP activists were executed by the army on Kingston's Green Bay firing range. The Green Bay Massacre, as it came to be known, marked the low point in Manley's 'disregard for law', said Perkins, who has devoted much of his radio air time to 'investigating' an event which occurred thirty years before.

In 1979, similarly disillusioned, John Hearne wrote a now notorious article for the *Gleaner*, 'Snoopy Go Home', in which he compared Michael Manley to the cartoon dog who could bark all right but did not know how to find his way home: Manley, Hearne implied, was full of sound and fury that amounted to little.

I liked 'Motty' Perkins more in person than on the radio, a tall, amusing man whose humour belied grave concerns. Perkins has received death threats and, by his own count, been sued fifteen times for libel. 'I don't disregard the death threats, but I hope not to be paranoid about them, either,' he told me. At the gates of his Kingston home an armed security guard sometimes walks 'Motty' to his car. There are certain things in Jamaica, he contends, that Jamaicans don't talk about. 'Not in public, anyway.' Such as?

'Such as our rapine political order. Yes, *rapine*,' said Perkins. Jamaican politicians and businessmen had been drawn into the state's parasitic embrace and metaphorically 'raped' the poor. Independence from Britain had been a 'squandered opportunity'. Forty years of unbroken 'democratic' constitutional rule had failed, in Perkins's view, to bring true democracy. Instead Jamaica had a winner-takes-all mentality, where the political elite were always asking themselves *cui bono*? (Who benefits?) What can we get out of the people?

Perkins refilled his glass with whisky. 'The British did terrible things in Jamaica, but whoever said we have a fair society in Jamaica today? True, we have reasonably open elections, but political oppression here is real.' Perkins was not, it seemed to me, making a general complaint about a government – the PNP – that might have taken up the struggle of the poor but had not done so. It was something more specific, a complaint that all Jamaican politicians (not just Michael Manley) had exploited the poor for their own purposes, in what Perkins saw as a pattern stretching back through the three centuries of slavery.

The attitude to power in Jamaica, Perkins said, remains that of the plantation system, where brutality is meted out against the defenceless, and every little shanty-town Napoleon wants to be an overseer with a team of servants at his call. 'The Jamaicans who live in the great houses today – black, brown, yellow, white – man, I tell you, they look *down* on the man in the street.' Perkins added, 'The prime minister, his cabinet, they're contemptuous of the poor. And the police, they *despise* those niggers down there, the poor.' It was a law of nature to 'hate those we oppress', said Perkins, and it was hard to disagree with him that Jamaicans had inherited a lot of social contempt from slavery. Or, as Perkins put it (a touch pretentiously): 'Our minds are *riveted* to the plantation paradigm.'

The book I had to read if I was to understand Jamaica, said Perkins, was *The Plural Society of the West Indies* (1965) by the Jamaican social anthropologist M. G. Smith. Post-independence Jamaica, as viewed by Smith, was an immovably hierarchical society riddled by anxieties (created partly by the slave-owning British) about social caste and colour. Jamaica is identified as a 'plural society', where groups of differing race, rank and colour might rub shoulders in the sugar, bauxite or tourist industries but – and this was Smith's point – without a common social will. The European, Chinese, East Indian and African Jamaican populations of Jamaica 'mix but they do not combine'; instead they are kept apart through opposed material interests and a 'division of labour along racial lines'. The upper strata of Jamaican society, Smith concluded, are characterised by the snobberies and racial prejudices attendant on the plantation great house – 'of which modern versions are still being built (though in different style)'.

One could argue, as Perkins repeatedly does on his radio show, that Michael Manley, far from ridding Jamaica of plantation inequalities, merely reproduced them. His politics of Black Power and racial equality had encouraged 'top ranking' ghetto dons to become the new lords of the manor; the privilege and money of the plantocracy was coveted now by a frustrated, angry people who wanted a say in their world.

While Perkins was emphatically not (he said) a colonialist, he claimed to find much to admire in Britain's colonial stewardship of Jamaica. 'Colonialism was in some ways a wonderful thing,' he said. 'It exposed the Jamaican people to opportunities – railways, education, democratic institutions – which we might not have been able – in fact, *have* not been able – to take up and develop ourselves.'

Surely, in identifying so much to admire in the Empire, there was a danger of ignoring the arrogance, racism and authoritarianism at the heart of the British imperial project? In Jamaica, as in the Raj, the British had professed *libertas* but practised *imperium*, subjugating the population to Britannia's rule in the name of freedom. Behind Perkins's admiration for aspects of Empire-era Britain, I suspected, was a question of colour. Perkins was a mixed-race or 'browning' Jamaican; and, as such, he thought of himself as middle class – middle class in the Jamaican way, meaning essentially British, with a pride at being a remnant of the old colonial 'brown' class. Such a class regarded all things West Indian as of inferior quality. British is best: education, food, health, the British Empire (even as it became moribund) was the definition of the very best.

Perkins is especially riled by Rex Nettleford, vice-chancellor of the University (or 'intellectual ghetto', as Perkins calls it) of the West Indies in Kingston. As an ideologue of Black Power and 'blackness', Nettleford had been the PNP's philosopher-in-residence during the 1970s and acted as something of a guru to Michael Manley, who consulted him on matters of Revivalist and Rastafari ritual. Nettleford's many books on Afro-Jamaican culture – *The Story of Jamaican Dance, Rex Nettleford: Selected Speeches* – are hard to read, being full of circumlocutory jargon and large, sonorous epithets. Perkins cannot abide them. 'Nettleford wastes a bitch of an amount of time talking about Africa and plantations, and all kinds of nonsense,' he judged, impetuously. Yet the desire to 'disrespect' Nettleford involved Perkins in contradictions and inconsistencies, as he too spoke a good deal about 'Africa and plantations', albeit in quite a different way to his rival.

For an Afro-centrist such as Nettleford, Africa forms the very bedrock of Jamaican culture: the rules in colonial Jamaica may have been British, but the *subterranean* ideas were African. Even the Jamaican deference for titles, far from being a British inheritance, derives from African honorific tribal forms of address. (Nettleford in fact is very mindful of titles and their correct use.) With his thick gold neck chain and fastidious Oxford accent, Nettleford invites a certain amount of ridicule ('Sexy Rexy', Jamaicans call him). But unlike 'Motty' Perkins, with his cynical demolition of Jamaica and Jamaican achievement, Nettleford has at least achieved something. In 1962 he founded the National Dance Theatre Company of Jamaica with the specific aim of introducing a Caribbean choreography to Jamaica. The company, now almost half a century old, was a not insignificant part of the PNP's project to 'decolonise' Jamaica of European influence. Nettleford reserves his greatest contempt for Jamaica's brown class. 'The "brownings" put on airs and see themselves as the natural heirs of the Raj,' he told me. 'We call them "Bounty Bars"– white on the inside, black on the outside.' He included in that ambiguous category Wilmot 'Motty' Perkins.

*

The red-brick Victorian church in Willesden, north-west London, was hung with wreaths for the bicentenary of Mary Seacole's birth. It was a spring day in 2005, and the pews were packed with uniformed nurses come from the former British West Indies to celebrate the occasion.

Mary Seacole, the Jamaican nurse and entrepreneur, was born in Kingston in 1805 to a mixed-race parentage. Her memoir, *Mrs Seacole's Wonderful Adventures in Many Lands* (1857), is justifiably upheld as an Afro-Caribbean masterwork. And Seacole herself has been appropriated posthumously as a 'black British icon', with her life story now on the National Curriculum in British primary schools. Seacole's was the first autobiography to be published in Britain by a non-white woman, yet it is hard to construe the book as an advertisement for 'black British literature', as political correctness demands one should.

For Seacole was not British – she was Jamaican. The argument might seem tortuous: Jamaica was part of the British Empire, and

Seacole's identification with Britain was in many ways inevitable. Yet neither Paul Bogle nor Marcus Garvey has qualified for the label 'British' (they are simply 'Jamaican'). Why? Because Bogle and Garvey had rebelled against the British establishment, whereas Seacole was an apologist for the British Empire who, moreover, lived in some denial of her African Jamaican roots. A rare chink in her self-constructed British persona is her endorsement of African slave remedies; Seacole knew how to apply herbal poultices to comfort the injured or dying, like a Maroon 'bush doctoress'.

In that curiously British church setting, however, with its air of Anglican pageantry, Seacole's patriotic spirit and 'service' to the mother country were enthusiastically applauded. She had been fearless under Russian fire in the Crimean War and rode to the front lines to help wounded British troops. She had gone to the Crimea in 1854 under her own steam, moreover, as the War Office in London (almost certainly on racial grounds) had turned down her application to serve there as an official nurse. For sixteen months in war-torn Balaklava she worked as a sutler (camp follower) by providing Britain's beleaguered troops with food and rum. It was in 'scenes of horror and distress', she firmly believed, 'that a woman can do so much'. Seacole was fifty-two when she set up the 'British Hotel' outside Balaklava and was admired for her cheerful and practical compassion.

After the war, in 1856, 'Mother Seacole' settled in London, where thousands of British ex-servicemen remembered her as their saviour. A bust of her was carved by Queen Victoria's nephew, Count Gleichen, and supposedly she acted as masseuse to the Princess of Wales. In 1881, following an 'apoplexy', or a stroke, she died and was buried in St Mary's Catholic Cemetery in Kensal Green, the future resting place (before he was repatriated to Jamaica in 1964) of Marcus Garvey.

It was not until 1954, with the centenary of the Crimean War, that Mary Seacole was officially honoured in Jamaica (a ward at Kingston Public Hospital was named after her). By that time, thousands of Jamaican women had migrated to Britain to work or train as nurses in the National Health Service. Many of them regarded nursing as a calling and honoured Seacole as the 'true mother' of their profession. Leeka Champagnie, ninety-two, has been recognised by the Jamaican government for her services to nursing. She lived in the 'Golden Retreat' retirement home off Seymour Avenue, Kingston, and I went to see her there one evening. Small and frail, with cataract-coloured eyes and a fluff of sparse white hair, she approached me down the hall on a Zimmer frame.

Britain in the early 1950s was, Champagnie recalled, derelict, dark and half-ruined after the war, the interiors of railway carriages and buses black with grime. Bomb damage was still visible round St Leonard's Hospital on Kingsland Road, east London, with bulldozers raking up the remains of the paediatrics block destroyed in 1941 by German bombs. On the men's ward where Champagnie worked she was surprised to find so many poor white patients. (That poor whites existed at all was a surprise to her.) The patients were fascinated by the underside of her hands – why were they pink when the rest of her was black? They wanted to know how you could tell if black people had jaundice. 'You have to look into the eyes,' Champagnie told them. 'It's the eyes that go yellow.'

Champagnie's arrival in Britain coincided with the West Indies' historic triumph at Lord's in 1950. This was a defining moment, not just in cricket, but in the history of the Anglophone Caribbean. England had been beaten by the West Indies on home ground at the game they, the English, had invented. Thousands of Caribbean 'immigrants' (according to *The Times*) calypso-danced round the Eros statue in Piccadilly armed with 'guitar-like instruments'. Champagnie was among them. Afterwards, at a victory party held in Fulham Town Hall, she joined Jamaicans in singing Lord Kitchener's calypso, 'Cricket, Lovely Cricket', written for the occasion.

> England was beaten clean out of time
> With the spin bowling of Ramadhin and Valentine

To me, Champagnie spoke of Mary Seacole as a 'pioneer and a beacon' to nurses everywhere. Between 1948 and 1969, the formative years of the NHS, Seacole's idea of service had been perpetuated by Jamaicans working in Britain with little expectation of much pay. Champagnie thought the NHS was 'marvellous'; some Jamaican women worked for the organisation all their lives. It offered a form of socialised medicine which accorded well with Seacole's vision of service to Britain and her injunction to fulfil one's societal function. 'The NHS allowed me to help people and give something back,' Champagnie said, in terms now unfashionable.

Jamaica's own public health service, founded in 1966, has not shown up so well. Universal health care is said to be the mark of a civilised society – one concerned about the well-being of its citizenry. In the 1970s under Michael Manley, accordingly, government expenditure on the health service increased more than 30 per cent. Yet in parts of the Jamaican countryside where 'bush medicine' is still practised, government health provision has yet to arrive.

More and more trained Jamaican nurses are migrating to North America or the Bahamas, or choose to work in the private sector. The Victoria Jubilee Hospital, a women-only hospital built in Kingston in the fifty-fifth year of Queen Victoria's reign in 1892, has one of the best midwifery schools in the West Indies. (The most promising students receive the Leeka Champagnie Award for Excellence.) Yet the infrastructure is crumbling and staff shortages are now so acute that specialist teachers have to be recruited from Cuba and Nigeria. The doctor-to-population ratio in Jamaica is currently 1 to 5,240, one of the lowest in the world.

The Sir John Golding Rehabilitation Centre, however, is a national treasure. Set up in 1954 to provide care for victims of a Jamaican poliomyelitis epidemic, the centre has served as a sanctuary and place of healing for half a century. Now that polio has been eradicated from Jamaica, most of the ninety patients today have been admitted for spinal cord injuries or congenital abnormalities such as muscular dystrophy. Nevertheless such medical care is wonderful to see. It was a Friday afternoon when I was taken on a tour of inspection, and an end-of-the-week cheer pervaded the centre. Work of some sort – sewing, tailoring, soldering – is provided for all the patients. Their handiwork is later sold in tourist gift shops; thus the long-term patients have an economic life and a purpose. Everywhere they went about their tasks, stitching together national flags, making laminated table mats. Minute tasks: one man was sterilising and repairing Air Jamaica headsets – thousands of plastic headsets were hanging out to dry on racks, their wires trailing like blue spaghetti. The atmosphere, friendly and full of industry, filled me with me a mood of optimism.

I was keen to see the place where the reggae album, *The Same Song*, by Israel Vibration, had been conceived. Bulgin, Craig and Spencer were three Rastafarians confined to wheelchairs by polio at the Sir John Golding centre – yet they managed to create a music of extraordinary hope. Released in 1978 on EMI's 'progressive' Harvest label, *The Same Song* was intended partly as a social commentary on Michael Manley's soured Jamaica, with its 'bandoolos' (crooks) and other compromised characters. Yet it also celebrated – with finely crafted harmonies and a spiritual Rastafarianism of unalloyed sincerity — the very human qualities of forbearance and overcoming of adversity that the Rehabilitation Centre nurtured.

Care, government-funded medical care of the simplest sort, was possible here; why could it not be extended to others in Jamaica? I wondered why it had to be a foreigner who had made this possible; John Golding, a man of culture, was an English Jew, a lecturer in orthopaedics. Was there something innately vulnerable – helpless, even – in the post-colonial condition that required it to seek an outsider's hand?

22

Scotland Yard

One of the great books to have come out of the Jamaican–British encounter is *Journey to an Illusion*: *The West Indian in Britain* by Donald Hinds. Published in London in 1966, it sympathetically conveys the plight of Jamaicans who, lost amid alien signs in Britain, tried to settle and earn a crust. The book is made up of a series of interviews with Jamaican (and other West Indian) migrants in Britain, interspersed with social commentary. The author is described on the dust jacket as a 'Jamaican-born journalist and former London bus conductor'.

A recurring theme in the book is Hinds's discovery that Britain was not only unmindful of the Commonwealth but disinclined to help Jamaicans. Italians in Britain after the war selling ice cream and confectionery were made to feel more welcome, despite having fought on Hitler's side in the conflict. The antipathy was especially galling to Donald Hinds, who as a teenager in Jamaica had read Dickens and Wordsworth, and watched endless genteel films – 'Tea Party Movies' – from the Gainsborough Studios. But, for all his immersion in British culture Hinds was, he recalled, 'struck dumb' on his arrival in Britain in 1955.

I met Hinds in a café in Eltham, south London, in 2006. He was looking relaxed (if ready for a run) in a pair of trainers and a tracksuit. His wife was a retired Jamaican nurse who had trained at the Victoria Jubilee Hospital in Kingston. Hinds spoke of his days on the London buses with nostalgia, even amazement. At London Transport's Brixton garage his driver, a Woodbine-smoking First World War veteran, was happy to have a Jamaican on board. 'I fought alongside a lot of coloureds in the trenches,' he would say.

Jamaicans were not numerous in 1950s London and an entire

week could go by on the double-deckers without Hinds seeing another black face. Passengers, astonished to encounter a black 'clippie' (bus conductor), asked him if they could pat his hair for 'good luck'. After the Civil Rights Movement asserted itself in America, Hinds came to resent such curiosity. Yet London Transport played its role, he now believes, in breaking down race prejudice in post-war Britain; the buses provided the British public with an opportunity to encounter West Indians for the first time and even (heavens!) talk to them. The sense of camaraderie did not last.

The race 'disturbances' of 1958 dramatically altered the way Donald Hinds looked at Britain. Tensions erupted first in Nottingham, then, more grievously, in west London. White youths ('Teddy Boys' to the press) went out to beat up West Indians in Shepherd's Bush and the area then known as Notting Dale between the factories of Wood Lane and the newly claimed middle-class streets of Notting Hill Gate. Oswald Mosley's Union Movement and other 'Keep Britain White' parties were rallying working-class youths to go out 'nigger-hunting'. So began four days of the worst rioting the United Kingdom had ever seen.

The Times, in a now celebrated editorial of 4 September 1958, 'A Family of Nations', announced: 'The time has come to admit that there is a coloured problem in our midst.' The following year, on the night of 17 May 1959, a thirty-two-year-old black carpenter from Antigua, Kelso Cochrane, was fatally stabbed under a railway bridge in Paddington. His killers have still not been found.

Cochrane's funeral in Kensal Green Cemetery adjacent to Mary Seacole's grave was attended by over 1,000 mourners, black and white. The show of white support did little to prevent the notion, fast growing among Jamaicans, that the mother country was not so welcoming. As Hinds put it to me: 'After Cochrane's death we had to rethink everything, we had to revise our faith in the Union Jack.'

Between shifts on the buses, Hinds began to write for the *West Indian Gazette,* Britain's first black newspaper, founded in 1958 by the Trinidad-born civil rights activist Claudia Jones. It was through the efforts of 'Miss Jones' (never 'Claudia') that Hinds became more politically aware. He interviewed Marcus Garvey's first wife, Amy Ashwood, in London, and offered trenchant reports on life in post-war black Britain. In her newspaper office at 250 Brixton Road (now the 'Marvellous Fried Chicken'), Claudia Jones received guests at all hours, like an alternative West Indian High Commissioner. Downstairs was London's first black music shop ('Theo Campbell's'), where Jamaican mento and boogie by Laurel Aitken and Monty Reynolds sold in quantities. Black London was finding a niche for itself. The Barbadian cricketer Gary Sobers, Donald Hinds recalled, made a point of visiting the record shop during the 1963 Test at Lord's.

Gradually, Hinds's reverence for Britain and the Empire diminished. As he and his mother stayed on in Brixton at their house on Crawshay Road, he noticed the shelves in white-owned grocery shops begin to stock tins of Jamaican ackee and Jamaican carrot juice. The 'Jamaicanisation' of London quickened apace after independence when more Jamaicans came to Britain and London was poised to become the most Jamaican city in Europe. Britain's indigenous culture is now so influenced by Jamaica that a Jamaican inflection is hip among white British teenagers. Black Jamaican culture *is* youth culture in London.

Donald Hinds, for his part, was proud that Jamaicans were predominant among West Indian migrants. They were, he let slip, 'better' than (certainly 'different' from) their British Caribbean brothers. Meaning? Well, he replied, apart from the accident of their having been under British control, Barbadians, St Lucians and Guyanese have very little in common with Jamaicans. 'Superimpose a map of Europe on the West Indies,' Hinds explained, 'and Jamaica is Edinburgh, Trinidad is north Africa, Barbados would be Italy – that's how far apart we are.'

As Hinds spoke the Polish owner of the café called out from the counter: 'Excuse me, where is Jamaica?'

*

As Jamaica is predominantly black, it might be thought that racial prejudice does not exist there. Jamaicans were always reminding me that they had no 'colour prejudice', only 'class prejudice'. Snobberies had been rife among British planters, as they ranged down the social scale from attorney to overseer to bookkeeper. But these were not British class distinctions (the typical Jamaican planter preferred to *forget* his class origin): rather, they were a variant designed by men who needed to keep their 'position' in West Indian society as a reward for their self-exile.

Planter snobberies were inevitably shaped and defined by colour (or, more properly, ethnicity). In order to bolster their social status, planters evolved an elaborate ranking of skin beginning with their white eminences at the top, and descending to the 'salt-water Negro' at the bottom. Between true black and pure white were mustees, mustaphinos, quarteroons or quadroons, octoroons, and Sambos (children of 'mulatto' and African mix). These names have a strange poetry in their sounds, but they conceal a mean-minded prejudice. Consequences of this 'racialised' system – the minutely calibrated hierarchy of skin tones devised by the British – have survived in Jamaica to the present day.

It is a nonsense to claim that 'colour prejudice' does not exist in Jamaica. Prejudice is strongest not between white and black, but, I came to realise, between black and 'browning'. Mixed-race Jamaicans, though 'structurally black' (in anthropologist's jargon), often seem more pugnacious in their disapproval and derision of Africa and African 'mumby-jumby' than white Jamaicans. Most 'brownings' who stayed on in Jamaica after abolition thought of themselves as staunchly British. Their Britishness was part of what it meant to be a cut above the poor, *patwa*-speaking Jamaicans who said 'Inglan' instead of 'England'. Even freed Jamaican slaves were at pains to reject their African origin; Anthony Trollope, in his travel account *The West Indies and the Spanish Main* (1860), wrote of how they refused to eat, drink or even work alongside slaves newly arrived from Africa. Their faces scarred with Congo tribal distinctions, these Africans were reckoned to lack British manners and upbringing, what Jamaicans call 'broughtupsy'.

Inevitably, in their move white-ward mixed-race Jamaicans identified with planter-class Englishmen. (There were even some 'brownings' who joined white slave-drivers in resisting emancipation.) On the other hand, many white Jamaicans today happily lapse into Afro-Jamaican patois; they have no reason to fear the mark of Africa. Such are the intricacies of skin colour in Jamaica.

Mary Langford, a Jamaican writer and historian of the island's

Quaker movement, is the sister of the author Evan Jones. Like many of her mixed-race class and colour, she lived in a smart Kingston house jammed with mahogany furniture, silver polo trophies, silver tea pots and, above all, maids. The maids were very black, and their blackness, contrasting with their pink blouses and pink skirts, served to highlight the 'whiteness' of their employers. Likewise, wealthy black Jamaicans may choose to exhibit their equality with whites by employing white servants imported from Eastern Europe.

In much of what Mary Langford said I detected a sense of 'African embarrassment'. She told me, 'I'm not afraid *ipso facto* of Africa, or of African culture. But there's too much ganja, too much dancehall, and too much sleeping in the afternoon.' She sighed. 'The *yout bwoys*, they have no work but what they do have is a gun.' That word 'yout' – youth, but with a connotation of delinquency – was a bad word with these brown people: it meant underdeveloped, non-English: in a word, African.

I asked Mary Langford, with one eye on the polo trophies: 'So Jamaica was better off under the British?'

'Oh I don't know about that,' she said with a cautious air. 'Mark you, there was better law and order. The British police were marvellous. They didn't boss it over others like the Jamaican police do today. Black Jamaicans – not that I have any prejudice – are just not as good at keeping law and order.' The PNP under Michael Manley, with its black nationalism and project to 'decolonise' Jamaica of its British influence, had taken Jamaica too far in the direction of Africa, said Mary Langford. 'Where is the place for us in Rex Nettleford's Afrocentric outlook? Where do we fit in?' Cecil Langford, her husband, had served in Edward Seaga's JLP government and was part of the middle class, from which Jamaica's political elite was drawn following independence. The world had moved fast for him and Mary Langford: what had long been consolidated by them – the status, the property – was being menaced by a new class risen up from the ghetto and the gulley. They found it uncomfortable to have to jostle for position with the newcomers.

Four dogs – Rhodesian Ridgebacks – bounded up to me as the Langford chauffeur came to take me back midtown. He was wearing a khaki drill uniform to signify his owners' wealth and he opened and closed the door for me, addressing me as 'sir'.

*

A white skin in Jamaica is associated with wealth and high social rank, yet there are exceptions. Scattered across Jamaica are pockets of poor white country folk sometimes known as 'rummers' after their fondness for drink, or 'redskins' from their sun-reddened skins. These white Jamaicans challenge the stereotype of dispossessed blacks and all-powerful whites.

Poor whites are to be found everywhere in the Caribbean. In Barbados they live in conditions of near-destitution along remote Martin's Bay; in Haiti is a community of *moun rouj* (red people), believed to be descended from the Polish troops sent out by Napoleon in 1803 to help quell the slave revolt. Most of the 2,570 Poles defected and, in 1806, following Haitian independence, they were granted the right to stay on the island and own property. But they would have to count themselves as part of the black majority; to my knowledge, this was the first time in history that the term 'black' had been used in an ideological sense.

Two distinct communities of poor whites exist in Jamaica: one is notionally 'Scottish', the other 'German'. The Scots live along the south coast in the parish of St Elizabeth, the Germans in Westmoreland parish deep in the interior. The whites of St Elizabeth – 'St Bess whites' – have Scottish surnames such as Heron, Hamilton, Paterson and (easily the most common in Jamaica) Campbell. They live in villages with Scottish names: Culloden, Scott's Cove, Ballards Valley.

The Germans are descended from indentured labourers drafted in by the imperial British during the 1830s as a 'civilising' presence. As white, conscientious, God-fearing folk, they were expected to set a good example in pre-emancipation Jamaica and, if necessary, take up arms in defence of the planters should the slaves revolt. Among the 1,500 original settlers were gunsmiths, metalworkers, cloth-weavers, stone-carvers, teachers, tinsmiths and cobblers. The British administration had promised them an amount of arable land in return for their labour. Inadequate preparation had been made for their reception, though, and before long Jamaica's extremes of heat and hurricane overwhelmed them.

Some 250 of the Germans were settled on a wild tract of land owned by Lord Seaford, a white Jamaican whose family had been on the island since 1685. In Seaford Town they cultivated yam, plantain and ginger. 'We was all of us poor in them days,' Olga Gardner, a ninety-two-year-old Seaford Towner, told me. 'Life was hard – hand to mouth – yes, we come from hungry-belly history.'

Bizarrely, some of their descendants later appeared as film extras in the prison saga *Papillon*, based on the novel by Henri Charrière and starring Steve McQueen and Dustin Hoffman. The film was shot partly in Jamaica, in 1972. The extras were required to play the part of prison inmates in French Guyana. Each day fifty of them were bussed to locations in Kingston and the north coast. ('There was no place for Negroes in *Papillon*,' one of them said to me. 'If some of us was too dark – if we had mixed Negro and German blood – we got floured up.') Filming went on for three weeks. Father Francis Friesen, the Catholic priest of Seaford Town, features in the film as the priest who administers the last rites to a poor devil about to be guillotined for attempted escape. Neither he nor any of the 'convict' extras is credited in the two-hour-long epic. Father Francis complained to the director, but to no avail, and when he died in 2006, at the age of eighty-five in his native Holland, apparently he was still aggrieved.

Today, only 157 'full white' descendants of the original German settlers survive in Seaford Town. The German word *Heimat* – homeland – occasionally occurs in their speech, which contains traces of Westphalian and Rhenian dialects. But most Seaford Towners have no idea from where in Germany their ancestors came. Some of their houses, with their lattice-work gables and pastel-coloured verandas, nevertheless have a Germanic aspect. Inside, certain items of furniture and kitchen utensils (ceramic-tiled stoves, scrubbing boards, sausage-making tools) enhance this impression. One elderly woman I met had been making pastry with a *Nudel-roller* and the grey dough clung to her hands. Her maiden name was Hacker. From a cupboard she removed two porcelain milk jugs with a pink floral pattern, which her great-grandparents hadbrought over in 1835, from Gottingen, perhaps. Holding one of them up to the light, she tried to remember the prayer she had been taught as a child. The prayer was recited, she said, during illness and natural disasters. She squeezed her eyes shut and opened them – the words had come back to her:

> *Ich bin klein.*
> *Mein Herz ist rein,*
> *Soll niemand drin wohnen*
> *als Jesus allein.*

She translated: 'I am small. My heart is pure, nobody may live in it but Jesus.' The hymn had gone down the generations of Seaford Town like the porcelain jugs as a talisman of *Heimat*. Yet, at this late hour in Jamaica's history, the fate of the 'Germaicans' is uncertain. In Seaford Town, cousins often marry cousins; and there are a number of deaf-mutes. 'Cousins boil good soup,' goes the Jamaican proverb.

*

Exactly when the 'Scots' came to St Elizabeth's is not known. But the isolation of the parish – with swamps to the east and west, mountains and desert savannah to the north, and sea to the south – has helped preserve them as a people apart. Legend has it that they came off a shipwreck some time in the seventeenth century, stayed and left their 'Scottish' names.

The first wave of Scots arrived as slaves to English planters in about 1655. A second wave, in 1745–6, was made up of Jacobite rebels captured after Culloden. Yet a third wave, in the years after Culloden, went voluntarily and comprised doctors, engineers and sugar estate managers. As professionals, they planned to return to Scotland as soon as they had discreetly amassed a fortune or, in the expression of the time, a 'comfortable independence'. Young Scots hoping to escape economic depression scoured the *Caledonian Mercury* and *Edinburgh Advertiser* for news of Jamaica-bound ships. Among them was the poet Robert Burns, who in 1786 was offered the position as a bookkeeper. Jamaica was then at the peak of its slave-based sugar boom, but Burns never took up the post.

The Scots, like the English, were ardent capitalists and agents of Empire. Yet they perceived themselves as oppressed by Empire and their Calvinist morality often recoiled against the luxury and dissolution of the English planter class. Zachary Macaulay, the future abolitionist, arrived in Jamaica from Scotland in 1784 at the age of sixteen. He began work as a plantation bookkeeper and, subsequently, rose to assistant manager. He was not initially opposed to slavery, yet he flinched from whipping the slaves in his care and disdained (so he later wrote) the 'grossly vulgar manners' of the English masters. After four years in Jamaica he returned to Scotland, apparently in disgust.

Other Scots were not so lucky. They failed to accumulate sufficient capital to go home and, seduced by the tropic warmth and women of the island (or their Calvinistic conscience silenced by drink), became ensnared. Tobias Smollett, the Glasgow-educated Scottish writer, aptly described Jamaica as 'the grave of the Europeans'. By the 1750s, Scots were estimated to form nearly a third of Jamaica's white European population. Place names in Scotland today attest to their migration: Jamaica Street in Glasgow; Jamaica Bridge over the River Clyde.

For years the 'whites' of St Elizabeth had kept to themselves along a fifteen-mile stretch of coast between Parottee Point and Great Bay. Ballards Valley, a little way inland, is still distinctly 'white'.

Lena 'Dimple' Henry, a Jubilee-trained nurse, lived in a house in St Elizabeth hung with pink curtains ruched into swags. She and her three sisters, Blossom, Puxie and Cherry, had been raised by their white grandmother, Lina Hyam, in the St Elizabeth village of Berlin. For the slightest misdemeanour 'Miss Hyam' would flog her charges; above all she prohibited them from mixing with black boys. The 'Quashees' had to know their place but, Miss Hyams complained, they were always trying to 'marry up' – marry light-skinned women in order to 'improve' the social colour of their children – and to add 'a bit of cream to their coffee'. As the only 'white' inhabitants of Berlin, the Henry girls would have to watch their backs.

One of the first St Elizabeth 'red men' to marry a black Jamaican was Zimroy 'Zim' James, a fisherman in the Treasure Beach area. His wife, Chrisida, had come from Brown Hill up country where no whites lived. 'Yes,' James said to me, 'she was a dark lady and I married her. Lord, everybody was fussing back when it happen, said

I was spoiling the family by marrying a black. Well, what happened happen – it can't unhappen.' Chrisida was among the early wave of Jamaicans who moved into the area in the 1950s as the bauxite industry expanded. St Elizabeth's demography changed as more outsiders came to work in the mines and tourism. As late arrivals – black, at that – they often found themselves unwelcome; today things have improved.

White Jamaican prejudice towards black Jamaicans works both ways. Sheila Hamilton, now seventy-three, is a Justice of the Peace in Treasure Beach, and regards herself as a woman of 'Scottish' descent. 'Sometimes people call me black,' she said. 'Maybe we Hamiltons *do* have African race in us – well, most Jamaicans do – but I'm not black. I'm brown. A light-brown lady.' She paused. 'Actually I'm virtually white.' In the 1950s, when she worked as a nurse in Mandeville Hospital, the black nurses there called her 'Redskin', 'Mulatto', 'Red Nurse' or 'Redibo'. ('Redibo', in modern Jamaica, designates a person of reddish-yellow complexion, and is usually derogatory.) 'We clear-skinned folk were thought to have advantages which the blacks couldn't have or get.' Such as? 'Well, the full-blacks were jealous of my skin and my tall [straight] hair.'

Mrs Hamilton concluded ruefully: 'Our Scottish colour's dwindling down – we're all getting Jamaicanised now.' Let us hope so. Colour prejudice in Jamaica is as subtle as it is pernicious. Eunice ('Cherry'), Lena's younger sister, has worked since 1979 in the Passport Office at the Jamaican High Commission in London. She said to me, 'There's no one more prejudiced than black Jamaicans. Why, blacks are prejudiced even against *themselves*.' Even the black Jamaicans of her acquaintance did not like being called blacks, she said. 'Maybe some of the young people. And those radicals. You know, Rastas. But not Jamaicans my age. Even people who really are black, they don't like it.'

Recalling her St Elizabeth childhood, Eunice told me of a friend of Miss Hyam's in Berlin, called Miss 'Goatfoot' Gertrude. 'She used to say the only thing she liked about black was the colour of her shoes. And you know what colour Miss "Goatfoot" was? Right. Black.'

*

'So would you like to go to Scotland?' My question, I realised, was ridiculous. Lancel Graham was an old Treasure Beach fisherman; how could he get to Scotland at his age? But he answered, 'I have a brother in Scotland.' Graham, a physically slight, quick-witted man, agreed that his surname was 'full-on Scottish'. He pointed to a LOCH NESS fridge magnet from his brother Aston in Scotland. Amazingly, Aston had been resident in Peebles on the Scottish Borders for seventy years now and (according to Lancel) spoke English with a Jamaican-Scottish accent. The strangeness of Aston's itinerary from the 'Scottish' shores of Treasure Beach to Scotland was not untypical of Jamaica's mixed bloods and destinies.

Lancel Graham had hints of blue in his eyes. 'I don't look right to black people,' he said, 'but I'm not white, either – I'm a red man.' His wife, Vanita Simmonds, was effectively white. To me she said, 'You'd be as brown-lookin' as my husband if you'd stayed in Treasure Beach – brown as a berry.'

'He'd be a red man,' Lancel offered.

'My husband,' Vanita said, 'is really a black Scotsman. Yes, he's a black man at heart, with a little Scottish blood.'

About the Scottish shipwreck Lancel knew very little, only that it had happened in 1690 or perhaps 1750.

In fact, as I discovered later in the British Library in London, St Elizabeth had been populated in 1699–1700 by the remnants of the 'Scotch Darien colony'. The planter-historian Edward Long, in his *History of Jamaica* (1774), tells how the Scots merchant entrepôt and colony was situated on the Darien coast of Panama near what today is the Colombian border. It was intended to be Scotland's gateway to the New World.

The five ships that set sail from Scotland in the summer of 1698 carried the hopes of a nation. Half the capital available in Scotland – a sum of £400,000 – had been raised for the Darien cause. The expeditionary force comprised over 1,000 Scottish volunteers and their families, among them doctors, ministers, lawyers and seamen, all of them skilled, and all of them anti-Catholic, Protestant-Calvinist. Having weathered the Atlantic, they anchored off a Panamanian jungle that the settlers named New Caledonia (marked on today's map as Punta Escoces – Scottish Point).

At first things went well: a site for a fort, St Andrew, was chosen, and a town, New Edinburgh, was built. The colonists wrote of an abundant 'Eden', and in the fertile plains round Darien they raised cattle, hogs and what crops they could. Within less than a year, however, it was a different story. The colony had begun to collapse owing to disease and attacks by the Spanish stationed in Panama. The failure of the first expedition was unknown to the second when it arrived in November 1699 at the swampy isthmus of New Caledonia, now a 'vast, howling wilderness'. Most of the original settlers had either perished or escaped to English colonies in the West Indies, where it was feared they had been sold into slavery.

By April 1700, Scottish imperial dreams had come to dust in the Panamanian hellhole. The governor of Jamaica, Sir William Beeston, reported to London: 'The Scotch are quite removed from New Caledonia, most of them dead and the rest in so lamentable a condition that deserves great compassion.' So ended Scotland's dream that it could compete with the other seafaring powers. In all, 2,000 men, women and children were sacrificed to the Caledonian trading expedition. Scotland was broken by the experience; English propagandists could therefore argue that the Scots were unfit for sovereignty. Five years later, in 1707, the Act of Union obliged Scotland to surrender its independence to England.

Only one ship, the *Caledonia*, made it back to Scotland. Two others, the *Hope of Bo'ness* and the *Duke of Hamilton*, were washed up on the southern coast of Jamaica. Crammed in stinking holds, the 500 Scottish survivors had had only spoiled oatmeal for sustenance. Edward Long, writing seventy years after the catastrophe, claims that they 'may now be traced by the names of several settlements hereabouts'. Curiously, St Elizabeth reminded me of Scotland, where the low-lying hills had a faint amethyst outline at sunset like the Cuillins of Skye.

*

'You've been asking me all the questions,' Dick Kinkead said to me. 'Now let me ask you some. Are you Scottish? You have a Scottish name.'

'My father was born in Glasgow,' I said. 'I don't have an English bone in my body.'

'I've never been to Scotland,' said Kinkead. 'I'd like to one day.' He added quickly, with a look of regret, 'But there won't be time now, not at my age.'

Kinkead was a pharmacist based in Kingston. The family business used to operate from 20 King Street (now the Hanna's Betta Buy clothes store where weeks earlier I had equipped myself with trousers and tie for a murder trial). It has now moved to a dishevelled harbour-side street near the Air Jamaica offices, where it stocks Victorian-sounding tinctures (Swimmer's Ear Drops, Witch Hazel Gel), as well as sick room and nursery requisites. Errol Flynn obtained his prescriptions for morphine there and the Duke of York, the future King George V of Britain, paid for some pills with a cheque simply signed 'George', now on display above the Kinkead cash till.

Kinkead's great-grandfather had run a sugar estate outside Kingston called Stirling Castle. 'They say he was a cruel man,' Kinkead told me. In fact it was his overseer, an Englishman named Sharkey, who was murderously severe. He lost no opportunity to flog his slaves into their graves if he felt like it. Sharkey is mentioned in the book, *Jamaica Plantership*, published in London in 1839, by Benjamin McMahon. The author, a Scot who worked for eighteen years in Jamaica as a doctor, writes with an awareness of the troubling ethical and religious issues involved in the 'Africa Trade'. 'Mr Kinkead was no lover of the whip,' McMahon comments of the pharmacist's Scottish forebear. However, he turned a blind eye to the butchery and draconian punishments meted out round him daily at Stirling Castle.

Very shortly after I met him, Dick Kinkead died. He was eighty-nine. His daughter, the photographer Cookie Kinkead (credited on the first Bob Marley and the Wailers album, *Catch a Fire*), informed me that the funeral service was to be held at the Scots Kirk of St Andrew's, downtown Kingston. During the service, the organist played a Scottish air. Around me, memorial tablets attested to the dedication of missionaries come here from Midlothian and Elgin. Beneath the polished mahogany pews other tablets were inlaid in the floor, commemorating the lives of engineers and 'gentle ladies' who had settled in Jamaica after Culloden. For Dick Kinkead, those memorials were the closest he got.

23

Herbsman Hustle

I was due to leave Kingston at first light for a journey to Black River, on the south coast. It was a relief to get out of the capital; the summer air had turned thundery and thick with car exhaust, and I could feel the pressure closing in. I had cadged a lift from Don Plunkett, who was driving down to visit relatives in the Black River area. In his mid-fifties, stocky and reserved, he spoke a thick *patwa* and carried himself with an air of mystery and importance. Big gold rings flashed on his fingers and mutton-chop sideburns enhanced the Johnny-Too-Bad appearance. He worked part-time as a driver for a Kingston tour operator. As we set off, Plunkett turned on the car radio and, adjusting his wraparound sunglasses, said, 'No problem.' *No problem*; when Jamaicans say that, invariably there is a problem.

We had no sooner left Kingston than an armed policeman stopped us. Roadside checks are frequent in Jamaica as they are an opportunity for the police to get a 'let-off' (bribe) for turning a blind eye to various offences. Having flagged us down, the sergeant asked me what was in my bag. I told him truthfully: a lavatory roll and a paperback copy of *The Ballad of the Sad Café*. He gave me a searching look. 'You an author?' When I said yes, he answered, 'Make sure you tell the truth about Jamaica.' In Plunkett's view, the sergeant 'kudda been more polite'.

Once out of Kingston, Ernest Ranglin's beaming, Nelson Mandela-like face loomed down at us from billboards advertising cures for diabetes; other billboards cautioned against speeding: 'DON'T BE IN A HURRY TO ENTER ETERNITY'. At Mandeville Plunkett stopped to enquire the way from an old man. 'OK, Dads,' he thanked him, adding, 'Walk good.' At dusk we had reached the outskirts of our destination in St Elizabeth parish. A sign – 'WELCOME TO BLACK RIVER' – was pointing into the ground.

Don Plunkett was full of enthusiasm: 'Black River!' he exclaimed. 'Check it.' I had read somewhere that Black River, capital of St Elizabeth, was a town surrounded by waterways and swampland and that crocodiles live in the river that had given the town its name. At first sight, Black River had the look and feel of a frontier outpost, with long-unused buildings and empty hotels serving no discernible purpose. It was easy to imagine that I was in Haiti, rather than Americanised Jamaica. 'Scandal bags' (black plastic grocery bags from supermarkets) of rubbish left dumped on street corners had long since bleached grey and gone dry as driftwood.

The town had begun life in the eighteenth century as a logwood warehouse. European – pre-eminently German – dye-makers had coveted the purple-red dye extract from logwood trees. The logwood timber would be floated upriver on lighters (flat-bottomed barges), then chipped, weighed and taken out to sea for shipment overseas. Black River, being at the head of the only navigable river in Jamaica, had been a good place for business; Mary Seacole ran a general store here in the 1840s before she left for London and the Crimea.

During the 1980s, government funds had poured into Black River for 'tourism development'. Boat trips were organised for tourists to see the crocodiles upriver and 'safari' hotels were built. But tourists, finding Black River too isolated and too touched with Caribbean confusion and decay, preferred the all-inclusive resorts on the north coast. So the town took on the abandoned air it has today.

On the High Street behind St John's Anglican church was a canteen or 'cook-shop' dingy with frayed postcards up on the wall of George Foreman and Muhammad Ali. I was here to talk to a retired schoolteacher, Albert Reynolds, resident in Black River since 1948. The canteen was run by one of his old pupils, Melford Headley. Though they were friends, Reynolds still pulled rank. Everyone in Black River addressed him as 'Teacher', even if they had not been taught by him.

Black River had begun to decline in the 1950s, said Reynolds, when artificial dyestuffs killed off the logwood business. Any logwood trees surviving today are chopped down to make fencing posts, or burned for charcoal. In the post-war years, as a boy, Reynolds had watched boatmen load the logwood planks at riverside wharves. The lighters, chained to each other nose to nose, were pulled out to sea by tugs. As well as logwood, the waiting ships would collect jute bagfuls of sugar. 'It was heavy work and sometimes very dangerous,' Reynolds recollected.

Melford Headley, who had been listening to his teacher, spoke of the day in 1962 when eight port-workers drowned while loading the HMS *Escalante*, a Royal Mail steamer, with sugar. The lighter capsized when the men rushed to the stern to avoid scalding water issuing from the *Escalante*. None of the men could swim. The *Escalante*, in Headley's memory, was 'the greatest tragedy in the history of Black River harbour'.

Back in the late 1940s, German sailors had begun to come ashore. Once off the logwood ships, they would get drunk and incoherent in the wharfside cook-shops and brothels, much to the annoyance of the Jamaican stevedores toiling thirsty in the timber depots. Few in port could understand a word they said. Melford Headley was not much inclined to like the Germans as Germany had been Britain's enemy in the Second World War. 'England! A great country!' Headley exclaimed, and added quickly, 'There are good things about America, too, but Jamaica doesn't adopt them.' Our conversation had touched on the American influence. Was it so bad? Easier access to college and university education in the United States has enabled many Jamaicans to prosper in business, sports, music and politics. Harry Belafonte, Grace Jones, Kool DJ Herc, Colin Powell, Louis Farrakhan – all are Americans of Jamaican heritage. Perhaps Headley exaggerated the ill effects, as perhaps I, in conversation with Jamaicans, had tended to exaggerate them too.

Like many Jamaicans of his generation, Headley did not (or did not want to) realise that Britain is now as much influenced by America as his own country is. When I told him that the London bus queue was mainly a thing of the past, Headley looked at me with incredulous eyes. 'I cyaan' believe it,' he said. By presenting the view that the United States alone had 'put paid' to some sort of

Jamaican golden age he was putting a rosy glow on what had actually been achieved by the British in Jamaica.

As I left the cook-shop, Headley looked at me with sadness in his eyes.

'Is true what you say jus' now about the bus queue?' He shook his head gloomily. 'I cyaan' believe it,' he said, 'I jus' cyaan' believe it.'

*

I splashed cold water on my face, brushed my teeth and left in search of Spiderman, a fisherman whose name had been given to me by Don Plunkett. It was five o'clock in the morning and a bright quarter moon was still in the sky. Spiderman lived in a shanty by Black River's disused logwood wharf. Once a week he punted upriver to check his fish traps laid amid the mangrove swamps.

Outside the shack two skinny dogs were disputing the rubbish. At my approach they trotted off in single file across a patch of wasteland. I rapped on the door and from inside came a noise of stirring, then a drowsy voice, 'Soon come.' Plunkett had forewarned Spiderman of my arrival. In a corner of the yard I could make out, in the half-light of dawn, orange-wire lobster pots prepared with halved coconut for bait. The moon sent little patterns of shadow over the door. The door opened and Spiderman looked at me: his face, mahogany-dark, had a piratical scar down one cheek. He beckoned me in.

The walls were smoke-blackened, with the remains of the previous night's meal in a cauldron on the table in the centre of the room. The odour here was of ganja smoke and curried vegetables. Spiderman had East Indian blood. He sniffed constantly – muscles twitched round his eyes – and it was not long before I realised he was addicted to (or heavily abused) crack cocaine. He spoke to me later about 'raw product' and I knew enough to understand that he meant powdered cocaine. His son, Dwilly, eight, stared at me moist-eyed from a corner of the room, a troubled-looking presence. He had been crying. After a breakfast of boiled perch we left the shack and went to Spiderman's boat moored under the small iron bridge that spanned the old logwood depot. On his shoulder Spiderman was carrying a wooden pole with a hook at one end to pull in the fish traps; Dwilly, running and skipping by his side, was carrying a jerry can full of diesel fuel.

The boat, of fibreglass, was tied up at a point where Black River debouched into the sea. Floating detritus – leaves, plastic bottles – indicated the current's slow pace there. I looked upriver, where daybreak had begun to spread like a slow, pink conflagration. We climbed on board the boat as children leapt and splashed about in the sludge-green shallows. Spiderman topped up the outboard's engine with diesel; we were about to leave, when Spiderman called out 'Delroy!' and another small boy came running up to us from a scattering of huts. Delroy stopped abruptly when he saw me. He was Spiderman's other son; his father commanded him, 'Delroy! Get some Rizlas and my cigarettes.' The boy ran back across the scrub, pursued by chickens.

Once Delroy had returned with the papers and tobacco, Spiderman fired the outboard and we headed off north towards the bauxite town of Maggotty. Further upstream the waters turned a curious deep brown-purple owing to the logwood chips that had fallen from the boats trafficking on the water, Spiderman said. Rio Cobana, the Spanish called it – Mahogany River.

So far we had seen no crocodiles, but they were lurking in the wild cane, said Spiderman, or in the mangroves, whose aerial roots stretched down towards us now like organ pipes. One hand on the tiller, in his other a lit spliff, Spiderman guided us upriver. Ganja, he explained, is cultivated deep within the Black River wetland – one hundred square miles of marsh forest and jungle known as the Morass. The crocodiles there are at their most dangerous during the egg-laying and mating seasons. 'When a crocodile get *really* vex,' said Spiderman, 'it make a bellowing noise – like a dog.' As a child he used to jam sticks into the jaws of baby crocodiles, then watch them sink, fight their way back to the surface, sink again until they died.

Spiderman had placed his traps where the current was slowest, under vegetation along the banks or amid the roots of riverside trees. We stopped to hook in a couple using the pole. Nothing showed inside except a few small crabs dug into the coconut or chicken bait. We lowered the traps and moved on.

Bright flowers rotated like tiny wheels on the river's surface.

Black River was now a soft, unnatural green. 'We're in the heart of the Morass,' announced Spiderman. The landscape, with its vast, aquatic distances, suggested Florida's Everglades or a South American mangrove wetland, with long-legged wading birds standing on the banks motionless as garden statuary. It was impossible to pass through these mangrove cathedrals – archways of great beauty and serenity – without feeling enchanted.

Spiderman pointed out to me a shape like a black log on the river. As we passed, it dropped below the surface in a wreath of bubbles. Sometimes crocodiles jostle ferociously over chicken scraps that Spiderman throws them for sport. At least 200 crocodiles inhabit the Morass but by midday most of them will have crawled off into the mangroves to be out of the sun's glare. One of them was lumbering out of the shallows now, and making for the riverbank on its short, hooked legs.

Along the way Spiderman identified birds, trees and plants with the knowledge born of a lifetime on the river. At times the jungle's aerial canopy seemed to shut off the sunlight, cloaking the water in black velvet; at others, the river widened into a flat expanse of apparently stationary water. Spiderman's skill with the steering-oar and pole was extraordinary as he punted us into a clump of bulrushes to retrieve another trap. (The trap- and boat-handling skills of Black River fishermen, intriguingly, are believed to be identical to those on the River Niger in West Africa today.) This time the trap held a good catch – a tarpon fish – and a big crab. The crab nipped Spiderman with its pincers as he pulled it out along with the fish, and threw them into the boat. 'I'll have them for breakfast,' he said, as the tarpon flapped on the bottom-boards.

After two hours, we turned the boat downriver, heading back for town, the current whispering soft and rock-steady past our hull. The final haul – six fish, three crabs – was respectable, said Spiderman, who had baited each of his eight traps again before submerging them into the mahogany-dark waters of Black River.

*

Due west of Black River is a seashore village called Bluefields. Philip Gosse, the Victorian naturalist, had lived there between 1844 and 1846, while conducting ornithological excursions into the Jamaican countryside. The books that resulted – *The Birds of Jamaica* (1847) and *A Naturalist's Sojourn in Jamaica* (1851) – are marvels of West Indian natural history, lyrical as well as informative. Jamaica, with its acacia scrub, forest and mountain, remains attractive to ornithologists, though narcotics and the trade in narcotics have helped to create an edgy atmosphere for them. One British birdwatcher complained in 2005, 'Even with the most friendly groups, conversations could be marred when our interlocutors were so heavily under the influence of ganja as to be of limited coherence.' Philip Gosse, in his desire to 'twitch' the rarest of Jamaican birds, nevertheless helped to popularise the science of ornithology in Britain's West Indian dominions, and I was keen to see the house where he had operated.

By the time I got there, stars had begun to stud the sky. The shadowy garden was perfumed and thick with trumpet-orchids and waxy, yellow-spattered lilies. The property had high-pitched gables and shuttered windows; on the sea side was a fretwood portico, and at the back a flight of wooden steps leading to the entrance. I climbed the steps. The house was in darkness except for a light that showed in a room upstairs. I called out 'Anybody home?' and the door opened.

A young woman, her hair in curlers, said she was the caretaker. I stated my business and she showed me into the hall.

I was given a room upstairs that overlooked the sea and, to the south-west, the swamplands filmed in *Papillon*. Gosse had been taken in as a lodger by Moravian Brethren, pietistic English evangelists based in Bluefields. Gosse himself belonged to the Plymouth Brethren, who likewise scorned Catholic ornament and believed (not unlike Rastafari) that the last days of Babylon were nigh. By the time Gosse arrived in 1844, slavery had been abolished definitively six years earlier, yet much work remained to be done in 'burying the chains'. Jamaica must have appealed to Gosse as a field of low-church missionary endeavour; the Moravian evangelists who housed him were opposed to Anglican prejudice against the freed slaves, and tolerant of mixed marriages. Once a week, Gosse preached in the Moravian church up in the hills of Content, a freed-slave village situated six miles north of Bluefields, where the church is still in use.

Gosse, having set sail from Gravesend in October 1844, caught his first glimpse of Jamaica from the southern coast of Haiti. He was entranced; Jamaica appeared to him like a 'midsummer night's dream' – magical. Every Bluefields forest was studded with insect and birdlife: a biblical Eden barely touched by man. Equipped with bottles of embalming fluid and tins of arsenic paste (for preserving bird skins), Gosse began to catalogue Jamaican ornithology, plant and insect life. Beetles were immersed in boiling water and stored in rum. Sacks of bulbs and palm-seeds, nets, traps and specimen boxes lay strewn across the floor of the room where I was now standing. In the course of his excursions, Gosse was swooped on by pelicans and stung by bees and hornets. Yet he managed to collect 1,500 native bird specimens. Shipped to Gravesend, the preserved birds either found their way into natural history collections or ended up as feathers in the hats of fashionable Victorian women. The 'Father of Jamaican Ornithology' has now given his name to the Gosse ornithology club of Jamaica (occasionally misspelled the 'Goose' Bird Club).

Years later, when writing of Jamaica in his east London home, Gosse found he was unable to recall the beauty and moonlit nights of Bluefields. Jamaica was an impossibly distant land to him now: he could have spent a lifetime there, he wrote, and 'still not found the answers to a hundred questions'.

Gosse was later criticised by his son Edmund for having been blindly convinced of the rightness of his Christian faith. His peculiar Creationist beliefs (animals and human beings were in a state of full maturity when God created them) invited the ridicule even of churchmen of that time. Edmund Gosse, having begun his own life 'puffed out' with a sense of evangelical holiness, later rebelled, and in *Father and Son*, that classic Edwardian memoir, he recorded the struggle between his own scepticism and his father's rigidly certain temperament. Edmund may have written of his father in derogatory terms, yet that does nothing to detract from his father's achievement, which in Jamaica remains unsurpassed.

*

'What's that?' I asked, as a bird flew up amid a clump of hibiscus.

'That's a rosy spoonbill,' said Ann Sutton. The bird vanished into the cedar tree forest stretching towards Shooters Hill. We were sitting in the garden of a mossed and crumbling mahogany-pillared Jamaican mansion called Marshall's Pen on the outskirts of Mandeville. In the 1790s, Marshall's Pen had belonged to the Earl of Balcarres, commander-in-chief of Jamaica, who imported Cuban blood hounds to track down the island's runaway slaves. Like many imperial servants in the British West Indies, he was a coarse man. Lady Nugent, visiting Balcarres in 1801, remarked on his dishevelled appearance: 'the black edges of his nails really make me sick'.

Ann Sutton was an English-born environmentalist who, with her late husband, Robert Sutton, had continued Philip Gosse's exploration of Jamaica's endemic bird species, cataloguing John Crow vultures, black-throated grebes and 'John-to-whits'. In 1997, they acted as consultants to David Attenborough's 'Life of Birds' BBC documentary shot partly in Jamaica. Five years later, in 2002, Robert Sutton was murdered at Marshall's Pen by intruders. Homicide detectives from Kingston have long since given up on the case owing to lack of evidence.

Ann Sutton put down her teacup and took a cucumber sandwich. 'Philip Gosse was a marvel,' she said. 'Have you seen the bird skins? The ones he prepared at Bluefields? They're in the British Museum – as fresh as if the birds had been shot the day before.' In her jeans and a yellow T-shirt she looked younger than her fifty-five years. 'I came to Jamaica at the age of twenty,' she said with a dreamy expression, 'hoping to see the world but I got married and never left.' Her husband's family had lived in Jamaica for over two centuries; and, like many settlers of Regency (and earlier) times, they had maintained their plantations against the odds through the boom and bust of cocoa, sugar and citrus. Robert Sutton's great-great grandfather had founded the London Stock Exchange in 1801.

'Robert could trace his ancestors back to the first white man born in Jamaica of English parentage,' Ann claimed. 'He was a true Creole.' The word 'Creole' usually denotes white or near-white descendants of European settlers in the Caribbean or America. ('I am a Creole,' wrote Mary Seacole on the first page of her memoir, 'and have good Scotch blood coursing in my veins.') Ann Sutton herself was very pale – the Jamaican sun had had no effect on her –

and in her paleness one might have detected the marks of strain. 'Requiem for a Bird Lover', the *Gleaner* obituary of her husband, had stated sensationally: 'Murder is now so common and so frequent in Jamaica that, for many of us, it fails to shock.'

Until now, Ann Sutton's face had remained calm, but now her blue eyes flickered with excitement. 'Oh look!' She pointed to a cluster of black-and-emerald birds that swirled away across the lawn. Doctor hummingbirds. 'The doctor's the gem of Jamaican ornithology,' she said. 'Robert loved them.' *Trochilus polytmus*, 'the doctor hummingbird', is so called because its two black streamer tails suggest the black tail-coat of the Victorian physician. The bird, black-green in colour and 'no larger than a schoolboy's thumb', according to Gosse, is found only in Jamaica.

Inside Marshall's Pen, floral chintz armchairs, brass candlesticks and pieces of chinoiserie created a curiously English atmosphere. A paperback Jane Austen – *Mansfield Park* – lay open on a table. Up a creaking staircase we came to the drawing room, where glass-fronted cabinets contained rare bird feathers along with decaying leather-bound memoirs of Victorian missionaries and traders in the West Indies. The humidity had mouldered the books and mildewed the leather of the chairs. Otherwise Marshall's Pen looked every inch the halcyon English country house of the high imperial era, transplanted to the West Indies. The only shadow cast across its genteel, book-lined rooms was the killing, on the night of 22 July 2002, of the owner.

*

It had rained hard during the night but next morning Bluefields harbour was bright with sunshine. Fishing boats were sliding down ramps into the warm Caribbean waters. The fins, head and intestines of a white shark, weighing 400 pounds, were being tossed into the shallows as the fishermen cleaned their catch. The boats, long and lying low in the water, were generally painted with all-seeing eyes and representations of the Virgin – a protection against death by drowning. The work is ordinarily hazardous, even more so now that fish stocks have depleted and the fishermen have to venture as far out as Colombian, Nicaraguan or Panamanian waters.

The fishing season – October to November – coincides with the hurricane season, and is therefore dangerous. Most Bluefield fisherman are poor swimmers – or not-at-all-swimmers – so if they ditch in high seas they are likely to drown. During the summer months, with most of the fish harvests in, the fishermen have nothing much to do except drink and sleep around. Havelyn Honeygan, secretary of a Bluefields fishermen's co-operative, explained that fishing villages were the most densely populated in Jamaica. 'Out of season it's either the bar or the bed,' he explained. He claimed that drugs had never come his way ('not one ounce or bag of cocaine') and that the 200 fishermen under his responsibility had been thoroughly vetted. 'Their characteristics have to be straightforward, otherwise they can't join the co-op,' he said.

Yet with 638 miles of coastline and over 100 unmonitored airstrips, Jamaica is wide open to smuggling. The narcotics come in through soporific, under-guarded places like Bluefields which, in 2001, became the site of one of the largest drug hauls in Jamaican history. Cocaine valued at US $37 million was seized by police at Bluefields harbour, along with a speedboat, two satellite telephones and bundles of e-mail printouts in Spanish. Later, two men in neatly pressed white trousers and monogrammed shirts checked in to the Culloden Cove guest house in Bluefields and, having settled the bill, went out with their silenced automatics and shot dead the six Jamaicans who had bungled the operation and been bailed pending trial. The murderers (Colombians operating within the Medellin cocaine cartel) were never caught.

The bulk of narcotics go through Kingston: it is the main transit point in the West Indies and vital to the shipment of cocaine from Latin America to the markets both in North America and – the most highly prized market – Britain. (Cocaine fetches three times as much in Britain as in other European countries.) Kingston opened as a container terminal in 1975; since then container traffic has increased twenty-fold and is now so great that only a percentage of shipments can be inspected. Over 450 acres of harbour lie sprawled out along the west Kingston shoreline, an invitation to smugglers from Liverpool, Miami, Hamburg, Rotterdam and Dover.

Some weeks earlier I had spent an afternoon in Kingston's

container terminal at Port Bustamante, watching vessels unload. An average of 1.5 million containers are handled by Port Bustamante each year. Up to six vessels can be emptied at the South Terminal at any one time; the din caused by the unloading was deafening. Yard tractors, ship-to-shore gantry cranes, forklifts: lifting, shunting, swinging. The harbour waters gave off a powerful smell; ships empty their latrines and clean their holds into the rubbish tip of the sea.

I continued past the north terminal, where seashore cranes loomed tall like prehistoric birds. Stockpiles of unloaded containers – P&O, Hamburg Süd – were stacked like giant Lego blocks along the wharves, among them 'reefers' (refrigerated containers) crammed with frozen fish fingers and TV dinners. A container ship from Beijing was unloading 'reefers' of meat and the sea's surface round the ship gleamed and glinted in the afternoon light. To the east of where I stood, the national Petrojam oil refineries belched a red-black fire.

Omar Williams, chief of the port's anti-narcotic security force, carries a pair of binoculars and a licensed firearm. He is on the look-out for 'high-risk containers' from Colombia, Venezuela and Nicaragua. As Colombia is Jamaica's nearest neighbour south, Kingston is a key passageway and warehouse for drug smuggling. X-ray equipment installed by US security experts in 2006 works only intermittently because 'certain employees' (Omar Williams would not say who) 'keep pulling the plug'. In return for bribes, that is, personnel turn off the cargo scanning equipment; Jamaica's 'guns-for-drugs' trade with Haiti is thought to be facilitated in this way.

The contraband comes by air, too. 'Mules' board planes at Kingston and Montego Bay, having ingested up to 100 condoms or (more dependably sturdy) latex surgical glove fingers filled with cocaine. Most 'mules' are single mothers in need of money to feed their families. On average they are paid between £2,000 and £5,000 for each trip – more money than some Jamaicans will see in a year. A rupture in just one of the latex packages can kill. Not that the drug dons care: the women are expendable. More than 300 Jamaican women are currently serving sentences in British prisons for carrying drugs.

I said to Omar Williams, 'Should Jamaica tighten its border controls?'

'You could say that. But it's not just Jamaica. The United States are part of the problem.' America's liberal gun laws have eased the transfer of firearms into Jamaica. 'American guns are dropping into Kingston like mangoes off a tree,' said Williams. 'To be truthful,' he went on, 'I don't see how the situation can improve.' The sun was now low in the horizon, and the rasping of cicadas in the grounds of the container terminal announced the beginning of Jamaica's short-lived dusk.

24

Investors in People ('Cargo')

The guest house where I was staying in Black River had a white picket fence and a breadfruit tree that rustled in the breeze. At night I could hear the sea folding across the rocks where a tanker carrying drugs had run aground in 2002; its hull lay rusted in shallow waters just beyond the fence.

At a little distance from the wreck was another hotel, grandly named the Invercauld Great House. With its baronial turrets and towers, the building reflected the confidence of Black River during the 1880s, when the town was lit by electricity, traversed by trams and bore names like Victoria Avenue and Jubilee Lane. Queen Victoria's new-look Empire, in all its imperial vigour and righteousness, had presented emancipation as the irrefutable proof of its virtuous motives. The crusade for the slave trade's abolition had taken place in an atmosphere suffused with self-congratulation.

Given Britain's role in shipping Africans to the New World, rhetoric celebrating 'British liberty' rang a bit hollow. In the eighteenth century, Britain had been the world's leading slave trader; slavery had, moreover, survived in the British Empire until the 1830s. Forgotten amid all the self-satisfaction was the mistreatment – sexual, mercantile – of the slaves. Over the course of 400 years, beginning in the late fifteenth century, eleven million Africans are estimated to have arrived in the New World. About three million more perished in the process of capture and enslavement in Africa, or on board ships.

The *Zong* – a Liverpool slave ship – was perhaps the most spectacular example of atrocity in the history of the British slave trade. In 1782 it sailed with a 'cargo' of 470 tight-packed Africans from the Gold Coast to Black River. Owing to headwinds alternating with spells of calm, however, the voyage took twice the expected time. After three months at sea more than sixty of the slaves were dead and many of the others looked set to die soon.

Dead slaves could bring a trader no profit. Before the *Zong* put into Black River harbour, the captain ordered his crew to throw the dead and sickest slaves into the sea and told them to say, if they were later asked, that because of the unfavourable winds, the ship's water supply had run out and caused shipboard death with a risk of disease. In British maritime law a captain was allowed to jettison some of his 'cargo' – slaves were included in the category – in order to save the remainder. Insurance would cover the loss because the slaves had died from 'perils' beyond the captain's control.

So the dead slaves were jettisoned along with fifty-four of the sickest survivors. Two days later, a further forty-two slaves were thrown overboard still alive. When a third group was selected, the slaves had begun to fight back; twenty-six of them were pushed over the side with their arms still shackled. The entire remainder, according to one eye-witness, 'sprang disdainfully from the grasp of their tyrants, and leapt to their death'.

Mass murder. Yet the Black River atrocity caused no immediate outcry in Britain and virtually no press coverage. No inquest followed and certainly no memorial service was held at the Black River Anglican church. The subsequent trial in London of the captain and crew, however, did attract publicity. The court found in favour of the accused, and the insurers lost: killing slaves ('cargo') was no different from killing horses, it was ruled. Nevertheless the *Zong* was to nag long at the British conscience. Abolitionists frequently referred to Black River, and prominent clergymen discussed the enormity in sermons, essays and letters. After the *Zong* (its horror later memorably evoked in Turner's painting *Slave Ship*), calls for an end to the slave trade were increasingly heard.

If the institution of slavery was doomed to die in Jamaica, it was thanks in part to the British abolitionist and missionary William Knibb. On his arrival in Jamaica in 1825 Knibb vowed to destroy the plantation system, and return dignity to the 'poor, oppressed, benighted, and despised sons of Africa'. Eighteen years had passed since the Imperial Parliament in London abolished the slave trade in

1807 but its official demise had not heralded the end of slavery. Slaves were systematically bred on Jamaican plantations like livestock, and worked almost to death. Slavery, in Knibb's view, was incompatible with Christianity because God had made all men equal; to be a Christian, therefore, was to be an abolitionist.

For twenty years this patriarchal figure – 'King Knibb' to his supporters – attempted to Christianise 'the swarthy sons of Africa'. His weekly newspaper, *The Baptist Herald and Friend of Africa*, promoted what became known in Marcus Garvey's day as 'Ethiopianism' – the generic term for an ideal of black self-improvement and salvation. Knibb's identification of black Jamaicans with the biblical Ethiopia foreshadowed the Afrophile wing of Michael Manley's PNP, as well as Rastafari and other religions devoted to an ideal of African autonomy. Many freed slaves joined Knibb's Baptist church for its Revivalist sympathies and its image as a black church – a church of Ethiopia. (Psalm 68: 'Ethiopia shall soon stretch out her hands unto God.')

Knibb's nonconformist sentiments, forged in the working-class Northamptonshire of his birth, were anathema to the establishment Church of Jamaica, with its planter prejudice. Knibb's most outspoken enemy, the Reverend George Wilson Bridges, was a leading Anglican advocate of slavery, whose two-volume *Annals of Jamaica* (1828) was perhaps the only work of Jamaican origin to argue the planter's case in any depth. The book reads like a primer on the British Empire's 'civilising mission' abroad: Africans need the 'civilising hand' of the white man, argued Bridges, because the 'spirit of the negro is to destroy the works of the past, and the hopes of the future'.

To the Reverend Bridges, Knibb was not only a vile dissenter, but a mortal threat to His Majesty's white subjects in Jamaica. Bridges blamed Knibb for the slave uprising of 1831–2 led by the Baptist preacher and former slave Samuel Sharpe. Sharpe was convinced (seven years before the date) that King George III had declared full freedom for his slaves and that the time had come to 'cast off the chains'. He was not mad or deluded. As news of abolitionist debate and agitation reached Jamaica from London, it was suspected that a recalcitrant local assembly or parliament was withholding their freedom.

Sharpe planned and led the rebellion. In the Montego Bay area where he preached he urged slaves not to work after Christmas, but to start a campaign of civil disobedience. 'If the black men did not stand up for themselves and take their freedom,' Sharpe was said to have proclaimed, 'the whites would put them out at the muzzles of their guns and shoot them like pigeons.' Though loss of life in the campaign was low, huge damage, valued at £1.25 million, was done to plantations across Jamaica. The disturbances were finally suppressed by British troops and Sharpe taken into custody awaiting execution. The imperial gallows claimed a further 340 'rebels'. Forty years before the Morant War of 1865, this was one of the most spectacular slave revolts in the history of Anglo-America. In the witch-hunt for agitators, the Reverend Bridges called for Baptist missionaries to be hanged; many were beaten and tarred. In the sugar port of Falmouth on Jamaica's north coast, where Knibb lived and operated, Baptist chapels were burned down by a white mob. Knibb was lucky to escape with his life.

The burning of Baptist churches profoundly shocked the British public and made their demands for emancipation the more clamorous. William Knibb, catching the mood, left Falmouth in 1832 in order to travel round Britain on a lecture tour. In packed church halls he told how planters loyal to the Anglican Church had jabbed him in the chest with bayonets; to further gasps he exhibited the tar-smeared neckerchief of a Baptist colleague who had been almost lynched in front of his children.

The Baptist uprising under Sharpe, and the retributions that followed, at long last convinced Britain that the price for maintaining slavery was too high. Freedom for Jamaica's slaves was the only alternative – Knibb argued – to island-wide race war on a Haitian scale. In the summer of 1833, fearing further unrest, British Parliament passed the Emancipation Bill. The bill fell short of what Knibb and his supporters had hoped for. To soften the blow for planters, Parliament had decreed that emancipation was to unfold in two stages. First, slaves had to become 'apprentices' obligated to work full time (and without pay) for their former masters, in most cases for up to five years. Only then – the second stage – could they be liberated entirely. The real victory came four years later, on 1 August 1838, when

Parliament officially declared that nearly 800,000 black men, women and children throughout the British Empire were at last truly free.

In his headquarters at Falmouth, William Knibb presided over a midnight thanksgiving service in the church that became known as the Knibb Baptist Chapel. The church still stands on King Street, a run-down section of Falmouth pervaded by wood smoke and a salt-fish odour. Behind the communion table a marble tablet (made in Birmingham) marks the high watermark of post-emancipation fervour in British Jamaica:

ERECTED
BY EMANCIPATED SONS OF AFRICA
TO COMMEMORATE
THE BIRTH-DAY OF THEIR FREEDOM
AUGUST THE FIRST 1838

On 31 July 1838 – the eve of emancipation – the Falmouth church was hung with branches and flowers and portraits of William Wilberforce. Into an empty coffin Knibb's followers placed a symbolic iron punishment collar, a whip and chains, and as twelve o'clock approached they sang, 'The death-blow is struck – see the monster is dying,' bursting into cheers at the stroke of midnight. Still cheering, they lowered the coffin into an open grave in the churchyard. The Union Jack was then raised above the grave.

Post-emancipation Falmouth became a place of Baptist zeal, where black 'freedmen' were exhorted to rise early, keep clean, work hard, build new homes for themselves and marry ('buy a ring and put on a feast', in the island expression). Only then could they bring up God-fearing Christian families. In this missionary vision of black self-determination, independent Jamaica was to be governed by black freeholders – a 'good society', said Knibb.

It was, of course, a white man's utopia. Falmouth after 1838 might have been made in the abolitionist image, but, in spite of Knibb's proto-'Ethiopianism', it took little account of Jamaica's existing black culture or the African Jamaican experience shaped by the Middle Passage. Knibb's project, in some ways, was to 'colonise the interior' according to deep-rooted British Christian assumptions.

*

At Bluefields village, not far from Philip Gosse's home, lives a British artist called Barney Walsh, who unintentionally gave me some insight into the predatory nature of white sexuality in Jamaica. Walsh was a stocky man with reddish skin, his demeanour seeming to hark back to a time when English raffs – often men of 'good family' – were packed off to Jamaica with few questions asked. He looked like an eighteenth-century buck, with his hair held in a ponytail. His pale blue eyes, if set in a livelier face, might have been described as 'penetrating', but in his they looked vacant, even burned out.

Walsh (who claimed to be a second cousin to Queen Elizabeth II) boasted among his associates the late Princess Margaret, the late Steve McQueen, the late Patrick Lichfield, the late Ian Fleming and the late Noel Coward, as well as Chris Blackwell. He dropped names as only insecure people can. He loved Jamaica yet he was careful not to become *too* Jamaican. His exaggeratedly English accent, like his name-dropping of royalty, made him a bit of a bore.

Once Walsh had been considered a good artist, but I found that hard to believe. Samples of his work were stacked on the veranda of his house. Sketches of half-naked women in fantasy chariots drawn by white horses; a lake covered in swans, dragons, castles, dreamy Italian villas, paintings of clowns and vaguely psychedelic seascapes like a Yes album cover. 'And I did this painting' – he pulled out a particularly lurid canvas – 'while I was on an acid trip with Steve McQueen, *Papillon*, you know.' It was really quite bad.

Walsh had lived in Bluefields since 1989. His house, Lush Life, stood on an eminence above the Caribbean Sea and seemed to creak and sway in the salt breeze. Dogs prowled round it, one of which bounded up to me, fangs bared. 'I'm actually known as quite a hard man locally,' said Walsh, 'or at any rate an eccentric. People leave me alone.' He added with some pride, 'Four locals have had their throats slit on my account.' The 'lawlessness and brutality' of twenty-first-century Jamaica, he said, excited him.

Walsh had been burgled three times and even been shot at. 'You have to be a bit of a danger-junkie to like Jamaica,' he went on. 'There's always fuckery of one kind or another going on here.' (His chauffeur, Jon, was a known crack-dealer.) Walsh said he was fascinated by the personality of Thomas Thistlewood, an English rake who ran a sugar estate near Bluefields in the years 1750–86, and who (by his own precise account) had had sexual intercourse on 3,852 occasions throughout his forty-year-long Caribbean rampage. Thistlewood's strenuous licentiousness, chronicled in schoolboy Latin in a diary he kept ('About 2 a.m., *cum* Negro girls'), suggested that sex was intertwined with the very imperial project.

It was not just slave-drivers but slave-trade sailors who were the sexual predators. The Reverend John Newton, in his abolitionist pamphlet *Thoughts upon the African Slave Trade*, published in London in 1788, painted a chilling picture:

> When the women and girls are taken on board a ship, naked, trembling, terrified, perhaps almost exhausted with cold, fatigue, and hunger, they are often exposed to the wanton rudeness of white savages. The poor creatures cannot understand the language they hear, but the looks and manners of the speakers are sufficiently intelligible. In imagination, the prey is divided, upon the spot, and only reserved until opportunity offers.

The British Empire had given Thistlewood and other planters the license to abuse captive women. Barney Walsh, the battered sensualist of Bluefields, said to me with imperial British coarseness, 'I've not fucked a white woman in years.' A Bluefields go-go dancer called Cherie had briefly been his wife; it was, apparently, love at first sight. 'And it was *real* love, not go-go love.' Hoping to impress his London friends, Walsh took Cherie to dinner at the Dorchester: a trophy poppet from the torrid zones.

After a second bottle of white wine Walsh spoke more candidly of the condition of young women in Jamaica today. 'Girls lose their virginity here at about the age of eleven. You should see them – tits out here! S'big!' I found myself despising him. In 2007, concerned by the rise of sex tourism in Jamaican resort areas, the government passed the Trafficking in Persons Act. Jamaica remains a significant source, transit and destination for women and girl-chile (young girls) trafficked for the purposes of sexual exploitation. It has been so ever since the days of slavery. 'They recruit them early here', Walsh said to me.

By six o'clock the sea beyond Lush Life had faded to a dyewood blue. Pelicans – great white slack-jawed birds – swooped out to feed as the artist urged me to watch for a green flash at sunset. A green flash? 'Yes. Princess Margaret used to say you could see a green ray where the sun vanished below the horizon.'

'Oh.'

'Yes. Now careful not to blink.'

The sun submerged.

'Well?'

'I don't know,' I said. 'It was a blur.' The sea view, I was made to feel, was rather wasted on me without the green flash.

25

Lord Creator

Tourism, even more than the narcotics trade, has transformed the face of Jamaica. Once Jamaica was a place of servile deference, where a wealthy few could languish in smart hotels. Noel Coward, in his doggerel poem 'Jamaica' evoked a paradise of the sort enjoyed by Ian Fleming, in the days of dinner jackets and 'native Calypsos':

> Every tourist who visits these shores
> Can thank his benevolent Maker
> For taking time off from the rest of His chores
> To fashion the Isle of Jamaica.

However, since the advent of the long-haul charter flight, Apex-fare tariffs and packaged hedonism, swathes of Jamaica have been marred by breeze-block resorts, shopping arcades and concrete sport-cabin villas. Older Jamaicans complain that tourism has corrupted the island's youth and brought drugs and crime to once-stable communities. The industry is undoubtedly a mixed blessing; it contributes US $1 billion a year to the island's economy and has become a part of Jamaican life, with hordes of vendors, hustlers and 'guides' ready to hound the unwitting tourist.

Montego Bay – MoBay to Jamaicans – is the island's main tourist destination and has nightclubs with names like Jiggy Time, X-Tra Naked and X-Tatic Moods. Tourists flock there for a promise of tropical oblivion, and rarely leave their stockaded resorts, spending their days instead on the golf course and their nights in the bars. In the travel brochures MoBay is depicted as a haven, where unbridled sex and drinking abound. Tourists can do things there that they would never dream of doing at home. They can get married in the nude on the beach (sadly, not an uncommon sight), or dress up as Henry Morgan and drink rum on a motorised pirate galleon.

*

In the hills above Montego Bay, in a village called Cotton Tree, Seventh Day Adventists were holding a 'crusade'. A large white tent had been hung for the occasion with light bulbs, and rows of chairs were occupied by locals come to hear the Jamaican preacher man. At the entrance an Adventist woman was calling out 'There's still room in the inn!' as she propelled latecomers into their seats. The word 'crusade' in Jamaica intends a church meeting held in one of these mobile tent-halls. The tent may stay erected for up to six weeks in one location before moving on. Every 'clap-hands' church in Jamaica – Revivalist, Pentecostal – has its army of salvationist preachers. Some are honest types who want only to spread the love of Christ; others are sharks on the lookout for the main chance. Nearly all of them are politically conservative.

At the far end of the tent was a raised rostrum for the preacher, who was now dancing across the stage and cajoling the audience. 'Come on, church! Oh *talk* to me church! Young man!' He turned his gaze on me. 'Does the candle of the Lord shine upon your soul?'

'Um . . .'

He returned the microphone to its stand. The organ burst out a few fierce notes and the preacher began to hector us again:

'Oh, you're mighty cold on me tonight, church! Sit up, my friends! *Stay* with the preacher!'

Next to me was June Gay Pringle, a thin Jamaican woman of ascetic appearance. She was the sister of Sally Henzell, the late film director Perry Henzell's widow; extremely committed, she had been a Seventh Day Adventist for over half a century. Even the vilest and most crime-infested alleys of MoBay were no deterrent to June Gay as she brought a happy joy in Christ to waifs and strays. She went to these places on foot and was probably the last middle-class woman in Jamaica to do so. But, like most Adventists, she believed that those who were not Adventist were misguided; no matter how holy and self-sacrificing their Christian lives, God would punish them, in their millions, for being *misguided*. I liked June Gay; she radiated a quiet gospel energy and, with her horn-rimmed glasses

Sellotaped at the bridge, evidently cared little for money. We were the only two white people in the audience.

The preacher sat down, apparently exhausted, while a female choir, eight-strong, stood up to sing a hymn. They began softly but gradually increased their volume, their faces transformed, eyes uplifted, by the wah-wah electric guitar and Yamaha organ music. Another figure on the rostrum now rose and led a prayer. Around me everyone was singing *Lead me to a rock that is higher than I.* June Gay, catching the mood, called out from her seat, 'Yes Lord, yessir. Very right. Uh huh. Right.'

Microphone in hand, the preacher sprang up to deliver a message of salvation. 'Oh my friends!' He spread out his arms in a gesture of crucifixion. 'Jesus will come to investigate. He will judge you! Yes, he will make executions!' Christ's imminent advent did not look too jolly to me: American evangelism had come to Cotton Tree.

The preacher wiped his brow with a folded white handkerchief, and began again, his voice amplified round the hills of Cotton Tree. 'Men marrying men!' he yelled. A group of women seated behind me tittered. 'I don't see men marrying men in the Bible. Oh, don't tell me about your natural tendencies! Tell me about your word of *God*.' He looked furious. 'What these . . . men need is Christ. Jesus Christ alone can change *any* natural inclination.'

'But hold on!' He stopped himself in mid-flow. 'I don't believe we should abuse these individuals. Are you *following* the preacher? What these . . . men need is the love of the Lord Jesus.'

'Lord Jesus!' a woman answered.

'Do *you* love the Lord Jesus?' the preacher asked her.

'Yes, preacher man, sir, me does *luv* the Lawd Jesus.'

'Good. Because what these . . . men have *not* found is Jesus. So don't light them a fire. Don't burn them. Don't stone them. Jesus *died* for them.'

'Preach it, pastor!'

He preached it. 'In the beginning,' he judged, 'was Adam and Eve. Not Adam and Steve!'

The choir rose and those on the rostrum rose with the choir, as the gospel music lifted and a wind whipped round the tent. The preacher, after a final burst of outraged godliness, said, 'Good night, church, and thank you for coming to tent.'

June Gay, adjusting her straw cloche, patted her Adventist hymnal and led me to a pick-up where a group of children was waiting in the hope of a lift. 'And what did you take away from tent today?' she asked them; the children looked doubtful.

'Well?' she persisted.

'Miss, I tek way one free book,' one of them piped up.

'I see,' she continued in her best Jean Brodie tone. 'And what "free book" was that?' The child held up a copy of *The Great Controversy* by Ellen G.White, the founder in 1860 of the Seventh Day Adventist denomination.

'Read it carefully,' June Gay advised. The child and his friends clambered on board as we set off downhill to Montego Bay. On the way, June Gay expressed disapproval of the preacher's more 'ranty' aspects. Quieter discussions of homosexuality were more to her liking. 'Glad to hear it,' I said. We dropped the children off at Spring Mount, an old freed-slave village, and continued on downhill until we drew up outside a 1950s home. The home was a monument to the era when houses were designed to look like ranches, with high timbered ceilings and big glass windows. June Gay and her husband Frank Pringle lived here, at a remove from the brash city centre of Montego Bay.

Frank was at home reading a newspaper. 'Oh God,' he looked at me. 'What's June Gay been *doing* to you?' Frank was not an Adventist (neither was he teetotal or a vegetarian). 'Darling, are you *sure* Ian wanted to go on a crusade?' he went on, I think teasingly. 'We can't assume he'd have wanted to go at all.'

'Actually we enjoyed every minute of it,' June Gay answered.

His wife having left the room, Frank said to me, 'Will you have a rum and pineapple juice? Or would you rather a whisky?' Splendidly English in appearance, he had on a pair of knee-length shorts, and exuded the relaxed air of a man who had given himself a holiday.

He came back with the drinks, lit a cigar and puffed out smoke. His grandfather had come to Jamaica from Scotland but along the way the Pringles had acquired Sephardi Jewish blood, and were now a typically hybrid West Indian family. Frank had served as minister of tourism under Michael Manley and was known to fellow PNP members as the 'White Neega' – apparently a compliment. Before that, he had been aide-de-camp to the Governor General of Jamaica Sir Hugh Foot.

Frank liked to tell stories. The time he checked Fidel Castro into a hotel in MoBay, for example. Or when he escorted Winston Churchill round Kingston in 1953. Churchill had landed in Jamaica on 9 January preparatory to a two-week holiday. In Kingston the roads were thronged with crowds – schoolchildren, housewives, shopkeepers – hoping to catch a glimpse of the British prime minister's motorcade. Churchill was seated high up in an open touring car, Captain Pringle beneath him. The roadside was hung with bunting and a huge banner proclaimed: 'MR WINSTON CHURCHILL – THE CITY GREETS YOU'. Churchill responded to the crowds with the familiar 'V' for Victory sign. It was, recalled Frank, a great warm-hearted, unforgettable welcome. 'Churchill was *weeping* at the sight of the Jamaicans come out to greet him.'

Frank added, 'It was still possible in 1953 to take the view, as Churchill certainly did, that the British Empire would go on for ever.' Haunted by the spectre of Britain's post-war exhaustion, Churchill and his right-wing allies did not want independence for Jamaica. 'They wanted to keep us in thrall,' Frank Pringle said. 'But,' he added in something between a sigh and yawn, 'we Jamaicans *had* to detach from the parent country. Otherwise how could we grow up?'

*

Next day I went to see the Governor General of Jamaica, Sir Howard Cooke, who was about to retire. Soldiers in khaki drill saluted me as my taxi pulled up at the entrance to King's House. In the hall I was invited to sign the governor's book, then the aide-de-camp, Captain Williams, came for me. In a red dress-tunic he extended a white-gloved hand, then turned on his heel to greet two unlikely new visitors, Rastas in green-and-yellow T-shirts and matching green-and-yellow puss boots. I recognised them as Michael 'Ibo' Cooper and Stephen 'Cat' Coore of the inter-nationally famous reggae band Third World. The Governor General was about to present them with a National Award for services to music, but now they were gently ribbing Captain Williams:

'What? You mean you have no *say* in what colour tunic you can wear?' Coore asked him.

'No, it has to be red,' Williams replied stiffly. 'Sandhurst red.'

'It could be green, maybe,' Cooper suggested.

'No, man,' Coore said to Cooper, 'it should be green and black and *gold*, man.'

'Or it could be just *all* gold,' Cooper added, taking care not to laugh.

Ignoring them, Captain Williams accompanied me upstairs to the Governor General's office. The stairway, carpeted in royal blue, was lined with portraits of George III and Queen Charlotte (his Queen Consort), as well as a full-length portrait of Queen Elizabeth II, commissioned in 1952 to mark her coronation the following year. In so many ways, the fabric of Jamaican life remained semi-imperial: Britain might have lost its Empire, but imperial procedures were ingrained in Jamaica's political and cultural life.

At the top of the stairway Captain Williams knocked on a door, heard a response, opened it to let me in, and saluted the occupant. The door closed behind me; it took a few seconds for me to focus in the semi-darkened room as the shade had been drawn down over the single window above the Governor General's desk. Sir Howard emerged into the light, a big man, with a wide girth, and with a big bald head.

'Please, sit down,' he said, indicating a chair by his desk. On the broad mahogany surface there was nothing but a copy of *The Times* and a bowl of wilting roses. Britain's legacy, I felt, could not be creatively adapted in this museum atmosphere. Surprisingly, however, Sir Howard was no unthinking servant of the Commonwealth. Over ninety, he had a background in Christian socialism and Garveyite black nationalism, and had been a founder-member in 1938 of Norman Washington Manley's PNP. Manley's dream of social equality and welfare for the Jamaican people was one he still shared. 'Norman,' Sir Howard said to me, 'was my hero.' In 1939, he had gone to teach in the Jamaican countryside, where he organised community projects, wayside cinema shows and religious classes. He wanted to show Jamaicans how to improve and take care of themselves.

His parents, black farmers, were not rich. Yet every year the colonial administration offered exhibitions to study in England, and in 1950, Cooke acquired one to go to London. At London University he met other West Indians engaged in independence struggles. Cooke was now convinced that Jamaica could no longer be ruled autocratically by Englishmen with their English public-school codes and public-school curricula. At the same time Jamaica was to remain, if Cooke had his way, thoroughly 'British'; by which he meant, in essence, non-American. And by American he meant the 'oppressive' (his word) US style and habits – the label-obsessed consumer culture – that have begun to crush local forms of black vernacular in Jamaica.

'I'm an old-world person,' Sir Howard said. 'I am what I am today because of my relationship with Britain, and the British way of life.' His right hand moved slowly as he said this, tracing meaningless patterns in the air.

I liked Cooke and his politics, but surely he was a symbol – an empty symbol – of continued British influence in Jamaica and further proof that Jamaica was not yet truly independent of its parent country. Politically, Sir Howard was required to be a 'yes man' who would perpetuate a belief that progress is English, education is English, the good things in life (in the world the coloniser had made) were English. His conviction that 'progress' might be obtained by turning one's back on America (pre-Barack Obama America) was itself a very English presumption.

'But your Excellency,' I said (aware of how ludicrous that address sounded), 'wouldn't Jamaica be better off as a republic?'

'No!' The Governor General looked at me with a startled expression. 'Even if Jamaica *were* a republic, we'd still be attached to the Commonwealth; besides,' the Governor General added with a gentle hopeful smile, 'we Jamaicans are not natural republicans.'

'But aren't Jamaicans becoming more American and less bound to Britain and the idea of the Commonwealth?'

'Well, until Thatcher came along' – Cooke pointedly did not say 'Mrs' Thatcher – 'until Thatcher came along we Jamaicans had enjoyed so much of Britain and the British way of life.' During Thatcher's tenure, however, Jamaicans began to look again to

America for opportunities and a new start. In the 1930s and 1940s, tens of thousands had left Jamaica to work in the United States: it was only later, in the 1950s, when America tightened its immigration laws, that Britain became an alternative destination. According to a 1990 census, the number of Jamaicans living in America reached 435,025 during the 1980s. With the quota of illegal immigrants, however, that number is thought to be nearer a million.

'Our closeness to America is not good for us.' Sir Howard frowned. 'After Thatcher – the Special Relation and all that – we became more and more materialist. We wanted only to boast of our new Lincoln, Malibu or Caprice car or whatever. But there's more to life than cars and dollars.' Margaret Thatcher unfortunately did not value the often affectionate and loyal relationships between Britain and its former colonies (as she did not value much that could not be measured and accounted for). She mistrusted what she saw as demanding Commonwealth countries; the acronym CHOGM – Commonwealth Heads of Government Meeting – stood for 'Compulsory Hand-outs for Greedy Mendicants', she liked to say. In her day, Jamaica drifted more decisively into the American camp.

There was a knock at the door. 'Come, come,' said Sir Howard. A waiter in a maroon-coloured tuxedo entered. Would we like anything to drink? Sir Howard looked at me. Tea, perhaps, I said. Sir Howard addressed the waiter, 'Tea for two.' The waiter said, 'Very good, your Excellency,' and slipped out of the room.

As we waited for the tea, Sir Howard began to speak in patriotic terms of Jamaica as a colony of 'marvellous antiquity', far older even than British India or Australia. 'Now hear me on this. When Australia was just a convict settlement, Jamaica was an established outpost of British commerce and British civilisation.' *Civilisation?* 'Yes – even during slavery the British were sending some very good people out to Jamaica – but, as I said, to Australia, just convicts.'

More: not all British slave-owners were cruel and illiberal, insisted Sir Howard. 'Think of "Monk" Lewis – he helped to *begin* the social revolution.' Slavery brought over some excellent missionaries, too, and created the great houses, said Sir Howard. These seemed a high price to pay for the Africans worked to death in their thousands on the cane fields; but Sir Howard would not see it that way. 'Jamaica's greatness is due *entirely* to slavery,' he claimed. Jamaica and Jamaicans would not exist, had it not been for slavery.

'But Jamaica was a brutal place – the plantation,' I said. Sir Howard was not going to condone slavery, was he? 'Well, I'm not one to harp on about the wickedness of slavery, either.' He smiled at me patiently. 'I'm past that.' With slavery, as with any human commerce, there were anyway many sides to the story. Yes, the iniquities; yes, the horrors; but slavery, for all its manifest brutality, had rescued Cooke and his forebears from a 'night-black' continent and shown them 'true' – that is, British – civilisation. The 'night-black' remark of Cooke's seemed to contradict his earlier black nationalist politics; but the Governor General, I decided, was thoroughly West Indian in his complexities and contradictions.

The tea arrived: Earl Grey.

Sir Howard, sipping from his cup, was put in a religious mood as he spoke of Jamaica's hoped-for 'salvation'.

'What Jamaica needs now is to go back to the religious spirituality that we've lost. Oh I'm not talking about 'Churchianity' – American-style big Church bonanzas. Tents. Crusades. I'm talking about the old-time Jamaican spirituality. The Jamaican Churches – Adventist, Catholic, Revivalist – must disregard their differences and unite to save Jamaica.'

'Save Jamaica?'

'Yes, save Jamaica. What else can you do to save a nation that's lost its way?' The question, undigested and acid, lay heavy on our conversation.

But now the Governor General had to see Michael Cooper and Stephen Coore of Third World. He stood up, and took my hand in his. 'It's been so nice talking to you – it's not often I get a chance to talk about the things that really matter.' And, as Captain Williams came to collect me, Cooke added with another smile, 'Best of British.' As I left the room the crimson-suited aide-de-camp closed the door softly behind me. I was driven home in a Bentley, the Governor General's flag rippling from the bonnet.

*

Of all the ska, calypso and mento songs that celebrated Jamaica's secession from Britain, 'Independent Jamaica' by Lord Creator remains one of the best. Not only was it the biggest hit in the post-Crown colony but fittingly it was the first record to be released on Chris Blackwell's fledgling Island label in England.

Though Lord Creator was born in Trinidad in 1940, he has lived for most of his life in Jamaica. I first met him in a hotel in Montego Bay for breakfast one day in 2005. Accompanied by his Jamaican wife Neselin ('Nes'), he arrived dressed like an old-time calypsonian in a three-piece maroon suit and black bowler hat stuck with feathers.

Heads turned as the singer made his way to my table.

'Mr Creator?'

'No man,' he replied. '*Lord* Creator.'

I apologised for the error.

Lord Creator's is the sweetest, if most sentimental, voice in popular Jamaican music. In 1988, after years of alcoholism and depression, he woke up in a hospital in Kingston to learn that the pseudo-reggae band UB40 wanted to record his song 'Kingston Town'. Having suffered a stroke and being virtually broke, Lord Creator did not hesitate to give UB40 permission to use his composition, and within weeks it had reached number one in the European charts. Royalties poured in, and with these Lord Creator built himself a house in the heights above Montego Bay, where the locals began to hail him 'Mighty' or just 'Cre'. UB40, as Lord Creator readily admitted to me, provided the break that saved him.

His story had the savour of an old blues ballad, and it was wonderful to come across it in Jamaica. Born plain Patrick Kenrick, he was the proud father of ten Jamaican children and a further five children in Trinidad (three of whom had sadly died). 'Right now I've got twelve children left alive,' Lord Creator said matter-of-factly. And, turning to his wife Neselin, 'You look fine as silk, lady, and plenty stronger,' he told her.

In 2007, after our first meeting, I went to see Lord Creator again, this time at his home in the Palm Springs neighbourhood of Montego Bay where, over the Christmas and New Year of 1831 and 1832, the Great Slave Rebellion led by Sam 'Daddy' Sharpe had taken hold. June Gay Pringle (who was keen to meet Lord Creator) accompanied me there on foot. The house, built with the proceeds of the UB40 recording, was situated at the end of a rocky path. It was of ugly concrete but well kept; a good deal of the singer's effort had gone into it. Two guard dogs, Castro and Saddam, barked from a pen round the back. Inside, the hardboard partitions were decorated with Chinese fans in homage to Lord Creator's half-Chinese mother, as well as photographs of the calypsonians Lord Kitchener and Lord Invader, personal friends.

The singer extended a hand towards June Gay, while his other restrained Castro. He looked thinner than when I met him two years earlier, and in fact had suffered another stroke. 'My tongue's a bit heavy now,' he said (without a trace of self-pity), 'and I move kind of slowly.' Lord Creator still had the brilliantined hair and well-trimmed moustache of the dandy, though.

It was this house that had anchored Lord Creator during his recovery from alcoholism. 'I was a bad fellow,' he said, with the serenity of a man who has cleared his conscience. 'A rum-drinker don't gain respect from anybody.'

'Praise God,' June Gay interjected.

'So I gave up on the drink.'

The drinking had started early, in Trinidad, where Lord Creator's father used to reward him with tots of rum after singing in bars. ('Good man, drink it now, it good for the worms.') A drunkard himself, his father had managed to survive until 1977; his mother died when he was only eleven. With his mother the young Patrick used to sing the sentimental ballad 'I Poured my Heart into a Song'; it would bring tears to their eyes, their voices sounded identical.

In the late 1950s, accompanied by a troupe of Guyanese midgets and three limbo dancers, Lord Creator went to Kingston to try his luck as a singer on the hotel circuit. Vincent 'Randy' Chin, the Jamaican Chinese record producer, was so impressed by what he saw that he signed Lord Creator to his label. And, as August 1962 approached, Chin commissioned Lord Creator to write the independence songs 'Welcome, Princess Margaret' (the recording now lost – probably just as well) and 'Independent Jamaica'. The latter was first performed at the Independence Ball in the Chinese Athletic Club, Derrymore Road, Kingston, on the night of 4 August 1962.

Lord Creator got up from the sofa, opened a cabinet with a set of keys, and took out a stack of old 45s still in their sleeves. He put one of the 45s on the phonograph, sat down and closed his eyes. By the time Neselin had returned with some cake for us to eat, 'Independent Jamaica' was playing. A soft croon – a West Indian Louis Jordan – filled the room.

> Manley went up to England to seek for independence,
> And although Busta was late, he still attended the con-fer-ence . . .

The music, upbeat, welled from the scratchy vinyl as Lord Creator rubbed a hand slowly over his face. 'Sometimes it grieve me to listen to my music,' he said. 'No matter how popular I became, I never got no money from it. I had praise – but no raise.'

During the 1960s Lord Creator cut a series of ballads ('Someday') and ska numbers ('Don't Stay Out Late'), as well as the beautiful duet with Norma Fraser, 'We Will Be Lovers', about a Guyanese girlfriend of his called Pinkie. 'I doubt Pinkie knows she's the subject of that song,' Lord Creator said, adding, 'assuming she's still alive.' The singer smiled with a rueful concern. 'But right now I'm feelin' tired, tired.'

'I think,' June Gay interrupted, 'we should now say a prayer.' Lord Creator and his wife compliantly bowed their heads as Mrs Pringle, a sympathetic Adventist presence, stood up and began, 'Dear Lord, in your mercy, please help Mr Creator –'

'Lord Creator,' the singer corrected her.

' – Lord Creator to continue to stop drinking and also to regain his health. And, Lord, I beg you to remember Lord Creator's songs, each and every one.'

She paused to glance at the singer. 'He is coming tonight, Lord Creator. Are you ready if He comes tonight?'

The singer declared that he was ready; and, exuding a polite concern that we had enjoyed our visit, said to us, 'Any time you want to come back, you're most welcome.'

26

Life of Contradiction

My last days in Jamaica were spent in Falmouth, a coastal township in the north with a typically rich island history. (The headstones in the Jewish cemetery, strikingly, had been manufactured at a stonemason's off the Mile End Road, London.) Following emancipation in 1838, Baptist freetowns had sprung up in the hills nearby, where the formerly enslaved were allowed to cultivate handkerchief plots of land. One of these was Barrett Town, named after Edward Barrett, great-grandfather of the English poet Elizabeth Barrett Browning and a former Falmouth sugar baron. Everything the Barrett family owned and all that emancipation forced them to give up came from the Falmouth slave trade.

In its heyday, Falmouth rivalled Kingston as a slave port; it had its own newspaper, the *Falmouth Post* (1835–76), and could hold up to thirty slave ships in the harbour at any time. It had been named after the Cornish port in England, from where HM packet ships routinely took mails to Jamaica. In the 1760s, Falmouth had been laid out to a New York-style grid plan; it remains the only town in Jamaica where eighteenth-century planter architecture prevails. Work is currently under way to restore this to its original (or near-original) Georgian state.

The Falmouth Heritage Renewal Company responsible for the restoration is run by an energetic, Oklahoma-born former US marine named Jim Parrent. By training a marine archaeologist, he had acquired an abrasive, no-nonsense manner in the US Navy, and is now one of the most revered (possibly also most feared) foreigners in Falmouth: 'Sir P', the locals call him. He had lived in Jamaica for thirty years and was married to a Jamaican.

Stocky, with close-cropped red-blond hair, Parrent was waiting for me outside the Baptist manse on Market Street, a cut-stone Georgian building inhabited once (so it is believed) by the British abolitionist William Knibb. As we set off on our tour of Falmouth Parrent explained how his work had been wracked by controversy. His restoration of Georgian courthouses, wharves and warehouses had led locals to believe, understandably, that he was trying to resurrect an image in Falmouth of slavery. Parrent refutes the charge. If his heritage enthusiasms had been redolent of planter class nostalgia, that was in the minds of Jamaicans only. 'Jamaicans can be very suspicious of outsiders,' he judged. Dr Parrent was viewed more favourably in Falmouth when he opened a vocational training centre for youths who, being homeless or illiterate or just prone to violence, were not suited for gainful employment elsewhere.

The forty-odd trainee carpenters and masons in his care have become proficient in replicating Georgian sash windows, weatherboards and panelled doors; the restoration of Falmouth is a source of pride for them, apparently, even if Dr Parrent subjects them to what he calls a 'tough love policy' where laziness, unpunctuality, drinking or drug-taking are countered with blasts of US navy slang and threats of expulsion. In gratitude the trainees help to chase off (sometimes beat up) the local crack-heads who broke into the workshop fourteen times in 2008 alone, hoping to steal equipment.

At the sea end of Market Street we came to Barrett House. Built as a town house for Edward Barrett in 1779, it had wrought iron balconies of smart Regency design, originally imported from Philadelphia. Though vandals had long since taken the balconies away, two boys were guarding the property against further theft. 'Peter! Claude!' Dr Parrent called out to them. 'Dr P!' they shouted back. There was nothing much left of the property for them to guard. The mahogany panel doors and louvred shutters had also been pilfered. In fact, everything was gone – mahogany columns, railings – that could be put to use.

In addition to being vandalised, Barrett House had become a public lavatory. What was left of the drawing room reeked of waste. But then why should the locals have any interest in restoring this or any other property in Georgian Falmouth? Barrett House was not a part of their history; it was a part of slave-driver history. Only when I shut my eyes could I reconstruct this place in any of its Adam-style period splendour, with its cedar panelling and decorative doorways. The house had been built for a man blinded by greed for money, his slaves labouring from dawn to dusk till in the end they literally dropped dead. Barrett House: let it fall down.

*

On Edward Barrett's plantation home of Cinnamon Hill outside Falmouth toiled 10,000 African slaves. They called him 'Edward of Cinnamon Hill'. (His home would become the property of country and western singer Johnny Cash 200 years later.) The underside of the slave system that brought Barrett such wealth was the mixed blood of the family line. Elizabeth Barrett Browning's father – named Edward after his forebear – feared that the 'sins' of his family would work themselves out in later generations. In fact many Barretts were of mixed race or, to use the old planter rankings, were mustees, mustaphinos and octoroons. Elizabeth's father, a fervid, controlling man, forbade any of his eleven children from marrying; the shame of 'blood desertion' weighed so heavy on Edward Barrett.

Elizabeth herself believed she had African blood and saw the Barrett family as somehow cursed by slavery. ('Cursed we are from generation to generation.') She was the only one of her siblings to be born in England, yet from an early age she would have heard tales of Jamaican slavery, with their flavour of legal wrangling, sexual scandal, rum and opium addiction, crop failure and other mishaps of the sugar life.

During her honeymoon in Italy in 1846 (kept a secret from Edward Barrett), Elizabeth completed the strange poem, 'The Runaway Slave at Pilgrim's Point', based on stories told to her by a Jamaican-born cousin. Published in 1848 in the Boston anti-slavery journal *The Liberty Bell*, the poem is narrated by a runaway slave girl who has murdered her half-white child after being raped by white men. 'I am not mad: I am black,' she cries. Early manuscripts indicate that the poem, provisionally entitled 'Mad and Black and Pilgrim's Point', was to have been written from the perspective of a black man. After the woman has buried her child, she reaches Pilgrim's Point in New England.

In defiance of her family, Elizabeth was an abolitionist, who longed to be rid of 'dreadful Jamaica' and her legal status in England as a slaveholder. Her father loathed William Knibb and his army of Baptist preachers, whose testimonies had poisoned the slaves' minds, he believed, inciting them to rebellion and violent crimes. The British may as well 'hang weights to the sides of Jamaica and sink it into the sea', Edward Barrett despaired, if the Emancipation Bill was passed.

It was passed, and on Emancipation Day in 1838 hundreds of freed slaves, young and old, rushed from their shacks on the Barrett estates to join 'King Knibb' in the victory celebrations in Falmouth. The Barrett family incurred enormous financial losses, yet they still owned 31,000 acres of Jamaican land, along with an elegant town house in Wimpole Street in the Marylebone district of London (a residential area long popular with West Indian slave-owners). Every day until his death in 1857 – the year of the so-called 'Indian Mutiny' – Edward Barrett had gone to the City to arrange for cargoes of Jamaican sugar and rum to be ferried to London on the two slave ships still in his possession.

*

On the eve of my departure from Jamaica I went to a country house called Greenwood. Built in the early 1800s by relatives of Elizabeth Barrett Browning, it stood on the ridge of a hill high above the sea near Falmouth. Inside, amid a jumble of books (Gibbon, Homer) and custom-made china was a fearsome saw-toothed 'man-trap' designed to catch runaway slaves. And, on the wall above the trap was a framed list of the British planter family's less compliant slaves, including 'Bob Trouble'.

At the rear of the house, a long veranda commanded giddy vistas of the ocean. The view was so extensive from up here that I could see the curve of the horizon. Perhaps forty miles of Jamaican coastline were in sight: at the sea's edge was the long fringe of sand from where slaves had loaded sugar on to vessels bound for Liverpool, Glasgow, Bristol; then a green ribbon of cane fields; and, behind these, hillsides dotted with the castle-like mansions of drug barons. I looked down at the beach far below me: from these heights, I imagined, the slave-owning British could be the privileged spectators of Jamaica's physical beauty; they would not have to encounter its human wretchedness, only this endless stretch of sea and sand.

As I was contemplating the view, Bob Betton, the current owner, said to me, 'Sometimes I think to myself that slavery *can't* have been a good thing, but *without* slavery I wouldn't be here now, in this house.' His eye left me for a moment and fell on the turquoise expanse of ocean. Some Jamaicans have never got over the wounds of slavery, Betton went on. But why dwell on the past? Jamaicans are a proud people triumphantly risen *above* slavery. Betton, born to a poor black family in the Kingston ghetto, relished the irony of this life of his in a white slave-driver's mansion. 'How the tables have turned,' he remarked.

In 1955, with his mother, Bob Betton had bought a house in Stoke Newington, north London, for £400. Marc Bolan (then Mark Feld) lived round the corner but, like many of the Jews in that part of London, the future pop star was reportedly not that friendly to the West Indians, though he later befriended the black American singer Gloria Jones. To belong, you must be included; to be included, you must be accepted, said Betton. In their semi-detached house on Norcott Road, he and his mother eked out the loneliest existence, banned from the whites-only pubs and clubs, feeling god-forsaken.

'Yes, English society was very, very hostile,' recalled Betton, 'and the hostility could come from even your neighbours.' The majority of his neighbours were Orthodox Jews, for whom he was merely a *shvartzer* odd-job boy who could run errands for them on the Sabbath. Only homosexuals or Communists were interested in him, Betton claimed. So he became a Communist – not to feel so alone. In his Stoke Newington house virtually the only book was the *Communist Manifesto*, which Betton never managed to read. 'I wasn't a true left-winger, only a pretend true left-winger.'

In 1965 Betton's father left Kingston to join his family in Stoke Newington. He had been making good money back home as a barman at the St Andrew's Yacht Club and the (now defunct) Myrtle Bank Hotel. He was a Jamaican who knew his place in colonial society, and was deferential to the clubmen with their rum punches and sundowners. In London, however, no matter how hard he tried Betton's father could not find a job. He ended up as a park-keeper in Bromley, tending the bowling green. Remembering this, Bob Betton gazed out over the veranda and shook his head sadly. 'England was awful for my father, awful.'

All this happened a long time ago, but, as Betton said, it was the story of his life. In 1974, after twenty years 'in foreign', he returned to Jamaica accompanied by his wife Ann, a New Zealander whom he had met in London one night at the Flamingo jazz club. Betton felt he had to go back. How can you ever be severed from that place you first called home? With money made in England from property development, he bought Greenwood great house from an Englishman who had wintered there with his dogs and servants. In 1980, having re-shingled the roof and removed the linoleum from the floors, he opened up Greenwood as a tourist attraction.

Betton was determined to cut a dash as a returnee, so he drove round Falmouth in his Triumph Stag like a Grand Prix contestant – fast – so that the Greenwood gravel sprayed up under his tyres. He wanted the locals to see how he had mastered the old-fashioned art of idleness. To that end, he employed a black female 'museum guide' to stand by the bar dressed as an eighteenth-century servant, a Disneyland emblem of the enslaved Antilles, of the 'Africa Trade'.

A part of Betton, I understood, admired Britain's colonial endeavour in Jamaica, even if Britain had left some damaging prejudices regarding race and colour. 'You Caucasians are much more on the ball with things,' Betton said in an unguarded moment. 'I mean, we Jamaicans just don't rate each other.' In Jamaica it was accepted that whatever came from abroad – especially from white abroad – was superior. 'And that's part of our problem,' Betton explained. 'That's why we've got a white man as a copper!' (He was referring to DCP Mark Shields.)

As we spoke, the evening sun flooded Greenwood with its yellow light, turning Betton's white shirt to a rose tint. 'All this,' he moved his hand in a slow, languorous motion along the ocean rim, 'all this is mine.'

His wife, Ann Betton, had been waiting for us in the bar. 'Would you like a drink?' She looked at me expectantly. 'We do a very good planter punch.' I asked for a glass of soda. No tourists had showed up so far and the 'museum guide' in her white blouse and long-flowing *Gone With the Wind* skirt stood at a discreet distance from us. The Bettons had been married for forty years; she, a white New Zealander; he, a black Jamaican. Yet they were united by member-ship of the British Commonwealth. The Commonwealth had enabled them to share a culture and a heritage, brought them closer together.

'It's true, isn't it?' Bob said to Ann; Ann smiled thinly, shrugged and said, 'I suppose so.'

Darkness was falling now, and Bob gave a sudden, uncertain laugh as he recalled the day in the summer of 1953 when he had stood under a hot sun on Hagley Park Road in Kingston, waiting for the newly crowned Queen Elizabeth II of Great Britain to pass him in her motorcade. In his hand he held a little Union Jack flag, one of thousands distributed to the crowd by the colonial administration. At that time, no one thought Jamaica would separate from Britain. By a coincidence, Bob's future wife was also standing on a roadside with a Union Jack flag, waiting for the Queen that coronation year of 1953.

'Only I was in New Zealand,' she said to Bob, deadpan, 'not Jamaica.'

'I know, darling, but the Commonwealth – it joined us together across time and space,' Bob insisted sweetly. He was now in grand good humour after a third planter punch.

Yet the Commonwealth, that increasingly ramshackle totem of former imperial glory, now has only the British Crown as its unifying element, and serves merely to sustain a mirage of British importance abroad. The Commonwealth's governing principle – that people get along better than governments – was a grandiose Anglocentric concept doomed to fail. Few people in Britain today have reason to admire the Commonwealth (the Commonwealth Institute on London's Kensington High Street was recently closed down). Benefits no longer flow like milk and honey from the mother country to its dependencies; the old loyalties have changed, and Jamaica's three million are left sheltering under Britannia's threadbare mantle.

343

In Greenwood, though, amid the Georgian antiques, Bob and Ann Betton could mourn for an idea of Empire they had known in childhood. The old Jamaica of order and snobbery, of deference to hierarchy and status (those most British of reflexes) still existed for Bob Betton, but only here, in this plantation great house fantasy.

*

Two sharp beeps from a klaxon indicated that a coach full of tourists had arrived. Ann Betton stood, smiling welcomingly, as she ushered them in. From their accents I guessed they were North American. Ann, behind the bar counter again, greeted her first customer, a big, sunburned man in shorts, who asked for a Diet Coke.

'Boy, this is some planter house,' another tourist said, looking back over his shoulder as he started on the tour. The serving girl in her plantation costume moved off with the group, pausing here and there to touch a termite-eaten book of poems by Barrett Browning or raise a hand to emphasise the significance of the 'man-trap'. I watched the group disappear into the garden through fragile-leafed jacaranda trees and mossy stone benches. Soon it would be quite dark.

As I took my leave of the Bettons, I walked away from Greenwood, and a solitary hawk wheeled overhead. From the direction of Barrett Town came a bonfire whiff of burning collie weed. I kept on walking towards Falmouth in the gathering dusk. A single coconut tree silhouetted against the sky looked like an advertisement for paradise. By the time I got to Falmouth the town was receding fast into the night. Dr Parrent's trainee craftsman, Peter, was waiting for me by the Baptist manse, where I was to spend my last night in Jamaica. A hardness about his eyes suggested a difficult home life (or no home life at all).

He unlocked the bolts and padlocks fitted to the huge doors against the crack-heads. As he did so he glanced menacingly down the street, taking in the shuttered front of the Chinese store and the East Indian cook-shop with its dark interior. I shook his hand, went in and chained the doors from the inside, then climbed the wooden staircase to my room. In the box-like quarters was a bunk-bed and, next to that, a dresser, with a small sink in one corner. The kitchen in the adjacent room contained a midget stove with a couple of back burners. I looked out of the window; the light of a street lamp, falling in a yellow swatch across the façade of the Chinese store, fizzed and crackled. Peter was sitting on the kerb opposite, just beyond the lamp's circle of light. He looked up at me as I stepped back into the shadows.

That night, memories of Jamaica kept turning over in my mind like pictures in an album: the Kingston murder trial; the warm hospitable days at PJ's; the botanical gardens at Cinchona; the dead yard ritual in St Thomas; the Spanish Town mortuary. How well had I understood this place? Alone in the dark, I had a sudden sense of how it must feel to see this part of the West Indies for the first time, the semi-tropic greens and blues and the shallows where the slave ships once anchored. A kind of corrupted Eden. I was in no hurry to go back to it.

Take Down the Union Jack

Each day the planes land, the cruise ships call, and the tourists arrive for their dream holiday in the Caribbean. Yet today for Jamaicans there is despair. Armed gangs, police corruption and the indifference of politicians have created inner cities of mayhem and violence, where killings take place in daylight. The violence is largely confined to the ghetto, however, so Jamaica has been able to promote itself as a haven for tourists. Without tourists – the majority of them white – the Jamaican economy would struggle; without tourists, the islanders would suffer.

Affection for Britain remains surprisingly strong in parts of Jamaica. But with this has come a political system fatally hidebound by the colonial inheritance. Jamaican pseudo-colonials, of the sort portrayed by Sam Selvon in his great West Indian novel *The Lonely Londoners* (1956), survive in the Kingston law courts, in the Sandhurst-educated echelons of the army and in the civil service. The social contempt shown by some Jamaican public servants towards the poor is a legacy, in part, of slavery, and the dry rot of mistrust and resentment left by the imperial project. Ideas of social welfare and responsibility fell on barren ground in the 1960s and 1970s, and soon withered. So Queen Victoria is still on her pillar, watching Jamaica collapse. A fatalism seems to be inherent in the island: change is not possible.

Attempts were made post-independence to develop a national culture free from British and American influence. Yet the struggle towards nationhood was hampered by the national character. Over the three centuries of British rule, a combination of servitude and race, climate and geography had resulted in a citizenry fiercely resistant to government. When, in 1962, independence was granted,

Jamaicans seemed cowed, conservative, materialistic. Initially they were enthusiastic for nationalism but displayed little civic or moral accountability beyond their family or parish. (As one Jamaican told me, 'The "I" is often more apparent in Jamaicans than the "We".')

In the half-century since 1962 the hopes for a fairer, better Jamaica have not been met. The discontent is felt especially by the older generation who worked with Michael Manley to combat the effects of colonialism. Tax evasion is widespread (as it is in Italy, a country that shares Jamaica's anti-statism); the orderly queue is unheard of; beaches are becoming polluted, archaeological sites semi-abandoned. The so-called values of the PNP – national unity, socialism – were dealt a further blow in recent years by the Jamaican drugs trade, which has dominated Jamaica far more effectively than Michael Manley ever did.

In addition, Jamaica has a powerful neighbour to contend with. The United States has worked hard to make the island conducive to American banana, sugar and bauxite interests, as well as tourism, drugs and anti-communism. By virtue of its proximity, Jamaica inevitably attracts America's attention and concern. And as China vies for economic supremacy in the Caribbean basin, America's involvement in Jamaican affairs is likely to intensify – America opened a super-fortified embassy in Kingston in 2006. Barack Obama, the newly elected president of the United States, is in a position to change the old era of Jamaican–Washington relations characterised by American Republican party interests. As a black man ascended to the most powerful office in the world, Obama has even won the approval of Castro's Cuba.

Nevertheless, Jamaica, a nation built on violence and morose vendettas, today stands on shaky political and economic foundations. The island is wonderfully fertile, yet manufactured food-stuffs from the United States continue to overwhelm the markets. There is growing disbelief among some Jamaicans that Queen Elizabeth II should still be their head of state, when other countries in the Caribbean have become republics or are moving towards republican status. For too long Jamaica has interpreted its history, its political and cultural life through Britain. Jamaica needs to banish its psychological dependency on the Mother Country –

'Auntie England' – and haul down the Union Jack.

Jamaica looks small on the map. Yet for a nation of less than three million, it exerts a disproportionate influence abroad. No other West Indian island has generated such a widespread diaspora. Jamaica is a beautiful place; the mountains, streams and coastline linger in the memory. But the Jamaican people, with their gift for humour and generosity, their creativity (and fabled aggression), are stuck in a post-colonial malaise. In the course of my visits, I saw how the heritage of plantation slavery had helped to make the malaise.

Jamaica's very social order bears the mark of the slaving past. In 1965, when a statue of Paul Bogle was unveiled in Morant Bay, riots ensued as locals objected to the way the Baptist preacher had been made to look too black. A more confident nation would not have reacted in this way. But Jamaica remains unsure of itself and of its past. Jamaican planters had regarded slaves on the same level with beasts. In the last analysis, many things in Jamaica still turn on the bias of class and colour.

When I visited Zede and Millicent Hudson, elderly returnees in Portland parish, Millicent was lying on a bed in a back room. She had lost most of her hair, yet her eyes seemed resilient. 'My wife's ill,' Zede said to me, 'she's had strokes and all that kind of thing.' She could hear us, though, and she smiled whenever a place of fond remembrance – the Peckham Mecca, a pub in Lewisham – was mentioned.

The Hudsons had left Jamaica in 1961, a year before independence. For thirty years they scrimped in south London, trying to assimilate. Zede's job was to operate the lift in the pedestrian tunnel to the Isle of Dogs beneath the Thames. ('Up and down I went, all day.') Through all their hardship and vexations, they dreamed of going home. Like many Jamaicans at this time, they saw their migration as an interlude, a stage they would survive sustained by the promise of return. And in the long term, one day, return would be possible.

In the meantime, their Jamaican pride had no greater satisfaction than to hear relatives back in Portland say they must be quite wealthy now, after their years in England. ('Wealthy', that is, by

Jamaican standards.) In 1994, Zede and Millicent decided to return. 'I wish we'd stayed,' said Zede, the muscles ridged out tense on his jaws. The moment they set foot in Jamaica, they were overwhelmed by a sense of hostility.

Each day a Revival church behind their new house began to chant and drum in praise of the Lord. The noise they made overstepped the limits of decency, Zede told me. He and his wife could no longer think of the congregation's 'rudeness' without flinching. 'From six o'clock every morning, every day seven day a week, they knock that drum,' Zede said. 'Yes, we've been battered a whole heap of devil noise and drumming.'

It was a shock for the Hudsons to find how unkind Jamaicans could be to home-comers. The church ignored their complaints and continued to shout their hallelujahs. 'Every one of them is still stomping their hymns and other racket,' Zede went on. 'Me and Millicent, we can nevva sleep.' Instead they cat-nap during the day, until the next burst of church-house rhetoric disturbs them.

Oddly, their story seemed to parallel my own impression of modern Jamaica. Zede and Millicent, quiet people trying to lead a quiet life, had come home to a place that had failed to achieve democracy – a true democracy – after independence. 'The Jamaica that we return to, nowadays,' Zede told me, 'it give me a bad feeling.' In many ways, theirs was a very Jamaican story – Jamaican in its frustration of a hope.

Further Reading

The following books and articles – academic and general – were of invaluable help to me in writing *The Dead Yard*. Dates in entries refer to the editions consulted, not to first publication.

General

Brodber, Erna, *A Study of Yards in the City of Kingston* (Kingston, Inst. of Social and Economic Research, University of the West Indies, 1975); Campbell, Leeroy James, *Grow Jamaica: A comprehensive look at the economic, social and spiritual impact of the cannabis (ganja) industry in Jamaica* (Ocho Rios, Bright Morning Star Press, 2002); Cargill, Maurice (ed.), *Ian Fleming Introduces Jamaica* (London, Andre Deutsch, 1965); Cassidy, Frederic G., *Jamaica Talk: Three hundred years of the English language in Jamaica* (London, Macmillan Education, 1982); Didion, Joan, *Miami* (Granta Books, 2005); Ferguson, James, *Traveller's Literary Companion to the Caribbean* (London, In Print, 1997); Gambrill, Linda (ed.), *A Tapestry of Jamaica: The best of Skywritings* (Oxford, Macmillan Caribbean, 2003); Howard, David, *Kingston: A cultural and literary history* (Oxford, Signal Books, 2005); Naipaul, V. S., *India: A wounded civilization* (London, Andre Deutsch, 1977); Palmer, Andrew, *A Diplomat and His Birds* (Wheathampstead, Herts, Tiercel Publishing, 2005); Senior, Olive (ed.), *Encyclopedia of Jamaican Heritage* (Kingston, Twin Guinep, 2003); Shaw, George Bernard, 'Interesting Interview with Mr. Bernard Shaw', *Daily Gleaner*, 12 January 1911; Thomas, Polly and Vaitlingam, Adam, *The Rough Guide to Jamaica* (London, Rough Guides, 2003); Wardle, Huon, *An Ethnography of*

Cosmopolitanism in Kingston (Lewiston, Edwin Mellen Press, 2000); Williams, Joan, *Original Dancehall Dictionary* (Kingston, Yard Publications, 2003); Winkler, Anthony C., *Going Home To Teach* (Kingston, LMH Publishing, 1995).

History

Brathwaite, Edward Kamau, *The Development of Creole Society in Jamaica 1770–1820* (Oxford, Clarendon Press, 1971); Brendon, Piers, *The Decline and Fall of the British Empire 1781–1997* (London, Jonathan Cape, 2007); Bridges, Revd George Wilson, *The Annals of Jamaica*, 2 vols (London, John Murray, 1828); Bryan, Patrick, *The Jamaican People 1880–1902* (London, Macmillan Caribbean, 1991); Curtin, Philip D., *The Two Jamaicas: The role of ideas in a tropical colony 1830–1865* (Cambridge, Mass., Harvard University Press, 1955); Ferguson, James, *A Traveller's History of the Caribbean* (Oxford, Windrush Press, 1998); Heuman, Gad, *'The Killing Time': The Morant Bay rebellion in Jamaica* (Knoxville, The University of Tennesse Press, 2000); Segal, Ronald, *The Black Diaspora* (London, Faber and Faber, 1995).

British–Jamaican relations

Appleyard, Bryan and White, Leslie, 'The Ghetto's in the Mind', *Sunday Times Magazine*, 10 October 2004; Bostridge, Mark, *Florence Nightingale: The woman and her legend* (London, Viking, 2008); Gilroy, Paul, *There Ain't No Black in the Union Jack* (London, Routledge, 1992); Glass, Ruth, *Newcomers: The West Indians in London* (London, George Allen and Unwin Ltd, 1960); Hall, Catherine, *Civilizing Subjects: Metropole and colony in the English imagination 1830–1867* (London, Polity, 2002); Hinds, Donald, *Journey to an Illusion: The West Indian in Britain* (London, William Heinemann, 1966); Johnson, Howard, 'Decolonising the History Curriculum in the Anglophone Caribbean', *Journal of Commonwealth and Imperial History*, XXX, 1, 2002; Lamming, George, *The Pleasures of Exile* (London, Allison and Busby, 1984); Manzoor, Sarfaz, 'Britain's Darkest Hour', *Observer*,

24 February 2008; Noble, Martin E., *Jamaica Airman: A black airman in Britain in 1943 and after* (London, New Beacon Books, 1984); Owusu, Kewesi (ed.), *Black British Culture and Society: A text reader* (London, Routledge, 2000); Patterson, Sheila, *Dark Strangers* (London, Tavistock Publications, 1963); Sedley, Stephen, 'No Law at All', review of 'A Jurisprudence of Power: Victorian Empire and the rule of law' by R. W. Kostal, *London Review of Books*, 2 November, 2006; Walmsley, Anne, *The Caribbean Artists Movement 1966–72: A literary and cultural history* (London, New Beacon Books, 1992); Winder, Simon, *The Man Who Saved Britain* (London, Picador, 2006).

Politics

Beckford, George and Witter, Michael, *Small Garden . . . Bitter Weed: Struggle and change in Jamaica* (London, Zed Books, 1982); Carroll, Rory, 'Jamaica slums locked in violence', *Guardian*, 1 April 2008; Foot, Hugh, *A Start in Freedom* (London, Hodder and Stoughton, 1964); Gray, Obika, 'Predation Politics and the Political Impasse in Jamaica', *Small Axe,* XIII, March 2003; Gunst, Laurie, *Born Fi' Dead: A journey through the Jamaican posse underworld* (London, Payback Press, 1999); Hart, Richard, 'Federation: An ill-fated design', *Jamaica Journal*, xxv, 1, 1993; Kaufman, Michael, *Jamaica Under Manley: Dilemmas of socialism and democracy* (London, Zed Books, 1985); Manley, Rachel, *In My Father's Shade: A daughter's insight into the man behind the prime minister's mask* (London, Black Amber Books, 2004); Nettleford, Rex, 'The Michael Manley–Kari Levitt Letters', *Small Axe*, 1, February 1997; Rodney, Walter, *The Groundings With My Brothers* (London, Bogle–L'Ouverture Publications, 1969); Schwarz, Bill (ed.), *West Indian Intellectuals in Britain* (Manchester, Manchester University Press, 2003); Small, Geoff, *Ruthless: The global rise of the Yardies* (London, Warner Books, 1995).

Slavery

Desmond, Adrian and Moore, James, *Darwin's Sacred Cause: Race, slavery and the quest for human origins* (London, Allen Lane, 2009); Hall, Douglas (ed.), *In Miserable Slavery: Thomas Thistlewood in Jamaica 1750–86* (London, Macmillan Caribbean, 1989); Hochschild, Adam, *Bury the Chains: The British struggle to abolish slavery* (London, Macmillan, 2005); Jack, Ian, 'Britain is built on sugar: our national sweet tooth defines us', *Guardian*, 13 October 2007; Lewis, Matthew, *Journal of a Residence Among the Negroes in the West Indies* (London, John Murray, 1845); McMahon, Benjamin, *Jamaica Plantership* (London, Effingham Wilson, 1839); Rediker, Marcus, *The Slave Ship: A human history* (London, John Murray, 2007); Shepherd, Verene, *I Want to Disturb My Neighbour: Lectures on slavery, emancipation and post-colonial Jamaica* (Kingston, Ian Randle Publishers, 2007); St Clair, William, *The Grand Slave Emporium: Cape Coast Castle and the British slave trade* (London, Profile Books, 2006); Turner, Mary, *Slaves and Missionaries: The disintegration of Jamaican slave society 1787–1834* (Champaign, University of Illinois Press, 1982); Walvin, James and Craton, Michael, *A Jamaican Plantation: The history of Worthy Park 1670–1970* (London, W. H. Allen, 1970).

Travel accounts

Abrahams, Peter, *Jamaica: An island mosaic* (London, Her Majesty's Stationary Office, 1957); Beckford, William, *A Descriptive Account of the Island of Jamaica*, 3 vols (London, T. and J. Egerton, 1790); Gosse, P. H., *A Naturalist's Sojourn in Jamaica* (London, Brown, Green and Longmans, 1851); Long, Edward, *The History of Jamaica or General Survey of the Ancient and Modern State of That Island*, 3 vols (London, T. Lowndes, 1774); Macmillan, Mona, *The Land of Look Behind: A study of Jamaica* (London, Faber and Faber, 1957); Nugent, Maria, *Lady Nugent's Journal of Her Residence in Jamaica from 1801 to 1805* (Kingston, The University of West Indies Press, 2002); Sloane, Sir Hans, *A Voyage to . . . Jamaica with the Natural History* , 2 vols (London, printed by B.M. for the author, 1707, 1725); Trollope, Anthony, *The West Indies and the Spanish Main* (London, Chapman and Hall, 1860).

Religion

Banbury, Rev. T, *Jamaica Superstitions or The Obeah Book: A complete treatise of the absurdities believed in by the people of the island* (Kingston, Mortimer C. De Souza, 1894); Besson, Jean, *Martha Brae's Two Histories* (Chapel Hill and London, University of North Carolina Press, 2002); Hopwood, Andrea, 'Jamaican "Dead Yard" Cultures and Customs Through the Years', *Death and Bereavement Around the World*, vol. 2, 'Death and Bereavement in the Americas' (New York, Baywood Publishing Company, 2003); Hurston, Zora Neale, *Voodoo Gods: An inquiry into native myths and magic in Jamaica and Haiti* (London, J. M. Dent, 1939) Langford, Mary Jones, *The Fairest Isle: History of Jamaica Friends* (Richmond, Friends United Press, 1997); Seaga, Edward, 'Revival Cults in Jamaica', *Jamaica Journal*, III, 2, 1969.

Africa, Rastafari, Maroon culture

Barrett, Leonard, E., *The Sun and the Drum: African roots in Jamaican folk* (Kingston, Sangster's Book Stores Ltd, 1976); Beckwith, Martha Warren, *Black Roadways: A study of Jamaican folklife* (North Carolina, Chapel Hill, 1929); Bilby, Kenneth M., *True-Born Maroons* (Gainesville, University Press of Florida, 2005); Chevannes, Barry, *Rastafari: Roots and ideology* (New York, Syracuse University Press, 1994); Dunham, Katherine, *Journey to Accompong* (New York, Henry Holt, 1946); Grant, Colin, *Negro With a Hat: The rise and fall of Marcus Garvey and his dream of Mother Africa* (London, Jonathan Cape, 2008); Hart, Richard, *Slaves Who Abolished Slavery: Blacks in rebellion* (Kingston, University of West Indies Press, 2002); Sandbrook, Dominic, *White Heat: A history of Britain in the Swinging Sixties* (London, Abacus, 2008); Smith, M. G., Augier, Roy and Nettleford, Rex, *The Rastafari Movement in Kingston, Jamaica* (Kingston, University of the West Indies Press, 1960).

Music

Bradley, Lloyd, *Bass Culture: When reggae was king* (London, Penguin Books, 2001); Chang, Jeff, *Can't Stop Won't Stop: A history of the hip-hop generation* (London, Ebury Press, 2007); Cooper, Carloyn, *Noises in the Blood: Duality, gender and the 'vulgar' body of Jamaican popular culture* (London, Macmillan Caribbean, 1993); Fordham, John, *Jazz Man: The amazing story of Ronnie Scott and his Club* (London, Kyle Cathie, 1995); Katz, David, *Solid Foundation: An oral history of reggae* (London, Bloomsbury, 2003); Reynolds, Simon, *Rip it Up and Start Again: Post-punk 1978–84* (London, Faber and Faber, 2006); Salewicz, Chris, *Rude Boy: Once upon a time in Jamaica* (London, Gollancz, 2000), and *Redemption Song: The definitive biography of Joe Strummer* (London, Harper Collins 2007); Steckles, Garry, *Bob Marley* (Oxford, Signal and Macmillan Carribean, 2008); The Clash, *The Clash: Strummer, Jones, Simonon, Headon* (London, Atlantic Books, 2008); Younge, Gary, 'Chilling call to murder as music attacks gays', *Guardian*, 26 June 2004; Zephaniah, Benjamin, 'Stop This Obscenity: . . . time to leave Brother Bob [Marley] alone', *Guardian*, 12 March, 2004.

Ethnic minorities

Chen, Ray, *The Shopkeepers: Commemorating 150 years of the Chinese in Jamaica 1854–2004* (Kingston, Periwinkle Publishers, 2005); Erickson, Edgar, 'The Introduction of East Indian Coolies into the British West Indies', *Journal of Modern History*, VI, 2, 1934; Henriques, Fernando, *Family and Colour in Jamaica* (London, Eyre and Spottiswoode, 1953); Karras, Alan L, *Sojourners in the Sun: Scottish migrants in Jamaica and the Chesapeake 1740–1800* (Ithaca, NY, Cornell University Press, 1992); Mansingh, Laxmi and Mansingh, Ajai, 'Indian Heritage in Jamaica', *Jamaica Journal*, X, 2, 3, 4, 1976, and *Home Away from Home: 150 years of Indian presence in Jamaica 1845–1995* (Kingston, Ian Randle Publications, 1999); Ranston, Jackie, *The Lindo Legacy* (London, Toucan Books, 2000); Sardar, Ziauddin,

Balti Britain: *A journey through the British Asian experience* (London, Granta, 2008); Stoppi, Maurice, *Hope Road* (New York, TFG Press, 2004).

Fiction

Berry, James, *Windrush Songs* (Tarset, Bloodaxe Books, 2007); Cezair-Thompson, Margaret, *The Pirate's Daughter* (London, Headline, 2007); Cumberland, Richard, 'The West Indian: A Comedy in Five Acts', in *The London Stage*: *A collection of the most reputed tragedies, comedies, operas, melo-dramas, farces and interludes*, vol. I (London, Sherwood and Jones, 1830); Ellis, Garfield, *For Nothing At All* (Oxford, Macmillan Caribbean, 2005); Hughes, Richard, *A High Wind in Jamaica* (London, The Harvill Press, 1995); Johnson, Linton Kwesi, *Mi Revalueshanary Fren*: *Selected poems* (London, Penguin Books, 2002); Jones, Evan, *Stone Haven* (London, Heinemann, 1993); Kennaway, Guy, *One People* (Edinburgh, Payback Press, 1997); Miller, Kei, *The Same Earth* (London, Weidenfeld & Nicolson, 2008); Ross, Jacob, *Pynter Bender,* (London, Fourth Estate, 2008); Thelwell, Michael, *The Harder They Come* (London, Pluto Press, 1980).

Index

marriage, 158, 182; Marshall's
 Pen, 312, 313
Martin, Vincent 'Ivanhoe', 255
Martin, Winston 'Sparrow', 37–8
Marx, Karl, 2
Masemure sugar estate, 67
Mass Marriage Movement, 158
Massie, Brian, 121
Matalon, Evelyn, 136–7, 140–2
Matalon, Isaac 'Zaccie', 136, 141
Maxwell, John, 193, 194
Maytals, 35, 256
medical care, 289–90
Melly, George, 258
Mengistu, President Haile Mariam,
 111
mental illness, 37
mento, 5
Metropolitan Coloured People's
 Housing Association, 158
Mighty Diamonds, 40, 44
Miles, George, 42–3
Mill, John Stuart, 139–40
Minott-Tait, Diana, 83–5
Minton, John, 260
Mintz, Sidney, 1
Mitchell, Harold, 106–8
Mitchell, Joni, 260
Mittoo, Jackie, 41
Monroe, Marilyn, 238
Montego Bay, 325–6, 328
Moonraker (Fleming), 247, 258
Moore Town, 207, 209–11, 215–18
Morant Bay, 227–9, 348
Morant Bay Rebellion, 136, 138–41,
 205
Morant Point, 172–4
Morass, 308–9
Moravian Brethren, 310
Morgan, Anthony, 100, 101
Morgan, Derrick, 3, 35
Morgan, Captain Henry, 57
Morrissey, 257
Ms Dynamite, 205
Mudahy, Patrick, 90–1, 92, 105

murder: capital punishment, 116–17,
 120–1; rate, 7, 269; reasons for,
 273
music: Chinese record producers,
 225–7; Kumina, 146–51, 152–3,
 247–8; overview, 33–48; Ranglin,
 252–4; *see also* reggae
Mussolini, Benito, 97
Mutabaruka, 161
'My Boy Lollipop' (Millie Small), 35,
 227, 253

N.W.A., 44
Nanking Massacre, 228
Nanny, 206
Napoleon Bonaparte, 234
National Dance Theatre Company of
 Jamaica, 286
Negril, 186–7
Negro World newspaper, 7, 43
Nettleford, Rex, 285–6
Nevis, 185
Newcastle (Jamaica), 268–70
Newland, Arthur, 99, 100
Newton, John, 60, 323
Nine Night ceremony, 146–51, 247–8
Niyabingi, 97
Nock, William, 131
Norwich, Blake, 78–81
Norwich, Hyacinth, 78–81
Notorious B.I.G., 277
Nottingham, 292
novels: Bond, 171, 227, 233, 234–6,
 247, 258, 261; 'Jamaican Gothic',
 171; Jamaican novelists, 122, 157,
 159, 171, 279–81; Thackeray on
 Jamaica, 54
Nugent, Lady, 54, 108, 265, 312
Nyerere, Julius, 98

Obama, Barack, 7, 24, 159, 192, 347
obeah, 216–17
Oberli, Andreas, 131–5
Ocho Rios, 236–7, 238
Octopussy (Fleming), 235